REGULATING THE BRITISH ECONOMY, 1660–1850

Regulating the British Economy, 1660–1850

Edited by
PERRY GAUCI
University of Oxford, UK

ASHGATE

Published by
Ashgate Publishing Limited
Wey Court East
Union Road
Farnham
Surrey, GU9 7PT
England

Ashgate Publishing Company
Suite 420
101 Cherry Street
Burlington
VT 05401-4405
USA

www.ashgate.com

British Library Cataloguing in Publication Data
Regulating the British economy, 1660-1850.
1. Great Britain--Economic conditions--17th century.
2. Great Britain--Economic conditions--18th century.
3. Great Britain--Economic conditions--19th century.
4. Great Britain--Politics and government--1660-1714.
5. Great Britain--Politics and government--1714-1837.
6. Great Britain--Economic policy.
I. Gauci, Perry.
338.9'41'009033-dc22

Library of Congress Cataloging-in-Publication Data
Gauci, Perry.
Regulating the British economy, 1660-1850 / Perry Gauci.
p. cm.
Includes bibliographical references and index.
ISBN 978-0-7546-6969-2 (hbk) -- ISBN 978-0-7546-9762-6 (ebk)
1. Trade regulation--Great Britain--History. 2. Free enterprise--Great Britain--History. 3. Great Britain--Economic policy. I. Title.
HD3616.G72G38 2011
330.941'07--dc22

2010049582

ISBN 9780754669692 (hbk)
ISBN 9780754697626 (ebk)

MIX
Paper from responsible sources
FSC® C018575
FSC www.fsc.org

Printed and bound in Great Britain by the MPG Books Group, UK

Contents

List of Figures and Tables

Figures

Tables

Notes on Contributors

Ian Barrett completed his doctorate in 2009, having been based at King's College, London. He examined the defence of the slave trade in the age of abolition, with particular focus on the social networks of the various organizations and actors involved, and on the discourses of anti-abolitionist groups. His first degree came from Oxford University.

Perry Gauci is VHH Green Fellow and Tutor in History at Lincoln College, Oxford. His published work has largely centred on the social and political resonance of economic change in the late seventeenth and eighteenth centuries, with particular interest on the ways in which merchants endeavoured to influence the political order at all levels of society. To date he has largely viewed them within a domestic context, but hopes to situate them within more challenging colonial and continental perspectives.

Bob Harris is Lightbody Fellow and Tutor in History at Worcester College, Oxford. His early work was on newspapers and the politics of the British Isles in the mid-Georgian period. Subsequently, he has published on Scottish reactions to the French Revolution, and for some years he has examined the political workings of the eighteenth-century British state. He is currently completing several articles and a book on Scottish urban history in the later Georgian period, products of a three-year AHRC-funded project on 'Scottish towns and urban society in the Age of Enlightenment, c.1745–1820'. He hopes soon to move onto a new project on gambling in Britain and its empire in the long eighteenth century.

Julian Hoppit is Astor Professor of British History at University College, London. His first book, on business failure in eighteenth-century England highlighted the importance of the legal, institutional and cultural environment within which business operated. His subsequent work on parliamentary legislation on the economy 1660–1800 led to a collaboration with Joanna Innes on a project which produced databases of acts, failed legislative initiatives and some sample sessions. He is now returning to these sources, supplementing them with some preliminary work on the bibliometrics of economic literature.

He plans to write a major new work, provisionally titled, 'Britain's Political Economies, 1660–1800'.

Jane Humphries is Professor of Economic History, and a Fellow of All Souls College, Oxford. She has worked on a range of issues dealing with growth and development, and has a longstanding interest in labour markets. She has also published extensively on gender, the family and the history of women's work. She is currently researching child labour in Britain during the Industrial Revolution and has recently published *Childhood and Child Labour in the British Industrial Revolution* (Cambridge, 2010).

Joanna Innes is a Fellow and Tutor of Somerville College, Oxford. Over the past 20 years she has published extensively in the field of legal and social policy. Some of her essays on this theme were published in 2009 under the title, *Inferior Politics: Social Problems and Social Policies in Eighteenth-Century Britain* (Oxford, 2009). Her current interests centre on the Age of Reform 1780–1830. Her broad interest in labour conditions has now led her to focus on wage regulation, and the development of political economy.

Daeryoon Kim is a Visiting Professor of History in the School of Humanities and Social Science at the Korea Advanced Institute of Science and Technology. His recently completed Oxford doctorate examined the political methods and ideas of colonial merchants in London in the period 1763–83.

Mark Knights is Professor of History at the University of Warwick. He has written extensively on the political culture of the late seventeenth and eighteenth centuries, and has shown particular interest in interdisciplinary approaches. His current interests include the early Enlightenment, petitioning from the 1640s to the 1840s, and the nature of polemic.

Philippe Minard is Professor at the University of Paris-8, and at the Ecole des Hautes Etudes en Sciences Sociales (EHESS, Paris). He is also a fellow of the CNRS-Paris (National Centre for Scientific Research). He studied at the Ecole Normale Superieure and at the University of Paris-1 (Sorbonne). He specializes in the economic and social history of France and England in the early modern period, and has published several books about work, economy and economic policy in eighteenth-century France.

Paul Minoletti is a D. Phil. student at Mansfield College, Oxford, researching the position of women in the textile industries during the Industrial Revolution.

He focuses on how the level of competition in labour markets affected the desire and ability of workers and employers to discriminate according to gender. He has presented papers at various seminars at Oxford and Uppsala universities, as well as at the 2010 Economic History Society annual conference.

William Pettigrew is Lecturer in American History at the University of Kent. He is completing his first book, *Freedom's Debt: Politics and the Causes of American Slavery*, which examines the part played by the constitutional changes of the late seventeenth and early eighteenth centuries in escalating Britain's involvement in the trans-Atlantic slave trade. He is now working on a broader study of how political change underpinned economic growth at the threshold of modernity.

Steve Pincus is Professor of History at Yale University. He has published widely on English, British, and European politics, political economy and culture in the later seventeenth and eighteenth centuries. Most recently he published *1688: The First Modern Revolution* (New Haven, CT, 2009). He is also very interested in socio-economic change on the ground, and is currently pursuing a project with an economist arguing for the central role of party politics and colonial consumption in causing British economic divergence.

Alice Wolfram is a graduate student at Yale University. Her interests lie in the social, economic and gender history of Britain and the British Atlantic world in the seventeenth and eighteenth centuries. Her dissertation will explore marriage, property and inheritance in the commercializing economies of London, Glasgow and Philadelphia during the long eighteenth centuries.

Preface

This book is the most tangible result of a series of workshops held at Lincoln College, Oxford between September 2008 and March 2010. An international assembly of younger and more established historians met on four occasions to present papers in an informal and supportive environment. As their contributions to this volume suggest, they came to the theme of economic regulation from a wide range of perspectives and interests, aiming to tackle this theme as a means to embed the economy within broader cultures of social and political life. This collection reflects their major conclusions, and their hopes for further work in the field. As co-ordinator, I have found it a real pleasure to work with such fine and generous colleagues, and these sessions will remain a source of constant inspiration for the rest of my career.

The workshops would not have happened without the generous financial support of the British Academy, and the John Fell Fund at the University of Oxford. Two other young scholars, David Todd and James Vaughn, were key participants in these sessions, and I eagerly anticipate their important contributions to the field in the near future. Professor David Hancock also provided vital support at an early stage of the project. I would also like to express sincere thanks to Aileen Mooney, research co-ordinator at the History Faculty at Oxford, for all her advice and enthusiasm. All the participants are also indebted to the staff at Lincoln College for providing superlative hospitality to ensure that the workshops were both convivial and productive.

The process of publication was generously supported by the Michael Zilkha Fund at Lincoln College, Oxford. I am also very grateful to Ashgate for their unstinting backing for this project, and particular thanks must go to Emily Yates for overseeing the most fluid of production schedules. The final stages of production have been much eased by the efficiency and expertise of Harry Smith. I would also like to acknowledge the Bodleian Library in Oxford for permission to reproduce the print on the cover, *England's Great Joy and Gratitude* (Firth a.3, fol. 123).

PG,
Lincoln College, Oxford

List of Abbreviations

Add. Mss	Additional manuscripts, British Library
BL	British Library
CJ	*Journals of the House of Commons*
Cobbett	*Cobbett's Parliamentary History of England* (36 vols, London, 1806–20)
EcHR	*Economic History Review*
EHR	*English Historical Review*
HJ	*Historical Journal*
HMC	Historical Manuscripts Commission
JMH	*Journal of Modern History*
LJ	*Journals of the House of Lords*
PP	*Parliamentary Papers*
Sessional Papers	*House of Commons Sessional Papers of the Eighteenth Century*, ed. Shelia Lambert (145 vols, Wilmington, 1975)
Statutes	*The Statutes of the Realm* (12 vols, London, 1810–27)
TNA	The National Archives

Figure I.1 *England's Great Joy and Gratitude*, c.1700

Source: The Bodleian Libraries, University of Oxford.

Introduction

Perry Gauci

The image on the cover of the present volume offers a rare visual insight into the core themes of this work. *England's Great Joy and Gratitude* celebrates the passage in 1700 of a measure designed to aid domestic manufacturers by prohibiting the import and sale of oriental wrought silks and calicoes. Re-export of such goods was still permitted as long as traders observed strict rules on their warehousing, but hefty fines were introduced to deter any who would seek to supply the domestic marketplace. The print envisages this measure of economic regulation as a cause for universal celebration, most obviously represented by the circle of men and women rejoicing around a bonfire. Around this happy scene the engraver has arranged a series of 14 images to highlight the wide social spectrum which will benefit from this act. Images of textile production predominate, from combers and fullers through to spinners, weavers and dyers. However, deliberate emphasis is placed on the joy that will come to farmers and landlords too, and to the sailors and shipowners who will soon transport the produce of a rejuvenated textile industry. Even an alehouse, the likely benefactor of the increased spending-power of the average textile-worker, is represented. The title of the act also made no secret of its ambition to provide work for the poor, thus proclaiming a universal communal benefit. As the legend proclaims in the middle of the human circle: 'now lett us all joyn hand in hand t'advance what most promotes our land'.[1]

While the print highlights common benefits, other details hint at the hard bargaining that had gone into its passage. For instance, the heraldic arms of three textile guilds are depicted, all of whom had had to work very hard to gain their point when battling with the East India interest, which may be represented by the chained wild beasts at the base of the picture. The Norwich Worsted Weavers

1 Two copies of the image can be found in the Bodleian Library – Firth a. 3, fol. 123. Scholars have usually dated it to c.1690, but there can be no doubt that it refers to the 1700 measure. For discussion of the broader significance of the print, see Roze Hentschell, *The Culture of Cloth in Early Modern England* (Aldershot, 2008), pp. 15–16. For its economic and political context, see Patrick O'Brien, Trevor Griffiths and Philip Hunt, 'Political Components of the Industrial Revolution: Parliament and the English Cotton Textile Industry, 1660–1774', *EcHR*, 44 (1991): pp. 395–423.

had first petitioned the Commons on this issue some four years before, and had seen three earlier attempts at legislation thwarted. Their ultimate success was clearly aided by the cumulative pressure from other sectional interests, including the London Weavers' Company depicted here, who had warned of the dire consequences which Indian imports represented to domestic silk manufacture.[2] However, a petition from Taunton came closest to claiming the communal benefit depicted in the print, arguing that defence of the clothing industry would be the best way 'to raise the value of our land, to lessen the number and charge of our poor, and to increase the riches and strength of the nation'. In a House deeply concerned at the impoverishment of English trade, and with a self-chosen mandate 'to consider the encouraging and improving the manufactures of this kingdom', the textile interest at last prevailed, and the bonfires of celebration could begin.[3]

This book endeavours to take a fresh look at the ways in which government and society sought to advance the British economy across a period of profound transformation. Its primary focus centres on the attitudes and processes which determined economic regulations such as the Silk Act. As we shall see, scholars have long argued over the importance of political institutions in economic advancement, and this collection will demonstrate how analysis of the debates on the regulation of trade can cast light on both political and economic development, as well as their interaction. The contributors will cast much light on the character and impact of economic regulation, but their primary concern remains the process of *regulating* at all socio-political levels. Not all economic regulation took on the formal character of statutory intervention, or involved

2 The strength of the early eighteenth-century Weavers' Company has been linked to its support from the lower social orders – Joseph P. Ward, *Metropolitan Communities: Trade Guilds, Identity and Change in Early Modern London* (Stanford, CA, 1997), pp. 125–43. For the longer-term importance of the London livery companies as lobbyists, see Ian Archer, 'The London Lobbies in the Late Sixteenth Century', *HJ*, 31 (1988): pp. 17–44.

3 *CJ*, vol. 11, pp. 496, 627; vol. 12, p. 308; vol. 13, pp. 97, 113–14, 176, 184, 189, 225; *Statutes*, vol. 7, pp. 598–9. Tim Keirn points out that a call for a complete ban on foreign silk imports had been rejected, for the 1700 act permitted re-export, and also the import of semi-finished calicoes (to aid English dyers) – 'Parliament, Legislation and the Regulation of English Textile Industries, 1689–1714', in Lee Davison, Tim Hitchcock, Tim Keirn and Robert B. Shoemaker (eds), *Stilling the Grumbling Hive: The Response to Social and Economic Problems in England, 1689–1750* (Stroud, 1992), esp. pp. 9–10. David Ormrod has argued that Parliament's backing for manufacturers represented a decisive advantage for the domestic textile industry over Dutch rivals, whose political leaders (within a weaker federal political structure) prioritized the commercial sector over manufacturers and other economic interests – *The Rise of Commercial Empires: England and the Netherlands in the Age of Mercantilism, 1650–1770* (Cambridge, 2003), pp. 49–51.

the complex interplay of interests represented in *England's Great Joy*, but the contributors will show through a wide variety of case-studies that the economy was a central preoccupation of governors and citizens alike, and that the processes through which it was discussed and managed can reveal much about contemporary attitudes to both a changing economy and a changing political culture. The time scale of 1660–1850 has been designed to address key narratives of political and economic development, as England, and subsequently Britain, was transformed from a secondary European monarchy to a global economic superpower with established parliamentary sovereignty.[4]

England's Great Joy again highlights some of these key themes of interest, most obviously the shift of power from Crown to Parliament. Even by 1700 it was clear that the enhanced role of the post-1688 Parliament had had a profound impact on the ways in which politicians and economic interests interacted, and the prolonged battle over imported silks was merely one of the more bitter struggles to secure parliamentary sanction now that it appeared a more accessible and secure route to economic advantage. Many of the contributions focus on the ways in which this shift of power influenced the processes by which economic interests sought favour, and they also question how political and economic actors conceived of the role of the state in economic affairs. The fierce protectionism of domestic industry highlighted by the Silk Act of 1700 can be regarded as the epitome of the 'mercantilist' mindset which many scholars attribute to ministers and traders alike for much of the period in question, and a central concern of the volume is to achieve a better understanding of how economic theory and knowledge influenced policy and contemporary attitudes.[5] The need for such perspectives only becomes more obvious from the later eighteenth century, when protectionist instincts were increasingly challenged by doctrines of free trade and by the appearance of new industries lacking the mooring of a supposedly traditional 'regulated' economy. The contributors will offer new insights into this liberalizing trend, but their greater hope remains the encouragement of

---

4 Contemporaries were very alive to the growing importance of trade to the international world order. As Istvan Hont has observed, the eighteenth century was 'the period in which the interdependence of politics and the economy first emerged as the central topic of political theory' – *Jealousy of Trade: International Competition and the Nation-State in Historical Perspective* (Cambridge, MA, 2005), p. 4.

5 A key account remains Ralph Davis, 'The Rise of Protection in England 1689–1786', *EcHR*, 19 (1966): pp. 306–17. For the importance of the balance of trade in debate on the textiles industry at the turn of the century, see Lee Davison et al. (eds), *Stilling the Grumbling Hive*, pp. 1–24. David Ormrod has identified the opponents of the East India Company as a key force behind the protectionism of 1690–1704 – *Rise of Commercial Empires*, esp. pp. 43–59.

further research into a field usually studied through particular economic sectors or within limited time-periods.

In order to provide an effective platform for the collection, this introduction will begin by focusing on some of the key historiographical trends which have helped to forge the overall character of the book. It will then provide a brief overview of the ways in which the regulation of the economy was conceived in the period, and how 'regulation' itself was understood by contemporaries. It will then outline the key findings of the volume, and stake out an agenda for future research. Encouraged by recent work which has highlighted how the economy can illuminate the social, political and cultural development of Britain, it will offer new insights into the ways in which contemporaries understood economic change and sought to influence it.[6]

Historiographical Perspectives

This book owes a great deal to significant historiographical developments over the last 30 years, and the contributors would acknowledge three trends as particularly important for framing their questions and approaches. First, its focus on the interaction of political and economic spheres reflects a growing conviction among economic historians that there is a significant political component to British economic development in the long eighteenth century. Conversely, political historians, especially those investigating state formation, have helped to re-conceptualize the ways in which government and civil society interacted, and have advanced new ways of understanding the process of policy formation. Finally, in a post-Marxian world, historians have begun to reassess the agency of economic processes and ideas, and placed them at the heart of social and cultural change. The research interests of the contributors to this volume reflect these important historiographical trends, for they come to the issue of economic regulation from a wide spectrum of approaches, and few would describe themselves as economic historians *per se*. However, all would attest to their common interest in economic regulation as a means to understanding societal change across a very broad spectrum.

The essential fluidity of debate about the character and causes of economic change in the long eighteenth century has been fundamental to the recent burgeoning interest in this field. While most historians can agree that Britain's economy and its economic fortunes were transformed in the 1660–1850 period,

---

[6] For fuller historiographical surveys, see Julian Hoppit's further reading section at the end of this book.

they can agree on little with regard to the timing, causes and consequences of this headline change. As a sign of this, in recent years it has become less fashionable to talk of revolutions in agriculture, commerce, finance and industry without significant qualifications in terms of the scale, pace and scope of change. In particular, the findings of these 'new economic historians' have forced scholars to reconsider the agency of economic change across a broad front.[7] With particular interest for this study, the conjunctures of dynamic ideas and practices have been unshackled, most notably in the case of economic liberalism and industrialization, thus providing opportunities to reconstruct key causative relationships. This unravelling of older narratives has obvious ramifications for our understanding of agencies of change, and leading historians have duly begun to re-assess the basic mechanisms for economic growth.[8] Significantly, the 'new economic historians' have remained sceptical of the impact of political institutions in the advancement of the economy, in keeping with their argument that the pace of economic growth was sluggish before 1815, if not 1850. As one commentator observed, their work was responsible for consolidating the view that 'the state was not an active participant, and that it might even have slowed down economic development'.[9]

Their views, however, have not gone unchallenged, and have faced searching criticism from proponents of 'new institutional economics' such as Douglass North and Barry Weingast, who regard legal and social frameworks as important determinants of economic change. Their intervention of 1989 was seminal, when they made the most powerful argument to date for the role of political institutions in fostering economic growth. As they termed it, 'the triumph of parliamentary interests in the Glorious Revolution' ushered in more stable institutional foundations for economic growth, curtailing the potential arbitrariness of both Crown and Parliament. In short, 'the emergence of political and civil liberties was inextricably linked with economic freedom', and, but for these changes, the country's political and economic future 'would very likely have

---

7 A seminal work in the re-casting of Britain's economic development remains Nicholas F.R. Crafts, *British Economic Growth during the Industrial Revolution* (Oxford, 1985).

8 For example, new research has highlighted the durability of European apprenticeships throughout the eighteenth century, thus demonstrating that it was not economic forces (especially industrialization) which brought about change, but political factors, most notably anti-guild ideology in the early nineteenth century – Stephan R. Epstein and Maarten Prak (eds), *Guilds, Innovation and the European Economy, 1400–1800* (Cambridge, 2008).

9 Martin Daunton, *Progress and Poverty: An Economic and Social History of Britain 1700–1850* (Oxford, 1995), pp. 11–18, 501. Others observed that 'the new history of the first industrial revolution ... seems devoid of any informed analysis of government' – Patrick O'Brien et al., 'Political Components', p. 396.

been very different, potentially more in keeping with that of France and Spain'.[10] Their core argument has not received universal support, but it has certainly helped to focus attention on the contribution of state institutions to economic growth. Most significantly, leading economic historians have begun to challenge traditional assumptions regarding non-interventionist governments, and have queried the creeping triumph of *laissez-faire* economics from the later eighteenth century onwards.[11] Martin Daunton's 1995 survey posed a significant question mark against the putative inactivity or even obstructionism of state institutions, arguing that 'a strong case' could be made for seeing them as 'remarkably effective and strong' in nurturing new industries, protecting home markets and securing overseas markets by military force. His overall conclusion remained opaque, however, merely suggesting that 'perhaps the development of the British economy was a political rather than a merely economic phenomenon'.[12] Ron Harris subsequently went as far as to suggest that the poles of politics and the economy could no longer be segregated, and that 'it seems more appropriate to speak now of the state *within* the economy rather than of the state *and* the economy'.[13]

---

10 Douglass C. North and Barry R. Weingast, 'Constitutions and Commitment: The Evolution of Institutions Governing Public Choice in Seventeenth-Century England', *Journal of Economic History*, 49 (1989): pp. 803–32. Other important comparative work remains Robert B. Ekelund and Robert D. Tollison, *Mercantilism as a Rent-Seeking Society: Economic Regulation in Historical Perspective* (College Station, TX, 1981); Stephan R. Epstein, *Freedom and Growth: The Rise of States and Markets in Europe 1300–1750* (London, 2000). The latter is critical of the North-Weingast model, and for a robust critique of drawing too close a connection between constitutional rights and economic change, see Robert C. Allen, *The British Industrial Revolution in Global Perspective* (Cambridge, 2009), pp. 4–5.

11 Many historians now see the rise of economic liberalism as a very slow process, and one that saw little momentum before the 1820s – Kenneth Morgan, 'Mercantilism and the British Empire, 1688–1815', and Anthony Howe, 'Restoring Free Trade: The British Experience, 1776–1873', in Donald Winch and Patrick O'Brien (eds), *The Political Economy of British Historical Experience, 1688–1914* (Oxford, 2002).

12 Daunton, *Progress and Poverty*, esp. Part V, 'Public Policy and the State'. His recent work has more confidently asserted that 'the growth of Britain as a major industrial power was aided rather than hindered by public policy' – *State and Market in Victorian Britain: War, Welfare and Capitalism* (Woodbridge, 2008), p. 2.

13 Ron Harris, 'Government and the Economy 1688–1850', in Roderick Floud and Paul A. Johnson (eds), *The Cambridge Economic History of Modern Britain, Vol. 1: Industrialisation 1700–1860* (Cambridge, 2004), Chapter 8. Focusing mainly on industrialization, Harris identifies important regulatory influences with regard to the ownership of enterprise, fiscal activity and property definition, although he notes that 'the British way seems to have been the middle-road' in terms of state/private initiative. He also remains opaque on the impact of regulation on growth, suggesting that 'hindsight shows us that something in this mix did the trick'. For recent evidence of the British government's

Both authors acknowledge that governments were prepared to contemplate intervention in the economy if it was sufficiently motivated, especially in the case of finance, or were even prepared to pass laws it did not seek to enforce properly. Ministers, however, were still largely dependent on vested interests to provide initiative, enabling Parliament to emerge as arbitrator to ensure a generally level playing-field. Significantly, even those sceptical of the positive impact of such interventions in fostering economic growth, such as Joel Mokyr, still accept that 'on all accounts formal institutions and politics mattered'.[14]

Political historians have shown more consistent interest in tracing the relationship between economic and political development in the long eighteenth century, most obviously through study of the impact of 'mercantilism' as a sovereign force in promoting economic growth as part of the European power struggle.[15] Domestic constitutional conflict has also been studied through an economic lens for the light it can cast on the battles between Crown and Parliament.[16] More recently, our understanding of the interaction of political and economic change has been further advanced by growing scholarly interest in the legislative business of Westminster, which has highlighted the growing pressures on MPs to answer interest-led demands from the late seventeenth century onwards. As Paul Langford observed, ministerial and parliamentary power 'was deployed in response to the demands of interests, groups and communities, not so much imposing a sovereign will as providing a legal service'. In light of this scrum of interests historians have remained sceptical of claims that the period

---

flexibility in enforcing its own economic regulations, see Adrian Pearce, *British Trade with Spanish America 1763–1888* (Liverpool, 2007).

14 Joel Mokyr, *The Enlightened Economy: An Economic History of Britain, 1700–1850* (New Haven, CT, 2009), pp. 392–448, quotation at p. 413. He regards the flexibility and adaptability of the British political system as supportive of economic growth.

15 The literature sparked by Eli Heckscher's *Mercantilism* (London, 1931) is extensive and contentious, problematizing the application of the term. For a sharp critique of its evolution and usage, see Donald Coleman, 'Mercantilism Revisited', *HJ*, 23 (1980): pp. 773–91, in which he observed that, 'whatever historians say about mercantilism, economists and social scientists simply use it today as a shorthand for protection and other sorts of state intervention'.

16 The successes of the rivals of the Crown-backed overseas trading companies have enjoyed long-standing interest among late Stuart political historians – George L. Cherry, 'The Development of the English Free Trade Movement in Parliament', *JMH*, 25 (1953): pp. 103–19. These companies continue to be viewed as key testing-grounds in political battles at all social levels – Gary De Krey, *A Fractured Society: The Politics of London in the First Age of Party, 1688–1715* (Oxford, 1985); De Krey, *London and the Restoration, 1659–1683* (Cambridge, 2005), pp. 321–5; Steve Pincus, *1688: The First Modern Revolution* (New Haven, CT, 2009), Chapter 12.

saw the development of clear economic 'policy', but few would doubt that from the late seventeenth century onwards the economy was an established concern for politicians at Westminster.[17]

The significance of the economy as a political issue has also been highlighted by reassessments of the role and character of the 'state' itself. John Brewer's study of the rise of the 'fiscal-military' state after 1688 was important for underlining the connection between constitutional change and Britain's subsequent rise as a commercial and naval superpower.[18] Subsequent work has further re-conceptualized the state, such as that of Mike Braddick, who argues for significant state expansion after 1688, or, as he puts it, an increase in the 'functional space' of the state. He emphasizes that this did not see an accompanying increase in the power of the state, for political authority was still a much negotiated entity, and such expansion needed legitimation, either through direct consent, or by the state's servants exhibiting precision and impartiality in the use of their powers.[19] Parliament's growing power and annual sessions were clearly vital to these processes, but scholars have been careful not to confine their conception of the 'state' to the precincts of Westminster. Most studies stress that the direct remit and interest of the executive remained limited to military and financial matters, and that much of the day-to-day regulation of national life was left to unpaid local officials. Thus, certain aspects of economic life, especially those which might raise significant revenues for the Crown, were closely monitored by Whitehall. Beyond matters pertaining to customs and excise, however, ministerial influence was more variable, and often economic lobbies were forced to turn to Parliament to put pressure on the executive to respond.[20]

---

[17] Paul Langford, *Public Life and the Propertied Englishman 1689–1798* (Oxford, 1991), pp. 139–206; Peter Jupp, *The Governing of Britain, 1688–1848: The Executive, Parliament and the People* (London, 2006). Increased interest in the economic business of Westminster also reflects growing acceptance that Parliament could and did play 'a crucial role in domestic government' – Joanna Innes, *Inferior Politics: Social Problems and Social Policies in Eighteenth-Century Britain* (Oxford, 2009), esp. p. 3.

[18] John Brewer, *The Sinews of Power: War, Money and the English State, 1688–1783* (London, 1989). As he observed, 'above all the government wanted to know about trade, for the balance of trade was seen as one of the chief indicators of England's success or failure as a commercial power', pp. 223–4.

[19] Michael Braddick, 'Civility and Authority', in David Armitage and Michael Braddick (eds), *The British Atlantic World 1500–1800* (Basingstoke, 2002), pp. 93–112. For his broader work on state development, see his *State Formation in Early Modern England, c. 1550–1700* (Cambridge, 2000).

[20] For a useful summary of the existing literature on government intervention in the economy, see Jupp, *Governing of Britain*, pp. 73–5, 166–74. Economic regulation does not feature strongly amongst the routine duties of the magistrate at a local level, although

The contingent nature of parliamentary and Crown intervention has also been highlighted by more intensive studies of the legislative process, which have shown that Parliament's role as arbitrator of national interests was not necessarily readily welcomed by politicians at Westminster. For instance, growing levels of parliamentary legislation cannot be used as a crude index of governmental interest, for such growth reflected only specific bursts of enthusiasm, a limited range of societal concerns and the influence of a variety of non-governmental interests.[21] From a range of social and economic studies a key collection of articles in 1992 concluded that the state was a reactive mechanism in the first half of the eighteenth century, and that 'its involvement in the promotion of economic growth and social welfare took the form of acting on initiatives emanating largely outside executive government'. These findings are most germane to the core concerns of this volume, in particular for stimulating the thoughts of the contributors on how political-cultural changes, such as the broadening 'public sphere', influenced both ministers and economic interests.[22]

All of this scholarship has highlighted the importance of the period for the relationship between politics and the economy, and further inspiration for study of this vital dynamic has come from new approaches to the role of the economy as a force for socio-cultural change. Although concerns have been expressed at the decline of 'hard' socio-economic studies since the 1980s, there has been huge interest in the ways in which the economy both shaped and responded to a broad range of societal changes, and these historiographies have proved enormously influential to the approaches of the contributors. Three historical literatures hold particular significance for this collection: consumerism, credit and empire. All capture the dynamism of the economy in terms of the challenges and opportunities of growth, and also highlight its centrality to our understanding of the developing fabric of British society. Indeed, historians of these fields have proved that economic phenomena can be seen as representative, if not causal agents, of major socio-cultural change. In short, akin to recent

parliamentary-supported improvement commissions clearly had a significant impact on economic infrastructure and development – David Eastwood, *Government and Community in the English Provinces, 1700–1870* (Basingstoke, 1997), pp. 117–54.

21 See Julian Hoppit (ed.), *Failed Legislation, 1660–1800* (London, 1997). This work rightly highlights the difficulties of discerning the original source of regulation, for, 'in truth, even in relation to fiscal measures, it is not always possible to draw a hard and fast distinction between governmental and non-governmental legislation' – p. 7. Whatever their point of origin, Cecil D. Chandaman pinpointed the 1670s as the key stage when parliamentary revenue acts were used systematically for the promotion of domestic trades – *The English Public Revenue* (Oxford, 1975), esp. pp. 9–36.

22 Davison et al., *Stilling the Grumbling Hive*, pp. xli, 10–11. For a recent critique of the 'highly schematic' formulation of a 'reactive state', see Innes, *Inferior Politics*, pp. 7–8.

historians of the law, who have transformed the arid statute-book into a guidebook for understanding societal relationships, the contributors do not regard the economy as a matter for specialist practitioners, but as a major force for constructing identities and determining social networks.[23]

Consumerism, in particular, has highlighted how production can be married to social and cultural change, for economic actors were linked to classes eager to define and express their perceived roles in society.[24] Credit is perhaps even more revelatory in demonstrating the importance of economic relationships for establishing networks of interest and for determining societal hierarchies. Both these themes highlight that the economy was not a specialist interest or practice, but a subject with an incredible social resonance, and historians have responded with innovative inter-disciplinary studies. As Margot Finn has observed, 'only by combining culture and economics, law and society can we understand the full repertoire of consumer activities that powered the English economy'. Of course, this does not mean that the force of economic change was well understood, or welcomed, especially among the higher orders, but these imaginative approaches suggest that closer scrutiny of its impact can reveal much about institutions and communities which are primarily non-economic in character or purpose.[25]

Above all, these fields pose some very useful questions for helping us to appreciate both the growing opportunities *and* potential difficulties for regulation of the economy. Credit and consumer historians have not tried to argue that attitudes towards the economy were changing very much at all, but their work has highlighted how the audience for such debate, and the perceived resonance of economic issues were transformed across the period. For certain, the potential direct constituency for economic regulation was growing in our

---

23 The work of Peter King has particular resonance in this context, for he has highlighted 'the two-way relationship between court practice on the ground and statutory or other initiatives at the centre', the former of which must be acknowledged as a key influence on reform in the late eighteenth and early nineteenth centuries – *Crime and the Law in England, 1750–1840: Remaking Justice from the Margins* (Cambridge, 2006), quotation at p. 3.

24 Neil McKendrick, John Brewer, and John H. Plumb (eds), *The Birth of a Consumer Society: The Commercialization of England in the Eighteenth Century* (London, 1982). For a recent challenge to the notion of a consumer society, see Maxine Berg, *Luxury and Pleasure in Eighteenth-century Britain* (Oxford, 2005). She suggests that the 'product revolution' might have a longer life, for it does not convey any necessary teleologies in terms of enhanced standards or living, and acknowledges the pre-existence of more historic 'consumer societies'. For an important study of the interaction of production, commerce and consumerism, see John Smail, *Merchants, Markets, and Manufacturers* (Basingstoke, 1999).

25 Margot Finn, *The Character of Credit: Personal Debt in English Culture, 1740–1914* (Cambridge, 2003), quotation at p. 22. See also, Craig Muldrew, *The Economy of Obligation: The Culture of Credit and Social Relations in Early Modern England* (Basingstoke, 1998).

period with the expansion of consumerism and credit networks. This enhanced participation in national markets may have forced a greater responsibility of intervention upon the state, without any sense of political will, or political empowerment, on the part of the people. Beyond questions of audience, their findings have also demonstrated the potentially complex set of assumptions which lay behind contemporary views on the workings and moralities of the economy. More generally, their exposition of the negotiated character of many socio-economic relationships also warns against simplistic top-down or bottom-up models of regulation.

The debate on empire has probably had an even more direct bearing on our thinking, for it is accepted as one of the prime areas for government intervention, and has been widely credited for promoting the politics of economic interest, particularly from a British perspective after 1707.[26] The literature sparked in this area is huge, but it is revealing that there is still a great deal of debate with regard to the actual character of imperial 'rule' within the international economy, and whether continuity or change characterized British governmental responses to the challenges of making money from its global territories.[27] Of course, ministers did not simply regard the empire as purely a matter of commerce, but much can be learnt about domestic economic policy from the state's experimentation in the imperial sphere. In particular, the keynote of restraint in imperial policy throughout the period, and metropolitan fears for uncontrollable growth do have domestic economic parallels.

---

[26] For particular emphasis on the interrelationship between economic growth and imperial policy, see Nancy F. Koehn, *The Power of Commerce: Economy and Governance in the First British Empire* (Ithaca, NY, 1994). For British perspectives, see Tom Devine, *Scotland's Empire 1600–1815* (London, 2003); Allan I. Macinnes, *Union and Empire: The Making of the United Kingdom* (Cambridge, 2007); Thomas Bartlett, 'Ireland, Empire and Union, 1690–1801', in Kevin Kenny (ed.), *Ireland and the British Empire* (Oxford, 2004), pp. 61–89; Trevor Griffiths, Philip Hunt and Patrick O'Brien, 'Scottish, Irish, and Imperial Connections: Parliament, the Three Kingdoms, and the Mechanization of Cotton Spinning in Eighteenth-Century Britain', *EcHR*, 61 (2008): pp. 625–50. Many studies have also focused on the politics of imperial interest post-1688 as crucial to subsequent British development and stability. Note, in particular, the 'gentlemanly capitalism' described by Peter Cain and Anthony Hopkins as a key force for the alliance of land, finance and commerce behind imperial growth – *British Imperialism, 1688–2000* (2nd edn, Harlow, 2002), esp. Chapter 2.

[27] For a useful summary of current thinking on the negotiated character of imperial governance, see Ian K. Steele, 'The Anointed, the Appointed and the Elected: Governance of the British Empire, 1689–1784', in Peter Marshall (ed.), *The Oxford History of the British Empire: Volume II, The Eighteenth Century* (Oxford, 1998), pp. 105–27. From a more comparative imperial perspective, Sir John Elliot observed that 'where empire was established, regulation was never far behind' – *Empires of the Atlantic World: Britain and Spain in America 1492–1830* (New Haven, CT, 2006), p. 222.

Furthermore, the hesitancy with which successive administrations took upon full responsibility for the risks of empire, and its reluctance to delegate powers is very revealing regarding the outlook and priorities of politicians *as governors* as they contemplated intervention in the economy. Conversely, the increasing centrality of empire as a root of national wealth and prestige argued for their taking responsibility for its regulation and management, and may well have facilitated regulation of the domestic economy too.[28]

These recent historiographical trends have been critical to shaping the work of the contributors, and have highlighted the rich opportunities for advancing our understanding of the interaction of politics and economy in the period. The liveliness of the field clearly attests to the contemporary importance of the economy as a 'public' matter, which held the attention of a growing constituency of interests, many of whom sought to work Britain's changing political mechanisms in their favour. To many contemporaries, the economy came to be regarded as a 'new' or distinct subject, which could be debated and directed in novel ways, and could potentially command a more favourable public reception. The excitement of the times is ably represented by the contributors, whose widely differing perspectives and approaches serve to communicate the importance and societal resonance of these processes. The next section will seek to clarify the ways in which economic regulation was conceived and attempted amid these debates, and how such attitudes influenced governmental intervention in the economy.

Practices and Perceptions of Regulation

In common with other key areas of eighteenth-century governance, British economic regulation in this period defies easy categorization.[29] At one end

---

[28] Elizabeth Mancke's work on empire and diplomacy is enlightening here, for she demonstrates how domestic constitutional battles and European competition argued for both greater and reduced regulation of empire – 'Empire and State', in Armitage and Braddick (eds), *British Atlantic World*, pp. 175–95. Peter Marshall has recently suggested that it was the state's rising capabilities for raising funds and waging wars which encouraged reform of imperial governance to boost metropolitan authority – 'State and Empire', in Peter Marshall, *The Making and Unmaking of Empires: Britain, India and America, c. 1750–1783* (Oxford, 2005), pp. 57–85.

[29] For instructive comparisons in the fields of crime and social provision, see Innes, *Inferior Politics*, 'Introduction'. For a case-study highlighting the flexible pragmatism of parliamentary regulation in a key economic field, see Raymond L. Sickinger, 'Regulation or Ruination: Parliament's Consistent Pattern of Mercantilist Regulation of the English Textile Trade, 1660–1800', *Parliamentary History*, 19 (2000): pp. 211–32.

of the spectrum, statutory interventions could dictate the parameters of international commerce through the Navigation Laws, or seek to resolve imminent emergencies such as the re-coinage crisis of 1696. Chapters in this collection duly focus on responses to these major measures, but equal attention is given to more routine prescriptions, such as the rules which governed the setting of wages or factory hours. Given this range of economic concerns, it was inevitable that regulatory practice varied enormously across sectors and regions, and its timing relied heavily on the self-interest and relative influence of the economic groups involved in the debate.[30] As Philippe Minard points out in his analysis of attitudes towards regulation, both ministers and economic actors often had decidedly mixed views on these interventions, and such confusion of motives did not aid consistency of regulatory policy or practice. However, the sheer scope and variety of regulation only highlights the perceived importance of public debate of the economy, and demonstrates that the institutions of the state were held to have a vital role to play in the promotion of economic growth. Political and economic developments only intensified such debate at all levels of society, and helped to shape conceptions of 'regulation' itself.

At the start of the period, government influence on the economy ranged from the direct to the very indirect, from active intervention to mere 'nightwatchman' duties involving minimal supervision.[31] Under Charles II and James II, the Crown still retained widespread powers to intervene in the economy, but the increasing authority of Parliament had a key influence on economic regulatory practice. As William Pettigrew demonstrates in the opening chapter of this volume, constitutional change helped to establish Parliament's central role as a forum for discussion of economic policy in this period, and most regulatory

---

30 The sheer range of parliamentary interventions in the economy is highlighted by the subject classification employed by the Failed Legislation project. The Economy forms one of the ten 'major categories' of legislation, and is subdivided into 43 sub-categories. Other major categories which cover economic interests include Finance (Money and Banking), Social Issues (Labour) and Communications, adding a further 26 sub-categories – Hoppit, *Failed Legislation*, pp. 30–32.

31 Jacinct Jordana and David Levi-Faur (eds), *The Politics of Regulation in the Age of Governance* (Cheltenham, 2004), offer a useful political-scientist approach to the models of regulation which governments might employ. The most direct form encompasses regulation as governance, in other words, the introduction of rules, often enforced by an appointed agency to monitor compliance. On the other hand, more general governmental regulation can seek to 'steer' the economy (which can include taxation and bounties). They also acknowledge yet broader forms of social control, which can include the setting of legal and quasi-legal norms, with or without monitoring agencies. This can include non-intentional regulation, and non-state influences, and the market itself acting as a regulatory force.

debate targeted its legislative services either directly or indirectly. With more regular sessions after 1688, and the supremacy of the statute generally recognized, economic interests bombarded Westminster with petitions with ever greater regularity, and secured ever higher success rates for their legislative endeavours.[32] At this most visible level, Parliament intervened in the economy directly, setting rules and on occasion appointing monitoring agencies for the enforcement of these rules. It also worked closely with executive bodies, most obviously the various incarnations of the Board of Trade, to gather information and review the impact of its regulations. Also on a regular basis, laws were passed which significantly influenced economic exchange via the imposition of tariffs. These measures did not always have clear economic objectives in mind, and could be motivated by the demands of the Treasury rather than any obvious rationale for economic growth. The offer of bounties, however, was a more positive incentive to economic development, and Julian Hoppit's chapter highlights the significant scale of these interventions. Predictably, these initiatives varied according to sector, and across time, but there can be no doubt that Westminster saw increasing regulatory debate after 1688, and that the opportunities for both regulation and de-regulation featured prominently in the minds of the economic lobbies who flocked to its precincts.[33]

Not all regulatory debate took place in Parliament, however, and it is important to acknowledge other channels through which state and society could influence economic development.[34] For instance, the executive retained an important role in the negotiation of commercial treaties with other countries, and helped to monitor overseas markets through consular officials. In its judicial capacity, it also exerted much influence on the operation of economic regulation. In fact, a complete re-codification of commercial law was masterminded by Lord

---

[32] Failure rates for economic measures dropped significantly between 1660–1688 (81 per cent) and 1760–1800 (25.5 per cent), with an overall failure rate of 34.2 per cent. Different sectors of the economy experienced different success rates: land-related measures, dominated by enclosure, only suffered a 24 per cent failure rate, external trade 33 per cent, and internal trade 69 per cent – Hoppit, *Failed Legislation*, pp. 9–10.

[33] The economy features prominently in recent discussions of the continuous interest in political arithmetic in the eighteenth century, which promoted the collection and dissemination of statistics in the public sphere – Julian Hoppit, 'Political Arithmetic in Eighteenth-Century England', *EcHR*, 2nd ser. 49 (1996): pp. 516–40; Innes, *Inferior Politics*, pp. 109–75.

[34] Note the important collection by Julian Hoppit (ed.), *Parliaments, Nations and Identities in Britain and Ireland, 1660–1850* (Manchester, 2003), whose contributors acknowledge the key integrative role played by the Westminster Parliament within the British Isles and its empire, but also suggest that not all significant reforms were mediated through it.

Mansfield in the mid-eighteenth century without any recourse to Parliament.[35] The chapters of both Bob Harris and Julian Hoppit also show the importance of regional bodies for debate of the economy, such as the Convention of Royal Burghs in Scotland. At a more local level, a great deal of economic activity was regulated by magistrates acting according to notions of local custom with variable guidance from the centre, as Joanna Innes highlights in her chapter of the regulation of wages. Paul Minoletti also demonstrates in his chapter on the gendered politics of the textile industry that wide discretion in implementation was practised at ground level, and regulations could be overlooked, evaded, manipulated or fall into disuse according to local circumstances.

Although such wide variation in the forms and forums of regulatory practice makes it difficult to generalize about state intervention in the economy, it can also pinpoint many key features of governmental attitudes towards regulation. For certain, 'direct' regulation in the form of rule-setting enforced by supervisory bodies was rarely attempted in our period, and can be attributed to a basic reluctance to pay or enable state agencies to monitor economic practice, or simply to a lack of consensus on the rules which might apply. Governments were much more likely to sanction regulation via tariffs and bounties, reflecting their predominant revenue interest, as well as their thinking on the most effective methods of ensuring protected markets to preserve jobs. MPs were also willing to delegate powers to local authorities to oversee the enforcement of regulations, often initially on a short-term trial basis, doubtless attracted by the minimum outlay of resources involved. These categories of regulation were not mutually exclusive either, and this provided many opportunities for both ministers and local politicians to seek a re-calibration of regulatory levels, without necessarily moving between the poles of a 'command' economy to a *laissez-faire* system. Regulatory practice was highly varied and fluid, but such characteristics can be seen as a positive response to the needs of both ministers and economic interests.[36]

---

[35] David Lieberman charts how Lord Chief Justice Mansfield's 'system of mercantile jurisprudence' was introduced via key court decisions without a major contribution from statute law – *The Province of Legislation Determined* (Cambridge, 1989), pp. 99–121.

[36] Jordana and Levi-Faur have also highlighted different *types* of regulatory aim, beyond the dichotomy of regulation and de-regulation. Most helpful for this present study is their conception of re-regulation (or the establishment of new settings of regulation). Re-calibration seems much more in keeping with the modesty of eighteenth-century state intervention, and accords with the short-termist and experimental nature of much parliamentary legislation – *Politics of Regulation*, esp. pp. 1–8. Lars Magnusson points out that even the free trade reforms of the nineteenth century did not constitute 'total deregulation' but rather 'implied the replacement of old forms of regulation with new ones' – Magnusson and Jan Ottosson (eds), *The State, Regulation and the Economy: An Historical Perspective* (Cheltenham, 2001), p. 107.

The fluidity of regulatory processes is most directly represented by the varying conceptions of 'regulation' in this period, and we must be wary of reviewing governmental intervention in the economy through the often-prejudiced perspectives of contemporary observers, especially of the retrospective nineteenth-century variety.[37] Mark Knights highlights in his chapter that at critical moments 'regulation' could gain widespread interest as a buzzword for reform, and economic measures could be regarded as essential elements of a wider campaign to restore the moral health of society. In parliamentary circles, the frequency with which 'regulation' was specifically sought increased across the period, but the employment of the term reflected a diverse scale of policy ambition.[38] In the late seventeenth century, it was associated with the spectre of increased state intervention, most notoriously in the shape of James II's regulators of corporations. On the other hand, a broad survey of its usage in legislation suggests that 'regulation' was often used in the rather literal sense of 'making regular' or standardizing, and this meaning was retained into the early nineteenth century.[39] Given the decentralized and diverse character of much eighteenth-century government, contemporaries may well have seen such standardization as most ambitious, but the application of the term remains occasional and conservative in tone. Even in George II's reign, when there was a notable increase in parliamentary usage of the term, its ambition was still limited. Significantly, it was often cited as an aspiration in tandem with other goals, often in the form of measures seeking the regulation *and* government of

37 The fluidity of political language has been highlighted by Joanna Innes, 'Reform in English Public Life: The Fortunes of a Word', in Arthur Burns and Innes (eds), *Rethinking the Age of Reform: Britain 1780–1850* (Cambridge, 2003), pp. 71–97.

38 The British Official Publications Collaborative Reader Information Service (BOPCRIS) suggests increasing use of the term 'regulation' in a parliamentary context. The reigns of William III to George I record only some four hits a year, but under George II the average rose to 20 p.a., and then 80 p.a. under George III, and 170 p.a. under George IV (although only 100 p.a. under William IV). The overall increase in parliamentary business clearly had a significant influence on the prominence of the term.

39 For instance, note the report of 12 May 1729 that shipmasters had been 'obliged to think of rules for some regulation' to ensure equity during the unloading of ships (for the first unladen coals might gain an advantage in price). The shipowners revealed that they already had 'entered' into a regulation, highlighting the opportunities for self-regulation. In a similar vein, on 18 April 1732 it was reported that 'a good regulation' of the fees of law-officers had 'been able to preserve itself for above 130 years', indicating that the best regulations encouraged good self-government – *CJ*, vol. 21, pp. 370, 892. A more interventionist usage of the term often occurred within the province of individual behaviour, where the meaning has much more obviously the intention of *control* or *restraint*, and this sense also reflects use of 'regulation' in non-parliamentary sources.

a particular sector. Furthermore, continuity with past practice was also implied, highlighted by the constant emphasis on the *further*, the *better* or *the more effectual* regulation of existing measures.[40]

Significant change in parliamentary usage, however, can be espied in the early nineteenth century, when regulation took on a much more polemical meaning, stemming from the ideological force of free trade agitation. In a landmark move against proposed timber duties, on 20 June 1820 a petition of London's North American merchants railed against 'every restrictive regulation of trade not essential to the revenue', while a witness later testified to 'that unprecedented and unprincipled Love of Regulation and Restriction exhibited in this bill'. The following year a dissenting vote on the measure in the Commons was even more forthright, lambasting it as a 'specimen of our predilection for that illiberal, artificial, and restrictive System of Regulation, which has long disgraced our Commercial Code'. Thus, even though previous administrations had been very wary of intervening in the economy, nineteenth-century critics fumed against the inconsistent and varied 'system' of regulation in operation, believing it to reflect a coherent mindset intent on ever greater government control. Regulation was thus thrust to the heart of economic debate, and was increasingly conceived in ideological terms.[41]

The discordance between practice and perception remains of immense interest to the contributors to this volume, and in their varied ways they seek to explore this relationship through consideration of regulation, regulators and the regulated. Ranging broadly across ministers, economic commentators and traders, they hope to show how state intervention was negotiated, managed and imagined. They also explore a wide range of economic sectors in order

---

[40] A good illustration of the limited innovation of 'regulation' comes on 7 April 1749, when the South Carolinian agent suggested that a proposed measure to reform paper credit would in fact suppress all such bills 'under the appearance of a regulation only' – *CJ*, vol. 25, p. 818. Among sectors to be 'regulated' or standardized, the economy appears to be one of the key areas for parliamentary concern. However, it did not predominate, and analysis of the 'regulations' of George IV's reign suggests that legislators were more inclined to standardize the fees and practices of the courts of law, rather than trade.

[41] *CJ*, vol. 75, p. 332; vol. 76, pp. 428, 430. For a useful summary of the course of free trade success in foreign trade from 1820 to 1860, see Peter Mathias, *The First Industrial Nation* (2nd edn, London, 2001), Chapter 11. He notes, on p. 269, the crucial role played by Riccardian political economists in the production of these petitions, such as Thomas Tooke, who regarded the government as 'far more sincere and resolute free traders than the merchants of London'. However, note Boyd Hilton's caution that ministerial policy was not determined by free trade ideology, and that 'the main purpose of theory was to justify, not originate, measures' – *Corn, Cash, Commerce; The Economic Policies of the Tory Governments 1815–1830* (Oxford, 1977), pp. 304–5.

to understand the reasons behind the variety in regulation across time and space. To this end, the 12 chapters are arranged in chronological order, and each takes a defined theme of economic regulation, and seeks to explore the attitudes which framed the success and failure of measures in that field. They all share a keen interest in questions of political process, the impact of economic and political ideologies, the interplay of vested interests, and the status of the economy as a political issue. From this common framework, the contributors seek to communicate some key messages about the development of economic regulation in this period.

Conclusions

This collection challenges a linear narrative of change over time, both with regard to state intervention in the economy and to putative liberalization. Instead, the chapters suggest that there were recurrent cycles of regulatory endeavour, usually sparked by crises, either of a governmental or societal nature. Thus, although the Glorious Revolution can be shown to be crucial to subsequent debate on the economy, it did not herald a long-term course of de-regulation, or necessarily set Britain on an exceptionalist path of political or economic development. Across the period, our findings suggest that the character of the state's intervention cannot be represented as the initial sovereignty of 'mercantilism' giving way to Smithian economic liberalism; primarily because our collection stresses political *and* economic competition as driving forces behind state intervention. Although more theoretical understandings of the workings of the economy might have advanced by 1800, there was little consensus here, nor with regard to the state's role in promoting economic growth.

In accordance with this finding, the contributors remain cautious on the transformative impact of specific events or ideas (whether economic, political or political-economic), even though they acknowledge that in certain contexts they *could* influence the relationship between government and economic interests. In the case of economic regulation, the contributors often accord as much importance to the growing sphere of economic discussion as to the theories themselves. Furthermore, even those reformers who were motivated by economic ideas could not rely on doctrinaire arguments to win the day, and had to adapt to the more interest-driven character of contemporary debate. The contributors do not discount the force of broader ideologies either, for the intensity of economic and political competition ensured that they would both be advanced and had occasional agency, as the joint chapter of Steve Pincus and Alice Wolfram points out. However, while acknowledging the richness of the economic debate in the period, the contributors would caution against identifications of 'winning' and 'losing' economic outlooks, for economy politics drove policy far more than conceptions of political economy.[42]

These conclusions also reflect the central finding that the government was not simply a reactive player in debate of the economy, but an active participant. Its arbitrational role was not merely that of umpire or nightwatchman, but of a very interested partner. Reasons of self-interest, especially of the fiscal kind, were evidently at work here, but politicians were also motivated by their responsibilities for ensuring welfare and order in a society increasingly threatened by the instabilities of national and global markets. International competition was also crucial here, as the major European powers sought every advantage to maximize national resources in readiness for conflict. However, it is important to see that the government was not simply interested in fiscal-military affairs. Sectional interests were keen to prey on ministerial fears for Britain's great power status, but also alluded to the broader impacts of economic change on society, and by the later eighteenth century were increasingly prepared to couch their pleas for economic support in comparative international terms.

From this perspective, it becomes apparent that British exceptionalism lay far more with the general freedom of the political process, rather than the liberalism of its economic outlook. This is not to subscribe to the position of institutional economists such as North and Weingast, whose emphasis on the importance of free institutions appears narrowly conceived by the evidence of this volume, but to highlight that the competitiveness and sheer extent of the economic public sphere was critical to forging ideas on the economy. Indeed, our collection highlights the need to see 'national' policy mediated through various spheres of debate, from the boards of Whitehall, to the parliamentary committee, the press, the quarter-sessions, the tavern and the household. Parliament may appear as the principal forum, as the locus of power, but change by necessity had to be mediated through a wide spectrum of political levels. In essence, thus, the advancement of the economy was intensely political, and was directly influenced by changes in political practice and ideology. Again, the contributors would not discount the force of economic ideas, but contemporaries usually had neither

---

42 The essential heterogeneity of the political economists should counsel caution in this regard – Donald Winch, *Riches and Poverty: An Intellectual History of Political Economy in Britain, 1750–1834* (Cambridge, 1996), esp. pp. 1–31; Boyd Hilton, *The Age of Atonement: The Influence of Evangelicalism on Social and Economic thought, 1785–1865* (Oxford, 1988). The Failed Legislation project also argued that the existence of strong lobbies may have helped the greater success rates for economic initiatives in some sectors, while more diffuse sectors (e.g. covering inland trade) may have struggled to secure agreements for change – Hoppit, *Failed Legislation*, pp. 9–10.

opportunity nor inclination to subscribe to them exclusively. Lower down the political ladder, the 'local' state was far from *laissez-faire* in outlook or instinct either, but in process it did provide many opportunities for the advancement of economic causes both great and small.[43]

Although an active participant, the government's intervention in the economy remained highly uneven, and varied significantly according to economic sector or region. As in other spheres of legislation, politicians remained tentative in outlining general rules to guide economic activity, often for fear of the impact of legislation in such a volatile and important sector. Furthermore, both the government and lobbies were heavily persuaded by arguments which stressed the importance of allowing economic processes to correct themselves, and for much of the period 'regulation' was generally understood as regularization, as returning economic affairs to their correct channel or level.[44] Such contemporary attitudes can help to explain the unevenness of government intervention in the economy, and why important reforms did not even require statutory force. However, there are signs that the middle decades of the century saw greater concern among governors at the evasion of its regulations, and they were more prepared to contemplate intervention as the pace of economic change appeared to quicken. The territorial expansion of empire played a famous part here, but domestic pressures such as population growth, urbanization and industrialization demanded a response from ministers and magistrates. Fundamental innovation was seldom attempted, and at times the most efficient methods often lay with relaxation of rules, most evidently in the case of Pitt's Commutation Act. By the later eighteenth century, another important trend had emerged with the regulation of labour supplanting the regulation of products as a matter of direct concern, and it is clear that industrialization was a prominent force behind this. Moreover, certain sectors of production, especially agriculture, also received renewed scrutiny under the pressure of demographic growth. In these ways, the regulatory picture remained varied well into the nineteenth century, but the onus on the government to intervene steadily mounted.

This broad social terrain of debate was also critical in ensuring that the economy was seldom regarded as a separate or 'specialist' sphere of activity,

---

43 This accords with the key insights of Anthony Howe's argument that British exceptionalist policy in the nineteenth century responded to domestic-political, rather than geo-political influences. He argues that a large consumer market (imbued with the struggles for political freedoms and the free-trade campaigns of 1820s–40s) defied vested interests calling for retaliatory tariffs, thereby preserving free trade – 'Restoring Free Trade', pp. 193–214.

44 Peter Jupp observes a similar outlook with respect to Peel's view of a divinely-ordered society, which argued for minimal government intervention – *Governing of Britain*, pp. 171–2.

and profits were far from the only criterion used for measuring the impact of new ideas. Its growing political importance ensured that economic interests ran increasing risks in becoming embroiled in partisan affairs, which most regarded with deep alarm, whatever the short-term gain. As a sign of this, even the economic innovators were largely conservative in their rhetorical outlook, and the concept of radical change in the economic sphere was rarely contemplated before the 1820s. Such conservatism was clearly a function of British economic success, and many a counter-petition would warn politicians of the dangers of trying to change a winning formula. More importantly, such caution was also a function of process, in that the participatory character of the regulatory process placed significant obstacles before would-be 'progressives'.[45]

This participation ran deep into society, and the great mechanisms of political-economic change were worked with many visible hands. In purely institutional terms, the British state appears endlessly adaptive to economic processes, and *was* capable of accommodating reform on the ground and of providing proactive leadership. Bob Harris's analysis of the political and economic integration of England, Scotland and Ireland highlights that politicians could rise to the greatest of challenges. However, we must also acknowledge that politicians and economic actors could regard regulation with very different priorities, and successful would-be regulators usually needed to graft themselves onto existing structures of government. On all sides of this dialogue, we have to acknowledge growing ambition, but also fears of failure; we also have to see that even if the economy achieved the status of special pleader, its claims were rarely seen as independent of other societal concerns, and there remained a general mistrust of theory. In all these ways, we can see the state's uncertain relationship with the economy as the price of free process, but our work highlights the importance of a participatory public and a participatory state for Britain's adaptation to the great economic changes of the period.

If the government might be more inclined to contemplate regulatory intervention and enforcement by the end of the eighteenth century, it did not necessarily regard regulatory bodies as essential to those aims. Although many European states did see the creation of government bodies to supervise policy change, the British economy saw little direct state monitoring, and it is not apparent that there was any 'regulatory' system against which the free-traders of the early nineteenth century could rail. Indeed, in common with Adam Smith's

---

45 For recent evidence of the importance of local political circumstances to the success of free trade principles in the nineteenth century, see David Todd, 'John Bowring and the Global Dissemination of Free Trade', *HJ*, 51 (2008): pp. 373–97. He highlights how in France free trade was introduced as part of an authoritarian regime's nationalist policy, and not on account of any attachment to economic liberal theory.

mercantile system, the Whigs of the 1820s can be seen to be responsible for creating their own chimera of widespread regulation to champion their political causes. At root, the general inertia of eighteenth-century local government hindered any regulatory agendas. Reforming pressure undoubtedly scored anti-regulatory successes after 1800, but the contributors are more struck by how slowly reform occurred, and many victims were either easy targets with lax enforcement, or capable of surviving without legislative sanction on account of their economic utility, as Jane Humphries demonstrates in her chapter on the apprenticeship laws. 1832, in common with 1688, may thus have provided opportunities for economic interests to secure greater public access, but the new parliamentary system did not guarantee them favour, or determine regulatory outcomes.[46] Put simply, politicians at all levels were alive to the great economic changes of the time, and knew that the state would seek to direct or control them. Given inherent limitations in the operation of the state, direct central intervention was limited in nature and application, but it did provide protective agencies vital for the advancement of the economy across a very broad front.

These general insights are meant to stimulate further work on regulation, and many of the contributors will continue to mine this valuable seam of socio-political history. The sheer range of interests and approaches represented in this volume reflects the manifold ways in which the economy was recognized as a central force within state and society in this period. By contemporary standards, the economy achieved top billing in terms of state interest and action, and more research is needed on the resultant dialogues between governmental and economic interests. The contributors would welcome further study of the discourses of economic debate, especially with a view to clarifying contemporary views on the nature of representation. Daeryoon Kim's sensitivity to the conventions which ruled debate of imperial trade, and Ian Barrett's study of the manipulation of inquiries and evidence, both demonstrate the necessity of understanding the political cultures in which economic questions were debated and resolved. Several chapters in this collection also highlight the importance of notions of equity and justice in debate of the economy, and it would be fruitful to probe the thinking behind these claims, especially as a means to test the perceived efficiency of Parliament as both legislator and governor. Although

---

46 Note Paul Langford's argument for continuities through the Age of Reform, and that even in the mid-nineteenth century, 'Parliament remained for most purposes a kind of glorified umpire, adjudicating the disputes of propertied interests' – *Public Life and the Propertied Englishman*, pp. 582–6. Martin Daunton has also seen the Victorian state as 'an honest broker between interests, the opponent of monopoly, and liberator of the individual and of associational life' – *State and Market in Victorian Britain*, p. 37.

generally cautious on the impact of theory, the contributors would also champion broader work on the development of attitudes towards the economy as a distinct discipline, and towards the wider role of regulation in society. In particular, research into contemporary views on the enforcement of legislation would be welcomed.

The contributors would also like to see further work on the forums in which these ideas operated. This collection has emphasized the significance of various sites of economic debate, and would argue for a more problematized conception of the public sphere. Economic actors clearly tailored their proposals to a variety of audiences, and much might be learnt of contemporary attitudes from the ways in which language and image was used to target particular audiences.[47] Furthermore, more research is needed on the role of information in public debate, both within governing circles and beyond. In all these ways, the economy could illuminate the broader relationship between state and civil society. Regional variation would also be a fruitful concomitant area of study. It is clear that the period was important for changing the economic landscape, and further work could be undertaken on the relationship between the development of regional economic networks and the alignment of interests in public debates on regulation, both within Britain and its empire. Comparisons with European states would also be particularly useful, especially to test the supposed exceptionality of Britain's political-economic experience, as Philippe Minard encourages us to do in this volume.

These perspectives would only enhance our appreciation of the dynamic force which the economy represented in the political world of the 1660–1850 period. In keeping with the universal benefits claimed by *England's Great Joy and Gratitude*, such work would deepen our understanding of the ways in which economic debate permeated all levels of society, and would further illuminate the workings of both state and society. If the collection contributes to the continuing convergence of political and economic history, and can help to revitalize student interest in the field, then its contributors will have had a rich reward for all their labours.

---

[47] An excellent model remains Clive Behagg's analysis of the 'social language' of political debate in early nineteenth-century Birmingham, in which he painstakingly reconstructs the economic and political influences on workers and small manufacturers in an era of rapid change – *Politics and Production in the Early Nineteenth Century* (London, 1990).

Chapter 1

Regulatory Inertia and National Economic Growth: An African Trade Case Study, 1660–1714

William Pettigrew

The Glorious Revolution created new opportunities for broad-based interest groups to influence the rules that governed England's national economy. These new opportunities derived from the shift in regulatory initiative from more unilateral state institutions to more deliberative ones. Before 1689, Parliament worked alongside the royal prerogative and rulings from Privy Council to regulate the economy. From the early 1690s, Parliament became the undisputed arbiter of national economic concerns. By the turn of the eighteenth century, statute substituted for the prerogative or King-in-council and became synonymous, in the context of economic legislation, with regulation. Parliament continued to supervise the economy and engineer economic growth via statute as the Privy Council had done through conciliar rulings. It was Parliament's representative remit that helped provide, however, a platform for interest groups to influence how the economy was regulated. A wider sphere of involvement in the regulatory process saw interest groups lobby against regulatory statutes. Without other constitutional means to occupy the legislative vacuums that resulted from these movements, legislative inertia became regulatory inertia, which became, in turn, deregulation and, in some cases, national economic growth. Pamphleteers rationalized the benefits of this economic growth by developing economic theory. This chapter details one important case study, the deregulation of England's trans-Atlantic slave trade, to illustrate this new phenomenon.

In the national economic sphere, Parliament's significance grew after 1689. Parliamentary statutes began to compete more successfully with Privy Council orders and Royal Proclamations as state-sponsored means to regulate the national economy.[1] From the Restoration to the arrival of William III, the Privy Council

[1] I use the same definition of economic to qualify legislative acts and petitions as that used by Mark Julian. It includes all public economic bills and private bills whose impact could be felt across the economy such as transport and infrastructure bills. Estate and

issued on average four royal proclamations about the economy a year.[2] From 1689, Parliament began to eclipse the Privy Council as the most important vehicle for macro-economic regulation. Parliament achieved four economic statutes on average per year from 1660 to 1688 and 11 per year between 1689 and 1714. Before the Glorious Revolution, the Privy Council, via Royal Proclamations maintained, on average, a 68 per cent control over state attempts to influence the national economy. After 1688, that proportion of control had reduced to just 7 per cent (at a time when the average yearly total state attempts to influence the national economy increased by 54 per cent across the periods 1660–88 to 1689–1713). The increased number of parliamentary statutes accounts for the majority of this increase in state interest in the national economy (yearly averages of statutes either side of the Glorious Revolution increased by 166 per cent while the decrease in proclamations was 79 per cent).

Shifting the initiative for national economic regulation from the Privy Council to Parliament affected the way in which the state reached decisions about the regulation of the economy. This shift transferred decision making about the economy from the more unilateral Privy Council to the more deliberative Parliament. The Privy Council sometimes received counter-petitions and in Parliament issues could often be thrown out without reason, but Parliament provided a more open forum, which allowed debate to be influenced by outside petitions and pamphlets to a greater extent.[3] Parliament's more deliberative nature endowed attempts to regulate the national economy with the legitimizing force of consent. It also encouraged more and larger lobbies to campaign against regulation.

---

private naturalization bills have been excluded. See Mark R. Julian, 'English Economic Legislation 1660–1714' (M. Phil. thesis, London School of Economics, 1979), p. 175. I derive information about legislative attempts in Parliament from Julian Hoppit (ed.), *Failed Legislation* (London, 1997) and information about Royal Proclamations from Robert Steele, *A Bibliography of Royal Proclamations of the Tudor and Stuart Sovereigns, 1485–1714, Vol. 1: England and Wales* (Oxford, 1910).

2 Much of the Privy Council's withdrawal from national economic concerns in this period has to do with the career of its sub-committee on commercial matters, the Lords of Trade and Plantations.

3 William Cunningham regarded autocratic political institutions as better suited to regulation. See William Cunningham, *The Growth of English Industry and Commerce in Modern Times, Vol. 1: The Mercantile System* (2 vols, 6th edn, Cambridge, 1925), vol. 2, p. 19. Ekelund and Tollison have argued that the additional cost of lobbying Parliament dissuaded interest groups from seeking to sustain monopolies after 1688 and therefore played a part in deregulating the economy, see Robert Ekelund and Robert Tollison, *Mercantilism as a Rent Seeking Society: Economic Regulation in Historical Perspective* (College Station, TX, 1981), p. 149.

Parliament remained, as it had been from its creation, a vehicle for the representation of diverse interests unevenly spread throughout the Kingdom. What changed after 1689 was how Parliament's representative remit became subsumed within the functions of the state.[4] Previously un-enfranchised representatives of the market now had access to the regulatory apparatus of the state via Parliament to create, enlarge and protect their economic interests. Petitions remained the primary means for such representatives to operate. Parliament therefore became a more important venue for appeals to influence the state's decisions about the nation's economy. Before the 1690s, the Court and (to a lesser extent) the Privy Council, with its executive powers, had provided a forum for petitioning about economic matters. In 1660, 77 per cent of all petitions about the economy were addressed to the King.[5] In 1696, that number had fallen to 12 per cent. From 1689, Parliament, and especially the House of Commons, became the majority recipient of petitions to do with economic matters. In 1660, the House of Commons received just 6 per cent of such petitions. By 1713 its share had risen to 92 per cent. A rising number of these petitions concerned economic matters. At a time when the total numbers of petitions to the House of Commons increased from 60 in 1660 to 118 in 1713, the percentage of those petitions concerning economic matters increased from 8 per cent in 1660 to 55 per cent in 1713. From the Restoration to the Treaty of Utrecht, the number, ambitions and effectiveness of commercial lobbyists increased. In 1660, 1 per cent of petitions to Parliament came from commercial interest groups. By 1696 this proportion had increased to 18 per cent and increased again to 35 per cent in 1713. In 1660, about a quarter of all petitions to do with the economy came from commercial lobbies. By 1713 this figure exceeded 70 per cent.[6]

Although it remained largely a landowners' club, Parliament's personnel and procedures became more responsive to commercial interests in this period. An increased proportion of MPs came from commercial backgrounds, echoing a developing belief that merchants rather than landowners ought to control commercial policy. The percentages of members of Parliament who were merchants increased from 3.7 per cent in the period from 1660 to 1690 to 7.9 per cent between 1690 and 1715. The House also began to take trade business more seriously. A 1703 ruling dictated that 'no bill relating to trade or the alteration of laws concerning trade be brought into the House until the proposition shall have been first examined and debated in the grand committee

---

4 For the way in which government became a function of the legislature, see Paul Langford, *A Polite and Commercial People: England 1727–1783* (Oxford, 1998), p. 706.

5 I compiled these lists of economic petitions from *CJ* and *LJ*.

6 I compiled these statistics about economic petitioning from *CJ*.

for trade, and agreed unto by the House'. Between 1690 and 1702, committees of the whole House heard 20 per cent of commercial bills. By Anne's reign the percentage had improved to 57 per cent.[7] The increased participation of merchants in the parliamentary process after 1689 confirms the extent to which merchants wished to serve as political representatives of their markets and how they increasingly viewed the state via Parliament as a means to protect their economic concerns.

In particular, Parliament provided a forum for the advertisement of the breadth of opposition to the monopoly companies. The great onslaughts against the London overseas trading companies accounted for nearly a third of all mercantile petitions in this period.[8] In 1692, in a discussion concerning the future of the East India Company, Gilbert Heathcote, the scourge of several monopoly companies during this period, complained to the Commons that ships had been hindered from sailing to India by the Privy Council acting upon the company's representations. Heathcote achieved a motion in the House of Commons (though only by the margin of a single vote in a Committee of the Whole House) declaring that it was the right of all English subjects to trade to the East Indies *unless* explicitly restricted by an Act of Parliament.[9] In doing so, Heathcote helped to strengthen the connection between statute and regulation and therefore, legislative failure and deregulation.

As a result of Heathcote's motion, the scale and persistence of non-governmental involvement with the regulation of the economy increased faster than the number of statutes relating to economic matters. Commercial interest groups began to lobby against statutory proposals to restrict the economy to ensure deregulation. The commercial interest group's counter-petition became an important macro-economic lever. In 1660, less than 1 per cent of parliamentary petitions could be classified as counter-petitions. By 1696 this had increased to 10 per cent and increased again to 24 per cent in 1713. The trend is even more striking for petitions relating to economic matters: in 1660, 1 per cent of petitions to do with economic matters were counter-petitions. In 1696, the figure was 20 per cent; in 1705 it became 33 per cent and in 1713 it reached 65 per cent.

The Glorious Revolution therefore provided the opportunity for broader involvement with the state's regulatory apparatus. It did not, however,

---

7 For growing mercantile interest in Parliament in this period and for the 1703 ruling see Perry Gauci, *The Politics of Trade: The Overseas Merchant in State and Society, 1660–1720* (Oxford, 2001), pp. 197, 227.

8 Ibid., p. 218.

9 For Heathcote's resolution see *CJ*, vol. 11, p. 50, 8 January 1693–94; and see also *The Case Between the African Company and the People of England* (1698?), p. 1.

necessitate the liberalization of the economy or its centralization. As soon as the primacy of Parliament as regulator of the national economy became fixed, the logical implications of that arrangement also became apparent: if a statute to regulate the economy failed in the legislature, then a legislative vacuum would assist deregulation. The improved powers of Parliament made the potential consequences of legislative failure greater because other branches of the constitution such as the monarchy and Privy Council could no longer be relied upon to resolve such issues. Broadening access to the discussion of the regulation of the national economy encouraged interest groups to lobby to engineer legislative vacuums that produced economic growth.

These legislative vacuums could be sustained with the help of another, famous example of legislative inertia: the expiration of the 1662 Licensing Act in 1695. A counter-petitioning campaign based on the anti-monopoly refrain prevented the licensing statute from being replaced in 1695. The expiration of this legislation allowed parliamentary deliberation to enter the extra-legislative public sphere.[10] By 1700, Parliament could not claim to monopolize the state's access to national means of representation. Increased use of petitioning provided an alternative representation of the public sphere, but the more discursive format of the pamphlet or broadside provided a means for lobbyists to craft public opinion outside as well as inside the House.[11] These lobbies used pamphleteering campaigns to convince public opinion that the result of legislative vacuum, deregulation, suited the public interest. Such pamphlets mentioned how deregulation and the ensuing competition would assist the growth of the national economy and how that growth would produce benefits for all.

With the important exception of the 1713 French Commerce bill, large counter-petitioning campaigns typically opposed attempts to monopolize overseas trade. There are numerous examples of such campaigns: versus the Hamburg Company in December 1696, versus the Royal African Company in November 1696 and again in January 1709. Large counter-petitioning campaigns also helped to discredit movements to limit the export of wool in December 1696 and November 1699, and the import of foreign lace in February 1699. In all cases, the weight of petitioning support proved critical to the defeat of

---

10 See Raymond Astbury, 'The Renewal of the Licensing Act of 1693 and its Lapse in 1695', *The Library*, ser. 5, no. 33 (1978): p. 301. However, Parliament remained very sensitive towards direct reporting of its debates until the 1770s.

11 See Mark Knights, *Representation and Misrepresentation in Later Stuart Britain* (Oxford, 2005), p. 127; and Rosemary Sweet, 'Local Identities and a National Parliament, c. 1688–1835', in Julian Hoppit (ed.), *Parliaments, Nations, and Identities in Britain and Ireland, 1660–1850* (Manchester, 2003), pp. 50–51.

the measure and pamphlets helped to circulate the benefits of the non-statutory outcomes.[12]

The lobbying campaign against the Royal African Company to deregulate the slave trade provides the best case study. Founded in 1672, Charles II granted the Royal African Company a monopoly of all English trade with the West Coast of Africa. Its monopoly allowed the company to engross the export trade from England to Africa (primarily woollens), the trade in slaves, ivory and gold from Africa, and, therefore, to dominate the trade in sugar from the Caribbean islands back to England. Prior to 1688, the company enjoyed close relations with the monarchy. In the 1670s, the Privy Council regularly intervened to prevent interloping slave traders from assaulting the company.[13] By 1689, however, after the flight of its leader and largest shareholder, James II, independent slave traders targeted the company in common law courts and insisted that the company pay compensation for the cargoes it had seized in the 1670s and '80s, under the jurisdiction of its now undermined prerogative-sponsored charter. In 1689, Chief Justice John Holt issued a default verdict in the Court of King's Bench in *Nightingale vs. Bridges* that sustained the crown's right to issue monopolistic charters, but did not allow such charters to forfeit the property of independent merchants, unless the charter received statutory endorsement. The African Company therefore made an appeal in 1690 to Parliament to obtain a statute to support its monopoly. A broad-based interest group representing the independent slave traders in London, the West Country, Barbados, Jamaica and the American mainland persuasively argued that deregulation of the trade would increase its capacity.[14]

The African Company, however, appealed to the parliamentary audience by noting how its monopoly better served the interests of the English state because it would continue to trade, unlike independent traders, when the prospects of profit looked bleak and could therefore better uphold the interests of the English state and its Atlantic empire. As a result, the company achieved a statute in its favour in 1698 (to last until the summer of 1712), but compromised to allow independent slave trading so long as those traders paid a 10 per cent duty to finance the African Company's West African forts.

---

12 See Gauci, *Politics of Trade*, p. 249. For the Hamburg Company see George Cherry, 'The Development of the English Free-Trade Movement in Parliament, 1689–1702', *JMH*, 25/2 (1953): p. 116.

13 See Roger Coke, *Reflections upon the East-Indy and Royal African Companies with Animadversions, Concerning the Naturalization of Foreigners* (1695), p. 10.

14 For a full discussion of the dispute between the Royal African Company and independent slave traders see William Pettigrew, *Freedom's Debt: Politics and the Causes of American Slavery* (Chapel Hill, NC, forthcoming).

By 1707, it had become obvious that despite the large expansion of the slave trade after 1698, the African Company was unable to gather enough benefit from the duty to finance itself. Another round of parliamentary deliberations began in 1708. The African Company interest again acknowledged that its monopoly required a statute to be enforceable.[15] The company's African forts provided its best argument in favour of a statute because financing their maintenance would involve a regulatory mechanism that would need to be agreed to in an Act of Parliament.[16] Regulatory statutes, such as that sought by the Royal African Company, proved difficult to achieve. The intervention of government improved the chances of achieving a regulating statute. Parliament became the state's primary provider of revenue in wartime and sessions lasted until the government had secured the means of financing its wars. Any regulating statutes that proposed to help with revenue matters would therefore benefit from the support of the ministry. Despite *Nightingale vs. Bridges*, Parliament countenanced a series of company charters in the hope of raising revenue. In 1692, Parliament levied duties on the East India, African and Hudson's Bay Companies and stated that their charters would be void if the duties were not paid.[17] The East India Company's monopoly survived this period because it offered governmental loans. Similarly, MPs achieved the South Sea Company Act in 1711, which transferred government debt that had been accrued during the War of Spanish Succession into the capital of a new joint-stock company, in 11 days and members of Parliament agreed to the bill's terms unanimously.

The African Company's opponents, the separate traders to Africa, sought, however, to deregulate the trade without a statute. Daniel Defoe, who observed the Africa trade debates and received payment from the African Company to write on its behalf, made it clear that it would be impossible to legislate free trade.[18] When explaining the failure of a bill to create a regulated company (one which broadened access to the trade), Defoe argued, 'the Bill was lost, because it was impossible to be found; it stop't because it was impossible to go on: There was no Act pass'd, because there was nothing to pass an Act upon; there was no Substance in the Bill'.[19] Defoe believed that a free trade statute was a self-contradicting act.

---

[15] See TNA, Records of the Royal African Company (T70 series), T70/58, fol. 407, the Royal African Company to Patrick Thompson and Thomas Stewart, 13 October 1713.

[16] See *Objections to the Bill for Establishing the Trade to Africa in a Regulated Company* (1712), p. 3.

[17] See *Statutes*, vol. 6, pp. 401–4: *Rot. Parl. 4 Gul. & Mar., c. 14*, p. 3, n. 9.

[18] See Tim Keirn, 'Daniel Defoe and the Royal African Company', *Historical Research*, vol. 61 (1988): pp. 243–7.

[19] Daniel Defoe, *A Review of the Affairs of France*, vol. 22, pp. 79–80 (30 December 1712).

The Africa trade dispute produced over 200 petitions and over 200 pamphlets.[20] No other legislative issue of the period, however, so persistently failed to produce a statutory outcome as the dispute about the management of the African trade. The extent of interest in the Africa trade debates need not make Parliament's failure to produce a statutory resolution surprising. The separate traders used the breadth of their petitioning support to derail the African Company's attempts at legislation. The separate traders cultivated a broader geographical petitioning constituency than the Africa Company. While the separate traders enjoyed the support at one time or another of 40 different petitioning locations, the company received support from just 11. The separate traders obtained 61 petitions from the English provinces in comparison to 11 for the company. Similarly, the Act of Union and the expectations it produced among Scottish commercial interests encouraged Scottish merchants to lobby Parliament when they believed the capital engrossed economic opportunity. Scottish boroughs submitted nine petitions, all against the company. This helped the separate traders' claim to better represent the national interest to ensure the sort of national economic growth that would produce social, political and economic benefits for all.[21]

This breadth of support enabled the separate traders to block the African Company's legislative attempts. The separate traders did not use their broad support to endorse statutes of their own. One pro-company pamphleteer pointed out, prior to the 1698 Act, that separate traders preferred obstructing African company bills to authoring their own:

> Ever since the Parliament voted that it was the undoubted Right of all the subjects of England to Trade to Foreign Parts – none of those Free Traders have ever brought to the Parliament a Bill to settle this Trade, but still opposed what was offered by the Company ... because those free traders ... had just cause to believe that under such a Regulation, whatsoever it should be, they must pay towards

---

20 Another issue of comparable dimensions was that surrounding the leather trade which saw the presentation of over 150 petitions from over 100 different locations between 1697 and 1699 in that interest group's two-year-long campaign to have the leather duties repealed – see John Brewer, *Sinews of Power: War, Money and the English State, 1688–1783* (London, 1989), p. 233.

21 For the rising importance of petitioning see David Zaret, 'Petitions and the "Invention" of Public Opinion in the English Revolution', *American Journal of Sociology*, 101/6 (1996); pp. 1497–555. For the increased incidence of provincial petitions see Gauci, *Politics of Trade*, pp. 214–15, 'the twenty-fold increment in provincial petitioning in the reign of William is unmistakable proof that extra-London forces were striving hard to influence policy in the Commons, and this momentum was maintained in the succeeding reign'.

> what by the Parliament should be thought necessary for the general interest of that trade whereas if they continue that heavy load upon the African Company only by opposing this bill, they should then enjoy their trade without that expence.[22]

The company's opponents initiated proceedings in Parliament in only three out of 16 sessions.[23] When anti-African Company proposals appeared, in the 1690s, the company's opponents seldom advocated statutory alternatives to the company's monopoly, using such vague terms as 'advantageous regulation' and 'a better, more beneficial, and equal establishment' and 'liberty, and freedom to trade'.[24] Later, separate trader petitions became explicitly anti-regulatory. In 1708 a separate trader petition pleaded to 'be relieved from the heavy duty of ten per cent'. In 1709 this had evolved to 'may be continued free and open to all the subjects of Great Britain, discharged from such part of the £10 per cent duty'. Calls for regulated company statutes typically emerged from cross-party drafting committees hoping to legislate through compromise measures, as in 1698, rather than from separate trader petitions, which preferred to argue in favour of an ill-defined notion of 'open trade' or simply for parliamentary consideration, knowing how it favoured their cause.[25]

Daniel Defoe described the separate traders' lobbying strategy in full:

> they [the separate traders] car'd not whether the Parliament did any thing or no, provided they did but delay the company; for then they knew the thing would fall into their hands of course, the company not being able to stand of themselves, without some act was passed in their favour, which they had nothing to do but to prevent.[26]

The African Company noted how the separate traders' filibustered parliamentary deliberations to sustain legislative inertia in a petition to Queen Anne in December 1710,

---

22 *Considerations Relating to the African Bill* (1698), p. 3. This was a reference to Gilbert Heathcote's resolution of 1694 in relation to the East India trade, see above.

23 These were 1710, 1712 and 1713.

24 *CJ*, vol. 10, p. 383, 'Petition of Merchants and Planters trading to and interested in the Island of Barbadoes' to the House of Commons, 22 April 1690; and p. 382, 'Petition of Clothiers of Suffolk and Essex' to the House of Commons, 21 April 1690.

25 *CJ*, vol. 15, p. 612, 'Petition of merchants, and planters, separate traders in Africa, and interested in, and trading to Barbadoes, and the other Leeward Islands', 16 March 1708; and vol. 16. p. 77, 'Petition of merchants and planters, separate traders to Africa, in behalf of themselves and divers others, interested in and trading to, the Island of Jamaica', 1 February 1709; and p. 235, 'Petition of divers merchants of London, traders to Africa', 8 December 1709.

26 Daniel Defoe, *An Essay upon the Trade to Africa* (1711), p. 25.

> some few Private Traders for selfish and particular ends had the art of propogating and imposing impractical notions on some members of the legislature in such a manner and possessing them with very groundless prejudice against the Company, that both the sessions terminated without any actuall care being taken for the preservation of the Trade.[27]

Encouraging parliamentary deliberation while discouraging statutory resolution became the separate traders' lobbying motto. The separate traders cultivated extra-parliamentary opinion. They steered a middle course in Parliament that aimed to achieve non-statutory parliamentary rulings that would modify public opinion in favour of open, deregulated trade and ensure that the legislative vacuum was tolerated. These rulings accrued more public significance the more interest in Parliament increased after 1689. The rulings were meaningful because of the ritualized nature of parliamentary deliberation. Once a legislative proposal had reached a certain stage, it gathered legitimacy even if the proposal ultimately failed.

Non-statutory parliamentary rulings in favour of deregulation appeared in several forms. First, and perhaps most important, was the precedent established by the Act of 1698 itself which could be deemed non-statutory after its expiration in 1712. The Africa Trade Act proved that open trade expanded British exports to Africa, enlarged imports of enslaved Africans to America, and increased the size of the Atlantic colonial commodity trades. One separate trader pamphlet argued that this Act had been designed to prepare the way for unregulated trade.[28] The 1698 Act was clearly an essential stepping-stone to total deregulation of the British slave trade.

The Board of Trade's reports to Parliament offer another example of a non-statutory parliamentary ruling. Parliament had, from 1708 onwards, instructed the Board of Trade to enquire into the African trade. Charles Davenant, another pro-company pamphleteer, noted how the board's findings in early 1709 offered much needed legitimacy to the separate traders' cause and 'the Transcribing them by way of report and intermixing them with such accounts as were demanded of ye Royal African Company, has happened to give them some more seeming authority than can reasonably be supposed to have been ever intended by the Lords Commissioners'. Davenant noted how such legitimacy proved influential with public opinion and helped, in turn, to influence the political process, 'for the Separate Traders have taken occasion, from thence to print certain paragraphs of there [sic] own base allegations by way of Extracts out of the said report, as

27 See 'Petition to the Queen', 3 December 1710, in TNA, T70/175, fols 200–201.

28 *The Case of the Separate Traders to Africa* (1710), p. 1.

vouchers to gain Credit to the very same allegations again without doors'.[29] A separate trader pamphlet acknowledged how the Board's report reflected a deliberate separate trader lobbying strategy:

> ... the Report is drawn up with such Exactness and Impartiality, that whensoever the Parliament will please to call for it, I dare take upon me to say, it will justify my present Undertaking, and verify the most, if not all the Suggestions and Allegations here laid down, and give Such a Light and Insight into the whole Matter, that the Publick will be kept no longer in the dark about it.[30]

The various stages that each legislative proposal reached provided a third category of non-statutory parliamentary rulings: from points scored in debate, to votes and resolutions, and to bills. Pamphleteers referred to the perceived outcome of parliamentary debates or to testimony deemed trustworthy because of submission in the House. One colonial representative of the African Company informed his superiors, 'The inhabitants [in Montserrat] think it in Vain to Sign Any More Papers in favour of the Company Since ye Parliament Countenance ye Separate Traders'.[31] One separate trader disputed the utility of the company's forts not through any investigation or reasoning on the part of the author but 'because it hath often been made appear at the Bar, that most of the Negroes brought from Africa are loaden where we have no settlements'.[32] Pamphleteers relayed the perceived outcome of parliamentary debates to undermine their opponents. The same was true of the parliamentary votes, which informed how the economy functioned, even if they did not lead to the passing of bills into Acts. A separate trader pamphlet described how a vote in favour of a regulated company bill led to expansion in the trade:

> ... since the vote of the honourable House of commons about eight years ago, that the trade thither was best to be managed by a regulated company, there has been a greater trade driven thither, notwithstanding all the difficulties at home, and hazards of war, than ever was carried on in times of peace.[33]

---

29 Charles Davenant's responses to the Board of Trade's 1708 report are contained in [Davenant], 'Some General Observations and Particular remarks on the Report made by the Lords Commissioners for Trade and Plantations the 3rd February, 1708 Touching the Contents of the Royal African Company's Peticion Referred to them by her Majesty' in TNA, T70/175, fols 87–96.

30 *Considerations upon the Trade to Guinea* (London, 1708), p. 26.

31 TNA, T70/8, William Fry to Royal African Company, 25 July 1710, fol. 106.

32 *An Answer to a Paper Called Short Remarks on the African Trade* (1711), p. 1.

33 *Reasons Humbly Offered by the Merchants and Traders to Guiney and the West-Indies, against the Bill for Settling the Trade to Africa* (1698), p. 1.

Parliamentary resolutions, unlike – at this stage – the content of the debates themselves (outside partisan pamphlets) were often printed which made them more influential outside the chamber. Parliamentary resolution conferred pseudo-statutory legitimacy for parliamentary proposals in the absence of a statute. A petition from Exeter cited how a resolution in favour of a regulated company in a previous session had 'so far encouraged the petitioners, that it gave a new life to their trade, and some thousands of pieces ... made more than usual, and the price advanced from 11 shillings and six-pence per piece to 15 shillings and six-pence per piece'.[34] Parliamentary resolutions confirmed, especially when originating from the committee of the whole House, that there existed broad parliamentary approval for the proposed scheme and that its translation into statute was undone by disagreement over the legislation's fine print. One pamphlet complained how the company's assumption that the law of the African trade revert to its 1672 charter after the expiration of the 1698 Act proceeded:

> ... without any regard to the many resolutions of this honourable House repeated last session, viz. that the African trade ought to be free and open to all her majesty's subjects ...

and went on to describe how

> ... Tis true the bill for the National Trade did not pass last year, but even the adversaries thereto did agree, 'twas not because they were against an open Trade, but that some clauses in that bill were excepted against.[35]

This pamphleteer believed a non-statutory parliamentary ruling from the reformed Parliament commanded more public authority than a charter derived from royal prerogative. We may assume that the separate traders intended these clauses to be objected to as the failure of the 1713 open trade bill allowed the slave trade to proceed without any regulation.

---

34 *CJ*, vol. 10, p. 579, 'Petition of Mayor, Aldermen, and Common Councilmen of the City of Exon and also of the merchants, serge-makers, fullers, and other trading people, employed in and about the woolen manufactury within the said city and county of the same and parts adjacent', 9 December 1691.

35 The belief that anti-company legislation failed for reasons other than a lack of support was commonplace. See also *The Present Case of the African trade Truly Stated, with Reasons for the Bill for Establishing the Same Now Depending* (1713), p. 1; and *The Case of the National Traders to Africa* (1714), p. 1; see also *The Anatomy of the African Company's Scheme for Carrying on That Trade in a Joint-Stock Exclusive, ...* (1713), p. 2.

The open trade bills themselves offered further evidence of parliamentary support and provided some of the information about how the trade might function without a statute. Pamphleteers deemed previous bills to be binding of future parliamentary deliberations, 'Who but this company would come to Parliament, to ask an exclusive trade, when but 7 or 8 months before the House passed a bill for a free and open trade?'[36] The separate traders also used their bills on the African coast to convince African traders not to deal with the company, as an African Company official warned, without fully grasping the separate traders' political strategy:

> We believe ye Separate Traders' captains and officers may impose on you and ye rest of our servants by magnifying the pretended advantages they gained this parliament, but we must observe to you, that tho' they had prevailed to far as to have ye liberty of offering a bill to the House in order to lay open the trade to Africa, the House did not think fit to pass that bill but adjourned it from day to day until ye session was ended.[37]

While blocking regulations in Parliament, the separate traders petitions and pamphlets helped to modify public opinion to support deregulation. In response to the African Company's refrain that a deregulated trade offered no security of slave supply when trade was low, separate traders argued that open trade would offer a vent for every citizen's natural and insatiable desire to truck and barter:

> There can be no greater security of the continuance of any branch of our foreign trade, than the absolute and everlasting necessity thereof, as is the case of the trade to Africa, by reason of its being founded on the computation of cloths, and other merchandize necessary to human life, for gold, Negroes, elephants teeth, dye-woods, and other useful commodities produced in Africa. So that till men cease to wear clothes and rather chuse to go naked; till the planters cease to cultivate their lands, and rather chuse to starve; till Gold becomes out of esteem, and mankind cease to seek farther after it; till our sheep cease to produce wool, and our poor chuse to perish rather than work; in short, till there is an end of all commerce in the world, there is a greater certainty of the continuance and security of our African trade, than any other Branch of foreign trade whatever.[38]

---

36 *The Anatomy of the African Company's Scheme for Carrying on That Trade in a Joint-Stock Exclusive, ...* (1713), p. 2.

37 TNA, T70/52, fols 223, 226, Royal African Company to Sir Dalby Thomas, 5 May 1709; and Royal African Company to William Hickes, 5 May 1709.

38 *The Argument Touching Security Necessary to Be Given for Carrying on the African Trade, Demonstrated to Be Groundless and Ridiculous* (1711), p. 1.

Separate trader pamphleteers described how open trade produced growth because it encouraged competition. One pamphleteer argued, '… when trade is confined to a few, who are in no apprehension to be outdone by any rival, they are not likely to take extraordinary pains to improve it. Whereas when many carry on a trade, their industry and ingenuity are always at work to outvie one another'.[39] Although the Royal African Company's monopoly had been critical to developing England's trade with Africa, the separate traders sought to develop the perception that free trade represented the default setting for the African trade by pointing to precedent for an open trade to Africa. Many anti-African Company lobbyists described how the Africa trade boomed in the 1660s before the formation of the Company of Royal Adventurers. A 1690 petition, from the clothiers of Suffolk and Essex, presented by Sir Gervase Elwes, MP for Suffolk, disputed a claim the African Company had made in the petition for the previous session that it had 'improved the manufactories of this nation' by recalling how open trade prior to the creation of the company had led to 'so quick a vent and so good prices given, that the petitioners were encouraged to carry on the making of far greater quantities of says and stuffs' and that the restraining of their market for woollen goods by the company would lead to 'the ruin of many poor families'.[40] The separate traders used these economic arguments to encourage public and state acceptance of the legislative inertia their political strategy sought.

The separate traders to Africa's victory was to convince the public at large that they could operate the trade for the benefit of all, unlike the African Company, and without statutory approval. By 1712 they had secured this outcome and the British slave trade began to expand. The annual average peacetime capacity of the trade when the African Company's monopoly came closest to being enforceable from 1673 to 1688 was 23 voyages. An equivalent period of peacetime after deregulation, from 1714 to 1729, saw open trade produce an average annual number of voyages of 77. Between 1687 and 1729 the company's market share reduced from 97 per cent to 4 per cent. The separate traders' non-statutory parliamentary rulings proved invaluable to achieving this outcome. The separate traders sought sufficient support from their constituents to block company attempts to achieve a statute in its favour and to influence the legislative vacuum, but not so much that a regulated company statute was secured that would have imposed a duty on their trade and, therefore, harmed their profit margins.

Comparing the African Company's fortunes after the expiration of the 1698 statute in 1712 with those of the Hudson's Bay Company after the expiration of its statute in 1697 confirms the importance of extra-parliamentary support to

39 *A Letter to a Member of Parliament Concerning the African Trade* (1709), p. 3.

40 *CJ*, vol. 10, p. 382, 'Petition of Clothiers of Suffolk and Essex', 21 April 1690. See also BL, Harleian Mss vol. 3710, fol. 221.

sustain a legislative vacuum in favour of open trade. For unlike in 1712, legislative inertia in the context of the Hudson's Bay Company favoured monopoly. Political interests opposed to the Hudson's Bay Company were far less broadly based than those against the Royal African Company, and they made less of an attempt to win over public opinion to discredit the Hudson's Bay Company's monopoly.[41]

The Africa trade debates shed new light on the late Stuart legislative process. They show how the public sphere interacted with Parliament in the context of state regulation of the economy. The Africa trade debates suggest that Parliament was a forum, which offered the means to defeat statute as much as it was an institution of legislation. Statute, the traditional measure of legislative success, usually resulted from Parliament acting in a supervisory capacity. Statute often derived from monarchical or oligarchic interests who wished to regulate and restrict the economy.

The Africa trade case study suggests that exclusive focus on statute as the primary product of parliamentary deliberation obscures much of the most important parliamentary activity. Because of the deliberate nature of legislative failure and because of the dramatic effects such failure could have on the economy, legislative failure represents a form of parliamentary success. The post-1689 legislative process is better examined beyond the narrow confines of statute and Parliament itself. The legislative process produced non-statutory results that could be as significant as statutory outcomes. What occurred and resulted from activity outside the chamber proved critical to the outcome of the parliamentary process. Legislative failure either resulted from Parliament's failure to supervise, or, as in the case of the African trade debates, its success as a *representational* body for diverse interests. Parliamentary consideration offered a means for groups to preserve the legislative vacuum and with it, in the case of the African trade, their economic interests.

Resolution of the Africa trade debates reflected alterations in how the British state might regulate its economy at the turn of the eighteenth century. The decline of royal prerogative as a regulatory device meant that monopoly companies required statutory backing. The British slave trade evolved without regulation because the separate traders cultivated more broadly based interests to convince Parliament to defeat the African Company's attempts to restrict the trade with legislation. Parliament's sovereignty as economic regulator made it more likely that the African Company's failure to legislate would lead to legislative vacuum because parliamentary sovereignty decreased the chances of other branches of

---

[41] For the Hudson's Bay Company see Edwin E. Rich, *The Hudson's Bay Company, 1670–1870* (London, 1958), vol. 1, p. 363.

the constitution settling an issue left unresolved by Parliament. The separate traders pitched for non-statutory parliamentary rulings that helped ensure acceptance of the legislative vacuum. These rulings proved formative in how the unregulated market that resulted from legislative failure operated, because their pseudo-statutory quality provided legitimacy and therefore helped to modify attitudes in favour of legislative vacuum in the extra-parliamentary public sphere. In short, the separate traders lobbied public opinion inside and outside Parliament to ensure that the legislative vacuum and the resultant unregulated slave trade would endure. Despite being instrumental to the escalation of the enslavement of human beings, legislative failure was a victory for representation and consent.

The Africa trade case study also demonstrates the importance of interest groups and a changing political landscape to the achievement of economic growth, in this case an expanded slave trade. It shows how markets deregulated more as a result of new political processes than due to any theoretical discussion of the benefits of deregulated economies. Although pamphleteers began to describe some economic benefits of deregulated markets to promote legislative inertia, their descriptions were secondary to their central aim of preventing statutory regulation in Parliament. The increasing sphere of discussion of economic issues was more important than the content of these descriptions. At the beginning of the eighteenth century, free trade and economic growth had determinants that are better essentialized as political than economic.

Chapter 2

A Proactive State? The Land Bank, Investment and Party Politics in the 1690s

Steve Pincus and Alice Wolfram

John Briscoe and Hugh Chamberlain, observed Charles Dickens, the eldest son of the novelist, 'met with some favour during the reign of William and Mary' and successfully incorporated their pet Land Bank scheme in 1696. The Land Bank was 'loved by the Tory country gentlemen who wanted to borrow money, [and] would perhaps have been looked kindly upon by the Whig merchants, who were prepared to lend it, had it not been at once apparent that it was intended to ruin the Whig institution' of the Bank of England.[1]

This Victorian assessment of the party political nature of the Land Bank scheme echoed the vitriolic party debates of the 1730s about the project. The establishment Whig newspaper *The Daily Gazetteer* castigated the Land Bank as the brainchild of 'the enemies of the Revolution', who claimed fatuously that the Bank of England 'was only profitable to a few traders' and had as its aim the destruction of 'the ancient gentry'. The Land bank, this Whig journalist opined, was a political scam. 'The scheme was so bad' and the projectors' 'credit and authority so low' that the project 'totally failed' with disastrous consequences for England. 'The nation was thereby reduced to the greatest distress and difficulty; for the low condition of public credit at that time, was entirely owing to this hopeful project'.[2] A contributor to the Tory/Jacobite *Fog's Weekly Journal* offered a rather different account of the Land Bank's rise and fall. The 'scheme' of the Land Bank was 'for supplying the public on reasonable terms'. However the worthy project was 'artfully clogged and rendered ineffectual' by the Junto Whig ministers.[3]

Victorian and Hanoverian accounts tying the history of the Land Bank to party politics in the 1690s sit uneasily with established interpretations of the Financial Revolution. Both those who insist on the fundamental continuity

1 Charles Dickens Jr, *All The Year Round*, 15/366 (4 December 1875), p. 223.

2 *Daily Gazetteer*, 26 May 1737, No. 598.

3 *Fog's Weekly Journal*, 25 March 1732, No. 177.

of political economic debate and those who insist on a radical caesura in 1688 deny the possibility that there should have been a party political squabble over competing banking projects.

Many scholars have denied that the Revolution of 1688–89 transformed England's political economy. Many of those interested in ideas, following the influential account of the relationship between political economy and the Glorious Revolution developed by John Pocock, argue that the vast majority in England lacked the conceptual tools to argue for the kind of political economic innovation implied by the creation of the Bank of England. For Pocock, commercial society, 'the assertion of the commercial order', was not 'a crucial issue in English ideological debate' at the time of the Glorious Revolution. Indeed the truly revolutionary consequences of 1688–89 – the reorganization of 'military, financial, and political structures in order to achieve effective participation in continental and imperial warfare' – were 'not fully foreseen or desired by those who invited' William to England. It was because William imposed these changes from without that he is to be seen as 'a revolutionary actor in the history of the British monarchy'. The Financial Revolution, then, was the result of foreign imposition rather than domestic ideological debate. It was at best an unintended, at worst an undesired, consequence of the events of 1688–89. The English, it turns out, deployed well-worn ideological tools to react against this foreign imposition. They used classical and Renaissance tropes to argue against modern financial institutions. In this interpretation of the relationship between political economy and the Revolution of 1688–89, the English turned almost unanimously against the new capitalist institutions of the 1690s. Indeed, in Pocock's view, whatever the differences between the defenders of the Financial Revolution and their critics, 'all Augustan analysts of political economy accept the interdependence of land, trade and credit'; both Whigs and Tories 'share not only the same reading of the economic facts, but the same underlying value system, in which the only material foundation for civic virtue and moral personality is taken to be independence and real property'. All groups in the English political nation shared the same economic assumptions, assumptions that scholars would later term mercantilist. In other words, they all believed that property was necessarily finite and was defined by landed property. Trade was merely the exchange of the products of the land. In such a world, landed property was necessarily the basis for political power.[4]

[4] John G.A. Pocock, *Virtue, Commerce and History: Essays on Political Thought and History, Chiefly in the Eighteenth Century* (Cambridge, 1985), pp. 108, 230; Pocock, *The Machiavellian Moment: Florentine Political Thought and the Atlantic Republican Tradition* (Princeton, NJ, 1975), pp. 423–6; Pocock, 'Early Modern Capitalism: The Augustan Perception', in Eugene Kamenke and Ronald S. Neale (eds), *Feudalism, Capitalism and*

Many economic historians have also argued that little changed in the wake of 1688–89. In their view the economic terrain changed little, making the Land Bank one among many apolitical attempts to address the acute crisis of wartime finance. Anne Murphy is the most recent scholar to emphasize the fundamental continuity of England's economic arrangements in the later seventeenth century. 'It was the liquidity provided by the financial market that had grown up to support the transfer of shares in private companies' before 1688, she argues, 'rather than action taken by the government' that proved crucial in supporting 'the public funds in the short term'. The Financial Revolution, in Murphy's view, was the result of private activity prior to the Revolution, rather than public legislation after the Revolution. Unsurprisingly, then, the creation of the Land Bank had little to do with party politics. The Land Bank, she insists, 'commanded support from across the political spectrum'.[5]

Those who emphasize that 1688 was a turning point in England's finances also find it difficult to account for the emergence of the Land Bank as an institutional competitor to the Bank of England. In the social sciences Douglass North and Barry Weingast have developed an equally influential, if radically different, interpretation of the relationship between political economy and the Glorious Revolution. Where the humanists have posited an emerging anti-capitalist consensus, Weingast and North have posited that the Revolution of 1688–89 created a new consensus in favour of capitalism and against state intervention in the economy. In 1688–89, they claim, a coalition of interests, acting rationally, individualistically, and self-interestedly, came together to solve England's 'financial problems' and provide 'appropriate constraints on the crown'. The Revolution, elaborates Weingast, ended many of the old disputes dividing Whigs and Tories and 'created a consensus about many disputed issues', a consensus that was 'codified through various constitutional changes'. The Revolution, in essence, established 'an elite pact'. In particular, North and Weingast suggest, the pact ushered in three institutional changes: parliamentary supremacy, Parliament's 'central role in financial matters', and the curtailing and

Beyond (London, 1975), pp. 68–71. Pocock appears to echo the conclusions of Peter G.M. Dickson, *The Financial Revolution: A Study in the Development of Public Credit, 1688–1756* (New York, 1967), p. 17. But Dickson's account of those who 'in the main' opposed the Financial Revolution focuses heavily on Tory writers including Jonathan Swift, Charles Davenant, and John Briscoe.

5 Anne L. Murphy, *The Origins of English Financial Markets* (Cambridge, 2009), pp. 57–8. In this she follows in the tradition of Dennis Rubini who insists on the 'apolitical nature' of the Land Bank: Dennis Rubini, 'Politics and the Battle of the Banks, 1688–1697', *EHR*, 85/337 (October 1970): p. 702. However, Rubini does believe that there were ideological tensions; these were simply tensions that did not map onto party politics.

subordination of the Crown's prerogative powers. All of these changes were more durable because the Revolution had 'established a credible threat to the crown regarding future irresponsible behavior'. So whereas in Pocock's view the Revolution of 1688–89 had given the state newfound power to create capitalist institutions against which English thinkers reacted, in the view of North and Weingast the Revolution had effectively created political institutions 'that limit economic intervention and allow private rights and markets to prevail in large segments of the economy'. The new institutions acted to limit mercurial governmental interventions in the economy and 'significantly raised the predictability of government'. The Bank of England, in the North-Weingast account, was exactly the kind of institution that made it possible for markets to prevail.[6]

Among social and economic historians, meanwhile, the notion that a new kind of 'reactive state' emerged after 1689 has become influential. In a widely cited essay Lee Davison, Tim Hitchcock, Tim Keirn and Bob Shoemaker have insisted against the proponents of the continuity thesis that the period from 1689 to 1750 was a major turning point 'in the relationship between the English state and society'. As important as social and economic issues became for the post-revolutionary state, in the view of Davison, Hitchcock and company, they were not the stuff of party politics. This was because, in their view, there was a fundamental divide between 'lower levels of discourse' that dealt with 'care for the poor, the suppression of vice, and the regulation of trade and industry' and 'the treatise-based high discourse surrounding state religious and constitutional issues'. Whigs and Tories fought over the church and the constitution, not political economy. So, 'the state took an active and leading interest in the affairs of defence, foreign policy, taxation, state religion and the constitution' – the stuff of party politics – 'it was more often than not reactive to the litany of domestic social and economic issues facing the nation, relying on those outside of central government and the legislature for information and instruction'. 'The early eighteenth-century state was essentially reactive' they conclude, 'its involvement

[6] Douglass C. North and Barry R. Weingast, 'Constitutions and Commitment: The Evolution of Institutions Governing Public Choice in Seventeenth-Century England', *Journal of Economic History*, 49/4 (December 1989): pp. 815–16, 819, 831; Barry R. Weingast, 'The Political Foundations of Democracy and the Rule of Law', *The American Political Science Review*, 91/2 (June 1997): pp. 252–3; Weingast, 'The Political Foundations of Limited Government: Parliament and Sovereign Debt in 17th- and 18th-Century England', in John N. Drobak and John V.C. Nye (eds), *The Frontiers of New Institutional Economics* (New York, 1997), p. 23. This story fits nicely with Crawford B. Macpherson, *The Political Theory of Possessive Individualism* (Oxford, 1962), pp. 1, 3, 27, 258.

in the promotion of economic growth and social welfare took the form of acting on initiatives emanating largely from outside executive government'.[7]

Against these divergent views of the relationship between political economy and the Revolution – that the Revolution changed little in the relationship between state and society on the one hand and that it changed almost everything on the other – we suggest that the Revolution made disagreement over the proper role of the English state a contributory factor to the nature of party politics in this period. This was so because there was no consensus in favour of or against capitalism, because the Financial Revolution constituted of much more than the creation of a stock market, and because the English in the seventeenth century understood that financial institutions shaped society as much as they were shaped by social forces. Our analysis of the debates surrounding the creation of the Land Bank and of those who invested in the National Land Bank reveal sharp ideological and social differences between the defenders of the Land Bank and the advocates and investors in the Bank of England. We suggest, therefore, that political economic issues came increasingly to inform party political preferences in the wake of the Revolution of 1688–89. And, that those party political preferences had a social as well as an ideological dimension. If party politics was about more than squabbles over the constitution and religion, we suggest, then any account of social and economic regulation in the eighteenth century must involve a discussion of party politics. Political narratives of the eighteenth century that ignore political economy miss a fundamental element of political contention in the Augustan Age.

Part I

Banks were a hot topic in the 1690s. The newly married James Brydges was probably one among many who found time to discuss them in London coffeehouses.[8] Far from uniting the English against them, most in England

---

7 Lee Davison, Tim Hitchcock, Tim Keirn, and Robert B. Shoemaker, 'The Reactive State: English Governance and Society, 1689–1750', in Davison, Hitchcock, Keirn, and Shoemaker (eds), *Stilling the Grumbling Hive* (Stroud, 1992), pp. xiii, xv, xli. We share many of the concerns with 'the reactive state' expressed by Joanna Innes – *Inferior Politics: Social Problems and Social Policies in Eighteenth-Century Britain* (Oxford, 2009), p. 8. When we refer to 'Proactive State', it should be clear, we mean narrowly within the area of finance, which precisely straddled the boundary between fiscal-military policy and domestic policy.

8 Henry Huntington Library [henceforth HEH], James Brydges, Journal, 12 September 1697, ST 26, unfoliated. The proliferation of bank schemes in the 1690s was a commonplace in the older literature: William Robert Scott, *The Constitution and Finance*

believed that some kind of a national bank was necessary. 'The usefulness of banks in England is not now controverted', began one essay among the Tory Duke of Leeds's papers.[9] The question was what type of bank.

In January 1692 two competing groups brought proposals to the House of Commons for a national bank. Dr Hugh Chamberlain, supported by John Briscoe and John Asgill, proposed a land bank to the Commons. A Commons committee 'composed of several knowing gentlemen of most exquisite sense' reported that 'the Doctor's proposal was practicable'. Chamberlain, who had long been floating land bank schemes both in England and Scotland, petitioned the Commons to reconsider his proposal in December 1693, but received little further encouragement.[10] A second group, headed by William Paterson presented a proposal that would become the germ of the Bank of England that was eventually awarded statutory authority in May 1694. The Whig politician Charles Montague, who helped shepherd the proposal through the Commons, had himself been a keen advocate of banks of credit since at least 1683.[11]

Political economic questions mapped ever more tightly onto party politics in the 1690s. Whigs and Tories – many of the same Whigs and Tories who debated the relative merits of the Bank of England and the Land Bank – squared off throughout the 1690s over the competing claims of the New and Old East India Companies.[12] Less well known, but equally party political, was the struggle that began in 1695 over the London wharfingers' cartel that pitted a Tory group led by Sir John Fleet and Sir Josiah Child – both Old East India Company men – against a Whig group led by Sir Gilbert Heathcote. Dr Chamberlain's former

---

of the English, Scottish and Irish Joint Stock Companies to 1720 (3 vols, Cambridge, 1910–1912), vol. 3, p. 199.

9 British Library, Add. Mss 28079, fol. 146r, 'Banks', c.1694. This may well have been taken from Sir Francis Brewster's essay on banks.

10 *CJ*, vol. 10, p. 616, 8 January 1692; *CJ*, vol. 11, p. 22, 7 December 1693; National Archives of Scotland [henceforth NAS], GD 158/901/2, Dr Hugh Chamberlain, 'Proposals to make England Rich and Happy', November 1690; NAS, GD 158/901/9, Dr Hugh Chamberlain, 'An Humble Proposal', 1690s; *Some Remarks Upon a Late nameless and Scurrilous Libel* (London, 1696), pp. 1, [3]; John K. Horsefield, *British Monetary Experiments 1650–1710* (Cambridge, MA, 1960), pp.156–65. Chamberlain had deep ties to Jacobitism. He had been called to witness the birth of the Pretender in June 1688 and did attest to the birth of Mary of Modena's second child in 1692: James E. Thorold Rogers, *The First Nine Years of the Bank of England* (Oxford, 1887), p. 50.

11 NAS, Adv. 31.1.17, fols 1–4, Charles Montague's Paper, 15 May 1683; Dickson, *Financial Revolution*, pp. 50–51. Scott, *Constitution and Finance*, vol. 3, pp. 204–5.

12 Henry Horwitz, 'The East India Trade, the Politicians, and the Constitution: 1689–1702', *Journal of British Studies*, 17 (1978): pp. 1–18.

partner, the Tory lawyer John Asgill, drew up the secret deed poll formalizing the cartel's association.[13]

John Asgill, Nicholas Barbon, and John Briscoe – all three with ever deepening Tory associations – seized upon the swelling fortunes of Tories in Parliament and the growing doubts about England's creditworthiness to revive their pet land bank project. While Asgill and Barbon initially created a land bank based in Lincoln's Inn to rival John Briscoe's scheme, it was almost inevitable that the two would join forces.[14] Not only had Briscoe and Asgill worked together with Chamberlain in 1692, they had also joined forces in a scheme for establishing fisheries in North America and in a joint-stock company for establishing workhouses.[15] In September 1695, the Court of the National Land Bank – Briscoe's concern – resolved to seek 'a parliamentary establishment'.[16] By February 1696, after a few months of trading rebarbative squibs, 'Mr National Briscoe and Dr Barebones are joined together'.[17]

When the Committee of the Whole House agreed to the proposal to support a National Land Bank 'by subscription' and stated that 'none concerned in the Bank of England should have anything to do with it', it set off several months of anxious party political squabbling.[18] The Tory leaders Robert Harley and the Duke of Leeds both collected memoranda defending the Land Bank against the Bank of England.[19] Sir Joseph Herne, the Tory Old East India Company

---

13 Henry G. Roseveare, '"The Damned Combination": The Port of London and the Wharfingers' Cartel of 1695', *London Journal*, 21/2 (1996): pp. 97–111; Henry G. Roseveare, 'Property versus Commerce in the Mid-Eighteenth Century Port of London', in John J. McCusker and Kenneth Morgan (eds), *The Early Modern Atlantic Economy* (Cambridge, 2000), pp. 66–72. Interestingly another land bank protagonist, John Briscoe, may have been working as a land surveyor in the Port of London during this period, *Calendar of Treasury Books*, vol. 9, p. 119, 14 May 1689.

14 For an example of the bitter tone of the short-lived rivalry between the Asgill/Barbon and Briscoe banks, see John Briscoe, *Mr. John Asgill his Plagiarism Detected* (London, 1696).

15 *Calendar of State Papers, Domestic*, William and Mary, 22 June 1691, p. 422; *Calendar of State Papers, Domestic*, William and Mary, 21 September 1691, p. 527. Briscoe had worked with a Jesuit in the reign of James II to establish a joint stock company to produce white paper: Petition of George Hagar, *CJ*, vol. 10, p. 343, 25 January 1690.

16 London University Library, MSS 61, fol. 8v, Minutes of the National Land Bank, 20 September 1695.

17 *An Answer to a Libel* (1696), p. 21; Narcissus Luttrell, *A Brief Historical Relation of State Affairs* (6 vols, Oxford, 1857), vol. 4, p. 13; Andrea Finkelstein, *Harmony and the Balance* (Ann Arbor, MI, 2000), p. 206; Horsefield, *British Monetary Experiments*, pp. 180–205.

18 Narcissus Luttrell, *Brief Historical Relation*, vol. 4, p. 16.

19 BL, Add. Mss 28079, fol. 146r, Duke of Leeds, 'Banks', c.1690s; BL, Add. Mss 70155, Richard Harley, 'The Land Bank', 1696?, unfoliated.

man and John Briscoe's partner in a copper mining concern, partnered with the great East India man and fellow Tory Sir Thomas Cooke to 'discourse' with the Treasury commissioners on behalf of the Land Bank.[20] The Whig polemicist John Oldmixon later recalled that Robert Harley 'had been at no small pains to carry [the Land Bank] so far as into an act of Parliament'.[21] Harley, as in so much else, was ably supported by Paul Foley, the Tory speaker of the House, and Philip Foley his younger brother. The Land Bank scheme was 'chiefly managed by Harley, Foley and the Tories', Gilbert Burnet later quipped.[22] Foley's old enemies, the Whig directors of the Bank of England, petitioned anxiously against the Land Bank proposal.[23] The Whigs Charles Montague, Chancellor of the Exchequer, and John Smith – who would later threaten to attack Paul Foley in the House of Commons – led the opposition.[24] In Parliament and outside it, 'party and faction' dominated the debate over the competing banks. 'The two Banks are striving who shall supply the King', observed one commentator. Many sought anxiously to hear which would prevail. 'I would willingly be informed of the present state and credit of the Bank of England and the Land Banks, and the project also now in agitation for a national bank', John Lord Ashburnham, a Land Bank supporter, wrote anxiously from his Sussex home.[25]

In the end, the Tories received their wish. In April 1696 the National Land Bank received statutory approval.[26] Abel Roper's Tory newspaper *The Post Boy and Historical Account* eagerly promoted the Land Bank, proclaiming in early July that 'several of the subscribers' believed 'that the subscription of one hundred thousand pounds will be full before the 21st instant'.[27] These predictions proved wildly optimistic. Narcissus Luttrell noted as early as the beginning of June

---

20 BL, Add. Mss 34355, fol. 10v, Charles Montague to William Blathwayt, 3 July 1696. On the Briscoe/Herne relationship: *Calendar of State Papers, Domestic*, William and Mary, 1690–91, 3 July 1691.

21 John Oldmixon, *History of England* (London, 1735), p. 140.

22 Gilbert Burnet, *Bishop Burnet's History of His Own Time* (6 vols, Edinburgh, 1753), vol. 4, p. 249; *Faults in the Fault-Finder* (London, 1710), p. 8.

23 John Barrow, *A New and Impartial History of England* (London, 1763), vol. 7, p. 326; *CJ*, vol. 11, p. 524, 19 March 1696.

24 BL, Add. Mss 34355, fol. 1v, Charles Montague to William Blathwayt, 29 May 1696.

25 BL, Add. Mss 34355, fol. 2r, Charles Montague to Blathwayt, 29 May 1696; HEH, HA 14767, John Forwad (London) to Sir John Coghill, 11 February 1696; East Sussex Record Office, ASH/840, 35, John Lord Ashburnham (Ashburnham) to James Mackburnye, 22 February 1696.

26 Narcissus Luttrell, *Brief Historical Relation*, vol. 4, p. 49; Henry Horwitz, *Parliament, Policy and Politics in the Reign of William III* (Manchester, 1977), p. 177.

27 *Post Boy and Historical Account*, 25 June 1695; *Post Boy*, 4 July 1695.

that 'most believe it will not be a bank'. By the beginning of August one of the Somerset Whig Edward Clarke's informants commented that 'it does not appear that the people of the Land Bank can succeed at present'.[28] And so it proved. In late November Charles Montague reported to the House of Commons that 'after all manner of expedients had been proposed by the Commissioners (for taking subscriptions to the Land Bank) to render their project palatable to the public' only £2,100 was collected above the initial £5,000 subscribed by King William – a tiny fraction of the £2.5m required.[29]

The causes of the Land Bank's failure were hotly disputed in the 1690s and throughout the eighteenth century. Whigs argued that it was a disastrous Tory boondoggle designed to fail and damage the war effort, while Tories argued that it was a virtuous and well designed plan that was doomed by unfortunate economic circumstances and Whig ministerial meddling.[30]

Whatever the causes of its failure, no one could doubt that the Land Bank was a Tory political project. Financial issues had become the stuff of party politics at least at the parliamentary level. The English were not united against the Financial Revolution as some scholars have maintained. Indeed, the one thing that Whigs and Tories agreed upon in the mid-1690s was the need for some kind of national bank. Robert Harley, the Foleys, the Duke of Leeds, and their Tory allies pushed through a land bank scheme against the virulent objections of Charles Montague, John Smith, and the Whigs.

Part II

The proponents of the rival banks engaged in a vitriolic and voluminous pamphlet war in the 1690s and beyond. Both sides advanced arguments that made it clear that each believed the struggle had the widest possible ramifications for English state and society. The struggle over the banks was over the nature

---

28 Narcissus Luttrell, *Brief Historical Account*, vol. 4, p. 67; Somerset Record Office, DD/SF/3088, John Danvers (London) to Edward Clarke, 3 August 1696.

29 *The History and Proceedings of the House of Commons* (London, 1742–44), vol. 3, p. 53. The report was presented on 24 November 1696.

30 For the Whig view, Abel Boyer, *Animadversions and Observations upon a Treatise* (London, 1718) p. 23; BL, Add. Mss 34355, fol. 10r, Charles Montague to Blathwayt, 3 July 1696; BL, Add. Mss 34355, fol. 14, Montague to Bathwayt, 17/27 July 1696; BL, Add. Mss 34355, fol. 37r, Montague to Blathwayt, 25 June 1697; William Anderson Steel, 'The Founders of the Bank', *Macmillan's Magazine*, 70/417 (1894): pp. 187–8. For the Tory view, John Asgill, *Remarks on the Proceedings of the Commissioners* (London, 1696), pp. 15, 20–22; *Post Boy*, 4 June 1696.

of English society, not merely a fight over the most expedient way to finance the Nine Years War. This was a debate over the relationship between state and society, not a narrow, erudite discussion over high finance.

The Whigs who had created, and now defended, the Bank of England believed that labour, rather than natural endowment, created property. They believed therefore that the most efficient way to increase a nation's wealth was to promote manufactures, since manufactures mixed human labour with natural resources to create valuable commodities for human consumption. The West Country Whig John Locke, one of the earliest supporters of the Bank of England, and not coincidentally closely associated with cloth manufacturers, classically argued, 'if we rightly estimate things as they come to our use, and cast up the several expenses about them, what in them is purely owing to nature, and what to labour, we shall find that in most of them 99/100 are wholly to be put on the account of labour'. No wonder he was convinced that for states 'the honest industry of mankind' and 'numbers of men are to be preferred to largeness of dominions'.[31] In the 1690s a number of Whigs echoed these sentiments. They insisted that labour and manufactures rather than land were the key to England's future strength and prosperity. 'It is manifest by experience', claimed William James echoing Locke, 'that where a manufacture and much people are settled in any part of the nation, there the lands are not only occupied, but yield the greatest rents, and the fruits thereof the greatest price'.[32] James Whiston, who had long been known for his publication of mercantile price lists, thought that 'industrious inhabitants', not land, were the 'original riches, as well as strength of the nation'.[33] The 'labours' of the people were capable of infinitely improving nature's blessings, thought the author of *England's Glory*, so that human endeavour indeed 'is the real riches and strength of the nation; and the more the merrier, like bees in a hive, and better cheer too'.[34] The Irish Whig Sir Francis Brewster was certain that those nations that combine natural resources with labour 'are more to be feared, than those that abound with the blessings of nature, but want that of industry'.[35] The

31 John Locke, 'Second Treatise of Government', in David Wootton (ed.), *Political Writings of John Locke* (New York, 1993), pp. 281–2. For Locke's support of the Bank, see John Locke to Edward Clarke, 30 June 1694 and Locke to Clarke, 6 August 1694, in Benjamin Rand (ed.), *The Correspondence of John Locke and Edward Clarke* (Cambridge, MA, 1927), pp. 395, 397.

32 William James, *England's Interest* (London, 1689), p. 2.

33 James Whiston, *A Discourse of the Decay of Trade* (London, 1693), p. 3.

34 H.M., *England's Glory; or, the Great Improvement of Trade in General by a Royal Bank* (London, 1694), pp. 20–21; sigs A2v–A3r.

35 Sir Francis Brewster, *Essays on Trade and Navigation* (London, 1695), p. 1. Brewster is often said, based on the evidence of this tract, to have been an opponent of the Bank of

radical Whig John Cary knew it to be 'the great interest of England to advance its manufactures'. It was through manufactures that:

> ... we not only employ our poor, and so take off that burden which must otherwise lie heavy on our lands, but also grow rich in our commerce with foreign nations, to whom we thereby sell our product at greater prices than it would otherwise yield, and return them their own materials when wrought up here, and increased in their value by the labour of our people.[36]

Cary's views, and those of Locke, were shared by the future president of the Board of Trade, the Whig John Egerton, Third Earl of Bridgewater. To guarantee England's economic future, Bridgewater advised, 'that new manufactures be erected and introduced into such counties as have now none'.[37]

Whigs celebrated the Bank of England not only because it could help finance the war, but also because it would help promote the manufacturing sector. Almost a decade before the Whigs founded the Bank, Robert Verney had argued that by a bank of credit 'the quality and quantity of manufactures will be improved'.[38] The Whig Bishop of Salisbury, Gilbert Burnet, recalled that many at the time argued for the Bank because 'the credit it would have, must increase trade and the circulation of money', presumably making it easier for capital intensive manufacturing concerns to get off the ground.[39] Upon the establishment of the Bank, one supporter enthused that it would lower interest rates, 'facilitate the circulation of money', and help finance the war. Significantly, the value of the circulation of money was that it would thereby funnel money to where it could be productive, to manufactures.[40] H.M., the most eloquent defender of the Bank, pointed out that the bank of credit could provide 'ready money' in case of 'a sudden emergency' to 'equip Armadas, supply armies, levy soldiers'. This ability to support the government financially will 'tend to the overthrowing our enemies by sea and land'.[41] But, H.M. was certain that the Bank would be much more than an instrument of the fiscal-military state. It would, he argued, have a proactive effect on English society at large, 'Money

England. But in fact his discussion of banks appears to have been written before 1694, and he proposed an amalgam of land and credit banks, with the specific intent of encouraging manufactures, pp. 109–15.

36 John Cary, *An Essay on the State of England* (Bristol, 1695), pp. 2, 6 12, 23, sig. [A7].

37 HEH, EL 8443, Earl of Bridgewater, 'State Propositions', 1690s.

38 Robert Verney, *Englands Interest* (London, 1682), p. 6.

39 Burnet, *History of His Own Time*, vol. 4, p. 181.

40 *A Brief Account of the Intended Bank of England* (London, 1694), pp. 1–4.

41 H.M., *England's Glory*, pp. 21–2, 31.

in a nation in trade, is like blood in the veins, if it circulates in all parts, the body is health; if it be wanting in any parts, it languisheth'. Banks guaranteed the circulation of money which would 'beget trade and people, and they will beget riches ... Riches are the conveniencies of a nation: but trade and people are the glory and strength of the kingdom'.[42] H.M. was sure that a bank would initiate a spiral of infinite economic growth. 'People will increase, for trade will bring in people as well as riches to the nation: where trade is, there will be employment; where employment is, there will people resort; where people are, there will be consumption of all commodities'.[43]

Whereas the supporters of the Bank of England insisted that labour was the basis of wealth and hoped the new bank would help to transform England into a manufacturing society, the Land Bank men insisted that land and only land was a secure basis of wealth and sought to reverse the social revolution which they believed had begun at the Revolution. 'The land of England is the fund and riches of the nation, by which the government is supported and the nation defended', argued one Land Bank proponent.[44] The West India merchant, long time co-projector with Hugh Chamberlain and Land Bank investor, Sir Dalby Thomas insisted that 'land (and that only) is the immoveable in place, and durable estate of the kingdom, and the *primum mobile* of all things therein'.[45] 'Native commodities' not manufactures, thought John Asgill, 'are the foundation of the greatest trade and commerce under heaven'.[46] John Briscoe made clear his view 'that land was the true and solid fund of credit', the only basis 'to settle a bank upon'.[47]

The Land Bank, in the view of its defenders, would resurrect the standing of the gentry and aristocracy against the new moneyed interest. The Land Bank, Abel Boyer recalled, 'at first seemed calculated only to advance the Landed-Men's interest, in opposition to the growing power of moneyed men'.[48] The Land Bank will 'be the support of the nobility and gentry of England', crowed one of its proponents in 1695.[49] The new post-revolutionary financial instruments were fomenting a social revolution. 'It's every day's experience', lamented John

42 H.M., *England's Glory*, pp. 11–12, sig. A3r.

43 H.M., *England's Glory*, pp. 18–19.

44 *An Account of the Land-Bank*, August 1695, p. [2].

45 Sir Dalby Thomas, *Propositions for General Land-Banks* (1695), p. [1].

46 John Asgill, *Remarks on the Proceedings*, p. 1.

47 London University Library, MSS 61, fol. 2r, Minutes of the National Land Bank, c.1696.

48 Abel Boyer, *The History of King William the Third* (3 vols, London, 1702–03), vol. 3, p. 164.

49 *An Account of the Land-Bank*, August 1695, p. [2].

Asgill, 'that a few years success in trade, renders moneyed men masters of so much wealth, as enables them to purchase the most considerable estates in the Kingdom; so that at this rate in some few years, the traders will invade the ancient gentry, and take way their place and nation'.[50] The new funds, including the Bank of England, would in 'but a few years' prove to be 'like a canker, which will eat up the gentlemen's estates in land, and beggar the trading part of the nation, and bring all the subjects of England to be the moneyed men's vassals', prophesied John Briscoe in 1694.[51] Briscoe made clear in subsequent tracts that he understood the social struggle of the 1690s would pit the Tory merchants and the landed men against the new moneyed classes. He marveled that those who sought 'a monopoly of the money and credit of the kingdom' so long and 'strenuously opposed' the establishment of the East India and African companies – two overwhelmingly Tory joint-stocks – alleging 'they are monopolies and infringements on the rights of the subject'.[52]

In the view of the supporters of the Land Bank, the post-revolutionary regime had been an unmitigated disaster for the landed men. The Whig war effort impoverished the landed classes. 'The landed men have chiefly contributed to the support of the war', complained one Land Bank proponent, 'do want money most, and are least esteemed'.[53] ''Tis the landed men who pay the great taxes, and feel the burdens of the rest', chimed in Dalby Thomas.[54] A land bank, by contrast, Hugh Chamberlain argued, would eliminate the need for the land tax, which after the Revolution had so devastated the landed classes.[55] The Whig directors of the Bank of England, the proponents of the Land Bank proclaimed in squib after squib, will never 'answer the ends of the landed-men'.[56] The Land Bank, concluded John Asgill, 'is the most beneficial thing to the landed men that ever was projected, and the [Bank of England] profitable only to a few traders'.[57]

---

50 Asgill, *Remarks on the Proceedings*, p. 3.

51 John Briscoe, *A Discourse on the Late Funds* (2nd edn, London, 1694), p. viii.

52 [John Briscoe], *Reasons Humbly Offered for the Establishment of the National Land-Bank* (1696), p. [1].

53 *An Answer to a Libel entituled, a Dialogue between Dr. H.C. and a Country-Gentleman* (1696), p. 14.

54 Thomas, *Propositions*, p. [1].

55 Hugh Chamberlain, *Dr. Hugh Chamberlain's petition, and proposals for a land-bank* (December 1693), p. 2.

56 Thomas, *Propositions*, p. [1]; *An Argument Proving that the Reasons given by Directors of the Bank of England* (1695), p. 3; *A New Ballad upon the Land Bank*; Asgill, *Remarks on the Proceedings*, pp. 34–5.

57 Asgill, *Remarks on the Proceedings*, pp. 2–3.

Both supporters and opponents of the Land Bank were convinced that the post-revolutionary state had the capacity to transform English society. Neither side believed that the state was merely reactive. Neither side believed that only religious and constitutional issues were the stuff of party politics. Whigs were convinced that because property was constituted by labour and therefore infinitely expandable, the state should develop financial institutions like the Bank of England that would transform the country into a manufacturing nation. Tories, by contrast, lamented the social revolutionary implications of the new financial institutions. They believed that the state needed to erect institutions which would restore the country to its natural rulers.

Part III

Were the ideological differences between the Land Bank and Bank of England supporters merely an elite phenomenon? Were the political stakes manifest only to those sitting in Parliament, while most ordinary investors were indifferent? Was there in fact a distinction between party politics and the social and economic concerns of the middling sort?

Proponents of the Land Bank schemes and proponents of the Bank of England were not only rhetorical combatants. There is substantial evidence to suggest that they were divided along socio-economic lines as well. P.G.M. Dickson's study of the subscribers to the Tontine of 1693 and the original subscribers to the Bank of England in 1694 led him to conclude that 'in its initial phase English government long-term borrowing leaned heavily on the financial expertise and accumulated capital of the London bourgeoisie and office-holders'.[58] Gary de Krey has shown that the directorate of the Bank of England in the 1690s was dominated by prominent London Whigs.[59] And Anne Murphy has demonstrated that, while London merchants and elites predominated among the initial subscribers to the Bank, a wider swathe of London's middling sorts subscribed to the enlarged capital in 1697, by which point the shareholders included numerous retailers and manufacturers.[60] The early Bank directors, then, were predominantly mercantile and predominantly Whig, and the early Bank subscribers were predominantly middling and predominantly metropolitan.

How did the subscribers to the various land bank schemes compare? This question is complicated by the fact that these projects were, ultimately, short-

[58] Dickson, *Financial Revolution*, p. 259.

[59] Gary S. De Krey, *Fractured Society: The Politics of London in the First Age of Party, 1688–1715* (Oxford, 1985), p. 127.

[60] Murphy, *Origins*, pp. 148–54.

lived. Few detailed subscription lists and no transfer books survive to provide information on the social or geographical origins of the subscribers to the Land Bank. However, it is possible at least to sketch out the socio-economic characteristics of the subscribers to the land banks by linking the names on the subscription lists to the names of those leaving wills in the Prerogative Court of Canterbury in the late seventeenth and early eighteenth centuries.[61]

Land Bank subscribers, particularly the subscribers to John Briscoe's Land Bank, were significantly less metropolitan than the subscribers to the Bank of England. Whereas more than half of the original subscribers to the Bank of England hailed from London, only about a fifth of subscribers to the John Asgill-Nicholas Barbon bank and a sixth of the subscribers to Briscoe's bank hailed from the Square Mile. One critic of the Land Bank suggested that the typical subscriber was 'a mighty stranger in the town'.[62] This contemporary commentator aptly captured the geographical bias of subscribers to Briscoe's bank. As Table 2.1 shows, the Briscoe bank subscribers were largely a provincial group, with the bulk deriving from the rural southeast and significant minorities from East Anglia, the Midlands, and the southwestern counties of Cornwall, Dorset, and Somerset.

If the Briscoe bank drew most of its subscribers from the provinces, with a particular concentration coming from the southeast, the Asgill-Barbon bank was rather more metropolitan, with just over 57 per cent of its traceable subscribers coming from London, Westminster or Whitehall. Though still less London-oriented than the Bank of England, which drew 69.6 per cent of its subscribers from London, Westminster, or Whitehall, the Asgill-Barbon bank drew many of its subscribers from the urban parishes of Middlesex. It seems likely that the greater reliance of the Asgill-Barbon bank on Westminster subscribers can be attributed to basic differences in how the Asgill-Barbon and Briscoe banks were funded. Subscribers to the Briscoe bank were to settle land in exchange for bills of credit whereas subscribers to the Asgill-Barbon bank were to settle specie which would in turn be loaned out on mortgage.[63] It is not surprising that the specie subscribers to the Asgill-Barbon bank were likelier to come from the immediate vicinity of London than the Briscoe subscribers. However, there were still clear

61 This method is necessarily imperfect: in cases in which several people with the same name left wills, no link could be drawn, and some scope exists for misidentification. Nonetheless, it is the best means available for sketching out at least a rough profile of the Land Bank subscribers.

62 *Reasons against a Land-Bank* (1696), p. [1].

63 For the best recent description of the constitution of the two proposed banks, see Richard Kleer, '"Fictitious Cash": English Public Finance and Paper Money, 1689–97', in Charles I. MacGrath and Chris Fauske (eds), *Money, Power and Print: Interdisciplinary Studies on the Financial Revolution in the British Isles* (Newark, DE, 2008), pp. 85–7.

Table 2.1 Geographical origins of bank subscribers

Region	**Bank of England, Original Subscribers**	**Asgill-Barbon Land Bank Subscribers**	**Briscoe Land Bank Subscribers**
London (square mile)	58.3%	22.0%	16.4%
Westminster or Whitehall	15.8%	35.2%	9.8%
South East	17.5%	22.0%	41%
South West	2.8%	2.2%	11.5%
East Anglia	0.8%	4.4%	9.8%
Midlands	2.1%	12.1%	6.6%
North of England	0.4%	0%	3.3%
Wales	0%	0%	0%
Scotland	0%	0%	0%
Ireland	0.3%	0%	0%
Netherlands	1.6%	0%	0%
Foreign (other)	0.3%	2.2%	1.6%
Total	N=1191	N=71	N=92

Source: For Bank of England: Murphy, *Origins*, p. 152. Murphy's data is adjusted to show the geographical origins of Bank of England subscribers whose places of residence are known, to make the data fully comparable to the data we have derived. For Asgill-Barbon Land Bank: *A List of the Names of the Subscribers to the Land Bank* (London, 1695). For Briscoe Land Bank: *A List of the Names of Such of the Subscribers of Land and Money Towards a Fund for the National Land Bank Who Having Paid in Their Subscription Money or Subscribed to the Last Instrument Are Intitled to Elect or be Elected Directors of the Said Bank* (London, [1695]). Prerogative Court of Canterbury Wills indexed at http://www.nationalarchives.gov.uk/documentsonline/default.asp.

differences between the geographical origins of the Bank of England subscribers and those of the Asgill-Barbon bank subscribers. The former were far more likely to hail from the Square Mile, whereas the latter were much likelier to come from West End parishes like St Paul Covent Garden and St James's Westminster. If the Bank of England subscribers derived overwhelmingly from the commercially oriented Square Mile, the Asgill-Barbon bank subscribers were more likely to come from the more genteel parishes of Westminster and Whitehall.[64]

This impression that the Bank of England drew from the merchants and tradesmen of the City while the Asgill-Barbon bank drew from the genteel suburbs is confirmed by analysis of the socio-economic profiles of the subscribers, which shows that both the land banks had considerably higher numbers of

64 On the development of the West End, see M. Dorothy George, *London Life in the 18th Century* (New York, 1965), pp. 64–5.

Table 2.2 Socio-economic status of subscribers to the banks

	Bank of England, 1694	**Bank of England, 1697**	**Asgill-Barbon Bank**	**Briscoe Bank**
Titled Aristocrats	6.2%	4.0%	2.8%	9.8%
Gentlemen and Esquires	35.3%	21.1%	50.7%	65.2 %
Professionals	11.1%	5.9%	16.9%	8.7 %
Merchants	19.8%	24.0%	1.4%	9.8%
Finance	0.9%	1.9%	2.8%	0%
Retailing	14.6%	19.9%	9.9%	0%
Manufacture	9.8%	16.9%	9.9%	4.4%
Transport	0.7%	4.5%	0%	0%
Agriculture	0.2%	0.0%	0%	2.2%
Building	0.6%	1.1%	4.2%	0%
Domestic Service	0.9%	0.4%	0%	0%
Corporate	0%	0.3%	0%	0%
Total	N=1015	N=793	N=71	N=92

Sources: Murphy, *Origins*, pp. 150 and 153. For sources for the Land Banks, see Table 2.1. Murphy's data is adjusted to show the occupations only of male Bank of England subscribers whose occupations are known, to make the data fully comparable to the data we have derived.

gentry subscribers than the Bank of England.[65] As Anne Murphy has shown, the original subscribers to the Bank of England were generally drawn from the ranks of the gentry, professional, and mercantile classes, but the 1697 capital enlargement drew in large numbers of more modest subscribers, drawn from London's retailing and manufacturing classes. Both the land banks, by contrast, drew far more heavily from the gentry, as Table 2.2 shows: in the case of the Briscoe bank, from the provincial gentry and in the case of the Asgill-Barbon bank from the gentry and professional men who inhabited the parishes of Westminster, Whitehall, and, to a lesser extent, the City. The Asgill-Barbon bank drew a few retailers and manufacturers and a scattering of men from the building trades, some of whom may have worked with or for Nicholas Barbon in one of his real estate ventures.[66] But the Briscoe bank drew almost exclusively

65 One contemporary commentator also contrasted the social prominence of the supporters of Dr Hugh Chamberlain's Land Bank scheme with the subscribers and directors of the Bank of England, *Some Observations by way of Answer to a pamphlet called England's Glory* (London, 1694), p. 6.

66 The carpenter John Foltrop, for instance, had worked with Barbon in the late 1680s, Elizabeth McKellar, *The Birth of Modern London: The Development and Design of the City 1660–1720* (New York, 1999), pp. 87–8, 101–3.

from the gentry and aristocracy, and even the Asgill-Barbon bank had only a little more than half as many retailers and manufacturers among its subscribers as the Bank of England did in 1697.

While we can sketch out the geographical and socio-economic characteristics of the subscribers, it is difficult to know whether the genteel Westminster and provincial subscribers to the land banks identified themselves as Tories. It is, however, possible to identify strong Tory leanings among the active commissioners of the National Land Bank. Dennis Rubini, relying on the list of 300 commissioners appointed to take subscriptions for the National Land Bank in early May 1696, has characterized the Land Bank as '"country" rather than Tory'.[67] However, the records of the actual meetings of the commissioners reveal that there was a much smaller inner circle of active commissioners and that these active commissioners were Tories almost to a man. Among the 20 men listed in the Journal of the Land Bank commissioners were Tory merchants, financiers and Old East India Company governors Sir Joseph Herne, his brother Nathaniel Herne, Sir Thomas Cooke, and Sir John Fleet, as well as Col. John Pery, who held various offices in the Royal African Company.[68] Also active were leading Tories Sir Thomas Meres, and Col. Robert Byerly; the London Tory and 1695 parliamentary candidate William Faulkner; Thomas Foley and Edward Harley.[69] Clearly, the core of active Land Bank leaders, even after the Bank received parliamentary endorsement, was an overwhelmingly Tory group.

The Land Bank projects of 1695 and 1696, then, drew together a group of subscribers that was much more genteel and much more provincial than either the original subscribers to the Bank of England or the subscribers to the Bank's capital enlargement of 1697. And it drew these subscribers together in a project headed by leading Tory merchants, financiers, and members of Parliament. The new financial institutions of the 1690s, then, helped to shape and delineate emerging, and very distinct, social and political constituencies. By linking the

---

67 Rubini, p. 703; TNA, T52/19, National Land Bank: Commission for Taking Subscriptions, 1 May 1696.

68 On Col. Pery, see Kenneth G. Davies, *The Royal African Company* (London, 1957), pp. 164–5.

69 BL, Add. Mss 70155/64, A Journal of the Proceedings of the Commissioners Appointed to Take Subscription. The 20 commissioners appearing were: Sir Thomas Jermyn, Sir Joseph Herne, Sir Robert Cotton, Sir Thomas Meres, Lord Richard Blackham, Sir Thomas Cooke, Sir John Fleet, Col. Robert Byerly, John Trenchard Esq., Col. John Pery, Dr Nicholas Barbon, Mr Joseph Hoskinstiles, Thomas Foley Esq., Mr Thomas Goodwin, Mr Edward Harley, Mr Francis Eyles, Mr William Faulkner, Mr Robert Lyddell, Mr Nathaniel Horneby, Mr Nathaniel Herne. On Faulkner, see Eveline Cruickshanks, Stuart Handley and David W. Hayton (eds), *The History of Parliament: The House of Commons 1690–1715* (Cambridge, 2002), vol. 2, p. 381.

fortunes of individuals ever more closely to the shape of the English state, these institutions and projects bound ever-widening groups of subscribers to particular positions in the party-political controversies over the kind of economy and society that the English state ought to foster.

Part IV

The rise and fall of the National Land Bank in 1696 was a seminal event in the history of the state. The failure of the Land Bank proponents to get their pet project off the ground was of far wider significance than the hundreds of other failed projects or the thousands of pieces of failed legislation.

An examination of the political wrangling over the banks, the ideological skirmishes, and the subscription lists of the two land bank schemes that combined to form the National Land Bank has revealed that there were deep divisions over the financial arrangements most appropriate for England. The vast majority of parliamentarians accepted that some sort of national bank was necessary. There was no consensus against the Financial Revolution.[70] The vitriolic party squabbles over the competing bank schemes in Parliament, in the press, and in the committee rooms of the City suggest that there was no Coaseian bargain among English elites in favour of capitalist institutions in the wake of the Revolution. The subscription lists suggest that far from being merely the stuff of elite politics, the divisions over the banks stretched well into the middling sorts. Englishmen and some women cared deeply about the kind of bank their state would endorse precisely because they knew well that financial institutions shaped society. They understood that the kind of bank they would create in 1696 would profoundly influence whether England would become a manufacturing or a landed society. They understood, in other words, that the post-revolutionary state was much more than a reactive state.

The struggle over the Land Bank was also an important moment in the development of party political identity in the long eighteenth century. Political economic struggles, like the 1696 battle over the Land Bank or the 1711 debate over the creation of the South Sea Company, have proved remarkably difficult for historians to relate to party politics. This has been because political historians have shown little interest in social and economic issues, while those who have focused on commercial society have accepted an overly narrow and anachronistic definition of party politics. So, while Gary De Krey has suggested that 'the 1690s

[70] Much of Dickson's evidence comes from supporters of the Land Bank. Pocock has relied on Tory literature as well, many of whom supported the Land Bank. Both fail to discuss the arguments of the proponents of the Bank of England.

were a decade in which commercial questions were of importance in clarifying the terms of both party competition and party debate at Westminster', he has assumed that in the City 'no issue was more important than religion in creating and sustaining party enthusiasm'. The 'religious question', he insists, created 'a permanent cleft in the City's electorate and political leadership'. 'The Whig party and the dissenting electorate were virtually interchangeable political interests', De Krey contends.[71] Similarly Bruce Carruthers argues that 'Whig-Tory conflict contingently and subtly shaped the London stock market' in the late seventeenth and eighteenth centuries. But for Carruthers party politics had little to do with social standing or economic preferences. 'Disagreements over the Church, toleration, and Non-conformity were at the heart of the Whig-Tory split', Carruthers concludes, 'and these disputes were not about economics'.[72] In many ways these scholars, like those who developed the 'reactive state' thesis, have relied on the conclusions of specialists in high politics and political argument. 'Party configurations after 1688', argue Linda Colley and Mark Goldie, were decisively shaped by 'attitudes to the Anglican church and the tradition of [the] "mixed constitution"'. The Whigs, in their view, were united on one decisive issue 'the legitimacy and the desirability of the Protestant Succession in the House of Hanover'.[73] Party preferences, then, in the view of leading historians of trade and finance and scholars of high politics had little to do with political economy.

Our findings suggest that with the Land Bank scheme social standing and political economy did come to shape party preferences. The mid-1690s were a critical moment in the reformulation of party politics. The migration of Paul Foley and Robert Harley – both men with long-standing associations with religious dissent – into the Tory camp was a significant development. Both were ardent supporters of the Land Bank, as was the long-time East India Company director Sir John Fleet. Fleet was the lone survivor of James II's purge of Anglicans from the London coopers guild and was chosen Sheriff of London in June 1688, just at the moment that James II was leaning most heavily on London dissenters for support.[74] Many of the subscribers to the Asgill-Barbon bank appear to have had ties to religious dissent. Among them were the Presbyterian Vincent Alsop, who had been among the small number of prominent dissenters who had rallied

71 De Krey, *Fractured Society*, pp. 21–2, 74, 128.

72 Bruce Carruthers, *City of Capital: Politics and Markets in the English Financial Revolution* (Princeton, NJ, 1996), pp. 8, 10, 26, 198. David Stasavage follows this reasoning in his otherwise excellent study: *Public Debt and the Birth of the Democratic State: France and Great Britain, 1688–1789* (Cambridge, 2003), pp. 99, 103.

73 Linda Colley and Mark Goldie, 'The Principles and Practice of Eighteenth-Century Party', *HJ*, 22/1 (1979): pp. 243–4.

74 William Foster, 'Sir John Fleet', *EHR*, 51/204 (October 1936): p. 682.

around James II's 1687 Declaration of Indulgence; John Reynolds, likely the Presbyterian minister who served as chaplain to Philip Foley; and Nehemiah Lyde, the son of the Herefordshire dissenting minister Richard Lyde, who had relied on Sir Edward Harley for support when he faced religious persecution in the 1670s.[75] Of course, Nicholas Barbon himself was the son of the dissenting politician Praisegod Barbon, and John Asgill had strong dissenting connections: he attended nonconformist services in his youth, studied under the dissenting lawyer Sir Giles Eyre at the Middle Temple, and published late in his life with the son of the Baptist printer John Darby.[76]

The bitter party political struggles over the competing bank schemes in 1696 appear to have been a pivotal moment in the redefinition of party political identity. For many both inside and outside Parliament political economy was beginning to join religion and constitutional issues as critical to defining party politics. This was an important moment in what Perry Gauci has called 'the elevation of trade to party issue'.[77] The social differentiation that we have found among the supporters of the land banks and the Bank of England, with the social elite being far more likely to support the land banks, parallels recent findings about the eighteenth-century electorate.[78] Interestingly, early eighteenth-century manufacturers and labourers in the manufacturing sector were also much more likely to vote for the Whigs, the party of the Bank of England.[79] While we are not claiming that religion was unimportant in determining party political identities in the 1690s, our evidence does suggest that any definition of party politics that relies predominantly on religion is insufficient. Such a definition makes it impossible to understand both the contemporary belief that the struggle over the banks was a Whig/Tory battle or the centrality of political economic projects and arguments to Tory politics in the eighteenth century.

Scholars, we believe, have misunderstood the significance of the failed Land Bank project of 1696 because they have too readily accepted a radical

75 On Alsop, Steven Pincus, *1688: The First Modern Revolution* (New Haven, CT, 2009), p. 167. On Foley, Douglas R. Lacey, *Dissent and Parliamentary Politics in England, 1661–1689* (New Brunswick, NJ, 1969), p. 396. On Lyde, Nehemiah Lyde, *A Narrative of the Life of Mr. Richard Lyde of Hereford* (London, 1731), pp. 30–32.

76 Richard D. Sheldon, 'Barbon, Nicholas (1637/1640–1698/9)', *Oxford Dictionary of National Biography*, online edn; Richard L. Greaves, 'Asgill, John (bap. 1659, d. 1738)', *ODNB*; Stuart Handley, 'Eyre, Sir Giles (bap. 1635, d. 1695)', *ODNB*; Beth Lynch, 'Darby, John (d. 1704)', *ODNB*, all consulted January 2008.

77 Perry Gauci, *The Politics of Trade: The Overseas Merchant in State and Society, 1660–1720* (Oxford, 2001), p. 272.

78 Christopher E. Dudley, 'Establishing a Revolutionary Regime: Whig One-Party Rule in Britain, 1710–1734' (Ph.D. thesis, University of Chicago, 2010), p. 61.

79 Dudley, 'Establishing a Revolutionary Regime', pp. 58–9.

divide between social and economic history on the one hand and political and intellectual history on the other. The Land Bank scheme only appears apolitical if one is not interested in party politics. The early Augustan state appears merely reactive, if one ignores the volumes dealing with social and economic projects that fill the papers of Augustan politicians. Similarly party politics appear to be largely about religion and the constitution only if one occludes the mass of party political publications about social and economic issues, and the vast amount of time that eighteenth-century politicians spent in gathering information about and proposing policies for remedying social problems. In the 1690s, men and women, both of the political elite and of the middling sorts, recognized that the state played a pro-active role in shaping the English economy and recognized that party political contests over the control of those regulatory processes had real and profound consequences.

Chapter 3

Regulation and Rival Interests in the 1690s[1]

Mark Knights

This chapter explores regulation achieved at a local level after the revolution of 1688, when the national context became more conducive to such initiatives.[2] It seeks to show that regulation was the result of a good deal of local debate rather than something imposed by the 'state' from above and hence part of the negotiated, dispersed and participatory state outlined by recent social historians of the state.[3] The schemes succeeded only after a long dialogue with interested parties. The parliamentary bills had to be negotiated at local and national level. That meant overcoming vested interests both in the locality and at Westminster, and, more positively, selling the virtues of the proposed development to the local and national public. Debate often centred on petitions that were necessary to show local support for or opposition to a proposal, and these articulated and exploited quite sophisticated concepts of public and private good, conflicts

---

1 I am grateful to the workshops' participants and to Koji Yamamoto for comments on earlier drafts.

2 For the context of 1688 as a key turning point see Julian Hoppit, *A Land of Liberty? England 1688–1727* (Oxford, 2000); Douglass North and Barry R. Weingast, 'Constitutions and Commitment: The Evolution of Institutions Governing Public Choice in Seventeenth-Century England', *Journal of Economic History*, 49 (December 1989): pp. 803–32; David Stasavage, *Public Debt and the Birth of the Democratic State: France and Great Britain, 1688–1789* (Cambridge, 2003); Steve Pincus, *1688: The First Modern Revolution* (New Haven, CT, 2009); John Brewer, *The Sinews of Power; War, Money and the English State 1688–1783* (London, 1989); Peter Dickson, *The Financial Revolution in England: A Study in the Development of Public Credit 1688–1756* (Oxford, 1967). For a view of the state from below at this time see Lee Davison, Tim Hitchcock, Tim Keirn and Robert B. Shoemaker (eds), *Stilling the Grumbling Hive: The Response to Social and Economic Problems in England, 1689–1750* (Stroud and New York, 1992), pp. xi–liv; Stuart Handley, 'Local Legislative Initiatives for Economic and Social Development in Lancashire 1689–1731', *Parliamentary History*, 9 (1990): pp. 14–37.

3 Michael J. Braddick, *State Formation in Early Modern England c.1550–1700* (Cambridge, 2000); Michael J. Braddick and John Walter (eds), *Negotiating Power in Early Modern Society: Order, Hierarchy, and Subordination in Britain and Ireland* (Cambridge, 2001); Steve Hindle, *The State and Social Change in Early Modern England* (Basingstoke, 2000).

of interest and profit. Such campaigns, and the accompanying pamphlets, were evidence of a sophisticated art of lobbying. They were also sensitive to the language necessary to persuade – and should be exploited much more by historians of discourse. The chapter also seeks to explore how regulation was, at certain moments such as the 1690s, sought across a number of related activities: regulation of the press, of elections, of the coin, of the poor and of morality were all on the agenda. This, it is argued, is important because economic regulation was linked to, and in part justified by, other regulatory activity and the moral dimension helped to legitimize the pursuit of private interest by suggesting that it could also benefit the public. The public–private dilemma was not, of course, new to the 1690s; but it was presented in a particularly urgent form and the debates achieved a remarkable degree of social depth.

The chapter takes the numerous river navigation schemes of the later seventeenth and early eighteenth centuries, and in particular one promoted for the river Tone in Somerset, as a way of illustrating these processes.[4] The Tone scheme, enacted in 1699, originated amongst a group of projectors who seem initially to have been motivated by a concern to regulate and alleviate the poor of Taunton by improving the river Tone. Hitherto water-borne trade had been able to reach a little past Bridgwater, to 'Coal harbour' at Ham Mills, from where goods had to be carted four miles or so over land to Taunton. The navigation scheme proposed to make the river fully navigable as far as Taunton, facilitating the easier transport of bulky goods such as coal, iron and wood to a town that was one of the centres of the woollen trade.[5] The regulation of the river nevertheless required legislation in order to make a binding decision on the various interested parties, which included the proprietors of the banks and an earlier improver of the river who had been granted a royal patent. In the case of the river Tone the royal patent granted to Sir John Mallet in 1638 had enabled the construction of a 'cut' in the river (a new course for it), and the patent had been renewed in 1684 in favour of his three daughters, but, it was said, the tolls that had been levied to recoup the investment had led to 'several disputes and suits in law' and a bill was sought 'to end those disputes and quiet all differences for the future'.[6] For Taunton, and elsewhere, the chances of legislative success were improved

---

4 Information about the scheme can be found in Joshua Toulmin, *The History of the Town of Taunton* (1791); Tony Haskell, *By Waterway to Taunton: The Bridgwater and Taunton Canal* (Tiverton, 1994).

5 For Taunton see William Gibson, *Religion and the Enlightenment 1600–1800: The Rise of Civic Humanism in Taunton* (Bern, 2007); Eveline Cruickshanks, Stuart Handley and David Hayton (eds), *The History of Parliament: The House of Commons 1690–1715* (5 vols, Cambridge, 2002), vol. 2, pp. 525–8.

6 *The Case of the Daughters of the late Earl of Rochester* (1692).

by the Revolution of 1688–89, because parliamentary sessions were longer. The town also elected an MP, Edward Clarke, who worked indefatigably on behalf of his constituents and who recognized that the success of the scheme was also necessary for his political support there.[7]

The debates about the river navigation highlight larger ones about private and public interests. Albert Hirschman long ago argued that 'interests' became a means of containing the destructive passions, thereby legitimating the rise of capitalism and neutralizing pejorative associations with the pursuit of wealth.[8] Yet Hirshman's analysis is essentially one of canonical writers who, he implies, were responsible for changing the mental landscape. Wonderfully perceptive though his argument is, Hirschman has very little to say about the everyday economic arguments through which the change of mindset is more likely to have come about.[9] Moreover, 'interest' for Hirschman is primarily about individual human motivation, a new way of talking about 'self-love', rather than as a tool for engaging with the complex concept of the public good and justifying how what might otherwise be described as selfish behaviour could be rationalized as working for the common wealth. But what we have in the debate about navigation is a contest about how best to promote the common wealth after the notion of a 'commonwealth' had been proscribed by its associations with the republican regime of the 1650s and after the decline of the godly commonwealth envisaged by Calvinism. Part of that story has been told by J.A.W. Gunn, Joyce Appleby and Steve Pincus, who have very usefully mined some of the pamphlet material that discussed interest and economic theory. They show how the language of interest, increasingly prevalent from 1640s onwards and particularly shrill in the second half of the seventeenth century, was applied to economic as well as to political and religious conflicts; that 'interest' helped to reconcile the pursuit of wealth and the common good; and that there were 'contending views of the role of the state' in terms of regulating trade, with some arguing for state protectionism and others developing a more liberal approach.[10] Even so, it is worth re-emphasizing

---

[7] Cruickshanks et al., *House of Commons 1690–1715*, vol. 3, pp. 576–97. For his relationship with Locke see my 'Locke and the Franchise', *Past and Present*, forthcoming.

[8] Albert Hirschman, *The Passions and the Interests: Political Arguments for Capitalism before its Triumph* (Princeton, NJ, 1977).

[9] Pierre Force, *Self-Interest before Adam Smith: A Genealogy of Economic Science* (Cambridge, 2003) is also useful but curiously lacking in the context of the everyday.

[10] J.A.W. Gunn, *Politics and the Public Interest in the Seventeenth Century* (Toronto, 1969), Chapter 5; Gunn, 'Interest Will Not Lie', *Journal of the History of Ideas*, 29 (1968), 551–64; Joyce Appleby, *Economic Thought and Ideology in Seventeenth-Century England* (Princeton, NJ, 1980), Chapter 5; Steve Pincus, 'Neither Machiavellian Moment nor Possessive Individualism: Commercial Society and the Defenders of the English Commonwealth', *American Historical Review*, 103/3 (1998), pp. 705–36.

that apparently mundane domestic economic struggles, such as those over river navigation, are also a fruitful resource for studying economic ideas, for it was there that the implications of conflicting private and public interests were being worked out amid controversies that involved the whole community, down to the illiterate labourers who signed petitions.[11] Indeed, such debates should be exploited more routinely to expand the context of political discourse and there is particular value in doing so for Taunton given Clarke's proximity to the arch-regulator John Locke, whose close friend he was.[12]

River improvement schemes resulted in the physical regulation of the river but also a fiscal regulation in the form of tolls and tariffs granted by patent or act of Parliament. Such projects were important since they provided the infrastructure necessary for trade, reducing the cost of transporting heavy or bulky items, and control of a waterway could also confer economic advantage on individuals, groups and sectors of the economy.[13] Regulation of rivers, before canals became widespread in the later eighteenth century, thus helped to facilitate or restrict local economies and was a key part of thinking about the promotion of national wealth. Indeed, the most zealous promoter of navigation schemes, Andrew Yarranton, was in the mid-nineteenth century hailed as 'the Founder of English Political Economy' because of the way in which he saw national wealth advanced by this type of regulation, backed by the force of the state.[14]

River navigation schemes were complex because of the need to negotiate with those who owned stretches of the river banks and because the customary commissions of sewers which did regulate the maintenance of rivers had questionable authority to alter the course of a river or to levy charges. Both parliamentary legislation and royal patents could overcome these difficulties, though for much of the seventeenth century it was not clear whether Parliament or the Crown should be appealed to. Many river navigation bills fell foul of the frequent breaks in parliamentary business imposed by the Crown. It was only after 1688 that seeking legislation in Parliament became the norm, a reflection of a shift away from the Crown's power to grant monopolies and the result of regular sessions. The greater role of Parliament as regulator in turn increased the

---

11 Much attention has focused on national interest and foreign trade, thereby conflating state interest with interest theory more generally, but the reconciliation of private and public interests was very much a domestic issue.

12 I have explored their friendship in 'John Locke and the Franchise', *Past and Present*, forthcoming.

13 For an overview see Thomas S. Willan, *River Navigation in England 1600–1750* (London, 1964).

14 Patrick Edward Dove, *Andrew Yarranton: The Founder of English Political Economy* (1854). Yarranton remains a very neglected figure.

number of applicants turning to it. As Dan Bogart puts it, 'the political changes following the Glorious Revolution reduced political risk and uncertainty for road and river undertakers and they responded by initiating and investing in more projects'.[15] Whereas in almost 30 years between 1660 and 1688 there were only nine acts of Parliament for river schemes, in the three years between 1697 and 1700 there were eight navigation acts, of which the River Tone was one (a further four failed) and between 1719 and 1721 there were another nine acts (with just one failure).[16] This scale of activity inevitably affected the process by which Parliament granted rights to regulate rivers, forcing a sophistication of lobbying techniques to achieve success.

We should not, of course, forget the skills honed by London Livery Companies in their bids in the fifteenth and sixteenth centuries to influence regulatory legislation; but a new era of lobbying seemed to have been entered after 1688.[17] For example, campaigns had to be concerted and national rather than individualistic and piecemeal. In 1720 six bills were passed as the result of a 'combination of the projectors' who had 'worked up the temper of both houses to such a love of navigation' that the raft of legislation was enacted.[18] Localities were forced to think about national lobbying. In 1707, when the promoters of the river Tone scheme felt it necessary to seek controversial further legislation to authorize a new lock, they sent letters to over 60 MPs in England and ten 'to ye North Britains'.[19] Common interests were increasingly formed with far-flung places with whom a measure of co-operation was prudent.[20]

---

15 Dan Bogart, 'Did the Glorious Revolution Contribute to the Transport Revolution? Evidence from Investment in Roads and Rivers', p. 27, unpublished paper. Available at: http://www.socsci.uci.edu/~dbogart/research_page.htm [accessed: 2 August 2010].

16 The River Weaver scheme was promoted four times in the early 1660s, again in 1670 but only reanimated in 1699, and even then it took another 20 years to achieve.

17 Mathew Davies, 'Lobbying Parliament: The London Companies in the Fifteenth Century', in Linda Clark (ed.), *Parliament and People: Parliament in the Middle Ages* (Edinburgh, 2004); David Dean, 'Pressure Groups and Lobbies in the Elizabethan and Jacobean Parliaments', *Parliaments, Estates and Representation*, 11 (1991): pp. 139–52; Ian Archer, 'The London Lobbies in the Later Sixteenth Century', *HJ*, 31 (1988): pp. 17–44.

18 BL, Add. Mss 36914, fol. 84, Seymour Cholmondelely to Sir Thomas Aston, 26 April 1720, cited by Willan, *River Navigation*, p.30.

19 Somerset Record Office [henceforth SRO], DD/TC9 part 2, book of copies of letters, petitions 1707–08, unfoliated.

20 Sir Godfrey Copley, the MP for Thirsk who was promoting the Don navigation, tried to enlist the support of Leeds, which had its own river navigation bill and urged them to 'consider what friends they can make, be they of what county they will ... I will engage all that are for our river to be for both' (Cruickshank et al., *House of Commons 1690–1715*, vol.

As this suggests, the co-ordination of efforts and resources intensified and took new forms.[21] It was increasingly necessary to provide both financial resources and administrative coherence. Money was necessary not only to pay for the organization of a campaign – printed cases had to be made, petitions promoted, bills drafted, evidence to parliamentary committees mustered and MPs courted – but also, once successful, to pay for the implementation of a scheme. In the case of the River Tone the challenge of co-ordination and finance was met by the creation of a joint-stock company, known as the 'Conservators' of the river. A deliberate decision was made to by-pass the town's corporation which, it was felt, 'would not have had the confidence' to resist opposition.[22] Taunton seems to have been precocious in this development, which became integral to infrastructural development in the eighteenth century. The joint-stock was a good example of the incorporation of private interests into a larger whole in order to pursue a collective interest.[23] The company was formally the product of legislation in 1699, and amended in 1708 when its governance was codified. Yet even before the passage of the act that created them, and specifically in order to obtain it, the Conservators had a semi-formal existence. In February 1697 a treasurer, Maurice Hammond, collected £41, 17s, 6d, from 30 investors.[24] This fund paid for a scrivener who prepared a petition that was sent to Parliament, but most of it went to buy out the patentees.

In January 1698 the Conservators, recognizing that their undertaking would require 'a great sume of money', signed a 'Heads of Agreement' that formalized the company: a majority of subscribers were to choose a director and two assistants, and when the work was finished the subscribers were to be repaid at a profit of 7 per cent.[25] This provided working capital but further funds were collected from the original subscribers when the bill was introduced in Parliament. Outgoings relating to the bill between January and May 1699

3, p. 716). Since many rivers ran across counties some schemes were themselves more than 'local' in any case.

21 See also Alison Olson, *Making the Empire Work: London and American Interest Groups 1690–1790* (Cambridge, MA, 1992).

22 SRO, DD/SF/13/2/72, John Parsons to Clarke, 23 January 1698/99.

23 Taunton seems to have had some sort of early land bank (Andrew Yarranton, *England's Improvement* [1677], part 1, p.27) and so had a history of economic precociousness. For navigation finance see Willan, *River Navigation*, pp. 65–77. For joint-stocks more generally see Kenneth G. Davies, 'Joint-Stock Investment in the Later Seventeenth Century', *EcHR*, 4/3 (1952): pp. 283–301.

24 SRO, DDTC/8, Treasurer's Accounts and memoranda 1697–1719.

25 SRO, DDTC/8, 10 January 1697/98, 'General Proposal or Heads of Agreement'. The interest was reduced to 6 per cent in the act.

amounted to £453, 12s.[26] Further subscriptions were raised when work on the scheme started. Indeed, between 1697 and 1701, as much as £2,633 had been advanced to the project; and by 1707 this had risen to £3,800. The scheme only started to make money in 1717, by which time £5,697 had been spent.[27] All this had been possible because Taunton's better-off citizens and traders – seven were described as gentlemen, five as merchants, seven as clothiers, three as vintners, two as grocers, two as fullers, one dyer, one mercer, one ironmonger and one doctor – had pooled their resources. This fund had enabled the fledgling company to pay not only for the engineering work involved but also to mount campaigns to show public support for the scheme, first in 1698–99 when the original bill was passed and again, even more energetically, in 1707 when the Conservators argued that new legislation was necessary in order to complete the scheme.

The way to demonstrate that support was through a petitioning campaign. There was, of course, nothing new about petitioning or about its application to economic issues;[28] but it is clear that petitioning played a major role in the calculations of both proponents and opponents of river navigation schemes. Petitions were numerous but also customised for each locality. As Peter Shakerley, promoting Chester's interests relating to the River Weaver put it, 'the more petitions the better (for one petition will not be so advantageous), but the words of each must be varyed'.[29] The numbers of petitions could be very large. In 1698, for example, there were 25 petitions in favour of the Aire and Calder navigation bill, with 21 more in opposition.[30] The promoters of the River Tone scheme did not achieve the same level of activity but were assiduous.[31] They followed another of Shakerley's maxims, that the first petition should come from the local JPs or grand jury, securing one from the quarter sessions in 1707. Even though later

---

26 SRO, DD/TC1, Conservators of the River Tone, memoranda book 1699–1791, pp. 25–9. The Wakefield promoters of the Aire and Calder navigation spent £421, 15s, 11d on securing the passage of their act in 1699 – Peter Smith, *The Aire and Calder Navigation* (Wakefield, 1987), p. 4.

27 Toulmin, *Taunton*, p. 104. £9,000 was put up by 14 investors for the Weaver's improvements but the total spent rapidly escalated – Thomas S. Willan, *The Navigation of the River Weaver in the Eighteenth Century* (Manchester, 1951), pp. 23, 30.

28 Julian Hoppit, 'Petitions, Parliament and the Political Economy of Britain, 1660–1800', forthcoming in Richard Huzzey (ed.), *Pressure and Parliament*.

29 Willan, *Navigation of the River Weaver*, p. 144. Numbers were not always vital – the Bristol bill passed in 1714 even though there were 16 hostile petitions to the single one in support (Willan, *River Navigation*, p. 48).

30 Smith, *Aire and Calder Navigation*, p. 4.

31 Information about the petitioning can be found in SRO, DD/TC9 part 1 and DD/TC9 part 2, book of copies of letters, petitions 1707–08.

that year the grand jury of the sessions reversed the supportive stance adopted earlier, a significant setback, seven more favourable petitions followed. The Tone investors paid for scriveners who copied out the petitions and for the gathering of signatures – in at least one case money was paid to an agent for 'rideing about to gett ye names of ye Taunton Deane Tenants to a petition' and further sums were spent on promoting petitions in the surrounding towns. The numbers of people who signed were impressive, a fact obscured by the physical loss of petitions sent to the Commons but which is recoverable from the Conservators' own accounts; 131 signatures from Wellington, 130 from Ilminster, 51 from Langport, 92 from Collumpton, 57 from Ilvelchester, all the result of careful co-ordination from Taunton. And they achieved considerable social depth. On one petition several names were written in the same hand, it was noted, 'because many poor people were not able to write' their own names.[32]

Such laborious activity was necessary partly because of the vigour of counter-petitioning activity by the bill's opponents. In 1707, 389 'labourers' and 526 'inhabitants' of Taunton signed petitions against the second Tone bill because it raised new tolls. The Conservators seems to have been so worried that they went to the trouble of alphabetizing the names so that they knew their opponents at a glance. In all, there were at least 13 hostile petitions in 1707.[33] It was testament to the battle for public opinion that the Conservators procured a declaration, to be set before the House of Commons, from the mayor and corporation of Tiverton, supported by a further 55 inhabitants, protesting that although they had signed a petition against the navigation scheme they now, 'upon better informa[ti]on in the meritts of their case', felt they had been ' imposed on ... by diverse false representations' and publicly recanted their opposition.[34] As all this suggests, petitioning was necessary to show public support even though the public may have been bitterly divided over the suitability and benefit of a river scheme.[35]

Besides petitioning, another important vehicle of the lobbyist was the press. Andrew Yarranton went into print in 1677 to enthuse about his vision of a national network of navigable rivers and printed a draft bill that could be promoted in Parliament;[36] the second part, published in 1681, was republished in 1698, presumably to coincide with the post-revolutionary spurt of legislation.

---

32 SRO, DD/SF/13/2/72, John Parsons to Clarke, 25 January 1698/99.

33 The Weaver scheme in 1720 provoked 18 hostile petitions.

34 SRO, DD/TC9 part 1.

35 For another division, see T.S. Willan, *The Early History of the Don Navigation* (Manchester, 1965).

36 Yarranton was familiar with Taunton, as is evident from his discussion on p. 27 of the town's registry of lands, which he praised highly.

Printed 'cases' were also distributed to MPs and in the localities. The River Dee proposal in 1732–33 stimulated at least four pieces of print; the River Weaver bill in 1719 prompted five and a further six when it was reintroduced in 1726/27.[37] Increasingly, too, local presses were used. Taunton used one in Exeter; the promoter of the River Dee scheme employed one at Chester, though on a small scale, with 'no more than 100 copies printed'.[38] As the level of printed debate became more elaborate, science became another tool in the rhetorical armour. The later prints offered mathematical calculations about inclines, the flow of water and hence also of velocity and particles.[39] By the 1730s the printed debate about river navigation depended 'upon the knowledge of natural philosophy and mathematicks, in all its branches'.[40] The pamphlets, petitions and counter-petitions reflect an intriguing contest over the public good and hence the proper relationship between private and public interest. Peter Shackerly had urged the need to gain a petition from the grand jury because it could claim to speak for the locality and its public good. Opponents of the Weaver bill argued that 'if it were for the common good of the county, for the advantage of trade, or the publick good' a petition would have been forthcoming from the grand-jury or quarter-sessions whereas it had been signed only 'by a very few of the lowest rank in the county'.[41] But the proponents of the Weaver scheme argued that the interests of private individuals should not prevent its success: 'when they come in competition with a greater and more general interest, [private interests] must give way to the public good'.[42] Moreover, the language of the public or common good was widely used to legitimize projects. Taunton thus assured the Scots that the counter-petitions against its scheme were 'false representations', for its promoters had 'nothing but a common good' in mind.[43] A printed account of the scheme specifically stressed its 'advantage to the publick' and the funeral

37 Willan, *River Navigation*, appendix 1.

38 Thomas Badeslade, *Reasons Humbly offer'd to the consideration of the Publick* (1735).

39 *An Answer to the Objections of the Citizens of York* (1698); Badeslade, *Reasons Humbly Offer'd*; Badeslade, *The New Cut Canal intended to improve the Navigation of the City of Chester* (Chester, 1736).

40 Badeslade, *The New Cut Canal*, p. 17.

41 *Reasons against making the River Weaver navigable*, printed copy at BL, Add. Mss 36914, fol. 123.

42 *Reasons Humbly Offer'd for Making the River Weaver in the County of Chester Navigable*, p. 3; cf. BL, Add. Mss 36914, fol.135, *Reasons for Continuing the Duty of Eight Pence upon each one hundred and twenty pounds weight of Rock-Salt* (printed, 1697), p. 10: Objection, that every freeholder is 'lord and master of his own freehold and may dig and dispose of it to his best advantage'; Answer, 'This is not so where the Public good of the Nation is concern'd'.

43 SRO, DD/TC9 part 2, letter sent 24 December 1707.

sermon of Robert Webb, one of the scheme's first promoters, alleged that he had often sacrificed 'his own private interest to that of the publick'.[44] In a printed proposal about the River Weaver it was argued that it was 'a very considerable national advantage, as well as beneficial in particular to that county and the parts adjacent'. The scheme proceeded, it was insisted, 'from no other interest ... than a true Patriot ought to have a desire for the publick good'.[45] Indeed, the tract claimed, river navigations 'do always and in course increase the trade of the Countries where they are'. They increased employment; reduced transport costs and hence commodity prices; helped to reduce costs of maintaining the roads; and trained seamen who could be used in the navy. Proponents of the River Wye navigation argued that 'the attempting of any thing wch is for the publique good, howe new soever, is not against but agreeing with both equity and reason, for both equity and reason wills the good and benefit of the whole body, rather then any particular member'.[46]

But the public good argument was frequently contested by highlighting private or selfish interests. *A Short Account of a Design for making the river Weaver in the county of Chester Navigable* hoped that 'this self-designing Project shall never be countenanced by Parliament to the great Prejudice and Injury of the Publick for the sake of a Private interest'.[47] The Aire and Calder navigation was said to be 'in no sort beneficial to the nation in general' and tended 'only to the private advantage of the undertakers'.[48] Indeed, the navigation schemes never simply benefited everyone; there were inevitable losers too. Thus the economic benefits of the improvement schemes were frequently disputed. They would cause unemployment of carriers;[49] tolls could alter competitiveness of goods; monopolies could be created;[50] trade would be diverted from one town

44 *A True State of the advantage to the Publick by making the River Tone Navigable* (n.d.), copy at SRO, DD/SF/13/2/72; Thomas Lucas, *The Afflictions of Good Men* (1728), p. 42.

45 *Reasons Humbly offer'd for making the River Weaver ... Navigable*, subtitle and pp. 2–3, 11; cf. Willan, *Weaver Navigation*, p. 144, transcribing a letter from Shakerley to Sir Thomas Aston, 8 December 1709, referring to it as the 'pernicious self-ended project'.

46 BL, Add. Mss 11052, fol. 82, undated answer to reasons against the Wye bill. For the scheme more generally see E.D. Evans, 'Wye and Lugg Navigation 1696', in *Transactions of the Woolhope Naturalists's Field Club*, 50 (2000), pp. 51–7.

47 Opposition to the scheme ran from the 1660s through to the 1720s.

48 *Reasons against the Bill for making the Rivers Ayre and Calder in the West-Riding of the County of York Navigable* (1700).

49 Willan, *Weaver Navigation*, p. 5; Willan, *River Navigation*, p. 47; *CJ*, vol. 11, p. 440.

50 Willan, *River Navigation*, pp. 44, 116; *A Short Account of a Design for making the River Weever Navigable* (n.d.), p. 1.

to another;[51] and there was a fear of increasing price of goods by creating new monopolies.[52] Even Yarranton condemned those who 'eat up the publick, that so their private interest may be advanced'.[53] As opponents of the Tone scheme alleged, private interest could masquerade as public good and should be resisted.[54] The petitions to Parliament were thus an appeal to an umpire that could discern the national interest – a regulator of interests – and the creation of the Board of Trade in 1696 was another manifestation of the desire for an informed umpire. Competing interests had to be carefully examined, with as much information as possible, and needed a regulating arbiter.

The relationship between private interest and public good was frequently fraught and nowhere more so than in Taunton. A tract published in 1710, critical of the Conservators, noted that whilst they had pretended that 'the true interest and aim of all their project of navigation ... is for the benefit of the country and the poor of the town of Taunton', it was 'more a design for their own interest than any thing else'.[55] The debate over the river Tone was sharpened because the Conservators had claimed from the start that the public good had been a key part of the initial desire to promote the scheme. Alongside benefits to trade, the preamble of the 1699 act specifically announced that it would be 'advantagious to the Poor' and the surplus receipts from the tolls and duties were enacted to be 'imployed and disposed of for the only Use Benefitt and Advantage of the Poor' by 'building One or more Hospitall or Hospitalls or otherwise from time to time according to their best Discretions for the better educating and maintaining such poor Children as are or shall become chargeable to the Towne'.[56] The philanthropic motive also shines through correspondence

---

51 Ipswich, for example, opposed the Irwell navigation in 1719, fearing trade would be diverted to Stowmarket; the Chelmer navigation benefited Chelmsford at the expense of Maldon; the Derwent scheme favoured Derby but disadvantaged Nottingham.

52 Willan, *River Navigation*, p. 44.

53 Yarranton, *England's Improvement* (1681), part 2, p. 2.

54 *Some Plain and True Remonstrances to the Country and Traders on the River Tone, in the County of Somerset of the Unreasonable Proceedings of the Conservators of the said River. And a Discovery of the Falsehoods in a Printed Paper, by them Entituled A True State of the Advantage to the Publick; and a short Answer to the Obstructors of making the River Tone navigable. By a Well-wisher of his Country* (Exeter, 1710); cf. *Reasons against the bill for making the rivers Ayre and Clader in the west-riding of the county of York navigable* (1700); Badeslade, *Reasons Humbly Offer'd* (1735).

55 *Some Plain and True Remonstrances to the Country and Traders of the River Tone* (1710).

56 William III, 1698: An Act for makeing and keeping the River Tone navigable from Bridgwater to Taunton in the County of Somersett, Chapter VIII. Rot. Parl. 10 Gul.III.p.I. n.8., *Statutes*, vol. 7, pp. 464–9.

with the town's MP, Edward Clarke. In November 1696 Clarke was informed about the design and told that, after re-paying the initial investors, the profit was designed for 'the poore, to ease the Towne of such vast charges as they are att'.[57] When the Conservators had pooled sufficient money, in 1698, they wrote to Clarke saying that they were now ready to proceed and again stressed the public good as their motive. They protested that 'we have proposed no advantage or particular interest of our owne but a general good to ye whole Town & parts adjacent, and ye profits for ye use of ye poor'.[58] It was on this basis that Clarke agreed to negotiate with the existing patentees, which was essential for the project's success. The Tone Conservators insisted that they 'designed a general good to ye Poor of this Town' and that:

> one principal reason wch putt us upon this undertaking, [was] to Raise in time a fund for Building a Hospital, for ye maintenance & Education of Poor Children yt are or may be chargeable to ye sd Parrishes of Taunton & Taunton St James, our Poor being already become so exceeding burdensome; & like to be more, that if some care be not taken, more then hath been hitherto, to break ye Generation of Beggars, and to putt our youth upon ye fund of Industry, this Town & Parrish must sink under ye burden of them. [They] designed for a Publick good, without any private Interest of our own.[59]

The debate over the public good also had a partisan dimension. Over 500 of the town's residents had been sentenced for complicity in Monmouth's rebellion and the town was deeply divided along political and religious lines, with the Tories dominant in the corporation. There was a local charity for the poor but it too was in the hands of the town's Tories, so the need for the Whigs to come up with a solution that could be claimed for the public good had political resonances.[60]

The River Tone navigation was also part of a wider moral, social and economic crisis that characterized the 1690s and which was part of a web of interconnected regulations. Of course, there was a long tradition of multi-faceted regulation, going back at least to the mid-sixteenth century.[61] Regulation of trade went hand in hand with regulation of the poor and regulation of the money supply – just as the fiscal crisis of the 1620s had also led to concerted thinking about the role

---

57 SRO, DD/SF/13/2/51, Rd Snowe to [Clarke], 6 November 1696.

58 SRO, DD/SF/13/2/72, Conservators to Clarke, 15 January 1697/8.

59 SRO, DD/SF/13/2/72, Thomas Baker et al. to Clarke, 7 December 1698.

60 It was administered by Clarke's Tory rivals in Taunton – Toulmin, *Taunton*, p. 49.

61 Paul Slack, *From Reformation to Improvement: Public Welfare in Early Modern England* (Oxford, 1999); Charles Webster, *The Great Instauration: Science, Medicine and Reform 1626–1660 (Studies in the History of Medicine)* (Bern, 2002).

of trade regulation and had produced the first wave of 'mercantilist' ideology. But the necessities of the 1690s were particularly pressing. It was fitting that the hardships of the poor were brought to Clarke's attention since he and Locke had played a major part in enacting a series of regulatory measures to recoin what had become grossly devalued and clipped silver money.[62] These, combined with poor harvests and the eighth year of war against France, had the effect in the winter of 1696–97 of dislocating trade, making money for everyday transactions scarce and consequently exacerbating poverty. Taunton was said by its mayor to be:

> in a very miserable condition in relation to trade & the increase of the poor, the Town cannot subsist them, and I much dread the consequence thereof, for they give threatening speeches, and its dangerous to medle wth them, but by perswation & putting them In hopes of a speedy amendent. The greatest trades are forced to lay down trade, by reason of the scaraceness of monys & the charge of Bank-bills, wch amounts to double the profit of the trade; God give some reliefe or else wee are all ruined[63]

The regulation of the river, the regulation of money and the regulation of the poor were thus intertwined in a period of crisis.

Edward Clarke had felt the effects of popular hostility against the regulation of the coin. In August 1696, when trying to return to his house near Taunton, he was threatened by an angry mob (encouraged by a political rival), and had to stay away from his wife, Mary, for the rest of the summer. In November 1696 Mary reported, 'Here is nothing but talke of the poor rising for want of trade'; 'it is enough to make them desperate to have no bread, no work, no fire nor no cloths'. There were actual disturbances elsewhere, such as in Manchester, Rochdale, Cumbria, Derbyshire, Lincolnshire.[64] Edmund Bohun wrote from Suffolk that, 'the People are discontented to the utmost ... and should the least accident put the Mobb in motion no man can tell where it would end'.[65]

---

62 For the re-coinage see Appleby, *Economic Thought*, Chapter 8; Patrick Kelly, *Locke on Money* (2 vols, Oxford, 1991); John K. Horsefield, *British Monetary Experiments 1650–1710* (London, 1960); Ming-Hsun Li, *The Great Recoinage of 1696 to 1699* (London, 1963); Debra Valenze, *The Social Life of Money* (Cambridge, 2006); Craig Muldrew, '"Hard Food for Midas": Cash and its Social Value in Early Modern England', *Past and Present*, 170 (2001): pp. 78–120.

63 DD/SF/13/2/51, Rd Snowe to [Clarke], 6 November 1696.

64 Craig Rose, *England in the 1690s: Revolution, Religion and War* (Oxford, 1999), p. 138; *HMC Kenyon*, p. 409; *HMC le Fleming*, pp. 434–4; Bodleian Library, Ballard ms 18, fols 16–17, Hugh Todd to Arthur Charlett, 10 June 1696.

65 BL, Add. Mss 5540, fol. 64, Bohun to Cary; David Hainsworth, *The Correspondence of Sir John Lowther of Whitehaven 1693–8* (Oxford, 1983), p. 319.

Clarke's regulation of the coinage had thus imperilled order and seemed to require regulation of the poor and of trade more generally.[66] Mary Clarke set up a serge-making scheme in her parish and, fearing on the one hand what 'necessity' might embolden the poor to do and on the other that 'a habit of begging' might erode their later inclination to work altogether, wrote to her husband, 'methinks tis a thousand pities there was not workhouses set up by the government like those in Holland where the poor might always be imployed and not be forced to depend upon the uncertain favour and humour of these ill-natured gripeing trades people'.[67] John Bellers, a Quaker mercantile philanthropist, had in 1695 specifically linked his proposal for 'colledges of industry' to the oppression of 'mechanicks' by 'tradesmen', and singled out Taunton as a possible location for one of his schemes. His *Proposals* (1695), like the Taunton scheme, urged 'first, profit for the rich ... secondly a plentiful living for the poor ... Thirdly a good education for youth'.[68] Taunton's navigation project may also have drawn inspiration from Andrew Yarranton's printed advocacy of river improvements, in which he explicitly couched them as part of a design to improve the lot of the poor and he praised a school in which children were taught for part of the day and worked the rest, a model that he though ought to be emulated.[69] John Cary, MP for Bristol, published proposals about the recoinage and about the need for corporations of the poor – whereby parishes could collaborate to provide workhouses – and he too wrote to Clarke in November 1696 about the need to take action.[70] In 1696 the Bristol corporation for the poor was established, followed by eight others in 1697–98. Clarke's friend John Locke, on the Board of Trade, produced a report on workhouses in 1697 and 14 bills were introduced in Parliament 1694–1705 seeking to overhaul the machinery of poor relief. In other words, local regulatory initiatives that tied philanthropy to trade had national importance.

---

66 For the moral reform agenda of the 1690s see David Hayton, 'Moral Reform and Country Politics in the Late Seventeenth Century House of Commons', *Past and Present*, 128 (1990): pp. 48–89.

67 SRO, DD/SF4515, Mary Clarke to Edward Clarke, 26 October 1696.

68 John Bellers, *Proposals for Raising a Colledge of Industry* (1695), pp. 1, 10.

69 Yarranton, *England's Improvement*, part 1; part 2, pp. 191–2. Yarranton recommended to his readers to see samples of salt at Richard's Coffee House, which Clarke frequented, so it is possible the two men knew each other. Yarranton was, like Clarke, a politically radical Whig.

70 SRO, DD/SF transcripts at the History of Parliament, Cary to Clarke, 16 November 1696; John Cary, *An Essay on the State of England in Relation to its Trade, its Poor, and its Taxes* (1695); Cary, *An Essay on the Coyn and Credit of England as they stand with Respect to its Trade* (1696).

Figure 3.1 *The Chase after Money*

Note: The image shows the moral dimension of discussions about the economy in the 1690s, though the print draws on a late sixteenth-century Dutch engraving. Frugality is pulled by dogs representing diligence and industry, whilst the vices of flattery, prodigality and covetousness are associated with deceit, rapine, hazard and the trampling of justice. Verses published in 1693 on the corruption of the times by money were printed with the 1709 edition. Yet the notion of 'interest' was increasingly re-orienting such condemnation.
Source: © Trustees of the British Museum.

The intertwined nature of the discussions about trade and the poor gave them a moral dimension. For all his evident sympathy with the poor, Tiverton-based Richard Newnam attacked at length the 'prodigious growth' among them of 'all manner of wickedness, filthiness and lewdness'.[71] Such moralizing was reflective of a wider attitude that embraced churchmen such as Cary and Clarke, but could also stem from the zeal of the dissenter. Yarranton was a non-conformist; Bellers was a Quaker; many of the Mersey and Irwell navigation bill's supporters were dissenters;[72] and the Tone Conservators were drawn from a dissenting-inclined group at Taunton who opposed the High Church-dominated Corporation.[73]

---

[71] Richard Newnam, *The Complaint of English Subjects* (1698), p. 46. The strong moral tone to these debates is represented in Figure 3.1.

[72] Willan, *River Navigation*, pp. 59–62.

[73] The alliance between Clarke and dissenters at Taunton was asserted in *The Taunton Dean Letter* (1701) and *A Letter from the Grecian Coffee House* (1701), both instigated

Regulation was thus multi-faceted. Regulation of trade, poverty and morality were interconnected; and the web can be extended further.[74] The 'regulation' of elections was promoted by Clarke in Parliament in a draft bill that included provision for penalties for corruption going to the poor and to hospitals.[75] Contemporaries also talked about the 'regulation' of the press.[76] In 1696 Edward Phillips defined the verb 'To regulate' as 'to maintain good discipline, to cause good order to be observ'd, whether in publick or in private families'.[77] So by definition it was wider than the economic, and, like a regulated clock, seen as part of an interrelated system. A 1694 tract, aimed at the Locke circle since it was dedicated to Locke's host, lady Masham, even talked about the regulation of love, viewed as a form of motion.[78] Regulation was thus like adjusting a clock to ensure regularity.[79] This meant ensuring that the potentially conflicting private and public interests were made to work in harmony. This sense of setting the balance for a system in motion is caught by Defoe, who in 1726 wrote that 'what is a publick Good to day, may be a publick Grievance tomorrow; and what a Law is made to encourage at one time may require a law to prohibit and prevent at another'.[80] The 1690s was a decade of regulatory intensity, when an entire system needed harmonizing.[81]

Regulation and harmonization was thus the outcome of a contest between rival claims to be promoting the public good – there was a conflict of interests that had to be mediated by a parliamentary umpire.[82] Indeed, 'interest' was

---

by Robert Harley and fleshed out by Charles Davenant. The Conservators included nine dissenters, one of whom was a minister (Gibson, *Taunton*, p. 173). In 1708 Taunton dissenters were rebuked with hypocrisy for pretending 'tenderness of conscience' for their separation from the established church but being ready to 'grind the faces of the poor' – Isaac Gilling, *The Qualifications and Duties of Ministers* (1708), p. 35.

74 See also Koji Yamamoto, 'Piety, Profit, and Public Service in the Early Financial Revolution', forthcoming.

75 Mark Knights, 'Locke and the Franchise', forthcoming.

76 On this issue Clarke and Locke were on the side of liberalization.

77 Edward Phillips, *The New World of Words* (1696).

78 John Norris, *The Theory and Regulation of Love* (1688).

79 David Wootton argues that the mechanical world picture provided metaphors for talking about political constitutions – 'Liberty, Metaphor, and Mechanism: "Checks and Balances" and the Origins of Modern Constitutionalism'. Available at: http://www.constitution.org/lg/check_bal.htm [accessed: 2 August 2010].

80 Daniel Defoe, *A Brief Case of the Distillers* (1726), preface.

81 The early 1720s were another such moment, in the wake of the moral and financial South Sea Bubble crisis.

82 The first usage of the term 'conflict of interest' that I have found is 1739, though certainly a notion that interests could *conflict* can be found much earlier, in spiritual as much as economic writing.

becoming an increasingly useful way of thinking about the struggle between public and private. Initially that struggle had been seen primarily in religious rather than economic terms, since divines condemned the pursuit of private and selfish ends; the good of the common wealth and of God were superior.[83] As John Audley put it in 1652, 'Personall and private interest, must give place to the Publike Interest of the People, and of the Commonwealth: And in the Cause of God, *Who is above all:* thy interest, and the Peoples interest also, must give way to the glory of God'.[84] Given that, men were 'ashamed to avow self-interest as a principle of their actions'.[85] Yet interest could have a much more positive connotation when identified as the national interest. Correctly identifying the national interest, the key to political economy, was at the heart of Andrew Yarranton's advocacy of river navigation. He argued that it was in the interest of gentlemen to set the poor to work, since that would raise rents, and that 'interest will not lie'.[86] He sought to show how the self-interests of particular groups should not simply be disregarded but be made to harmonize and how the pursuit of private interests was justifiable when the beneficiaries were also the poor and that necessitated regulation by a public body: it was 'very apparent and clear, we cannot get that Trade well fixt, unless the Publick will give the helping Hand for some numbers of Years'.[87]

Applying interest to economics therefore led to a change in how wealth was conceived and promoted: the pursuit of private interest was not condemned as intrinsically wrong; rather it was recognized that interest was a human characteristic and would always prevail. Accepting that, public and private interest need not be antagonistic if the latter worked for the former. Yarranton and the river navigators believed in regulation that would enhance the national interest as well as the private when tied to, and legitimized by, a moral agenda. As the promoters of the Weaver navigation put it, the benefits would be 'public as well as private'.[88] For Joyce Appleby, the strengthening notion of the poor

---

83 For the medieval theological position see Matthew Kempshall, *The Common Good in Late Medieval Political Thought* (Oxford, 1999). For the continuing importance of religious notions of the common good see Brodie Waddell, 'Poverty, Property and Profit in English Popular Culture 1660–1720' (Ph.D. thesis, University of Warwick, 2009).

84 John Audley, *Englands Common-wealth* (1652), p. 3.

85 Isaac Barrow, *Of the Love of God and our Neighbour* (1680), p. 124.

86 Yarranton, *England's Improvement*, part 1, p. 110.

87 Yarranton, *England's Improvement*, part 2, p. 179. His first tract hoped it might be taken seriously by 'the powers above' (part 1, p. 194). Bellers, too, used the language of interest, trying to show that it was in the interests of the rich to care for the poor, and that this would in turn also be in the national interest (*Proposals*, p. 1).

88 *Reasons Humbly Offer'd for making the River Weaver in the County of Chester Navigable*, p. 2.

as a productive resource was evidence of a 'moral economy in retreat'; yet the 1690s suggest a moralized if not a moral economy: moralized to ensure that private and public interest were reconciled. Of course, the moral language that legitimized the pursuit of interest could also wane over time. Neither the school nor hospital for the poor promised by the Tone Conservators was ever built, whilst they profited from a 6 per cent per annum return on their money for almost 20 years and even charged compound interest.[89] The contrast between private profit and public rhetoric is striking. At worst, the Conservators could be accused of having cynically used the language of the public to disguise self-interest; that may have been increasingly the case but we should not ignore the context that produced their initiative and which drove them to attempt to reconcile private and public interests.

The Conservators had successfully pushed for state regulation from below. Yet it must also be recognized that the acceptance of 'interest' could also push against regulation if the latter could be shown to be advocated by interested parties who really sought their private or sectional interest. Thus interest could legitimize regulation but it could also be used to argue against it. Nicholas Barbon, for example, used the concept to attack the mercantile interest almost 80 years before Adam Smith.[90] Writing in 1690 Barbon attacked the 'mercantilism' of Thomas Mun, whose treatise of 1664 had, in his view,

> better set forth the Rule to make an Accomplished Merchant, than how it may be most Profitable to the Nation ... The Reasons why many Men have not a true *Idea* of *Trade*, is, Because they Apply their Thoughts to particular Parts of *Trade*, wherein they are chiefly concerned in Interest; and having found out the best Rules and Laws for forming that particular Part, they govern their Thoughts by the same NOTIONS in forming the Great BODY of *Trade*.[91]

Barbon, by contrast, argued in favour of free international trade and that consumption and fashion, far from being morally reprehensible, were beneficial.[92] Similarly Charles Davenant, writing in 1696, argued that while 'the wisdom of the legislative power consists in keeping an even hand to promote all'

89 The failure to build the school or hospital provoked legal action in 1730.

90 Barbon profoundly disagreed with Locke and Clarke about the recoinage and argued in favour of devaluation which he thought was a benefit rather than a hindrance to national prosperity.

91 Barbon, *A Discourse of Trade* (1690), preface Sig. A4. Mun had written *England's Treasure by Foreign Trade* around 1630.

92 For the broader context of arguments by economic liberals see Appleby, *Economic Thought*, Chapter 7.

trade, laws which gave trade 'Rules and Directions to Limit and Circumscribe it ... are seldom Advantageous to the Publick'.[93] He believed that all 'Traffick' was beneficial to the nation. The writings of Barbon, Davenant and others are a warning that *identifying* and *regulating* the national interest were not, therefore, necessarily the same task, a tension that was to underline discussions of political economy well into the eighteenth century.

93 Davenant, *An Essay on the East India Trade* (1696), p. 25.

Chapter 4

Towards a British Political Economy: An Eighteenth-Century Scottish Perspective

Bob Harris

This chapter asks how far, if at all, we can talk about a *British* 'political economy' in the eighteenth century. It is certainly arguable that this is not a meaningful question at all. There is, in the first place, a problem of terminology. The term 'political economy' was first used systematically at the beginning of the nineteenth century to describe a new enquiry into the sources of 'happiness and improvement of political society', including 'wealth' and 'population', which was becoming distinct from its parent, moral philosophy.[1] On the other hand, this has not prevented historians applying it to earlier periods to refer broadly to writings on and policy towards trade and economic development; and it is in this latter, less specific sense that the term is used here. Secondly, the politics of the regulation of trade and industry in eighteenth-century Britain simply did not and could not work in the way in which the title of the chapter might seem to imply. As historians have long emphasized, there was no 'mercantile system', a term invented by Adam Smith to refer to the (in his eyes) reprehensible responsiveness of the British state to special pleading on the part of particular groups of merchants and manufacturers at the expense of consumers.[2] Ministers were generally pragmatic and reactive in their approach to economic regulation, where indeed they took a close interest in this area. To a significant extent, moreover, their attitudes and actions were governed or largely controlled by fiscal imperatives. Their priority was more often than not raising money to fight wars or fund a climbing national debt.[3] Nor do notions

---

1 See 'The System of the North: Dugald Stewart and His Pupils', in Stefan Collini, Donald Winch and John Burrow, *That Noble Science of Politics: A Study in Nineteenth-century Intellectual History* (Cambridge, 1983), esp. p. 37.

2 Donald Winch, 'Scottish Political Economy', in Mark Goldie and Robert Wokler (eds), *The Cambridge History of Eighteenth-Century Political Thought* (Cambridge, 2006), esp. pp. 446–7. See also Joel Mokyr, *The Enlightened Economy: An Economic History of Britain 1700–1850* (New Haven, CT and London, 2009), pp. 393–4.

3 See e.g. Peter D.G. Thomas, *British Politics and the Stamp Act Crisis* (Oxford, 1975); *The Townshend Duties Crisis* (Oxford, 1987); *Tea Party to Independence* (Oxford, 1991));

of national economic interest stand up to close scrutiny, in that 'interests' were constructed things, usually comprised of unstable alliances of groups and bodies; they excluded and marginalized other groups and bodies. Lobbying bodies in this period usually spoke in terms of national interest, but this was a political and rhetorical ploy, hardly a statement of fact.

Nevertheless, if all this is true, there was still a 'British' dimension to the politics of commercial regulation in this period, even if it was intermittently present and usually but one element of a complex interplay of interests. The maintenance of political stability and national power within a competitive European and increasingly global states system required that ministers and the Westminster Parliament pay at least some regard to ensuring that economic benefit spread to all the nations which made up the British state and indeed British Isles. This might mean favouring particular industries which were strongly represented in particular nations – linen in the cases of Ireland and Scotland; or it might mean a different kind of state intervention to support particular regions or areas, as in the Highlands of Scotland or Ireland. The latter type of intervention became more visible and sharply defined from the end of the eighteenth century; just as, of course, arguments for less state intervention in economic life were gaining ground.[4] Above all, the interests of Scotland and Ireland could and did intrude into the economic and commercial politics of the time, very significantly so at various moments.

Commercial politics might also take on a British character in a different sense. This was a function of the modalities of representation at Westminster and in London at the Treasury and the Board of Trade. Lobbying encouraged the construction of alliances of different mercantile and manufacturing groups in pursuit of influence at the centre. To this extent, it worked to integrate lobbies at the British level. This was a tendency, and as a process it was inherently fragile and often transient, as was well illustrated by the General Chamber of Manufacturers of Great Britain, which flickered briefly into life in 1785 only to collapse in the following year.[5] Interest group politics

Bob Harris, *Politics and the Nation: British Politics in the Mid Eighteenth Century* (Oxford, 2002), chapter 6. Pragmatic motivations as drivers of economic and commercial policy in the early nineteenth century are emphasized in Boyd Hilton, *Corn, Cash and Commerce: The Economic Policies of the Tory Governments 1815–1830* (Oxford, 1977).

4 On this, see Anna Gambles, 'Free Trade and State Formation: The Political Economy of Fisheries Policy in Britain and the United Kingdom circa 1750–1850', *Journal of British Studies*, 39/3 (2000): pp. 288–316; Robert B. McDowell, 'Administration and Public Services, 1800–70', in William E. Vaughan (ed.), *A New History of Ireland. V: Ireland under the Union I. 1801–70* (Oxford, 1989), p. 547.

5 For this body, see John M. Norris, 'Samuel Garbett and the Early Development of Industrial Lobbying in Britain', *EcHR*, 10 (1958): pp. 450–60; John Money, *Experience and Identity: Birmingham and the West Midlands 1760–1800* (Manchester, 1977), chapter 2.

was by its nature fissiparous and unstable, something which tended to limit its influence on ministers and Parliament. Nevertheless, it may well have been precisely in the dynamic tension between integration and separation, or the maintenance and nurturing of a separate national interest, that Ireland and Scotland gained their particular leverage in the battle in London for advantage among commercial and economic interests. In Scotland, the Treaty of Union might add extra political weight, in that Scots were only too ready to appeal to its terms if they thought this might be to their advantage.[6] This was certainly not the whole story since much also depended on the preparedness of ministers, officials and MPs to listen to their claims, something which varied significantly over time. Success was also relative, and we should not exaggerate the achievements; but the important point may be that there was success alongside failure.

The chapter focuses particularly on the fate of Scotland and certain Scottish interests after 1707. This is partly because the case of Ireland is rather better covered in the existing literature; but also because the Irish and Scottish perspectives while in several respects running in parallel, as we will see further below, differ in very important ways. The key difference was political. Ireland in the eighteenth century was a dependent kingdom, while Scotland was after 1 May 1707 part of the new state of the United Kingdom of Great Britain. Mercantilism for Ireland in a British context meant, before 1779, dependency; it also usually meant, with one exception, the absence of a broader vision of commercial integration as a tool of political integration. This can be explained in part by how limited the main goals of ministers were in relation to Ireland – essentially stability and, related to this, stable management of politics and the Irish Parliament – and their normal pre-occupation with war and diplomacy.[7] Liberalization and encouragement of Irish trade by Westminster before the later eighteenth century occurred

---

6 This tendency to appeal to the Union led Sir John Sinclair to observe at the end of the eighteenth century: 'It is too often said that the Scotch are apt to claim the benefit of the Union, when it is in their favour, and to reject it when it is otherwise. But it is certain that where the two parties are united together, the one superior in power and wealth to the other, that in all unforeseen or doubtful cases, the balance must be given to the weaker' – Sir John Sinclair, *The History of the Public Revenue of the British Empire. Part III* (1790), p. 362.

7 See esp. David W. Hayton, *Ruling Ireland, 1685–1742: Politics, Politicians and Parties* (Woodbridge, 2004), esp. chapters 7 and 8. As Louis Cullen has emphasized, measures directed against Irish economic interests were not a product of government policy, but of the power of English vested interests. The limitations on trade implicit in the navigation acts were also subject to important qualifications, especially from 1731 – Louis M. Cullen, *An Economic History of Ireland since 1660* (2nd edn, London and Worcester, 1987), pp. 36–9.

because it was in or did not interfere with English or British interests.[8] John Foster, Irish chancellor of the exchequer from 1784 and speaker of the Irish House of Commons from the following year to the abolition of the Irish Parliament in 1800 and staunch defender of a conservative, Protestant interest in the later eighteenth century, observed somewhat tartly to John Baker Holroyd (later Lord Sheffield) in 1777:

> The woollen trade, home brewery and fisheries are matters in which we [i.e. the Irish] might enrich ourselves, and of course enrich England; but the narrow policy of prejudiced men, and the timidity of such English ministers as see, but will not venture, prevent us for hoping the restraints [are] to be taken off, except in the fisheries, for which we have not capital to drive a beneficial trade ...[9]

As Lord North discovered in 1778 (or rather had confirmed), and Pitt the Younger a few years later in 1785, reconciling Irish and British economic interests was a politically fraught business.[10] 'Free trade' for Ireland was only granted by a weak and divided North ministry in December 1779 under an extraordinary set of political circumstances produced by British failure in the War of American Independence. More broadly, the tendency to view Britain, or at times England, and Ireland as economic rivals remained deeply ingrained throughout the eighteenth century. Foster complained again in 1790, in the context of discussions about changes to the British Corn Laws: 'I hate the mistaken policy of deeming the two countries as rivals'.[11] One of the reasons why Pitt's commercial propositions made such halting progress in 1785, and ultimately failed, is precisely because the natural tendency was to debate them in terms of whether they would benefit, on the one hand, Britain or, on the other, Ireland. When the Irish chief secretary Thomas Orde introduced them into the Irish Parliament he spoke of them as being to Ireland's advantage, while Pitt in introducing them in the British Commons emphasized the opposite. The Whig opposition quickly produced a broadsheet placing these remarks alongside each other, which was circulated throughout England and Scotland. Pitt's supporters in the press, George Rose and George Chalmers, who defended his initiative on the grounds that British and Irish economic interests were complementary, ended up arguing, more or less explicitly, that England had nothing to fear

8 See e.g. Cullen, *Economic History of Ireland*, p. 59.

9 Anthony P.W. Malcomson (ed.), *An Anglo-Irish Dialogue: A Calendar of the Correspondence between John Foster and Lord Sheffield, 1774–1821* (Belfast, 1976), p. 6.

10 On this, see esp. James Kelly, *Prelude to Union: Anglo-Irish Politics in the 1780s* (Cork, 1992), *passim*.

11 Malcomson (ed.), *Anglo-Irish Dialogue*, p. 9.

from Irish competition and would be the gainers from the adjustment in trade relations.[12] If more and more people came to argue that union with Ireland was desirable, the logic could easily seem narrowly English or British; the assumption of 'metrocentric primacy' was not easily discarded in London.[13] Potentially more difficult was to demonstrate that union held out a solution to Ireland's troubles or more specifically a future of increased prosperity. It was precisely here, however, that Scottish experience after 1707 was seen as offering a powerful lesson for the Irish; and it is to Scotland and 1707 that we now turn.

If Scotland's experience in the eighteenth century was seen by the later eighteenth century as constituting proof that union could work for all parts of the state thus created – that the poorer partner would benefit as well as the richer – in 1707 most Scots who thought about these things appear to have been sceptical if not downright unconvinced that this would be the probable outcome. The reasons were various, and included the impact of higher rates of taxation as a consequence of fiscal integration and the effects of competition from English goods in the Scottish market. At bottom, however, what mattered was who would possess political power. The matter was bluntly put by Andrew Fletcher of Saltoun in 1703 in his *An Account of a Conversation concerning the Right Regulation of Governments for the Common Good of Mankind*. Fletcher made his case in relation to the conduct of the English Parliament in passing the Woollen Act of 1699, which banned the export of woollen goods from Ireland overseas in the interests of the powerful English woollen industry.[14] As this episode showed, Scottish industry and trade would find no succour, Fletcher urged, from a Westminster Parliament dominated by English MPs and peers. Matters might be put in slightly different terms; the challenge was the power and force of *English* political economy, as tradition and practice. This was exactly the point of course which Foster would make, as we saw above, decades later in relation to Ireland.

At the time of the Union, pro-unionists had no easy answers to Fletcher's prognosis, although the Treaty of Union did incorporate a number of important protections for key Scottish industries, for example, salt and coal, as well as a range of fiscal concessions.[15] Pro-Union propagandists urged the complementary

---

12 George Rose, *The Proposed System of Trade with Ireland Explained* (1785), esp. pp. 32–56; George Chalmers, *The Arrangement with Ireland Considered* (1785).

13 The phrase 'metrocentric primacy' is Peter Miller's – see Peter Miller, *Defining the Common Good: Empire, Religion and Philosophy in Eighteenth Century England* (Cambridge, 1994), p. 165.

14 The act did not ban the export of woollen goods to England, but this was effectively made impossible by prohibitive duties there.

15 The significance of these has been emphasized particularly by Christopher A. Whatley – see his 'Salt, Coal and the Union of 1707: A Revision Article', *Scottish Historical*

natures of the English and Scottish economies. Textiles featured heavily in this context, along with the fisheries – ever the un- or under-exploited treasure of the Scottish economy.[16] Scots were encouraged to consider linen as their economic future rather than woollens. One problem here which was noted (of which more below) was that this was precisely the solution which had been envisaged for Ireland in the 1690s and early 1700s. Responses were also unconvincing on the issue of whether Scottish representation in the new Parliament – the Parliament of Great Britain – was adequate protection for its interests. Defoe, for example, argued that with 45 MPs Scotland was, in fact, better off than Middlesex, an argument spoilt perhaps by his also observing that the English county was nearly as populous as Scotland, was 'vastly richer' and will pay at least ten times more in taxation than Scotland; its representation was eight MPs. It may have been true; it was hardly sensitive to Scottish national sensitivities. Defoe, however, went on:

> But suppose the whole Parliament of *Scotland* was assumed in its full Members, yet our Barons and Burrows wou'd make up little more than a Fourth part of the House of Commons of *Great-Britain*; so that you see, let us put our Representation in what shape we please, yet if *England* will violate the sacred Ties of an *Union*, and join to oppress us, it will be impossible to prevent it; but this last is no more to be supposed, than that the *English* will ruine and destroy themselves, by the Factions and Divisions that must inevitably happen upon a Breach between the Two Nations.[17]

Another riposte was to suggest that natural solidarity among Scottish MPs would be more than a match for the inevitable divisions among England's MPs.[18] Anti-Union addresses in 1706 commonly echoed Fletcher's concerns, which may be an indication of how little headway Defoe's and others' arguments made in this context.[19]

Review, 66/1 (1987): pp. 26–45; and, 'Economic Causes and Consequences of the Union of 1707: A Survey', *Scottish Historical Review*, 68/2 (1989): pp. 150–81.

16 For the fisheries, see Bob Harris, 'Scotland's Herring Fisheries and the Prosperity of the Nation', *Scottish Historical Review*, 79/1 (2000): esp. pp. 46–7.

17 Daniel Defoe, *A Letter to a Friend, Giving an Account How the Treaty of Union has been Received Here* (Edinburgh, 1706), p. 15.

18 *A Sermon Preach'd to the People at the Mercat Cross of Edinburgh on the Subject of the Union* (1707), p. 7. As with many other pro-Union pamphlets, the author also argued that English prosperity was the result of its tradition and system of political liberties; Scottish accession to this system would necessarily, therefore, bring prosperity.

19 For analysis of the anti-Union petitions and reactions in the burghs more generally to the prospect of union, see Christopher A. Whatley, *The Scots and the Union* (Edinburgh, 2006), pp. 282–6.

Modern historians have not by and large dwelt overly long on the issue of defence of Scottish economic interests after 1707 or how this was resolved, if at all.[20] There is debate among modern historians about whether union was the cause of economic progress, but by and large this is not focused on what Westminster and the Treasury or Board of Trade did or did not do.[21] Nor to be fair can it be said that the issue was especially controversial in the eighteenth century. From the central decades of the eighteenth century onwards, most Scots were only too ready to recognize the benefits of union, and to see its advantages as far outweighing its disadvantages. When, for example, the issue of whether the Union had benefited Scotland was debated by the Stirling Port Club in 1783, those present were unanimous that advantages had far outweighed disadvantages. As the relevant minute of the club reported:

> Several members spoke upon this subject and set forth the advantages of the union of the two kingdoms in such a distinct and clear point of view as gave the highest satisfaction – all of them considered it as the basis of that wealth, power and grandeur which Britain had since arrived at – any disadvantages derived therefrom entirely disappeared.[22]

There was a pamphlet published in 1745 alleging Scotland's economic marginalization under union, although its anti-English tone was unusual by this period.[23] On the other hand, as we will see towards the end of this chapter,

---

20 Although, see relevant comment in Alexander J. Murdoch, *The People Above: Politics and Administration in Mid-Eighteenth Century Scotland* (Edinburgh, 1980); Christopher A. Whatley, *Scottish Society, 1707–1830: Beyond Jacobitism Towards Industrialisation* (Manchester, 2000), pp. 96–141; Bob Harris, 'The Scots, the Westminster Parliament and the British State in the Eighteenth Century', in Julian Hoppit (ed.), *Parliaments, Nations and Identities in Britain and Ireland 1660–1850* (Manchester, 2003), pp. 124–45; Gordon Jackson, 'Government Bounties and the Establishment of the Scottish Whaling Trade, 1750–1800', in John Butt and John T. Ward (eds), *Scottish Themes: Essays in Honour of Professor S.G.E. Lythe* (Edinburgh, 1976), pp. 46–66. Two historians of an earlier generation who emphasized the importance of the economic role of the state were Henry Hamilton, *An Economic History of Scotland in the Eighteenth Century* (Oxford, 1963) and Edward Hughes, *Studies in Administration and Finance, 1558–1825* (Manchester, 1934).

21 See esp. Whatley, *Scottish Society*, chapter 2; Tom M. Devine, *The Scottish Nation* (London, 1999), esp. chapter 3. See also, more recently, Allan I. Macinnes, *Union and Empire: The Making of the United Kingdom in 1707* (Cambridge, 2007).

22 National Library of Scotland, Acc 7862 no. 3, Minutes of the Stirling Port Club, entry for 22 November 1783.

23 *The Present State of Scotland Consider'd And its Declining and Sinking Condition Charg'd Upon the Conduct of the Landed Gentlemen &c* (Edinburgh, 1745).

criticism of disregard for Scottish interests at the centre of power can still be found in the later eighteenth century.

The question might seem less relevant too because if there was a Scottish or Scottish-British political economy in the eighteenth century we could reasonably expect this to have been focused not on Parliament or the British state *per se* but on bodies within Scottish civil society or newly established for the purpose of economic improvement or indeed on patriotic ventures of other kinds established for public good and profit. There is undoubtedly much to this proposition, as a cursory glance at the activities of the Convention of Royal Burghs, several fisheries societies, the Linen Society of Edinburgh and, most famously of all, the Board of Trustees for the Improvement of Manufactures and Fisheries, founded in 1727, would show. Local government – burgh councils and commissioners of supply – pursued economic improvement in a variety of ways, often in cooperation with improvement-minded landowners. This was not a peculiarly Scottish phenomenon; there are clear parallels with Ireland and to a rather lesser extent England. But the point nevertheless is that Scottish national economic development was usually envisaged at a remove from Westminster and the British context; it was something which Scots would do for themselves in Scotland.

It was the Board of Trustees which constituted one of the principal foci for debate about economic improvement in Scotland for much of the eighteenth century. Significantly, from the perspective of the 1780s, the writer on economic affairs John Knox saw 1727 and not 1707 as a key turning point in the story of the nation's present and future, although not solely because of the foundation of the Board.[24] The Board was the vehicle for the distribution of the monies from various sources, including the equivalent fund established in 1707, and its foundation can be seen as a rare moment of British political economy directed by ministers in the early Hanoverian period. It was Sir Robert Walpole who delivered a stark lesson on this to the Commons in March 1726 against the background of the unrest provoked by the renewed attempt to levy a malt tax on Scotland in the previous year. Walpole urged his fellow MPs to learn the lesson that Scottish prosperity was in British interests; constructive intervention of this kind was much better than military rule, which was the alternative. According to George Drummond, many-time Lord Provost of Edinburgh and a notable force in Edinburgh's later re-casting as the modern capital of North Britain, and who was in London as the agent of the Convention of Royal Burghs, Walpole's speech was the 'finest I ever heard in that house'.[25] Nevertheless, at the level of

24 John Knox, *A View of the British Empire, More Especially Scotland* (1784), preface.

25 Edinburgh City Archives, Convention of Royal Burghs, Moses Collection, SL 30/242, George Drummond to the annual committee of the Convention of Royal Burghs, London, 19 March 1726.

discourse and ideology, the establishment of the Board reinforced a tendency for discussion of political economy in Scotland to develop within an explicitly national framework. Thanks to Roger Emerson's work on Archibald, 3rd Duke of Argyll's library, we know that political economy was a matter which was taken very seriously by Scotland's political managers of the first half of the eighteenth century, a further symptom of which was the establishment of the British Linen Company in 1746.[26] Broadly similar remarks could easily be made about the discourse of economic improvement in the later eighteenth century and in particular the promotion of the fisheries as a British and national project in the mid-to-later 1780s and the later investment in communications infrastructure in the Highlands. One might say in this context that Scottish political economy was British political economy; it was about unlocking the full potential of a Scottish contribution to British power and prosperity. As Knox put it, 'Upon the whole, the interest of Scotland is in every possible respect the interest of England'.[27]

As Knox also made clear, however, common and mutual benefit did not mean that Scottish interests did not require special or different treatment or consideration from England. One of Knox's proposals was to remove all taxes in Scotland, other than the land tax and those required for the regulation of trade. The proceeds of the latter were to be conferred on an expanded and re-configured Board of Trustees which would become a Commercial Parliament for Scotland.[28] This was implicit recognition that not only did Scotland need to be treated differently from England, but that it also needed bodies which could take a national as well as British view of economic development. Scotland was a special case.

Some might also argue, finally, that the natural trajectory, if this is at all a meaningful formulation, of eighteenth-century Scottish political economy was in any case towards 'free trade', towards the elimination of economic privileges and restrictions of all kinds. We might put Paterson and the Darien project at one end of this path and Smith and the *Wealth of Nations* at the other.[29] A contrast can be drawn here with Ireland, where 'free trade' meant something entirely different. One could argue, of course, with an eye to Josiah Tucker, David

---

[26] Roger Emerson, '*Catalogus Librorum A.C.D.C.*, or the Library of Archibald Campbell, Third Duke of Argyll (1682–1761)', in Paul B. Wood (ed.), *The Culture of the Book in the Scottish Enlightenment* (Toronto, 2000), pp. 13–39.

[27] Knox, *View*, p. lxi.

[28] Knox, *View*, pp. 100–112.

[29] This view is implicit in Michael Fry's essay, 'A Commercial Empire: Scotland and British Expansion in the Eighteenth Century', in Tom M. Devine and J.R. Young (eds), *Eighteenth Century Scotland: New Perspectives* (East Linton, 1999), pp. 53–69.

Hume, Arthur Young and Adam Smith among others, that free trade in the end did represent the only genuinely British language of political economy in the eighteenth century. What would be much less convincing would be to argue that it was a dominant one, especially, but not solely, in the Scottish context.

Undoubtedly, these factors tell some of the story of Scottish political economy in the eighteenth century. Yet it is far from the complete story, as the rest of this chapter will argue with reference primarily to the linen industry.

The linen industry offers us, in fact, a particularly powerful lens through which to explore further the question of Scottish and British political economy. This is partly because of its overwhelming importance to eighteenth-century Scottish economic development. Without its rise, which was spectacular, industrial growth in eighteenth-century Scotland would have been unimpressive, at least before the 1780s and the rapid rise of the cotton industry.[30] Secondly, because of this importance, and its significance as a source of employment and prosperity, it was viewed as the Scottish national industry. One memorial from the later eighteenth century stated of the industry, with pardonable exaggeration, that it was the 'staple manufacture of Scotland, and the source of its improvements and most useful wealth'.[31] Earlier in the century, its supporters tended to emphasize its significance as a vital source of subsistence to the poor, including women and children.[32] Thirdly, if it was the Scottish national industry, it could also be and was indeed argued that it was peculiarly 'British', in that it was also critical to Irish economic development in this period and had important branches in the north of England. As one writer on linen put it in 1744: 'The Encouragement ... of the Linen Manufacture is the immediate interest of England, Scotland and Ireland; and is more, perhaps, a common concern than any one Manufacture or Branch of Commerce whatsoever'.[33] Fourthly, and not the least important,

30 Christopher A. Whatley, *The Industrial Revolution in Scotland* (Cambridge, 1997), esp. pp. 21–9.

31 National Library of Scotland, MS 653, memorial representing the expediency and necessity of continuing the present duties on foreign linen, and the bounties granted by parliament on the exportation of British linen, and enacting the same for a fixt period of years, 1788.

32 See e.g. Perth and Kinross Council Archives [hereafter PKCA], A. K. Bell Public Library, Perth, B59/24/8/5/9, letter from provost of Perth to Patrick Haldane Esq., Perth, 21 November 1719; B59/24/8/7/2, petition of the provost, magistrates and common council of the burgh of Perth in North Britain ... about the making and trading in linnen [sic], 1722.

33 *Some Observations in Relation to the Linen Manufactures of Great Britain and Ireland* (1744), p. 1. For a similar argument, see *Thoughts on the Linen Manufacture of Great Britain* (1771), esp. pp. 1–2. In the Irish context, it was also argued that support for their linen industry was not just due recompense for restriction of their woollen industry by Westminster,

its development was directed by a body of mercantilist legislation passed by the Westminster Parliament and by financial support facilitated by parliamentary statute.[34] This is not a novel observation, but its ramifications for our view of how union worked or was made to work in terms of political economy have not hitherto been examined systematically.

How, then, did Scottish linen manufacturing depend on or benefit from state support in the eighteenth century? The biggest fillip delivered from Westminster came in the form of a bounty on exports of coarse linen. This was imposed in 1742 and raised in 1745, and continued throughout the rest of the century, albeit with a brief and, for the industry, disastrous intermission between 1754 and 1756. The 'very best thing ... got for Scotland since ye Union' was how one Scot described this bounty in July 1742.[35] Forty-six years later George Dempster of Dunnichen declared to Henry Dundas, no fan of bounties (presumably influenced by Adam Smith), 'the bounty upon linen, not only has done no mischief, but a great deal of good – more good perhaps than ever was done by any single measure of political eoconomy'. The son of a Dundee corn merchant, Dempster went on by way of illustration of the wider effects of a buoyant linen industry: 'May I draw your attention particularly to the encrease of the Town of Dundee. From a dirty Hole in which I was born, it has grown into a beautifull city'.[36] The bounty enabled domestic producers to compete with foreign produced linen in colonial markets overseas, especially the West Indies. Duties on imported foreign linen were drawn back on export. Linen producers called for the abolition of these drawbacks on exports from

---

but to enable them to support the charge of maintaining 12,000 British troops on the Irish establishment – *An Answer to Reasons (so-call'd) against the Bill for Exporting Irish Linen to the British Plantations Duty Free* (1717). For the sometimes underestimated significance of the English linen industry, see Negley B. Harte, 'The Rise of Protection and the English Linen Industry, 1690–1790', in Negley B. Harte and Kenneth G. Ponting (eds), *Textile History and Economic History: Essays in Honour of Miss Julia de Lucy Mann* (Manchester, 1973), pp. 74–112.

[34] Successive pieces of legislation sought to create a series of standard sizes and standards of manufacture in respect of linen yarn and cloth, as well as laying down required methods of bleaching. This framework of regulation was designed as an assurance of quality to facilitate trade and exports. The background to this was problems with low standards of manufacture in the early eighteenth century. For a summary of this regulatory framework, see *A Collection of the Acts of Parliament, Now in Force, Relating to the Linen Manufacture* (Edinburgh, 1751).

[35] Mitchell Library, Glasgow City Archives, Hamilton of Barns Papers, TD 589/588, William Hamilton to James Hamilton of Barns, 10 July 1742.

[36] National Library of Scotland, MS 653, George Dempster to Henry Dundas, 31 January 1788.

the later 1730s, but Parliament, anxious about continental retaliation against English manufactures, rejected this in favour of bounty.[37] It is important to note that the bounty was payable only on unprinted coarse linens. Following its re-imposition in 1756, the bounty was renewed several times – in 1770 being also extended to sheetings and table linens, while a new bounty was imposed on British checks and stripes – until 1825, when 20 per cent of the value of the bounties was withdrawn, thereafter falling by a further 10 per cent annually until their final demise in 1832.[38]

If bounties enabled domestic producers of coarse linens to squeeze foreign competition out of colonial markets, prohibitions and duties on imports protected linen manufacturers in domestic markets. Fine linen manufacturers, who were concentrated in Scotland in and around Glasgow, benefited from a prohibition on the import of French cambrics and lawns imposed by Parliament in 1745 and reinforced in 1748. This was renewed in 1756, again in 1770, when it was extended to cover checked and striped linen; further renewed in 1779, when it was extended to include Ireland; and extended once again in duration and range in 1781. In 1779 a proposal to end the prohibition was greeted with outrage in and around Glasgow. Looking back from 1798, an early historian of the city declared that North's bill had 'threatened the starvation of many families, [and] could not fail of meeting with a powerful opposition'.[39] A year later, Robert Frame reflected on the strength of the opposition in Paisley to another proposal to allow the import of French cambrics and laws. 'What a cry', he asked, 'did it not justly raise in this country? We all, then, foresaw the ruin of our infant manufactures established at Paisley'.[40] The competitiveness of foreign imports in the domestic market was also reduced by increases in customs duties during wartime. The mid century surge in linen manufacturing was, thus, aided by wartime demand (for shirts and sheetings of various kinds) but also by general increases

37 See esp. *A Letter from a Merchant to a Member of Parliament* (1738), *passim*; PKCA, B59/24/8/4, letter to Perth magistrates from Glasgow magistrates, 7 April 1742, enclosing petition to the House of Commons calling for abolition of the drawbacks on exports of foreign linen; *Report from the Committee to whom the Petition of the Merchants, and Others, of Great Britain and Ireland, Dealers in, and Manufacturers of, LINENS, THREADS, and TAPES, made in Great Britain and Ireland ... was Referred* (1744).

38 In 1822, a bill was passed that bounties on export from Great Britain should continue only as long as Irish bounties remained. The latter had been introduced from 1780. In 1825, it was decided to reduce them by a tenth each year, with payments finally being abandoned in 1830. Conrad Gill, *The Rise of the Irish Linen Industry* (Oxford, 1964 edn, first pub. 1925), pp. 303–4; Alexander J. Warden, *The Linen Trade: Ancient and Modern* (1967 edn, first pub. 1864), pp. 666–8.

39 James Denholm, *The History of Glasgow and Suburbs* (Glasgow, 1798), p. 41.

40 Robert Frame, *Considerations on the Interests of the County of Lanark* (1799), p. 32.

in duties.[41] In 1767, import duties on certain kinds of linen cloth were raised, almost certainly by way of a sop to Scottish producers facing declining demand after the end of the Seven Years War. This move was linked to the passage of an act designed to support flax cultivation in Britain and thus reduce dependency on imports of this raw material.[42] Duties on imports of raw materials were reduced or removed entirely, while in 1717 export duty on British linen was abolished.[43]

State support of various kinds for textiles – whether permissive, positive or protective in nature – was the norm in Britain in this period; and what happened in respect of linen was a natural extension of a policy framework which extended to other branches of the industry, notably wool, but also silk, worsted and cotton.[44] However, several points about this pattern do require special emphasis. In the first place, we need to acknowledge just how far linen manufacturers and merchants looked to support from the British state and Westminster, and equally the degree to which they saw such support as crucial to the fortunes of the industry. This could be illustrated many times over. In 1753, faced with the end (temporary as it turned out) of the bounty on exports, William Tod declared that if nothing was put in its place, 'the manufacture and industry of this country will receive a blow which cannot be recovered in our age'.[45] It was later claimed that 8,000 looms had been 'thrown idle' by the suspension of the bounty between 1753 and 1756.[46] In 1768 Dundee's linen merchants petitioned

---

41 Customs duty rates were raised across the board by 5 per cent in 1756 and a further 5 per cent in 1759. In the War of American Independence, similar subsidies were imposed in 1779 and 1782. For the impact of customs duties on English production, see Harte, 'The Rise of Protection', pp. 76–100.

42 This measure included provision for a fund of £15,000 to support flax cultivation. The increase in duties was to finance this fund. In 1770, £7,000 of this sum was allocated to Scotland.

43 Harte, 'The Rise of Protection', p. 98.

44 See, *inter alia*, Patrick O'Brien, Trevor Griffith and Philip Hunt, 'Political Components of the Industrial Revolution: Parliament and the English Cotton Textile Industry, 1660–1774', *EcHR*, 44 (1991): pp. 395–423; Tim Keirn, 'Parliament, Legislation and the Regulation of the English Textile Industries, 1689–1714', in Lee Davison, Tim Hitchcock, Tim Keirn and Robert B. Shoemaker (eds), *Stilling the Grumbling Hive: The Response to Social and Economic Problems in England, 1689–1750* (Stroud, 1992), pp. 1–24; Harte, 'The Rise of Protection', pp. 74–112; Raymond L. Sickinger, 'Regulation or Ruination: Parliament's Consistent Pattern of Mercantilist Regulation of the English Textile Trade, 1660–1800', *Parliamentary History*, 19/2 (2000): pp. 211–32.

45 Alistair J. Durie (ed.), *The British Linen Company 1745–1776* (Edinburgh, 1996), p. 54.

46 *Extracts from the Records of the Convention of the Royal Burghs of Scotland 1759–79* (Edinburgh, 1918), p. 562.

the Convention of Royal Burghs, declaring their fears that the linen trade, which they argued gave daily subsistence to 'the greatest number of inhabitants' would be lost if the legislature did not act by raising bounties and spending the £15,000 which had been promised under legislation in the previous year (referred to above) to help develop a British flax growing industry.[47] The following year, George Chalmers wrote to George Grenville about an application on the part of Dunfermline linen manufacturers for duties on foreign diapers and table linen to be raised. Chalmers, whose estate was close to the town, which specialized in the production of table linen, reassured Grenville: 'The principal manufactures assure me that they are in a condition to supply the great part of the English consumption if they have proper encouragement', also urging that with a small additional duty, local production would 'at least double or triple' its value in a few years.[48]

Meanwhile, the early 1770s saw a major campaign to solicit parliamentary support for the industry in the context of a sharp depression partly triggered by the Ayr Bank crisis (1772), and which saw a parliamentary enquiry into the state of the industry in 1773. The campaign, which had its origins in the later 1760s, was focused primarily on the aim of raising duties on imports, which led to concerted opposition, ultimately successful, from the powerful Hamburg merchants – the importers – and a woollen interest concerned about retaliatory action to deny or reduce their access to continental markets.[49] One memorial in support of the campaign warned starkly:

> Neglect or inattention in government to the due execution of the laws, or in framing new ones, when an alteration in circumstances renders it necessary, cannot fail of being attended with the most direful consequences.

It also declared:

---

47 Edinburgh City Archives, Convention of Royal Burghs, Moses Collection, SL 30/4/6, Linen Financial Papers, 1724–1821, petition of the merchants of Dundee to the Honourable Convention of Royal Burghs, 1768. I am grateful to Professor Chris Whatley for this reference.

48 Quoted in Jeremy Black, 'Introduction', in Jeremy Black (ed.), *British Politics and Society from Walpole to Pitt 1742–1789* (Basingstoke, 1990), p. 8.

49 See e.g. *Thoughts on the Linen Manufacture of Great Britain* (1771); *Memorial Addressed to the Honourable Convention of Royal Boroughs in Scotland. By a Friend to the Linen Manufacture* (Edinburgh, 1772); *Report from the Committee Appointed to Enquire into the Present State of the Linen Trade in Great Britain and Ireland* (1773); *Some Thoughts on the Present State of the Linen Trade of Great Britain and Ireland* (1774); PKCA, B59/24/8/28, letter by the lord provost of Edinburgh relative to the linnen manufactures, 28 September 1773; *Extracts from the Records of the Convention ... 1759–79*, pp. 326–491.

> It is surprising, that a trade, of so great importance to the three kingdoms, has so little attracted the attention of government, that foreign linens are allowed to be imported upon such small duties as enable the importers to undersell our own manufacturers, and that we should be supplied with the products of foreign countries, while our own industrious people are in want of employment.[50]

The explicit comparison was support for the English woollen industry, so often the benchmark in these appeals. Dempster's letter to Dundas, referred to earlier, was written in support of a memorial from Forfarshire linen merchants, manufacturers and dealers calling for the extension of bounties on exports of coarse linen and duties on imports of foreign linen. This memorial emphasized both the dynamic growth of the industry, but also the disadvantages under which it operated relative to other countries, meaning here German states predominantly.[51] The growing cost of flax imported from Russia was emphasized – this had allegedly risen by 30 per cent since 1743 – as was the dependency on exports to the West Indies. (The West Indies accounted, it was said, for two thirds of coarse linen exports from the county.) In what was certainly an allusion to Smith, the memorial referred to the threat from and lack of substance of 'ingenious theories'. What the petitioners sought was the extension of the duties for sufficient time to allow the industry to improve to the point where they were no longer necessary. The threat of competition from Irish manufacturers of linen was also raised.

This relationship to Ireland and the Irish linen industry is the second point which needs drawing out. A British political economy had to reconcile not just English and Scottish interests, but also Scottish and Irish; and the latter had long been a potentially politically combustible area. Moreover, Scottish thinking on political economy was, certainly from the later seventeenth century, deeply conscious of Ireland and likely competition from Irish agriculture and manufactures.

Irish linen manufacturing had been strongly encouraged by the English Parliament before the Union in compensation for the restrictions on Irish woollen exports imposed by the Woollen Act (1699), as indeed was the continued importation of Irish 'victuals' into Scotland, after 1707 in direct contravention of the Treaty of Union. Irish linen was allowed duty free entry into the English market from 1696. In 1704 Parliament passed an act which allowed English and Irish traders to ship brown and white linen manufactured in Ireland to any of the British colonies. The duration of this act was extended indefinitely in

50 *Memorial Addressed to the Honourable Convention of Royal Boroughs in Scotland. By A Friend to the Linen Manufacture* (Edinburgh, 1772), pp. 3, 7–8.

51 National Library of Scotland, MS 653.

1716. Following the Union, efforts in the 1710s by the Scots to secure measures from the Westminster Parliament supportive of their linen industry, but also to inhibit Irish competition, were defeated or emasculated owing to the power of the powerful Irish lobby. Worse than this, in 1711 and 1715, linen was subject to new Westminster-imposed duties on exports, while in 1714 woollen manufacturers were able to obtain a drawback on soap which was refused to the Scottish linen industry. The Jacobite George Lockhart of Carnwarth expressed Scottish frustration when he predicted that the result would mean that 'the Irish must and will undersell us and our linen become a meer drug'.[52] The travails of the Scots linen producers after 1707 formed an important, sometimes overlooked, part of the background of anger and disillusionment with union which made the 1715 Jacobite rising so potentially threatening to Hanoverian rule in Scotland.[53]

Later in the eighteenth century, and against a very different background, Scottish sensitivity to supposed Irish advantage in linen production again became a major source of concern. What partly lay behind this was a perception that the Irish industry was benefiting from unusually strong support from the Irish Parliament. Secondly, lower rates of taxation and lower labour costs made Irish production more competitive than in Scotland or England. It is this, and rising levels of taxation in Britain, which explain the intense hostility with which Scots and Scottish manufacturers responded to the proposals for liberalization of trade with Ireland in 1778 and Pitt's commercial propositions of 1785. The only equitable solution was union: Ireland should follow Scotland's lead in this respect.[54] By the end of the eighteenth century, it was being argued that while bounties may have been appropriate only for new industries, their continued existence was justified by the degree of support in Ireland for the Irish linen industry.[55]

---

52 Quoted in Whatley, *Scots and the Union*, p. 337.

53 For contemporary comment on this, see National Archives of Scotland, Edinburgh, Montrose Papers, GD 220/5/468/19, Charles Cockburn to John Cockburn, 9 July 1715.

54 See e.g. the letter under the pseudonym 'Anglo-Hibernus-Scotus', in the *Edinburgh Evening Courant*, 23 March 1785 recommending union; Sir John Dalrymple, *Particular Consequences of Mr Orde's Irish Resolutions to the Landed, Manufacturing and Trading Interests of Scotland, and General Consequences of them to the British Empire, and to the Interest of His Majesty and His Family* (Edinburgh, 1785), pp. 31–2.

55 Mitchell Library, GB 243/TD 76.1, minutes of the Glasgow Chamber of Commerce, 1783–88, fol. 319. In 1784, the Scots sought an extension of the bounties on printed goods to prevent the Irish damaging the interests of Scottish manufactures and merchants. See esp. PKCA, B59/34/71/2, scroll letter from provost Faichney to Mr Dempster as to the bounties on printed goods, 23 January 1784, which noted: 'You will no doubt remember, that the

What the linen industry shows, therefore, is that debates at Westminster and amongst ministers in London were critical to the Scots and Scottish economic fortunes; and certainly felt to be critical. This was true in a negative as well as positive sense; it might mean defeating measures which could adversely affect the industry, such as the proposed ban of wearing printed linens in 1719, a bill against pedlars and hawkers in England dealing in the linen trade in 1730, or Pitt's proposed tax on printed linens and cotton in 1784, as well as securing measures which might actively encourage and support expansion.[56] The deeper point is the same: it was Parliament (and the Treasury) where, as much as if not more than anywhere else, solutions to the Scots problem of political economy were to be found after 1707. The matter of British political economy resolves itself again into one of political representation in London.

There is not space here to make other than some fairly general comments on this particular strand in our story; research to date on Scottish fortunes at Westminster is in any case rather limited.[57] Scottish chances of success at Westminster were obviously increased if Scottish MPs were capable of uniting in support of Scottish interests. As James Erskine, Lord Grange set out optimistically in 1708:

> It would be a strange conceit ... that they ought not to be united for the common and visible welfare of the country: and why not for the welfare of north Britain? Do not the Members for York, or any other county, join for the common advantage of that country without being suspected to divide from the rest of Britain? And since Scotland has particular trades to pursue and advance, such as linen, fishing, cattle, etc., as well as the clothing or tin counties of England have theirs, why should Scots Members uniting to advance these be reckoned a setting up a separate interest, inconsistent with the Union, more than theirs? ... And after all our small representation can hardly become ever so considerable, as to give the South Britains [sic] any great ground for jealousy.[58]

Unity proved elusive before the 1720s or thereabouts, but thereafter seems to have come more readily. There is evidence, for example, of considerable

---

Irish have these Bounties on their printed goods & if not renewed to us would deprive us altogether of this valuable branch of trade'.

56 For these measures, and the campaigns to defeat them, see *inter alia* Harris, 'Scots, Westminster and the British State', pp. 128–31; John Ehrman, *The Younger Pitt: The Years of Acclaim* (London, 1969), p. 253; PKCA, B59/24/8/10–12.

57 See esp. Harris, 'Scots, Westminster Parliament, and the British State', *passim*.

58 Quoted in David W. Hayton, 'Adjustment and Integration: The Scottish Representation in the British House of Commons, 1707–14', *Parliamentary History*, 27 (2008): p. 419.

organization and coordination during the malt tax crisis in the 1720s.[59] In 1783–84, at the other end of the century, MPs for the royal burghs appear to have met regularly during the session at that frequent haunt of Scots in the metropolis, the British Coffee House, to discuss national matters under the leadership of Edinburgh MP James Hunter Blair.[60] The particular traditions and configurations of Scottish politics and civil society also aided the creation of a Scottish interest on economic matters. In the first half of the eighteenth century, this was in part owing to the system of political management which emerged after 1725 presided over by the 2nd and then 3rd dukes of Argyll, but also to the important role of the Convention of Royal Burghs which, with its annual committee and agents in London designated to keep close watch on the legislature, spoke for the nation on matters of trade and manufactures, or at least the national interest as defined before 1761 by the Argyll interest. In the second half of the eighteenth century, the Edinburgh Linen Society (a somewhat shadowy body, but which seems to have comprised linen manufacturers and merchants in and around the Scottish capital) and, more saliently, from 1783, the Glasgow Chamber of Commerce added new elements to this picture, although both were in no way rivals to the Convention or the Board of Trustees; rather they sought to work in close conjunction with them.[61]

Scotland had, moreover, a tradition of direct parliamentary representation, which survived the Union and indeed the potentially sclerotic effects of political management. Scottish MPs were expected to act both individually and collectively to support and defend Scottish interests at Westminster, often in response to instruction from burgh authorities. County MPs were from an early stage regularly written to by burghs to support their interests, as well as the local burgh MP. This practice is particularly well documented for successive MPs for Perth Burghs, owing to what appears to have been an extraordinary diligent and methodical series of town clerks who kept full records of council business. Among this material are letters detailing some of the parliamentary activities of

59 Harris, 'Scots, Westminster Parliament, and the British State', pp. 129–31.

60 PKCA, B59/60/66, scroll letter from meeting of annual committee of the Convention of Royal Burghs, 31 January 1783, where a request was made to Hunter Blair to convene meeting of all members of parliament for the royal burghs to consult and advise on measures which may be brought relating to grain shortages; 67/2, minutes of meeting of members of parliament for the royal burroughs of Scotland held at the British Coffee House, London, 10 February 1783.

61 Mitchell Library, GB 243/TD 76/1, *passim*. At the first meeting of the Chamber, Patrick Colquhoun, as chairman, informed members that a list of its membership had been communicated to the Board of Trustees, as well as to the Lord Justice Clerk and Lord Advocate. The annual reports of the Board were conveyed to the Chamber, where they were commented on.

George Dempster, MP for Perth Burghs between 1774 and 1790.[62] What comes across in these is just how assiduously Dempster performed his role representing local and Scottish interests in Parliament and London, including supporting the linen industry, which was crucial to the town's and region's economy. In 1787 he was behind the dispatch of an agent to France to investigate the likely effects on the linen industry of the Anglo-French commercial treaty of the previous year. Dempster explained to William Alison, then Provost of Perth, that he 'would have gone myself without an Expence to my constituents had I not been obliged to do down to Scotland'.[63] In 1784, he was made an honorary member of the newly-formed Glasgow Chamber of Commerce in recognition of his role in defending Scottish economic interests, especially the linen industry, at Westminster.[64]

Dempster, a genuine independent in politics – 'honest George' was his soubriquet – was probably unusual in the extent of his activities; but not that unusual. The MPs for the two main cities – Edinburgh and Glasgow – as well as those for counties which included important mercantile and manufacturing interests – for example, Renfrewshire in the west or Angus and Fife in the east – seem to have been generally diligent supporters of local interests. Ironically in light of local reactions to his role in the malt tax affair in 1724–25, Daniel Campbell of Shawfields seems to have been very assiduous in representing Glasgow tobacco interests at the Treasury in the early 1720s.[65] Ilay Campbell, MP for Glasgow Burghs between 1784 and 1789 and lord advocate (1783–89), was very active in support of Glasgow and Scottish economic interests in the 1780s. A supporter of the ministry, he nevertheless opposed Pitt's new tax on printed linens in August 1784, while in early 1785 he supported a motion for delaying the Irish resolutions until Scottish representations had been heard, and in the following year opposed any reduction in the bounty on the Greenland fishery.[66] At the beginning of December 1780, the new lord provost of Glasgow,

---

62 PKCA, B59/60/3, 4, 10, 63, 67/1, 68, 69, 71/2, 74/1.

63 PKCA, B59/24/8/33/1, George Dempster to William Aiton, provost of Perth, 4 June 1787. See also B59/24/8/33/2, Dempster to John Pitcairn, Esq., provost of Dundee, 4 June 1787.

64 Mitchell Library, GB 243/TD 76.1, fols 30, 56. Dempster's role as a spokesperson for the Scottish linen industry went back certainly as far as the late 1760s, when he was representing St Andrews at the Convention of Royal Burghs; for which, see *Extracts from the Records of the Convention ... 1759–1779*, p. 307.

65 Jacob M. Price, 'Glasgow, the Tobacco Trade, and the Scottish Customs, 1707–1730', *Scottish Historical Review*, 63 (1984): p. 18.

66 Michael Fry, 'Campbell, Sir Ilay of Succoth, first baronet (1734–1823), judge and politician', *Oxford Dictionary of National Biography*. Available at: http://www.oxforddnb.com/view/article/4504 [accessed: 21 May 2010]. Campbell frequently appears in the

Hugh Wylie, wrote a letter to John Crawford, Ilay Campbell's predecessor as MP for Glasgow burghs in which he declared that he had read in the *Votes* (the regular record of parliamentary business) that leave had been given to bring in a bill to alter the Corn Laws. Crawford was directed to send a copy 'as soon as you possibly can'. Wylie directed him further: '... I must request you to give me the earliest Intelligence of every Bill that may hereafter be brought into Parliament, which may in any respect affect the Trade or manufactures of this country'. He was also to inform another individual that Wylie would be corresponding soon with him 'upon our city business'.[67]

On their own, 'perseverance and keenness', and reasonable unity among Scottish parliamentary representatives, were of course insufficient; what mattered was influence at Westminster and other key organs of the state, notably the Treasury, and this in turn meant, usually, building alliances with interests elsewhere in Britain and indeed, in some cases, with the Irish linen interest. It also meant reconciling the rather different interests of the coarse and fine linen manufacturers. Ireland was both competitor and potential ally of the Scots linen interest in the eighteenth century. More widely, the ability to work across national boundaries was a crucial part of the growing success of the Scots in securing a favourable hearing at Westminster and in achieving a growing number of their legislative goals. In the 1740s, cooperation between Scots and the West India interest in London was forthcoming, perhaps unsurprisingly given the importance of the West Indies as a market for Scottish coarse linen.[68] Scots merchants in London, linen factors for example, could facilitate this process of connection and building of consensus, as well as providing a further point of contact at the heart of the political system. Alliances were also forged with fine linen manufacturers from the north west of England and with the Irish linen interest. The latter was undoubtedly very important in securing the bounty on coarse linen exports in 1742.[69] In the late 1760s and early 1770s, the strategy was very deliberately to solicit support from the north west of England and the

minutes of the Glasgow Chamber of Commerce as a contact point at Westminster for west coast manufacturing and mercantile interests (Mitchell Library, GB 243/TD 76.1).

67 Mitchell Library, TD 200/111, Hugh Wylie to John Crawford, Esq, MP, London, 1 December 1780.

68 For the perceived benefits of this alliance, see relevant comment in PKCA, B59/24/8/4, provost of Edinburgh to the magistrates of Perth, 1 November 1744. To some extent, this alliance was adventitious, in that it emerged during opposition to a new duty on sugar proposed by Henry Pelham; the West India lobby proposed a further tax on foreign linen as an alternative.

69 Public Record Office of Northern Ireland, Castleward Papers, D 2092/1/5, fols 49–50. There was a meeting in early February 1742 between linen merchants and representatives of Scotland, Ireland and England.

Irish Linen Board. In 1770, for example, two agents of the Convention were sent to the principal linen manufacturing towns in England to explain 'the plan [for support of the industry] intended to be adopted and solicite their interest & concurrence therein'. The same individuals also met with 'several gentlemen from Ireland' at Chester who recommended that the Convention write to the Linen Board in Ireland to gain their support.[70] One individual closely involved in lobbying activity on behalf of the Convention, the Edinburgh merchant George Chalmers, took the 'logic of concert' a stage further, in so doing offering a sobering assessment of the conduct of the British Parliament in relation to Scottish and Irish interests:

> ... in his opinion, the chief reason why the linen manufacture was not so much considered or encouraged by parliament was that Scotland and Ireland seemed chiefly interested in that question & England but little concerned, but if the matter was rightly considered, from what he had learned by conversing with persons concerned in that manufacture in England, after laying before them how much they were interested, he had reason to believe England might take the lead in any future application to parliament ...[71]

As a lobbying body, the Glasgow Chamber of Commerce sought from the outset to operate in conjunction with relevant English bodies and interests.[72] This in part reflected the growing importance of sectoral lobbying, as, for example, in the cotton industry, where from the start Scottish interests worked alongside those from the north west of England as part of a broader industry lobby. Viewed very broadly, as referred to towards the beginning of this chapter, it was precisely the balance achieved between integration within a developing and fluid world of parliamentary lobbying and a continuing ability to form and mobilize a national interest which explains Scottish relative success in achieving legislative

---

70 *Extracts from the Records of the Convention ... 1759–1779*, pp. 398–402. This source makes clear the work done to reconcile the various interests of the various manufacturers in different parts of the British Isles so as to prevent opposition to the appeal for further parliamentary aid for the industry.

71 *Extracts from the Records of the Convention ... 1759–1779*, pp. 421–2. Chalmers was the author of *Thoughts on the Linen Manufacture in Great Britain, Humbly Offered to the Legislature* (1771), written, in his words, 'with a view to excite the English to join and even take the lead in this affair'.

72 See e.g. Mitchell Library, GB 243/TD 76.1, fol. 11, minute of meeting of 18 February 1783, which noted that several members and the secretary were to draw up a memorial on ready money duties on the sugar and tobacco trades and send this to merchants in London, as well as chambers of commerce in Bristol and Liverpool 'in order to have their assistance in procuring redress of the hardships complained of'.

support for their economic interests and the emergence, as much unplanned as in any sense by design, of what, from a Scottish perspective, could reasonably be described as a British political economy.

Nevertheless, the process had important limits, and these need to be fully acknowledged. The failure of the campaign in the early 1770s to gain parliamentary support to relieve the industry in a phase of depression is instructive in this context; in this case, it was the continuing power and influence of crucial English interests which won out. It was against this background that a pamphlet was published in Edinburgh in 1780 presenting the 'union' of England, Scotland and Ireland as union frustrated or incomplete.[73] According to the author, this union had to date brought only distress to Scotland and Ireland and their peoples, as demonstrated by the rise of emigration from both countries in the previous decade. The sole viable solution, which did not involve its dissolution, was to encourage Scottish and Irish exports, and this meant primarily through support for the linen industry. Primary responsibility for this lay, in turn, with a legislature which had only a few years previously favoured the interests of a 'few merchants' rather than the 'poor of their country'. 'The interposition of the legislature is ... not only requisite, with a view to the further advancement of the linen trade in Ireland and Scotland', the author declared, 'but also to preserve it from a decline'.[74] In 1781, there appears to have been a further drive, equally unsuccessful, to get Parliament to take measures to equalize conditions confronting Scottish and Irish linen manufacturers, presumably a response to the granting of 'free trade' in 1779 and worries about Irish competition under the new dispensation, but also the granting of bounties on exports of linen from Ireland by the Irish Parliament.[75] This probably failed because it was politically inopportune, given the then state of relations between Dublin and London, but perhaps also because it coincided with the end of the North ministry and ensuing political turmoil. In the early eighteenth century, as David Hayton has recently emphasized, the Scots proved less adept than the Irish at extracting advantage from the Westminster Parliament, and it took them some time to learn the game of politics in the new legislature.[76] Even in the later eighteenth century, there were those who argued vehemently that the linen industry was

---

73 *Observations on the Importance of National Manufactures: and Particularly on the Linen Manufacture* (Edinburgh, 1780).

74 *Observations*, p. 27.

75 Mitchell Library, TD 200/111, fols 17–18, David Stewart, Lord Provost of Edinburgh, to Hugh Wylie, Provost of Glasgow, 21 July 1781. See also further letters from Wylie to John Crawford, Lord Frederick Campbell, Andrew Stewart on the same subject (fols 21–3, 26).

76 Hayton, 'Adjustment and Integration', pp. 410–35.

not an appropriate sector for support, given its dependence on imports of raw materials, although such arguments tended to be heard from defenders of the English woollen industry.[77]

British political economy was always, thus, a contested, fluid, intermittent, even adventitious phenomenon. It was but one element, as referred at the beginning of this chapter, in the scramble for parliamentary and political advantage among manufacturing and commercial groups within the British Isles in this period. There is much more that could be said about Scottish representation and treatment within and by Britain's fiscal-military state in the eighteenth century, and a full picture would need to include much more detail on the attitudes of successive ministers in London, as well as such things as patterns and relative levels of taxation; the role of the customs and excise services and the postal service, increasingly viewed as a crucial aspect of an effective commercial economy; the role of the Admiralty and defence of Scottish coasts from privateers; support for the development of the Highland economies through, for example, the establishment of the British Fisheries Society in 1786 or Telford's construction of communications infrastructure in the early nineteenth century. Nevertheless, the basic conclusions stand even on the partial evidence presented here – the state was a crucial actor in economic development in eighteenth-century Scotland; and equally importantly there did develop in this period a British political economy, albeit a limited, unsystematic one, a product as much of compromise and struggle as design. Thus it was that George Chalmers, the Edinburgh merchant quoted from earlier, who for 40 years was closely involved in lobbying for Scottish interests in London, could declare with tempered optimism in 1789: 'May the union ... be perpetual; may all its articles be fairly and candidly executed; may the English act like real mothers to Scotland, and the Scotch receive it with proper gratitude and respect'.[78]

---

[77] See e.g. *A Letter Occasioned by the Application to Parliament for Farther Encouragement to the Linen Manufactures of Great Britain and Ireland* (1774); *The Contrast; or a Comparison Between the Woollen, Linen, Cotton and Silk Manufactures: Shewing the Utility of Each, Both in a National and Commercial View* (1782).

[78] [George Chalmers] *Considerations on the Union Between England and Scotland, and on some Commercial Matters in Both Kingdoms. By a Citizen of Edinburgh, and member of its Chamber of Commerce* (Edinburgh, 1789), p. 68.

Chapter 5

Learning the Ropes of Sand: The West India Lobby, 1714–60

Perry Gauci

This chapter assesses the regulatory impact of an economic lobby generally considered to be one of the most successful of its age. Significant victories such as the Molasses Act of 1733, or the defeat of the Pelham sugar duty in 1743–44, have led historians to declare that the reigns of the first two Georges represented 'the heyday of the planting interest'.[1] Lillian Penson was the first to highlight their political resourcefulness, and in recent years Andrew O'Shaughnessy and Christopher Brown have added considerably to our understanding of its influence as a commercial lobby both before and after the Seven Years War.[2] The perceived importance of imperial discourses to domestic political development from the 1730s onwards has only served to highlight the potential resonance of the West Indians, and their common cause with domestic interests has also been flagged up by David Armitage, Kathleen Wilson and Bob Harris.[3] In common with research into the North American lobbies, this work has made a significant contribution to our general understanding of politics and economy in this age. This chapter seeks to take a closer look at the ways in which the lobby regarded the political process in

---

1 Christopher Brown, 'The Politics of Slavery', in David Armitage and Michael Braddick (eds), *The British Atlantic World, 1500–1800* (Basingstoke, 2002), p. 226.

2 Lillian Penson, 'The London West India Interest in the Eighteenth Century', *EHR*, 36 (1921): pp. 373–92; Lillian Penson, *The Colonial Agents of the British West Indies* (London, 1924); Andrew J. O'Shaughnessy, 'The Formation of a Commercial Lobby: The West India Interest, British Colonial Policy and the American Revolution', *HJ*, 40 (1997): pp. 71–95; Brown, 'The Politics of Slavery', pp. 214–32. Richard Sheridan's major economic survey also provides important political insights, *Sugar and Slavery: An Economic History of the British West Indies 1623–1775* (Kingston, 1974), esp. pp. 54–74.

3 David Armitage, *The Ideological Origins of the British Empire* (Cambridge, 2000); Kathleen Wilson, *The Sense of the People: Politics, Culture and Imperialism in England, 1715–1785* (Cambridge, 1995); Bob Harris, 'Parliamentary Legislation, Lobbying and the Press in Eighteenth-Century Scotland', *Parliamentary History*, 26 (2007): pp. 76–95.

the course of seeking regulatory advantage, and at the strategies they evolved to gain such significant leverage.[4]

Although it will seek to shine light on the foundation of their achievements, the broader priority of the chapter remains an examination of how the political actors involved in the regulatory process adapted to the great economic and political changes of the era, for this volume has recognized the reign of George II as particularly important for discussions of the state's regulation of the economy. In this regard, the West India lobby have particular significance as an economic interest with an uncertain political constituency before 1715, and with acute anxieties concerning the international battle for trading supremacy in the Atlantic. Thus, in order to achieve their economic goals they were forced to accommodate both domestic forces such as the growing centrality of Parliament and the expansion of the press, as well as international influences such as the growth of the British empire and imperial rivalries. Furthermore, the main actors in view here, the absentee planters and their correspondents, present a particularly interesting perspective, and not simply for their success. In particular, as political-economic actors, they represent an interesting bridge between various sectors of the economy, and between various political developments in train at that time. Although highly successful as a lobby, their success was conditional on adapting to British political processes and priorities. This will become clear from closer study of the relationship between their aims, their strategies and their general views on the political system.[5] From these perspectives, it will appear that the West Indians were far from confident of success, and that they found it difficult to work the regulatory mechanisms of the state. Furthermore, their political achievements cannot be represented as a watershed in British economic

---

4 For the most comprehensive survey of the representation of the North American colonies, see Alison Olson, *Making the Empire Work: London and American Interest Groups, 1690–1790* (Cambridge, MA, 1992). The title of the chapter acknowledges the important contribution of Michael Kammen to this field, *A Rope of Sand: The Colonial Agents, British Politics and the American Revolution* (New York, 1968).

5 They also represent a different model to the northern colonists so ably studied by Alison Olson, particularly for the size of the absentee group in the metropolis, *Making the Empire Work*. Recent work on the West Indies lobby has stressed that its success was highly conditional on anticipating the views and needs of metropolitan government – see O'Shaughnessy, 'The Formation of a Commercial Lobby', pp. 93–4, where he observes that 'lobbies frequently gain their mystique of power by apparently influencing a government which is already predisposed to act in their favour'. Trevor Burnard has also argued that the lobby's success was in part due to the fact 'that their advocacy fitted government policy' – 'Passengers Only: The Extent and Significance of Absenteeism in Eighteenth-Century Jamaica', *Atlantic Studies*, 1 (2004): pp. 170–95.

thinking or politics, and their experience casts doubt on the putative 'reactive' nature of the government on social and economic matters.[6]

Aims and Organization

Although this chapter will concentrate on the views of lobbyists in action, some preliminary observations are needed concerning the scope of legislation the West Indians sought, for, in common with economic lobbies more generally, the aims of the lobby were crucial to the strength of the interest, and to their regulatory strategies.[7] The basic aims of the lobby were fairly consistent and predictable – to keep the price of sugar and its by-products as profitable as possible. In common with many overseas traders, however, this involved a regulatory scope which ran far beyond conventional economic determinants, which reflected the socio-economic character of the colonies, the complexity of colonial trade, and international competition. Although the Atlantic traders have been heralded as free-trade's spiritual forefathers, the sheer breadth of their potential imperial needs ensured that the West Indians were prepared to contemplate significant government intervention, especially in the face of foreign competition. Beyond a basic resistance to monopoly companies, in itself a principle largely fired by self-interest, they looked to the government to protect their markets through every link in the economic chain, from the supply of slaves, through to the levy of domestic taxes, and drawbacks on re-exports. The regulatory goals of the West India lobby more obviously betray a common fear of the weakness of colonial societies and economies, as much as any increasing sense of imperial ambition.[8] Moreover, such was the indivisibility of imperial governance and imperial profitability, particularly with regards to slave systems in which economic

[6] Lee Davison, Tim Hitchcock, Tim Keirn and Robert B. Shoemaker (eds), *Stilling the Grumbling Hive: The Response to Social and Economic Problems in England, 1689–1750* (Stroud, 1992). Significantly, Tim Keirn argued that the executive had 'a powerful influence on commercial policy', and it would be 'foolish' to deny state priorities in economic legislation, pp. 10–11.

[7] By 1715 the state had evolved clear patterns of handling economic affairs, with the Board of Trade increasingly acting as a filter for directing economic petitioners through political channels, according to substance of the demands, and their general significance. For Parliament's increasing efficiency in processing mercantile business, see Perry Gauci, *The Politics of Trade: The Overseas Merchant in State and Society, 1660–1720* (Oxford, 2001), pp. 220–33.

[8] This chapter will principally deal with major issues affecting the interest, but this is not to ignore the potential resonance of more private matters, such as the recovery of a particular cargo, or the settlement of a personal estate.

priorities were particularly brutal, that the boundaries between the political and the economic were peculiarly blurred in imperial minds. For instance, continuing demands for troops to ensure the submission of slave-workers, and the deterrence of foreign invaders, highlighted most directly the critical dependence of the West Indian economy on wide-ranging state support. In this way, they could not expect the state to be a merely, or even a largely, reactive force, and often invited state intervention, even if they had natural cause to fear the government's financial demands.[9] In this way, the growth of empire and the activities of the absentees probably accelerated the processes by which the economy became a more central part of national politics, although without necessarily aiding the process of distinguishing it as a specialist field of activity or knowledge.

This reliance on state support had ensured the steady development of political links with the metropole from the late seventeenth century onwards, most obviously through the appointment of colonial agents from the 1670s. West Indian interests had paid constant court to executive offices since 1689; the pressures of constant war put great strain on the Atlantic trade routes, and even threatened the security of the islands themselves. At this stage, the islands were accustomed to petitioning separately, although common concerns, such as the timing and manning of convoys, encouraged some degree of co-ordinated action. Moreover, merchants and planters were ready to petition together, probably in the hope of raising a sufficient number of signatories to impress ministers.[10] Their petitioning to Parliament also became more frequent and sophisticated in the wake of the great debate over the Royal Africa Company in the reigns of William and Anne, which raised fundamental questions with regard to the supply of slaves to the Caribbean.[11] Nonetheless, the numbers of MPs with direct ties to the colonies remained small before 1714, and the

[9] Note the key arguments of Jack Greene here, who stressed how the increasing dependence of the West Indian islands on British military protection compromised their own claims to their liberties as Englishmen – 'Liberty, Slavery and the Transformation of British Identity in the Eighteenth-Century West Indies', *Slavery and Abolition*, 21 (2000): pp. 1–31.

[10] Centre for Metropolitan History, Merchant Petition database, which contains evidence of some 50 signed representations by West India interests in the 1670–1720 period. Most petitions were signed by 15–25 self-identified merchants and planters, although a handful mustered over 40. For analysis of the economic and political impact of colonial merchant associations in London, see Nuala Zahedieh, *The Capital and the Colonies: London and the Atlantic Economy 1660–1700* (Cambridge, 2010), pp. 55–136.

[11] William Pettigrew, 'Free to Enslave: Politics and the Escalation of Britain's Transatlantic Slave Trade, 1688–1714', *William and Mary Quarterly*, 64 (2007): pp. 3–38. However, the reign of George I saw few debates with regard to sugar or the slave trade in the Commons, and Caribbean business only became more prominent from 1729.

most active colonial representatives were London merchants, led by Sir Gilbert Heathcote, Jeffrey Jeffreys and Sir Joseph Martyn. With widespread commercial influence, and political clout in the Bank and the City, Heathcote could play a valuable role as a spokesman for colonial interests, but it was not until the 1720s that the West India interest took on a more coherent form.[12]

The establishment of an absentee planter group in the capital was clearly critical to the success of the West Indies lobby.[13] As scholars have highlighted, the number and influence of absentee planters remains debatable, but it is no coincidence that Parliament began to take regular notice of the sugar colonies at the same time as a significant increase in the numbers of absentees settling in the metropolis.[14] Not only did this provide a pool of rich and well-connected political lobbyists, but also permitted a continual internal debate on the future of the Caribbean, both amongst the West Indians, and between them and domestic interests. Although rivalries between merchants and planters, and between the islands, threatened to upset the unity of the lobby, its potent mix of landed and commercial interests presented powerful opportunities for engaging with their domestic and imperial counterparts.[15] In particular, the landed wealth

---

12 Significantly, the History of Parliament Trust volumes for the 1690–1715 period do not provide a separate survey of colonial interests, although they note that 25 transatlantic merchants sat in the Commons, and a further 14 MPs specialized in African commerce (including several slave traders). Few are recorded as having planting interests, Eveline Cruickshanks, Stuart Handley and David Hayton (eds), *The History of Parliament: The House of Commons 1690–1715* (Cambridge, 2002), vol. 1, pp. 734–5.

13 Burnard's systematic study of absentees estimates that at any one time there were 150 Jamaican landowners in Britain in mid-century (representing 11 per cent of island proprietors, and some 3–6 per cent of the island's white population). He also notes that they owned some 23 per cent of the land on the island. He argued strongly that the absentees were significant representatives for Caribbean interests in Britain, although not always gaining their point – Burnard, 'Passengers Only', pp. 183–5, 190–91. For the development of the economic management of absentee estates, see Barry Higman, *Plantation Jamaica 1750–1850* (Kingston, 2005), esp. chapters 2 and 3.

14 Trevor Burnard's database of Jamaican inventories reveal that only 11 Jamaican property-holders were listed as inhabitants of Britain at their death before 1730, while 18 were identified as such in the 1730s (including eight esquires/planters). A further 49 were listed in the next 20 years, including 16 of a gentle or planter status. No one factor can be attributed to an increase in absenteeism, although the consolidation of great plantation estates during the reigns of William and Anne provided some families with the wealth necessary to establish themselves in the mother country. West Indians were certainly aware of the heavy expenditure this would involve, and in 1751 Samuel Martin of Antigua thought that £20,000 was insufficient to set up a family in Britain, Add. Mss 41346, fol. 32.

15 For a useful review of the conflicting scholarly views on the core membership of the West India interest, see O'Shaughnessy, 'The Formation of a Commercial Lobby', pp. 72–5,

of the planters, and their close connection with mercantile interests, gave them significant advantages as politicians in terms of access, time and opportunity. The absentees also provided vital links to the British provinces and may have helped to heal some of the divisions between London and the colonial outports.[16] Recent work has rightly questioned the reality of their influence, for the West Indian lobby was a very fluid organization, and the defence of sugar could not obviate fierce rivalries within it and real differences over the future of the British in the Caribbean. However, it was the overall diversity and versatility of the lobby which was vital for its preservation and success, both in terms of countering the overt opposition of others, and for preserving its own discipline.[17]

The role of the Planters' Club of the 1730s onwards is indicative of the importance of greater co-ordination for the lobby as it sought greater state support. It remains a shadowy organization, but it is clear that in George II's reign it played an important political role.[18] The Jamaican William Beckford clearly regarded it as politically important by 1741, thinking it 'very proper that a number of gentlemen should meet together in order to consult on everything that shall be thought for the good of their country, for in the multitude of

---

where he concludes that in the Parliaments of the later eighteenth century some 40–50 MPs had direct connections with the Caribbean through land, business, office and family. For the 1715–54 period, a total of only 27 MPs had significant Caribbean connections, two thirds of whom were either born there, or had spent significant time there, see Romney Sedgwick (ed.), *The History of Parliament: The House of Commons 1715–54* (London, 1970), vol. 1, p. 153.

16 Historians and contemporaries have been quick to credit the sheer wealth of the Beckfords and Fullers as crucial for their growing interest, largely in terms of buying seats. However, it is important to see how their great wealth also gave them time for political activity, permitting them to delegate business operations to family or agents. Their business also provided them with contacts in the outports, with William Beckford establishing agents in both Bristol (John Curtis and Michael Atkins) and Liverpool (Richard Savage) – Hoare's Bank archive, Ledger 64, fols 426v–427v; Beinecke Library, General mss b. 4, folders 77–8. The development of the commission system, whereby the colonists lessened their dependence on British-based merchants by acting as their own principals, clearly aided their political authority. However, several London merchants and bankers still played a wide-ranging role as mediators within the absentee group, such as the firms of Barclay and Fuller, or Drake and Long, see Sheridan, *Sugar and Slavery*, pp. 282–305.

17 Indeed, the absence of an obvious consensus amongst the West Indians was a key rationale behind greater organization within the lobby, and was never easily achieved. Evidently, such co-ordination helped them to meet the challenge of their rivals, but it also performed the key role of presenting a united front to the ministry of the day.

18 O'Shaughnessy, 'The Formation of a Commercial Lobby', p. 75, notes that the club 'became little more than a social group with no apparent political activities', although an absence of records precludes any precise timing here. There was also a merchants' meeting in the 1730s, which has left little trace of activity.

counsels there is wisdom'. However, even for an observer convinced of the 'infinite consequence we are to Great Britain', Beckford was cautious over the club's regulatory role, only suggesting that 'many useful hints may be started which may prove of great advantage for the colonies'.[19] The club can thus be seen as providing a key function in *starting* ideas about regulation, but leaving a great deal of the detail to be filled in via discussion within the lobby itself, with the authorities, and with rival interests. Interestingly, even after the success of the campaign for the war against Spain in 1739, Beckford was convinced that the lobby needed to work harder to convince the British public of the value of the colonies, 'for surely we have been grossly abused and misrepresented by a pack of scoundrel writers, who know nothing either of our situation or constitution', thus highlighting the potential perils of becoming too prominent in the public view. Such awareness advised the club to keep a low profile, but would also propel Beckford and the other absentees on a wide campaign to gain influence and allies, and would fortify the importance of the club for securing a common front among the Caribbeans within the metropolis.[20]

As the Caribbeans became more successful, they had to work harder to gain leverage, because rival interests sought to challenge their supposed public spiritedness and right to special consideration.[21] The North Americans could prove particularly truculent. For instance, four northern colonies represented their opposition to the Commons in the spring of 1751 when the West Indians tried to crack down on illegal trade between North America and the Caribbean. A flurry of letters within the West Indian group survives to highlight the

---

19 Add. Mss 12431, fols 116, 120, Beckford to James Knight, 11 October 1740, 19 August 1741.

20 Add. Mss 12431, fol. 125, Beckford to Knight, 18 June 1743. The chequered reputation of the colonies must in part be seen as a consequence of the propensity of colonial interests to employ the metropolitan press to advance sectional interests. With ultimate authority centred in London, few colonial rivals stopped to think how their attacks might reflect on the reputation of the Caribbean as a whole.

21 Brown, 'The Politics of Slavery', pp. 219–20, notes that the success of the West Indians directly helped to create 'a rival set of ideas' among interests opposed to their influence in commercial policy. Interestingly, even as early as 1733, the Barbados agents warned the island assembly not to use the Molasses Act as a springboard to demand the direct export of sugar to Europe, reasoning that 'we thought it prudent to rest satisfied at present with what the legislature was most inclined to give us'. Even with the Molasses Act itself, they had not pushed for a complete prohibition (of exports to the mainland colonies), and settled for high duties, for 'it would have been construed as an affront to the House of Lords to attempt a bill in that very shape which had met so cold a reception ... the preceding session' – National Library of Jamaica, Ms 1021, S. Foster, P. Leheup and J. Yeamans to Barbados committee of correspondence, 8 June 1733.

strengths and weaknesses of a metropolitan presence, when the North American challenge left them with only 48 hours to organize a petition to support their cause. First, they had ready access to expert legal opinion, which could advise on the wording of the petition and the short case for MPs, the form of the latter which Beckford was still 'not so very conversant' with after several years in the House. They also had access to superior commercial statistics, which were not deemed to be 'exact', but certainly better than the 'random conjecture' of other lists.[22] They also were able to rustle up an impressive roster of signatures by circulating it to a limited number of sites within the City, and at the Bedford Head Tavern, off Tottenham Court Road, close to the residences of many of the leading planters. As the last link in the political chain, they also had a last-minute agreement from the London MP, Slingsby Bethel, to present the matter to the House. Interestingly, there remained great concern that public campaigns might expose internal divisions, with clashes recorded between the colonial agent John Sharp and Beckford's brother Julines, but the planting team were quick to smooth over these differences in the common cause. These *processes* of petitioning were thus vital both for organizing interest groups to pursue their objectives, and to give the lobby vital advantages. Nonetheless, on this occasion the Americans defeated the bill, largely due to a lack of parliamentary time.[23]

Regulatory Strategies

The West India lobby thus derived particular strengths from its membership, but what of its strategies for regulatory success, and its views on the authorities they lobbied? Given the wide variety of its demands, it was inevitable that the lobby sought regulatory satisfaction from a wide array of authorities, including just about every major executive department, but with particular reference to the Treasury, Customs and Admiralty. Their choice was usually dictated by the powers which they sought to appropriate for their own cause, and thus they had

---

22 National Library of Jamaica, Ms. 1792, John Gray to John Sharpe, 9 December 1750, 5, 6 March 1751, Thomas Cole to same, 5 March 1751; Ms. 1792a, William Beckford to John Sharpe, 5, 6 March 1751. Stephen Fuller's papers show that he was most concerned to assemble comprehensive statistics of Jamaica's commercial growth and importance in the early 1750s, Somerset Record Office (Taunton), DD/DN/513, agent papers.

23 For the strategies of the northern colonies, see A.G. Olson, *Making the Empire Work*. Richard Sheridan also identifies the sugar bakers as a key rival of the planting interest, and argues that the Direct Export Act of 1739 was simply a measure to alarm the bakers that low prices in Britain might lead the planters to supply European markets instead, *Sugar and Slavery*, pp. 69–70.

to focus increasing energies on Parliament when tariffs were so crucial to their future. Furthermore, as the colonies loomed larger in the national consciousness by the 1730s, they had to be prepared to defend themselves in the parliamentary arena, which by that time had become the ultimate forum for matters of national economic interest.[24] However, contrary to claims made to the centrality of empire for the development of popular politics, but in common with their northern colonial brethren, the West Indians remained ambivalent about the effectiveness of public campaigns, and it is clear that they regarded the public sphere with misgiving. Closer inspection of their tactics suggests that their instinct was to secure support amongst ministers, although often in the knowledge that it was merely a prelude to the campaign in the Commons. Their tactics also suggest that they had little faith in the economic understandings of most politicians, and of the public still less.[25]

The reluctance of the absentees to drag the 'public' into their affairs was rooted in a variety of concerns, most evidently their fear that they might antagonize the ministry unduly, and by their worry that their cause might be misunderstood or trounced by populist counter-arguments. Clearly, there was some recognition of the value of taking the fight to the public, and we see this in the resolve of Barbadian absentee Henry Lascelles in January 1744, when faced with an additional sugar duty: 'nothing shall be wanting to make the clamour popular, and if possible to get this dammed bill as much abhorred as the excise scheme'. Shortly afterwards he admitted, however, that 'the accumulated weight of all the people of this great City [of London] is nothing in competition with the influence of the ministry'. Indeed, he accepted that their ultimate victory over the duty was secured by 'the aid of our new allies, most of the Scotch and some of the Irish members', whose support was won by West Indian backing for a duty on foreign linens.[26] The Jamaican Rose Fuller was even more explicit in

---

24 As an illustration of this, in 1718 a spokesman for Bristol merchants at the Board of Trade queried its competence to debate the establishment of a company for marine insurance, reasoning that their rivals 'have not, as it might be expected they should, applied to the legislature in an affair of such importance to the trade of this kingdom', *Journal of the Commissioners for Trade and Plantations, 1715–18* (London, 1924), p. 385.

25 Key works to have highlighted the importance of the growth of empire in stimulating popular politics include Nicholas Rogers, *Whigs and Cities: Popular Politics in the Age of Walpole and Pitt* (Oxford, 1989) and Wilson, *Sense of the People*. Olson notes the distaste of the northern colonists for popular agitation in this period, *Making the Empire Work*, pp. 123–5.

26 *The Lascelles and Maxwell Letterbook, 1739–69*, ed. S. Smith (Microform Academic Publishers, 2002), pp. 82–3, 139. A year later he was worried by the prospect of an additional duty again, and was keen to get a new convoy act against the threat of French privateers (as in the preceding war). The episode does suggest that economic interests had more to fear from

his concern for the impact of the public sphere in their affairs, arguing against the use of the press 'by reason that the doing thereof would be an appeal to the public in a matter wherein they are not judges or concerned'. He also revealed that he had resisted the temptation to answer his personal critics in the press, even though 'a scandalous pamphlet was published throughout the nation, exposing me as the greatest villain and blockhead upon earth'.[27] Some Jamaicans took evident comfort from the jurisdiction of the executive in matters affecting their future, for in June 1757 William Wynter was able to dismiss the threat of petitions to the Commons from the merchants of London, Bristol and Liverpool by stressing that the matter (the removal of the Jamaican capital from Spanish Town to Kingston) was 'unparliamentary', and that the petitions would thus have little impact.[28]

Another sign of their adaptation to Whig oligarchy is their bipartisan assault on the grandees of Westminster politics, which represents a significant difference from the policy of the northern colonies, whom Alison Olson found much less inclined to play factional politics in this period.[29] Their pursuit of 'the great men', as they regarded them, was a significant feature of their strategies in the 1740s and 1750s, and thus Beckford pursued the likes of Bedford, Fox and ultimately Pitt, while the Duke of Newcastle was courted by Rose Fuller.[30] Indeed, the willingness of the Caribbeans to attempt any political persuasion is striking, and at root must be attributed to their mistrust of a very fluid, interest-dominated

---

each other than from the public, although their appeals to national utility did necessitate public activity. Bob Harris notes that the Convention of the Royal Burghs was keen to co-ordinate lobbying activity with the West Indians in 1744, 'Parliamentary Legislation, Lobbying and the Press', p. 93.

27 Somerset Record Office (Taunton), DD/DN/487, Rose Fuller to John Fuller, 10 July 1754. He probably was referring to the pamphlet penned by James Smith of Kingston, *A Letter from a Friend at J----- to a Friend in London: Giving an Impartial Account of the Violent Proceedings of the Faction in that Island* (London, ?1747), in which he was labelled 'a monstrous absurd fellow ... a busy, bustling, blockheaded booby', p. 6.

28 East Sussex Record Office, uncatalogued Fuller mss, William Wynter to Rose Fuller, 25 June 1757.

29 She notes that pre-1756 the northern colonists only sought opposition support in 'extraordinary' cases such as the Excise bill of 1733, and, even then, the colonial interests could be divided, *Making the Empire Work*, pp. 122–3. See also Jacob Price, 'The Excise Affair Revisited: The Administrative and Colonial Dimensions of a Parliamentary Crisis', in Stephen Baxter (ed.), *England's Rise to Greatness, 1660–1763* (London, 1983), pp. 257–321.

30 O'Shaughnessy notes that the divided political loyalties of the West India interest after 1763 may have bolstered its influence, especially its ability to weather changes of ministry. However, he saw their number as insufficient to dominate the House, 'The Formation of a Commercial Lobby', pp. 89–90, 93.

political system. Despite their reservations, absentee leaders recognized that they had to play the game with the political instruments at hand, and that such liaisons bore fruit both behind doors and in the Commons itself. The value of a good spokesman was noted by Lascelles in 1744, when he excitedly mentioned that Pitt had undertaken to speak for them – who 'far excels all the rest (some say every man in the House)'. The exhilaration of Lascelles was later shared by Rose Fuller, who relished the prospect of gaining the Duke of Halifax in 1756, who 'from his parts, knowledge and industry will be in a short time the first man in power in this kingdom'. However, the dangers of such associations were also recognized, for Beckford was censured by the Antiguan Samuel Martin in March 1762 for being too close to Pitt, and this friendship was blamed for 'the little regard paid to the extension of our sugar colonies' after Pitt's fall. More generally, there were great fears among colonial leaders that the price of governmental favour could be too high, and that metropolitan governors would exploit the Caribbean for their own purposes. For instance, a Jamaica lawyer warned in 1756 that if the court felt it could choose the island's agent, 'all their [own] purposes and designs and instructions would be instantly communicated to, and as instantly defeated by the ministers, unless they perfectly quadrated with their own schemes'.[31]

While uncertainties remained regarding the favour of the great men, the planters sought to establish a more durable platform for their interest by securing an increasing number of seats in the Lower House from 1747 onwards. As an alarmed governor warned Henry Pelham, 'there is a scheme, or I am greatly mistaken, among the West Indians to make themselves formidable; as many as can are to get into the House and keep together; all governors that will not be at their devotion are to be cried down'.[32] For certain, Samuel Martin left his son in no doubt of the importance of Caribbean voices in the Commons, urging him in 1750 to 'speak often and be not overnice to avoid the declamatory', in order to serve 'the country, your friends and yourself'. He regarded it 'a real defect in a moral character' not to aspire to ministerial rank, for this was the best way to support 'your country, your relations and your friends in the most effectual manner'. Fifteen years later he was still harping on this theme, warning his son to represent colonial grievances 'emphatically

31 *Lascelles and Maxwell Letterbook*, Smith, p. 119; East Sussex Record Office, Fuller mss 21/74, Rose Fuller circular letter, 2 November 1756; 21/88, F. Paris to Stephen Fuller, 16 November 1756; Add. Mss 41347, fol. 131, Samuel Martin snr to Samuel Martin jnr, 20 March 1762.

32 National Library of Jamaica, Ms 306, Governor Edward Trelawny to Pelham, 13 April 1749. Trelawny also speculated 'how easily' the City might be 'inflamed' by these moves.

to the public', or else to pass 'the materials' to others who would. He saw a parliamentary seat as vital, the loss of which would see the incumbent 'lose all weight of influence, not with men of power but with all the world'.[33] Although there were colonial misgivings about the attentiveness of the absentees to Caribbean affairs at Westminster, hamstrung as they often were by their political obligations to their electoral patrons and domestic constituents, islanders did welcome their electoral success. For instance, Jamaican planters were much encouraged by Rose Fuller's return at New Romney in 1756, 'from which this island has reason to hope for great advantages in having the power and influence of so able an advocate and friend to support its true interest, with which he is so intimately acquainted, not only in that august body, but more immediately among the ministry'. Nevertheless, while such political access was deemed increasingly vital, British politics appeared a necessary evil to most of the absentees, and their frustrations with its impact on economic regulation were at times very palpable.[34]

Significantly, this equivocal regard for metropolitan politics led several absentees to question the character of the political system, even as the Seven Years War seemingly marked a new high tide for empire. We can sense the powerlessness and suspicion of the lobby through Samuel Martin's censure of the commercial understanding of the average MP in June 1754. 'The utter ignorance' of ministers and MPs had been a recurrent theme of discontented economic lobbyists for some time, but it is interesting to note that Martin thought that commercial principles could be communicated, and that this ignorance was in fact founded on 'a wrong opinion of the mysteriousness of trade and the difficulty of setting up a regular system upon plain evident principles'. This misunderstanding could be rectified by reference to the best judges and books, and it is significant that several French works were on his list, including Colbert – 'if that minister's advice had been pursued with vigour, it is highly probable that Britain had been this day a province of France'. This view did not herald a sea-change in attitudes to the politics of trade, but it highlighted the readiness of the colonists to seek the reconciliation of landed

33 Add. Mss 41347, fols 18, 205, 232–3, Samuel Martin snr to Samuel Martin jnr, n.d. (c. November 1750), 5 August 1765, 10 July 1766.

34 East Sussex Record Office, Fuller mss, SAS-RF/21, Charles White to Rose Fuller, 19 March 1757. In turn, Fuller regarded his influence as an MP more prosaically, especially in the company of senior politicians such as the Duke of Newcastle, to whom he observed on 14 March 1761 that if he had become 'a man of some consequence', it was due to 'being the object of the Whig interest in a very great trading town [Maidstone], and ... in a very great county', Add. Mss 32920, fol. 196.

and commercial interests, which assisted domestic calls for a greater primacy to be given to economic matters in national affairs.[35]

In the case of Beckford, his entire career was spent fostering accommodations between gentlemen, planters and merchants. His parliamentary speeches likened the sugar planter to the country gentlemen of the shires; his political connections linked the polite West End to the commercial City; and his economic networks facilitated communication between the metropolis, the outports and the Caribbean. Inevitably, he found opposition in the process of forging these networks, and it even led him to question the constitutional structuring of Parliament, and to back moderate parliamentary reform. Significantly, this stance was shared by Samuel Martin senior and other colonial figures, who regularly censured rotten boroughs even though their general interest clearly benefited from them. Their reformist agenda can be plausibly linked to their familiarity with opposition groups, and their ideological attacks against the Old Whig oligarchics.[36] However, while Beckford and his allies did seek political capital from these domestic discourses, he was also reflecting a broader colonial suspicion of the failures of the current system to adapt to empire, and to dynamic commercial forces within the British economy more generally. Even before the troubles sparked by the more proactive imperial government of the post-1763 era, such views highlight how political processes worked both for *and* against the aims of the imperial lobbies. Whatever regulatory success they may have achieved, their metropolitan betters retained ultimate control both domestically and imperially.[37]

Regulatory Conclusions

There was clearly much to cheer the countenances of the West Indian lobby by the mid-eighteenth century, and one senses their excitement through the

35 Add. Mss 41346, fols 108–9, Samuel Martin snr to Samuel Martin jnr, 1 June 1754. Certainly this does seem a much more conciliatory stance than that taken by those lobbying for a commercially-experienced Board of Trade in the 1690s – Gauci, *Politics of Trade*, pp. 180–94.

36 Bob Harris, *Politics and the Nation: Britain in the Mid-Eighteenth Century* (Oxford, 2002), pp. 50, 53, 57; Rogers, *Whigs and Cities*, pp. 88, 92–3.

37 Colonial views on political reform deserve far wider discussion than can be supplied here, but the ease with which absentees adapted to discourses of freedom and independence reflected the interaction of their essentially British sensibilities and their colonial experiences. See Trevor Burnard's discussion of slavery and white egalitarianism in *Mastery, Tyranny and Desire: Thomas Thistlewood and His Slaves in the Anglo-Jamaican World* (Chapel Hill, NC and London, 2004), pp. 69–100. Beckford's support for the middling sort was clear by 1754, and his planterly roots clearly influenced the development of his anti-aristocratic position in the 1760s.

observation of Rose Fuller in September 1755 that 'the people of England are very serious upon the present disputes with France, and I think [are] convinced that the southern colonies depend upon the northern, and the nation upon the southern; this idea must be cherished'.[38] However, behind the scenes we can see common misgivings with the imperial Parliament and a strong sense of its unwillingness to back the colonies sufficiently. This poses interesting questions as we consider the strengths and weakness of the lobby in the pre-1760 period. Although historians have rightly highlighted the potency of the pro-imperial stance adopted by opposition politicians from the late 1730s as a sign of the colonists' adaptation to metropolitan politics, in reality, colonial interests were far readier to work with government, and were all too aware of the uncertainties of factional politics. Although largely metropolitan in character, they saw obvious common cause and backing in the English provinces and Scotland, and developed their strategies to match those natural associations. In this way they harnessed their natural economic interest, which may not have evolved into a political force independently, and struck deals with other economic forces to potent effect. In terms of overall achievement, they did make progress as a political regulatory force, particularly in developing a discourse of public utility, although crucially tuned for the ears of ministers *and* the wider public. They even managed to navigate the treacherous waters of party politics to tolerable effect, although only by remaining bi-partisan in their alliances.

These read as very healthy headlines for the West India lobby, but there remained limits to their influence, and even to what they might ask of the government. They also had some reason to doubt the effectiveness of the legislation they achieved.[39] From every angle, they remained intimidated by government influence, and rarely challenged the control of the ministry of the day, which was the price they paid for regulatory favour. Moreover, for every backstairs manoeuvre, they had to be prepared to defend their interest in the Commons and in the press, and their success did see a vocal opposition develop, which forced them onto the defensive. In this light, their experience highlights the opportunities provided by a participatory parliamentary system for all

---

38 East Sussex Record Office, Fuller mss 21/25, Rose Fuller to ?, 3 September 1755. For a recent review of ways in which creole planters identified themselves as industrious, useful Britons, see Christer Petley, '"Home" and "This Country": Britishness and Creole Identity in the Letters of a Transatlantic Slaveholder', *Atlantic Studies*, 6 (2009): pp. 43–61.

39 Significantly, Richard Sheridan argued that the planters found limited success in their determination to uphold the Navigation Laws in the Americas. However, while it remains unclear whether the North American market was secured for British-produced sugar, he concluded that Georgian legislation did help to gain the planters 'an enlarged and protected home market which was superior to the foreign market', *Sugar and Slavery*, pp. 71–4.

economic interests by the middle of the eighteenth century, but the resultant competition would continue to put them on their political mettle, and argue for even greater organizational vigour in the next half of the century.

The experience of the absentees thus fully endorses the dynamism of the politics of trade in the reign of George II. However, while the period has become an exciting one for historians wishing to espy novelties regarding political structures, interests and discourses, the absentees demonstrate that the state managed to harness these forces to achieve mutual satisfaction. In terms of economic thinking, these colonials had very little to offer to challenge accepted ideologies, other than perhaps in the urgency with which they demanded commercial mastery over foreign competitors. Politically, they were prepared to consider more radical options when blocked, but generally sought to adapt to the political *status quo*. Their success may have been remarkable, but it should be seen as a victory for opportunism and hard work, rather than as a paradigm shift in the state's relationship with the economy. Both the state and the Caribbean interests benefited enormously from having the absentees at the heart of the empire, where both they and ministers could learn the ropes of sand at much closer inspection.

Chapter 6

Political Convention and the Merchant in the Later Eighteenth Century

Daeryoon Kim

> The interest of the dealers ... in any particular branch of trade or manufactures, is always in some respects different from, and even opposite to, that of the publick. ... [They constitute] an order of men, whose interest is never exactly the same with that of the publick, who have generally an interest to deceive and even to oppress the publick, and who accordingly have, upon many occasions, both deceived and oppressed it. – Adam Smith, *Wealth of Nations* (1776)[1]

Writing in the midst of the imperial crisis, Adam Smith famously argued that the unnatural economic restraints imposed on the American colonists under the navigation system had rendered inevitable some fundamental changes to Britain's relationship with the colonies. This mercantile system, Smith contended, had been driven primarily by self-interested merchants and manufacturers at the expense of the public good. Lacking necessary policy devices and knowledge concerning the 'mysteries' of commerce, Britain's governing elites had often looked to the 'expert' counsel of the commercial classes, and had been repeatedly duped by their 'sophistry' and 'clamour'.[2] Smith's condemnation of merchants in particular resonated with many of his contemporaries. A leading figure among the moderates of the Edinburgh ministers thus wrote to Smith, 'You have done great Service to the World by overturning all that interested Sophistry of Merchants, with which they had Confounded the whole Subject of Commerce'. Politicians, usually guarded in what they said, did express similar

---

1 Adam Smith, *An Inquiry into the Nature and Causes of the Wealth of Nations*, eds. Roy H. Campbell and Andrew S. Skinner (2 vols, Oxford, 1976), vol. 1, p. 267.

2 Smith, *Wealth of Nations*, vol. 1, pp. 115, 144, 266–7, 493, vol. 2, pp. 570, 584. On Smith's critique of businessmen, see, for instance, Donald C. Coleman, 'Adam Smith, Businessmen, and the Mercantile System in England', in Donald C. Coleman, *Myth, History and the Industrial Revolution* (London, 1992), pp. 153–63; Donald Winch, *Riches and Poverty: An Intellectual History of Political Economy in Britain, 1750–1834* (Cambridge, 1996), pp. 92–112; Istvan Hont, *Jealousy of Trade: International Competition and the Nation-State in Historical Perspective* (Cambridge, MA, 2005), pp. 54–5, 304–5.

uneasiness about the power of merchants. Lord Germain, for instance, exploded at Westminster, 'I would not have men of mercantile cast every day collecting themselves together and debating about political matters'.[3]

Smith's critique may serve to illustrate the 'reactive' nature of the eighteenth-century British state, which Tim Keirn and Lee Davison have posited to underline the vital importance of regulatory initiatives from economic interests.[4] Smith's characterization of merchant influence, however, would have convinced few eighteenth-century merchants. Although fairly successful in broadcasting their political credentials as 'patriotic traders', especially through the mid-century imperial wars, merchants could never afford to take their political influence for granted. Their influence, if any, had to be earned by demonstrating to the state, and to a lesser extent to the public, their contributions to the national economy and their usefulness within the political system. To this end, as recent work by Perry Gauci and others have demonstrated, merchants had to adapt to the political system rather than try to dictate their wills to the state.[5] Its sheer intellectual force notwithstanding, Smith's criticism, then, should not be considered as reflective of the realities of merchant political influence. It may rather be viewed as part of the continuing, yet still unresolved, arguments about the political merits (or demerits) of merchant interests, and more broadly about the operation of the eighteenth-century British fiscal-military state. It is therefore necessary to examine more closely the particular circumstances in which a criticism of Smith's sort acquired renewed persuasiveness and the ways in which merchants adapted to this changing political climate.

A case in point here are the merchants trading to North America. Scholars have highlighted the political failure of the American traders to intervene more effectively for the peaceful resolution of the imperial crisis, but this work has

---

3 Hugh Blair to Smith, 3 April [1776] in, *The Correspondence of Adam Smith*, eds. Ernest C. Mossner and Ian S. Ross (Oxford, 1977), p. 188; *Cobbett*, vol. 17, p. 1195.

4 Tim Keirn and Lee Davison, 'The Reactive State: English Governance and Society, 1689–1750', in Lee Davison, Tim Hitchcock, Tim Keirn and Robert B. Shoemaker (eds), *Stilling the Grumbling Hive: The Response to Social and Economic Problems in England, 1689–1750* (Stroud, 1992), pp. xi–liv.

5 On the efforts of merchants to construct their 'patriotic' image, see James Raven, *Judging the New Wealth: Popular Publishing and Responses to Commerce in England 1750–1800* (Oxford, 1992); Perry Gauci, *The Politics of Trade: The Overseas Merchant in State and Society, 1660–1720* (Oxford, 2001); Bob Harris, *The Politics and the Nation: Britain in the Mid-Eighteenth Century* (Oxford, 2002). On the relationship between the state and merchant interests, see Andrew O'Shaughnessy, 'The Formation of a Commercial Lobby: The West India Interest, British Colonial Policy and the American Revolution', *HJ*, 40 (1997): pp. 71–95; Perry Gauci, *Emporium of the World: The Merchants of London, 1660–1800* (London, 2007), esp. ch. 8.

rarely acknowledged the magnitude of political challenges facing the merchants and the logic underlying their extremely cautious political positions towards the crisis.[6] Although sandwiched between the increasingly polarizing positions towards the crisis, they had to exploit what political means they could muster to get their specific political requests through the layers of administrative and legislative machinery, and this alone proved sufficiently difficult to achieve.[7] This crisis, however, demanded of the merchants more than their usual tactfulness, for, as this chapter will demonstrate, the escalating tensions between Britain and its American colonies rendered the political activities of American merchants more problematic than ever in the eyes of the state and the public. This profound challenge compelled the American traders to demarcate sharply their political contribution by stressing both their role as provider of commercial information and the necessity for the state to comprehend more clearly the economic ramifications of the crisis. From these perspectives, it will appear that political conventions informing the operation of merchant lobbies still largely dictated the course and substance of economic arguments between the state and the American merchants even in the midst of burgeoning radical reform movements. An appreciation of this will perhaps help us to understand why the unreformed political system persisted without significant reform in the later eighteenth century.

The imperial debates since the end of the Seven Years War had great significance for the ways in which merchant politics was discussed in both state and public arenas. As the debates were sparked by the fiscal and commercial measures introduced in the aftermath of the war, economic concerns underlying the relationship between Britain and its colonies were not entirely buried in

---

6 The literature on the attitude of the commercial classes on the American crisis is extensive, but on the failure of American merchants in particular, see Alison G. Olson, 'The London Mercantile Lobby and the Coming of the American Revolution', *Journal of American History*, 69 (1982): pp. 21–41; Paul Langford, 'The British Business Community and the Later Nonimportation Movements, 1768–1776', in Walter H. Conser, jr, Ronald M. McCarthy and David J. Toscano and Gene Sharp (eds), *Resistance, Politics, and the American Struggle for Independence, 1765–1776* (Boulder, CO, 1986). Also relevant here are the older studies focusing on the operation of American colonial agents: Jack M. Sosin, *Agents and Merchants: British Colonial Policy and the Origins of the American Revolution, 1763–1775* (Lincoln, NE, 1965); Michael Kammen, *A Rope of Sand: The Colonial Agents, British Politics, and the American Revolution* (Ithaca, NY, 1968).

7 There is not enough space here to fully address this issue except offering some general observations whenever necessary. For a more detailed discussion, see Daeryoon Kim, 'In Search of "Affectionate Regard": American Merchant Lobbies and the State during the Atlantic Imperial Crisis', *Parliamentary History* (forthcoming).

the subsequent constitutional conflict.[8] Merchants, especially those interested in the American trade, were therefore closely involved in these arguments through lobbying and other channels, and their political activities invited much comment, often of a very critical nature. Their interventions in such key policies as the Stamp Act, the Townshend duties and the Coercive Acts made their political presence far more conspicuous than they would have wished, and this brought to the fore the question of whether merchants were sufficiently qualified to take such a prominent position in matters of commercial and imperial policy. Here two related arguments gained wide currency: first, that merchants were too preoccupied with their immediate economic interests to provide informed and impartial judgments on matters of national significance; and secondly, that their parochial, short-sighted perspective would not allow merchants to discern whether a particular policy would be beneficial to their longer-term interests.

The charge against the self-serving nature of merchant politics was already in circulation while the American traders were conducting a well-orchestrated lobbying campaign for the repeal of the Stamp Act. Condemning the colonial resistance to this supposedly innocuous fiscal measure, a pseudonymous writer argued that his case deserved more serious attention precisely because he was not affiliated with any mercantile business. 'I am sure', he wrote, 'if I was a Merchant, I should reckon myself utterly unqualified for speaking on the Question which stands at the Head of my Paper. Actual Merchants are so ingrossed by the Gain or Loss of their own particular Branches, that it is impossible for them to perceive the Hurt or Benefit of the whole Body'.[9] While defending the wisdom of the stamp duties and other imperial measures, many opposition writers made a similar point. Charles Lloyd thus announced that, by endeavouring 'to attain that degree of popularity, which the interested followers of some interested traders could bestow', the Rockingham ministry let 'the temporary and partial views of a junto of interested traders held at a tavern' hold sway over imperial affairs.[10]

With the escalation of the imperial crisis, similar charges were made more frequently and forcefully. In the winter of 1774–75, when London's merchants

8 Nancy F. Koehn, *The Power of Commerce: Economy and Governance in the First British Empire* (Ithaca, NY, 1994).

9 Cato, *Thoughts on a Question of Importance Proposed to the Public* (London, 1765), pp. 45–6.

10 Charles Lloyd, *The Conduct of the Late Administration* (2nd edn, London, 1767), pp. 148, 119. See also Soame Jenyns, *The Objections to the Taxation of our American Colonies* (London, 1765), p. 19; *Constitutional Considerations on the Power of Parliament to Levy Taxes* (London, 1766), pp. 11–12; *The Justice and Necessity of Taxing the Colonies* (London, 1766), p. 31.

trading to North America were contemplating the necessity of petitioning to Parliament for conciliation with the colonies, their leaders were called 'a few interested, mercenary Firebrands'. This endeavour was attributed to their selfish pecuniary motives, as 'when Merchants are suffered to give Advice to Statesmen, even in Matters which appear of a commercial Nature, they seldom fail of mixing a self-interested Dash with their Counsels'.[11] Although slightly more moderate in tone, several newspaper articles and pamphlets nonetheless advised that merchants should not allow their 'phantom of private interest' to cloud 'the general concern', and instead should follow the guidance of sensible politicians who were in a better position to decide what would be their long-term benefits.[12]

These criticisms would dovetail well with the more refined arguments of some economic writers on the limits of merchant political contributions. In this respect, Malachy Postlethwayt's case is perhaps representative. Although hardly an opponent to mercantile interest, he still observed that the aims of merchants were not always compatible with the public interest, and more importantly that the merchant was not capable of admitting that, 'taken up with his own detail', he 'seldom has an eye to what is general'.[13] It was perhaps inevitable, as Thomas Pownall suggested, for merchants to consult only their own gains, as commerce naturally 'supersede[s] all particular laws and customs, and operate by those which the nature and actual circumstances of the several interests require'.[14] Instead of relying on merchants, it would be therefore safer

---

[11] Quotes from the letter of Baliol and the letter of Britannicus, respectively printed in *Public Advertiser*, 12, 26 January 1775. See also several letter-runs in the same paper, 7, 14 February, 6, 8, 20 October 1775.

[12] Quote from Anthony Bacon, *A Short Address to the Government, the Merchants, Manufacturers, and the Colonists* (London, 1775), p. 36. See also William Knox, *The Interest of the Merchants and Manufacturers of Great Britain* (London, 1774), pp. 49–50; *Public Advertiser*, 2, 3, 7, 10, 18, 21 January, 1, 4 February 1775; Israel Mauduit, *Considerations on the American War* (London, 1776), p. 148; *An Address to the People of Great Britain in General* (Bristol, 1776), pp. 66, 71. The North ministry was indeed concerned with the reaction of merchants trading to North America when introducing the punitive measures against the American colonists in the aftermath of the Boston Tea Party. Lord North was reported to remark in his speech of 14 March 1774 that 'he hoped that all would agree with him, both peers, members, and merchants, to proceed unanimously to punish such parts of America as denied the authority of this country'. See, *American Archives*, 4th ser., ed. Peter Force (9 vols, 1837), vol. 1, p. 38.

[13] Malachy Postlethwayt, *Britain's Commercial Interest Explained and Improved* (2 vols, London, 1757), vol. 2, pp. 390, 368–70. Josiah Tucker conceded the validity of this sort of argument in *A Brief Essay on the Advantages and Disadvantages* (London, 1753), pp. vi–vii.

[14] *The Administration of the Colonies* (4th edn, London, 1768), p. 8.

for the nation to leave commercial policy in the hands of those independent gentlemen at Westminster. These impartial deliberators would ask themselves whether:

> the Basis of all Deliberation on our Connection with the Colonies abroad, ought to be Not – how will they bring the greatest immediate Wealth into the Coffers of a few Merchants? Or how will they bring the greatest immediate Splendor of the City of London? – But how will they continue to promote the Population of the Island, and the Industry of the People of Great Britain?[15]

This would in fact benefit merchants themselves, some emphasized, as Parliament would protect them from any unfair infringement on their interests by other competing interest groups. Merchants trading to North America, for instance, had been granted legislative protection from the excessive use of paper money by the American colonists.[16]

These observations were occasionally challenged in public forums, but it seems that merchants were wary of being involved too deeply in this debate over the limits of merchant interest for fear of their mercantile identity being disclosed to the public.[17] They instead took a decidedly cautious tack. Their primary concern was to preserve their credibility with the state and with the public. To that end, they found it necessary to distinguish very clearly where they believed their values lay within the political system, and strived to keep their actions and arguments within bounds. In this respect, one of the strategies to which they consistently resorted was to confine their political role to that of information provider, leaving decision-making to politicians and public officials. This strategy was certainly reflective, as John Brewer and others have suggested, of the growing importance attached to commercial information throughout the eighteenth century.[18] More immediately useful for the American traders,

---

15 Cato, *Thoughts on a Question of Importance*, pp. vi–vii.

16 Thomas Whately, *The Regulations Lately Made with Respect to the Colonies Considered* (London, 1765), pp. 39, 43–5.

17 There is not enough space here to discuss this strand of opinion, but see some arguments in John Mitchell, *The Present State of Great Britain and North America* (London, 1767), p. 313; Edmund Burke, *Observations on a Late State of the Nation* (London, 1768), pp. 21–2; *To the Electors of Great Britain* (London, 1768); Arthur Lee, *The Political Detection* (London, 1770), pp. 120–26; James Burgh, *Political Disquisitions* (3 vols, London, 1774–75), vol. 1, p. 54.

18 John Brewer, *The Sinews of Power: War, Money and the English State, 1688–1783* (London, 1989), pp. 221–30; Julian Hoppit, 'Political Arithmetic in Eighteenth-Century England', *EcHR*, 49 (1996): pp. 532–5; Alison G. Olson, *Making the Empire Work: London and American Interest Groups, 1690–1790* (Cambridge, MA, 1992).

this strategy served to reassure the state that they fully understood what their duty as the king's loyal subjects was – making available for the state whatever information they learnt from their business activities. Once fulfilling this duty, they would leave 'the political to those who should best know how to discuss it', as one leading American trader pointedly announced at a public meeting in January 1775.[19]

When seen in this context, the apologetic language often used by merchants in their petitions and other forms of representation may not be dismissed as a mere rhetorical flourish. Admittedly, such formulaic expression as 'intreating relief, as to the House [of Commons] shall seem expedient' was quite commonly used in parliamentary petitions, but the fact that merchants felt obliged to make the same apologetic gesture repeatedly is still revealing.[20] David Barclay, jr, for instance, professed at the hearing of London merchants' petition against the New England fishery bill that the merchants submitted their petition in the belief that 'they have it in their power, to give such information as may enable the honourable House, consistent with its wisdom, its justice, and its dignity, to adopt measures the most advantageous to the landed and commercial interest of the whole British Empire'. Similarly, a merchant witness declared in support of the petition of the West India lobby urging conciliation with America, 'I came here as an evidence of facts, which I hope will influence the opinions of the House, but not to obtrude my own'.[21] Summarizing the testimonies given by the West India merchants and planters, Richard Glover expanded on this point:

---

19 An extract of a letter from London, 6 January 1775, *American Archives*, vol. 1, p. 1087; *London Evening Post*, 5 January 1775. The American traders in London had taken the same position when requesting Parliament to consider the repeal of the Townshend duties. When preparing their petition, they followed Lord Hillsborough's advice that their representation should be confined strictly to the difficulties the duties had caused for British manufacturers. To the protest of Dennis De Berdt, merchant and agent for New England, who warned this would not satisfy the colonists, the merchants answered, 'they had no other regard for America apart from the resumption of trade. Political matters were the concerns of the agents' – De Berdt to Thomas McKean, 15 February 1770, 'Letters of Dennys De Berdt', *Publications of the Colonial Society of Massachusetts*, 13 (1911): p. 399.

20 Quoted from the petition of London merchants to the House of Commons for the repeal of the Stamp Act (read on 17 January 1766). See *CJ*, vol. 30, p. 462.

21 Richard C. Simmons and Peter D.G. Thomas (eds), *Proceedings and Debates of the British Parliament Respecting North America, 1754–1783* (5 vols, Millwood, NY, 1982), vol. 5, pp. 496–7; *The Evidence Delivered on the Petition Presented by the West-India Planters and Merchants to the Hon. House of Commons* (London, 1775), p. 40. At the same hearing, an MP asked 'whether, if the Americans were prevented from trading with the French islands [in the West Indies], it would be advantageous to Great-Britain'; the merchant witness answered, 'a speculative opinion is asked; I spoke only to facts' (ibid., p. 43).

> when presented in their genuine simplicity, untainted by prejudice, passion, or party, not looking towards any one quarter in preference to another, without courting any; meaning to offend none; but soliciting the attention to all; information and knowledge in such a shape must be acceptable to any assembly, and I am confident will be accepted here. To throw lights into the Committee is the sole object of your Petitioners, limiting themselves to the line of facts, which from their peculiar situation none can fully explain, but such as themselves.[22]

Glover's remark pointed to another important political consideration at work in merchant politics. By stressing the neutrality of information they offered, these merchant petitioners and witnesses answered the accusation of being manipulated by factional politicians and at the same time the allegation of their manoeuvring other commercial interests for their political patrons. Owing to their close relationship with the Rockingham ministry, London's American traders found themselves exposed precisely to these suspicions. At the hearing of 11 February 1766 on the petitions for the repeal of the Stamp Act, an MP thus challenged, 'what are the means or arts used to procure those petitions?' To this blunt question, their leader Barlow Trecothick replied, 'Many of the manufacturing towns sent for the form of a petition which we declined, particularly at Bristol. We thought it too indecent and desired them to speak from their own feelings and that none should complain but what were aggrieved'. At the same hearing, a witness from Manchester was asked twice whether there was 'no member of parliament soliciting the petition'. To this, the witness countered, 'the merchants determined of themselves'.[23]

Merchants also highlighted the spontaneous nature of their political representation by following certain conventions concerning the organization of petitioning. In order to prevent the possibility of favouring one sectional interest at the expense of others, eighteenth-century Parliaments and government departments tended to require petitioners to specify the purpose, scope and expected consequences of their particular requests, and then to let competing interests have their opposing views known to both original petitioners and the state. From the same concern derived another requirement that subscription to a particular petition ought to be confined to those whose interests bore direct relationship with its subject matter.[24] Evidence from government and

22 Richard Glover, *The Substance of the Evidence on the Petition Presented by the West-India Planters and Merchants, to the Hon. House of Commons* ([New York], [1775]), pp. 7, 8.

23 Simmons and Thomas (eds), *Proceedings and Debates*, vol. 2, pp. 192, 224.

24 Paul Langford, *Public Life and the Propertied Englishman 1689–1798* (Oxford, 1991), pp. 139, 174–87; Julian Hoppit, 'The Landed Interest and the National Interest,

parliamentary papers shows that merchants adhered fairly consistently to these conventions. Thus, if an issue under consideration affected several merchant interests in various sectors or localities, each group submitted its own petition, respectively setting out the precise nature of its interest in the matter at hand. The number of subscribers to a particular petition was also carefully regulated, and it was not even a primary concern for merchant petitioners how many signed a petition. There were indeed several petitions submitted by merchants trading to North America in which less than ten merchants took part, and yet they encountered little difficulty in getting their wishes granted. By defining their requests clearly and regulating participation, merchants were able to claim the authenticity of their applications, at the same time avoiding the undesirable impression that they tried to exercise an unsolicited collective power to force their wills on decision-makers.[25]

While following these conventions of lobbying, merchants seldom ventured to boast their extensive experience and knowledge concerning overseas commerce, in contrast to economic writers in pamphlets, periodicals or learned treatises. As Postlethwayt noted, there were of course some merchants who were perfectly capable of doing so:

> as some of the body of merchants have occasionally manifested an eminent knowledge, in the national interests of trade, it has never been deemed unbecoming them, or foreign to their character. On the contrary, it has been thought as a great merit for merchants, on public conjunctures, to have afforded satisfaction to their fellow-citizens, in their associations in this metropolis; and the highest honour to have given the legislature an acceptable judgment, in matters of weighty concernment to the traffic of the kingdom.[26]

One should notice the qualification Postlethwayt attached here: he did not mean that all merchants were qualified to undertake such a dignified role. A more immediate help most merchants could offer to both the state and the public was based on their command of details concerning particular branches of trade. Postlethwayt made this point, when writing, 'It is ... necessary to know them [details of trade]; but that knowledge cannot be gathered but from merchants. One cannot converse with them too much in order to learn; but in deliberating,

---

1660–1800', in Julian Hoppit (ed.), *Parliaments, Nations and Identities in Britain and Ireland, 1660–1850* (Manchester, 2003), pp. 90–91.

25 For evidence supporting the general observations made above on the patterns of lobbying, see Kim, 'In Search of "Affectionate Regard"'.

26 Malachy Postlethwayt, *The British Mercantile Academy* (London, 1750), p. 38.

their advices are to be received with caution'.[27] Josiah Tucker would have readily agreed with this conditional endorsement of the merchant contribution to the formation of commercial policy, for he also believed the merchant 'is more *skilful* in the *Practice* of *Trade*, and *a better Judge*, whether the Project, perhaps so fair in *Theory*, is *feasible* in *Fact*'.[28]

In public forums, where they could take advantage of anonymity, merchants had opportunities to present their views in broader contexts. It seems, however, that, even when addressing more general issues concerning trade and empire through the medium of pamphlet or newspaper, merchants were still wary of behaving like a 'person of liberal and learned education'. Although stressing whenever possible the vital importance of their particular line of business to the nation's economic and strategic interests, merchants were sure to underline that their opinions were based on their personal experiences. One case in point centres on contributions to the debate over post-war trading arrangements between Britain and the United States. With peace at last in sight, the Atlantic traders immediately started to voice their wishes for Britain's Atlantic trade to be restored on its pre-war footing through the concession of certain commercial privileges to the Americans. Their proposal, however, was forcefully renounced by Lord Sheffield, who claimed that preferential measures for the former colonists would not make any economic sense but only help the new republic to become a naval power sufficiently strong to pose a military threat to Britain.[29] Against Sheffield's case, merchants advanced an argument that, as naval power should be considered a by-product of a flourishing carrying trade rather than an end in itself, their proposal would eventually help Britain to maintain its strategic superiority in North America. What is interesting here, however, is not this rather familiar mercantile case but the ways in which these writers constructed their argument. While drawing on the work of some celebrated economic writers – some of whom were of merchant origin – and official statistical accounts, they persuaded themselves that their most credible source had to be found in their own personal experiences. Thus, criticizing Sheffield's omission and misrepresentation of

27 Postlethwayt, *Britain's Commercial Interest*, vol. 2, p. 390 (quote); Postlethwayt, *British Mercantile Academy*, p. 54.

28 Tucker, *A Brief Essay*, pp. vi, vii. Adam Smith also noted the same point, when writing, 'Their [merchants' and manufacturers'] superiority over the country gentleman is, not so much in their knowledge of the publick interest, as in their having a better knowledge of their own interest than he had of his' – *Wealth of Nations*, vol. 1, pp. 266–7.

29 Lord Sheffield, *Observations on the Commerce of the United States with Europe and the West Indies* (London, 1784); see also John E. Crowley, 'Neo-Mercantilism and *The Wealth of Nations*: British Commercial Policy after the American Revolution', *HJ*, 33 (1990): pp. 339–60.

certain statistical data, merchants claimed that their long mercantile experience did not allow them to accept his conclusions.[30]

As they were willing to content themselves with their limited role within the political system, merchants wished to witness the consistent operation of a kind of division of labour between the merchant as information provider and the state as the decision-maker. The realities they faced, however, were much more complicated. For one thing, for this partnership to work smoothly, it was vital for the independent landed gentlemen, who constituted the mainstay of the political elites in the late eighteenth century, to educate themselves in the secrets of trade and its connections with the landed and national interest. A self-styled mercantile educator Thomas Mortimer announced:

> The present and future grandeur, fame, riches, and happiness of Great Britain, depend so entirely on the ingenuity, industry, and commercial spirit of its inhabitants, and on the wisdom of its legislature, that no study seems more important than that which tends to convey proper ideas of those most essential subjects, COMMERCE, POLITICS, and FINANCES; especially for those, who, by their rank, fortune, or connections in life, may hereafter be called upon to direct and improve, or to patronize and reward the exertions of genius and honest labour in their fellow-citizens; either by representing them in parliament, or by taking a part in the administration of government, as ministers, or magistrates.[31]

Such appeals, however, seem to have remained unanswered, as is attested in frequent expressions of frustration about the lack of commercial knowledge and

---

30 Richard Champion, *Considerations on the Present Situation of Great Britain and the United States of America* (London, 1784), esp. pp. 76–8 (where Champion faulted Lord Sheffield for depending exclusively on the customs accounts which he believed were not fully reflective of the number of ships built in America); Bryan Edwards, *Thoughts on the Late Proceedings of Government* (London, 1784), p. 21 (pointing out Sheffield's omission of the customs accounts, especially on the size of American trade with the West Indies), p. 147 (claiming he drew on not only the customs house books but his 15-year experience as a merchant). See also *Considerations on the Present State of the Intercourse between His Majesty's Sugar Colonies and the Dominions of the United States of America* (London, 1784); Edward Long, *A Free and Candid Review, of a Tract, entitled, 'Observations on the Commerce of the American States'* (2nd edn, London, 1784).

31 Thomas Mortimer, *The Elements of Commerce, Politics and Finances* (London, 1780), p. i. See also Postlethwayt, *British Mercantile Academy*, pp. 38–9, 63–4, 68. Dedicating his edition of *Works of Charles D'Avenant* to Lord Hillsborough, Charles Whitworth wrote in the same spirit, 'The subjects treated of are such as every nobleman and gentleman ought to be well acquainted with, viz. The Trade and Revenue of England, the Plantation Trade, the East-India Trade, and the African Trade' – *Political and Commercial Works of Charles D'Avenant* (5 vols, London, 1771), vol. 1, p. v.

reliable information on commerce and trade.[32] While the ruling elites of Britain's rivals were busy acquiring 'a thorough knowledge' of commercial interests, 'the study of trade and commerce, has been more neglected and despised [here] ... than in any other nations, and especially by our great men'.[33]

The lack of commercial knowledge on the part of Britain's landed elites perhaps did not hinder the operation of merchant lobbies in any profound way, as real decision-making power rested primarily with ministers, public officials and parliamentary men of business. This vital fact was rarely lost on merchant lobbies. Through their frequent dealings with these decision-makers, they knew only too well how difficult it could be to get their proposals through the administrative and legislative machinery. They, therefore, attempted to make the most of their political contacts within both the executive and the legislative; they carefully regulated their internal organization and their relations with other sectional interests; they developed their political roles to answer the expectations of policy-makers; they endeavoured to comply with frequent requests from the state for information and opinion. None of these tasks were as simple as merchant interests would have liked. On top of the necessity to adapt to rapidly changing political conditions due to the frequent ministerial changes and the deepening colonial crisis, they often found themselves involved in serious debates with policy-makers over the factual grounds of their particular requests and the ramifications of their trading activities for the fiscal imperatives of state and the national economy. This often required much more of them than their limited role as information provider.[34]

Although they did not question their inferior position within the policy-making process, merchants were still able to claim certain rights, and to request the state to perform certain roles. One of the arguments merchants often employed was their entitlement to regular consultation and fair treatment by the state. For instance, Henry Eustace McCulloch, agent for North Carolina, registered a complaint to the Board of Trade against the application of London merchants for stricter enforcement of a bounty on tar. Asking the Board to suspend any further deliberation on this matter, McCulloch declared, 'The

32 Arthur Young, *Political Essays Concerning the Present State of the British Empire* (London, 1772), pp. 317–18, where he deplored, 'It is a misfortune that these capital interests of this nation are no better known. Such a scarcity of authentic materials to compile such a work as this ... makes it too often necessary to have recourse to conjecture'.

33 *A Letter to the Right Honourable Sir Thomas Chitty ... by an English Merchant of London* (London, 1763), pp. 42, 60 (quote); *Monthly Review*, XXXV (1766), p. 440, where Thomas Bentley, the famous partner of Josiah Wedgwood, argued, 'the subject of commerce ... is far from being so well and universally understood'.

34 For a more detailed discussion, see Kim, 'In search of "Affectionate Regard"'.

application [is of] the most partial nature, from some gentlemen of the port of London only, without the Planter abroad ... and without the merchants at Bristol, Liverpool, Hull & other outports, having ever been apprised of such an application'.[35] Similar sensitivity was revealed in a petition of merchants trading to New England concerning a bounty of 40 shillings per ton for the Greenland and Davis Straight whale fisheries. The merchants argued, 'it cannot be the design of Parliament, to grant a bounty to one part of his majesty's subjects; in order to encourage the importing of oyl and whale finn and to discourage another part of them by laying a duty upon the same materials'.[36]

Equally persistent was the claim that mercantile contributions to the national economy should not be disregarded simply for the sake of the fiscal, administrative or political needs of the state. In early 1771, a request of London merchants for speedy grant of bounties on American timber was turned down by the Customs as its commissioners believed it would not only cause the larger importation of timber but also take up too much of its administrative resources. To these objections, the merchants responded by claiming that the increased import of American timber would cause the proportional growth of British manufactures. The value of timber imported, they pointed out, had already amounted to no less than £99,000 a year and it would increase many times in the next few years. Considering the commercial value of this trade, the merchants concluded, it should be regarded as 'an Object of National Concern', and 'the Difficulties attending the Survey of Staves are by no means such as ought to conterballance [sic] the commercial Advantages which will arise from their Importation and which only can be effected by the Bounty proposed'.[37]

It was of course common for merchants to emphasize the commercial value of their particular trade and hence its contribution to the nation's wealth. This strategy was indeed used consistently throughout the imperial crisis by the American traders.[38] What should be noted here is that, by stressing the

---

35 The letter of McCulloch to the Board, 14 April 1769, CO 388/56, fol. 88.

36 The petition was originally submitted to the Treasury, and deliberated at the Board of Trade in January 1764. See CO 388/51 (not paginated).

37 The original memorial of the merchants to the Treasury, was read on 23 January 1771 (CO 323/27, fol. 30); the Treasury forwarded the Customs report with the memorial to the Board of Trade on 16 February 1771 (ibid., fols 31, 33–4); the answers of the merchant were received and read on 1 March 1771 (ibid., fol. 35). The Board eventually found the answers 'full and satisfactory' (1 March 1771, CO 324/18, fol. 184).

38 The best example is probably Barlow Trecothick's testimony at the House of Commons hearing for the repeal of the Stamp Act, where he offered an impressive array of statistical figures illustrating the value of Britain's trade with the American colonies – Simmons and Thomas (eds), *Proceedings and Debates*, vol. 2, pp. 185–93. For similar examples, see CO 388/52, fols 168–9, with timber merchants claiming the value of import

importance of a particular trade, merchants could make a powerful case that the state should look beyond the immediate needs of state revenue. When the petitioners challenged the alleged administrative difficulties attending the grant of timber bounties, they were in fact questioning whether the Customs was willing to examine their application in the broader context of Britain's economic development. In the same vein, merchants often invoked the original intention and spirit of trade laws against the 'restrictive Construction' of commercial regulation by policy-makers.[39] It was precisely in this spirit that the 24 petitions for the repeal of the Stamp Act were drawn. This would remain an essential element of merchant argument in favour of reconciliation with North America. As a merchant declared at a parliamentary hearing in 1775, the American merchants hoped that Parliament would understand that:

> Her [British imperial] system is commerce; her strength and resources are wholly derived from trade. ... On the firm ground of such authority let enquiry be made, whether we should not remain content with the lot assigned us, which hath raised us so high among the modern nations, where all are in rivalry for manufacture and trade.[40]

These appeals, however, were not always answered in favour of merchants. Indeed, interpretations of the intention and spirit of a particular policy were deeply contested; these issues had to be constantly negotiated between the merchant, the state and the public. In that sense, Smith's attack on the political power of merchants cannot be accepted without qualification. Far from 'holding the state hostage' whenever their own interests clashed with those of the state,[41] merchants had to work hard to invite state intervention for their particular branches of trade. This proved a very difficult task for those trading to North America, as

substitution to be £1,300,000 per year; CO 388/57, fols 135–6, 'Memorial of the Merchants of Hull concerned in the importation & traffic of naval stores, stating Objections to any alteration in the premium on naval stores from America'; *CJ*, vol. 29, p. 527, merchants trading to North America discussing the impact of bounties on rice; *CJ*, vol. 35, p. 71, the petition of the merchants, traders, and others of the city of London, concerned in the commerce of North America, 23 January 1775.

39 The phrase is taken from the memorial of Francis Ingram and four other merchants in Liverpool trading to the coast of Africa, where they argued, 'if this Act [concerning the embargo imposed of exportation of corns] admits of *this restrictive Construction* the African Trade must suffer and those who have provided their Cargoes sustain great Loss' – 4 April 1766, T1/448, fol. 24.

40 *CJ*, vol. 30, p. 462; vol. 35, p. 71; *Evidence Delivered*, p. 59.

41 Quoted from Vivien E. Dietz, 'Before the Age of Capital: Manufacturing Interests and the British State, 1780–1800' (Ph.D. thesis, Princeton University, 1991), p. 14.

their political activities were inevitably entangled with the far more explosive imperial constitutional debates. In the face of the increasingly frequent charge against their pursuit of profit at the expense of national unity, the merchants had to adapt by strictly adhering to their perceived role as information provider for policy-makers and thus separating their economic concerns from political and constitutional issues. Even in these unfavourable circumstances, however, these merchants never failed to remind the state of their entitlement to regular consultation and fair treatment, and of the necessity on the part of the political elites to acquire a fuller understanding of commercial affairs.

The Atlantic imperial crisis, then, did not mark a significant turning point in the relationship between the merchant, the state and the public. While struggling to come to terms with many difficulties caused by the crisis, merchants still demonstrated their trust in the virtues of Britain's political system. This was inevitable, as they knew from their experience that they needed the state as both the protector and mediator of diverse commercial interests. From the perspective of the state and the public, the economic contributions of merchants and their knowledge of commercial affairs were too valuable to dismiss. It was perhaps because of this profound mutual understanding that the unreformed political system continued to operate during and after the American crisis. It is true that some merchant and manufacturing interests played with new forms of national lobbies to achieve a more effective system of economic regulation and commercial policy, but these efforts did not lead to a fundamental questioning of the political system itself.[42] Instead, attention was still given to the question of how best to utilize the expertise of merchants without compromising the broader interests of the state and the nation, as was testified by a proposal for recruiting retired merchants to the reorganized Board of Trade. That the exact same scheme had been proposed at the creation of the Board in the late seventeenth century should serve as an apt reminder of the problematic, yet still necessary, connection between the merchant and the state in the long eighteenth century.[43]

42 Dietz, 'Before the Age of Capital', pp. 94–196; O'Shaughnessy, 'The Formation of a Commercial Lobby'.

43 *The First Measures Necessary to be Taken in the American Department* (London,1768), pp. i–iii, 4, 9, 21–2. The earlier proposal had been given in Francis Brewster, *Essays on Trade and Navigation* (London, 1695), pp. 37–40, cited in Gauci, *Politics of Trade*, p. 186.

Chapter 7

Bounties, the Economy and the State in Britain, 1689–1800

Julian Hoppit

It is well known that almost all expenditure by central government in eighteenth-century Britain was on the military and to repay war debts; little was left to spend elsewhere.[1] Thus O'Brien noted that 'Patrick Colquhoun's [1814] estimates imply that only 0.5 per cent of total public revenues collected during the long reign of George III was devoted to objectives that might nowadays be defined as developmental'.[2] Such figures buttress the view that economic regulation then depended overwhelmingly on prohibitions, obstructions and legal requirements. They are similarly compatible with depictions of 'rent seeking', as well as of a 'reactive state', of the power of particular interests, private and corporate, seeking public authority, but rarely direct funding, for example to reorder estates and form companies.

Yet Adam Smith suggested otherwise in 1776 when he first conceptualized the 'mercantile system' in *The Wealth of Nations*. If unquestionably he saw restraints as crucial to that system, in two chapters he also considered the role of 'drawbacks' and 'bounties', that is payments by the state to traders when certain goods were exported or imported (or, very occasionally, produced), though he also briefly noted the state's capacity to make other *ad hoc* payments. To Smith both were important ways that politicians encouraged certain types of economic activity, though he was clear that they also showed another facet of the utilization of the state's power by merchants and manufacturers for selfish ends. That is, to Smith the state was both reactive and mercantilist, as well as willing to use some public funds for economic ends.

---

1 Patrick K. O'Brien, 'The Political Economy of British Taxation, 1660–1815', *EcHR*, 41/1 (1988): p. 2; John Brewer, *Sinews of Power: War, Money and the English State, 1688–1783* (London, 1989), pp. 39–40; Brian R. Mitchell, *British Historical Statistics* (Cambridge, 1988), pp. 578–80.

2 Patrick K. O'Brien, 'Political Preconditions for the Industrial Revolution', in Patrick K. O'Brien and Roland Quinault (eds), *The Industrial Revolution and British Society* (Cambridge, 1993), p. 228.

If parts of Smith's analysis might be questioned, this chapter establishes that via bounties rather more public funds were used to stimulate economic activity in Britain between 1689 and 1800 than has previously been thought.[3] Hitherto, despite the rich literature on mercantilism, no general survey of bounties has been attempted, though the extent of some particular cases has been made clear: more than £6m was paid out in corn export bounties before 1766; £1.5m on imported naval stores between 1705 and 1775; £2.0m on whaling between 1733 and 1800; and £0.8m on fisheries between 1771 and 1796.[4] Here such studies are put alongside other fragmentary evidence to produce some general estimates of spending on bounties that suggest important differences with regard to time, space and sector. A case study of a short-lived bounty upon domestically produced hemp and flax fleshes out those statistical bones. Some general observations on the nature and significance of bounties are offered in the final part of the chapter, especially that they often had both economic and non-economic objects in view and had a number of structural limitations. There is not space here to provide a full account, simply to point up the main aspects of the topic.

Bounties were usually paid upon the quantity not the value of the goods produced or shipped, most commonly upon exported goods, which in turn were mainly funded from particular customs duties; only rarely were other revenue streams exploited.[5] Another type of payment made at ports, 'drawbacks', the repayment, in whole or in part, of a duty already paid, are not considered here because others have studied them, usually in the context of the vibrant

---

3 For convenience, these are simply termed 'bounties' hereafter, though in fact contemporaries sometimes called them 'allowances' or 'premiums'. Moreover, 'bounties' were also offered to attract soldiers and sailors into the armed forces, or to help them at demobilization and were also paid as pensions or gifts, usually to public servants and their dependents, including the clergy (via both Queen Anne's bounty and other funds). These are not considered here.

4 Arthur H. John, 'English Agricultural Improvement and Grain Exports, 1660–1765', in Donald C. Coleman and Arthur H. John (eds), *Trade, Government and Economy in Pre-industrial England: Essays Presented to F.J. Fisher* (London, 1976), p. 59; Joseph J. Malone, *Pine Trees and Politics: The Naval Stores and Forest Policy in Colonial New England, 1691–1775* (London, 1964), p. 45; Gordon Jackson, *The British Whaling Trade* (London, 1978), p. 264; Anna Gambles, 'Free Trade and State Formation: The Political Economy of Fisheries Policy in Britain and the United Kingdom circa 1780–1850', *Journal of British Studies*, 89/3 (2000): p. 314.

5 In 1799, 91.8 per cent of bounties paid in England and Wales were paid from customs receipts. *Accounts Presented to the House of Commons, Respecting the Public Expenditure of Great Britain, for the Year Ending Fifth of January 1800* (London, 1800), p. 16, reprinted in *Sessional Papers*, vol. 118, p. 264.

Table 7.1 Commodities able to claim bounties and drawbacks (excluding re-exports), 1770

Export bounties	Import bounties	Drawbacks on exciseable goods
Cordage	Hemp and flax*	Candles
Corn	Indigo*	Hides
Fish and flesh	Naval stores*	Lace, thread & fringe
Fisheries, incl. whaling	Portage	Leather manufactures
Gunpowder	Raw silk*	Paper
Linens	Tobacco, damaged	Printed, stained, painted or dyed calicos, linens and stuffs
Sail cloth	Wine, damaged	Salt
Silk, manufactured	Wood	Soap
Sugar, refined		Starch

Note: Bounties limited to plantation goods are marked *.
Source: Samuel Baldwin, *A Survey of the British Customs* (London, 1770), part 2, pp. 19–20.

re-export trade, and because while much larger sums were involved their cost implications to the state were largely neutral.[6] The immediate task is to describe what bounties were available, when they were introduced, how much they were worth and where the money was claimed.

As is well known, external trade regulations were extremely complicated in Britain in this period, making it difficult to identify all bounties. One informed observer in 1757 noted that bounties and drawbacks were not 'so immediately obvious to the officers of customs', not least because 'they are now become very numerous, and in regard to bounties and premiums a very extensive and formidable branch of the business of the customs'.[7] Such guides to duties provide, in fact, useful snapshots of bounties at particular moments, with a particularly clear summary being provided in 1770 (see Table 7.1).

Most bounties were enacted in the first three quarters of the eighteenth century, though often later extended or modified. These included bounties on naval stores in 1705; herring fisheries in 1707 (based on earlier Scottish bounties); sailcloth 1713; fish 1719; manufactured silks 1722; whale fishery 1733; linens 1742; indigo 1748; hemp and flax 1764; and raw silk 1770.[8] In considerable measure this was because of the growth of customs and excise

6 The English customs system paid out an annual average of £1.9m on drawbacks and bounties between 1756 and 1766, 87.7 per cent upon the former. TNA, T1/462/43-4.

7 Henry Saxby, *The British Customs* (London, 1757), p. xiv; on the title page Saxby was accredited to 'the customhouse, London'.

8 Naval stores, 3 and 4 Anne, c. 10; sailcloth, 7 and 8 William III, c. 10; herring fisheries, 5 Anne, c. 29; fish, 5 George I, c. 18; manufactured silks, 8 George I, c. 15; whale fishery, 6

after 1689, not least because duties often produced the revenue utilized, while bounties might be offered up as part of the negotiation between the state and different interests when duties were under consideration.[9] The most notable seventeenth-century bounty was that upon corn, initially in place from 1673–78, but reintroduced remarkably quickly at the Glorious Revolution, being given the royal assent in late April 1689, less than two weeks after the coronation of William and Mary.[10] This was, indeed, the first major economic policy after the Revolution, and, as will be seen, was financially and ideologically the most significant bounty available.

Outlining the cost of these bounties is difficult because no consistent figures appear to have been produced at the time. Crucially, most bounties were paid out of gross customs receipts, subtracted along with administration and other charges to produce net receipts. As such, they are often missing from available statistics of public expenditure, thereby failing to catch the eye of most historians. Thankfully, because bounties often came up for renewal or revision statistics were prepared from time to time as aids to both the executive and legislative branches of government, sufficient indeed to allow some general findings.

Unfortunately, no figures of total expenditure upon bounties have yet been found before 1740, and there remain many gaps in the following 60 years, especially relating to import bounties and Scotland.[11] The figures in Table 7.2 do not, therefore, constitute a consistent time series and are indicative only.

Total bounties paid in England and Wales annually averaged about £74,000 from 1740–42 and £258,000 in 1764–66, but nearly £460,000 in 1786–90 for *Britain*. It is possible to deflate this last figure to allow like to be compared with like. In 1799 Scotland received nearly 17 per cent of bounties paid out in Britain, a share that had almost certainly grown since 1750.[12] Assuming

George II, c. 33; linens, 15 George II, c. 29; indigo, 21 George II, c. 30; hemp and flax, 4 George III, c. 26; raw silk, 9 George III, c. 38.

9 Ralph Davis, 'The Rise of Protection in England, 1689–1786', *EcHR*, 19/2 (1966): pp. 314, 316–17.

10 1 William and Mary, c. 12; *CJ*, vol. 10, p. 103. The standard history remains David G. Barnes, *A History of the English Corn Laws from 1660–1846* (London, 1930).

11 TNA, CUST37/62; CUST24/19, overlap between 1740–50 to provide annual totals paid, by commodity. TNA, T1/462/43-44 provides only annual totals for 1755–66. Annual totals for 1786–90 are in *Report from the Select Committee on Accounts and Other Papers, Relating to the Public Income and Expenditure* (London, 1791), p. 90, in *Reports from the Committees of the House of Commons 1715–1801*, vol. 6 (London, 1782–1802). These are the sources for the following discussion.

12 *An Account of the Amount of Bounties paid in England and Scotland Out of the Public Revenue Between the 5th January 1799 and the 5th January 1800* (London, 1800), p. 16 in *Sessional Papers*, vol. 129, p. 264; Mitchell, *British Historical Statistics*, p. 11.

Table 7.2 Selected annual totals expended on bounties, 1740–89

Year	£	War or Peace	Scope
1740	51,968	War	From customs, England and Wales. May not include naval stores
1750	373,442	Peace	Ditto
1760	231,226	War	From customs, England and Wales
1786	440,419	Peace	From customs system, Britain
1789	434,422	Peace	Ditto

Note: It is possible, though unlikely, that the figures for 1786 and 1789 include other types of bounties, not just trade bounties.
Source: See note 11.

Scotland's share in 1786–90 was 15 per cent, expenditure on bounties in England and Wales then was £391,000. Because inflation set in around 1750, this figure might in turn be deflated, by 20 per cent using O'Brien's indices, to £312,800.[13] In real terms, therefore, total payments on bounties grew at a compound rate of 3.0 per cent from the early 1740s to the late 1780s, though growth was twice as quick in the first compared to the second half of this period. The significance of such growth is aided by considering expenditure on bounties against an appropriate benchmark. Two might be offered, bounties expressed as a percentage of total public civil and military expenditure and customs revenue (see Table 7.3).

Neither of these benchmarks are ideal, but both show that bounties were a minor but growing element in public finances across the half century 1740–90, albeit from a low base. Some sense of the dynamics involved can be gained by considering on what commodities the money was spent.

Detailed figures of the composition of expenditure on bounties is only available from 1740 to 1750, when 85.4 per cent went to corn, 6.4 per cent

Table 7.3 Expenditure on bounties expressed as a percentage of civil and military public expenditure and net customs revenue

Year	Civil and military expenditure	Customs revenue
1740–42	1.4	5.4
1764–66	4.2	10.9
1786–90	7.2	12.1

Sources: Table 7.2 above; Mitchell, *British Historical Statistics*, pp. 576–7, 579–80.

13 Patrick K. O'Brien, 'Agriculture and the Home Market for English Industry, 1660–1820', *EHR*, 100 (1985): pp. 773–800.

Table 7.4 Annual averages of corn bounties paid by 10-year periods

Year	1708–17	1718–27	1728–37	1738–47	1748–57	1758–67	1768–77	1778–87	1778–87
£	58,532	77,168	74,584	100,383	167,578	91,699	12,637	40,508	21,864

Source: 'On the Corn Trade and Corn Laws of Great Britain', *Farmer's Magazine*, 12 (November, 1802): pp. 407–8.

to silks, 3.1 per cent to refined sugars and 5.1 per cent on the rest. Corn's dominance is unsurprising, but it was liable both to short-term fluctuations caused by variable harvests, and structural changes as the nation's population grew from 1750. On the second point, it is well known that corn exports grew about four-fold from 1700 to 1766, reaching a notable peak in 1749–51. After 1766, however, net imports became increasingly the norm.[14] Table 7.4 shows the pattern of payments of corn bounties that resulted, though it hides suspensions of the bounties on many occasions from 1765, especially in the years 1767–73.[15]

Recalling the figures of total bounties paid since 1740 allows the estimates in Table 7.5 to be constructed.

Table 7.5 Total bounties and corn export bounties, 1740–86

Year	**£ total**	**£ corn**	**% corn**
1740	51,968	36,296	69.8
1750	373,442	325,405	87.1
1760	231,226	134,087	58.0
1765	210,137	72,373	34.4
1786	440,419	c. 41,000	9.3

Note: figures for 1740, 1750, 1760 and 1766 are for England and Wales. That for 1786 is probably for Britain, though again it may include non-trade bounties.
Source: totals, note 11; corn bounties TNA, T64/274/67, except for 1786, estimated from Table 7.4.

In the 1740s corn generated 90 per cent of the increase of total spending on bounties. But in the next four decades corn bounties fell substantially, off-setting increases that must have been experienced by other bounties – which of course were growing in number. Moreover, just as bounties on the corn trade were on the wane, accounting for only 5 per cent of all bounties paid by 1790, American

14 *PP*, 1826–7 (XVI), pp. 487–8; John, 'English Agricultural Improvement'; David Ormrod, *English Grain Exports and the Structure of Agrarian Capitalism, 1700–1760* (Hull, 1985).

15 Barnes, *Corn Laws*, pp. 38–45.

independence must also have largely ended a number of import bounties, especially naval stores, raw silk, indigo, hemp and flax. Consequently, the general rise in bounties paid after around 1760 must lie elsewhere. But quite which other commodities became more bountiful is far from clear because records are sparse. There appear, however, to have been at least three areas of growth: linen, whaling and refined sugar.

Bounties upon the export of British and Irish linens from Britain were enacted in 1742 and soon judged to have 'greatly increased' output, Harte concluding that 'between about 1740 and 1790 the English linen industry enjoyed a flowering'.[16] A total of nearly £500,000 was spent on these bounties by 1771, though figures for the rest of the century have not been found. In 1750 they were worth a little over £8,000 annually and in 1770 nearly £37,000. Given the stable levels of total linens exported from Britain between 1770 and 1790 the bounties paid probably did not rise. But in the final decade, linen exports tripled, meaning that bounties may now have been worth £95,000 annually.[17] A second area of growth of bounties between 1766 and 1790 was in whaling, the annual average paid to the Greenland whaling rising from £17,573 in 1750–76 to £50,855 in 1787–92 despite a reduction in the rate of the bounty by 25 per cent between the two periods.[18] But figures for linen and whaling bounties were dwarfed by those for refined sugars, which were worth £216,660 in 1798 (up from an average of only £4,500 in the 1740s), though Smith thought, not altogether convincingly given the importance of the processing stage, that the bounty 'may be considered as a drawback of the duties upon the [imported] brown and muscovado sugars from which it is made'.[19]

The final stage of this statistical overview considers which parts of Britain experienced bounties, something that was bound to be significant because bounties were available on only a restricted range of goods, often produced or traded in certain regions only and were usually paid at ports. As before, the

---

16 BL, Add. Mss 35,910, fol. 5v. Negley B. Harte, 'The Rise of Protection and the English Linen Trade, 1690–1790', in Negley B. Harte and Kenneth G. Ponting (eds), *Textile History and Economic History: Essays in Honour of Miss Julia de Lacy Mann* (Manchester, 1973), p. 108.

17 *Report from the Committee Appointed to Enquire into the Present State of the Linen Trade, in Great Britain and Ireland* (London, 1773), p. 46, in *Sessional Papers*, vol. 25, p. 436; Elizabeth B. Schumpeter, *English Overseas Trade Statistics, 1697–1808* (Oxford, 1960), pp. 31–3.

18 Jackson, *Whaling*, p. 264.

19 *An Account of the Quantity of British-Plantation Sugar and Rum Imported into and Exported from Great Britain* (London, 1799), in *Sessional Papers*, vol. 121, p. 291; TNA, CUST37/62; Adam Smith, *An Inquiry into the Nature and Causes of the Wealth of Nations*, ed. E. Cannan (Chicago, IL, 1976), part 2, p. 29.

Table 7.6 Total English and Scottish corn exports, 1707–66 (quarters)

	Barley	Malt	Oatmeal	Rye	Wheat and flour	Total
England	2,296,051	12,975,842	126,979	2,177,372	13,684,107	31,260,351
Scotland	155,264	495,854	383,095	16,093	108,595	1,158,901
Total	2,451,315	13,471,696	510,074	2,193,465	13,792,702	32,419,252
% Scotland	6.3	3.7	75.1	0.7	0.8	3.6

Source: TNA, T64/274/66, 68.

Corn Laws provide the obvious starting point, the main direct beneficiaries of which were the merchants shipping corn out of the arable areas of southern and eastern England. In 1752 11 ports there accounted for 84 per cent of the corn bounties.[20] There was also a national dimension to this because the corn laws favoured some types of grain more than others. Thus though they were available to the Scots from 1707, they were much less heavily involved in the corn trade than the English, as Table 7.6 shows.

Measured in crude volume terms, Scotland's share of corn exports was very small, being significant only in oatmeal, a crop not much exported; by volume, English wheat exports were 36 times larger than those of Scottish oatmeal between the Union and 1766. Nonetheless, as Whatley has emphasized, bounties were one of the issues keenly considered at the Union in 1707. Recognizing that Scottish agriculture was unlikely to produce much surplus wheat, the corn bounties were extended to include oatmeal for the first time in the first session of the Union Parliament.[21] But because Scottish exports of oatmeal were never large, the bounties reaped must have been modest in terms of the whole. By one report, bounties paid in Scotland on exported oatmeal totalled only £5,583 between 1746 and 1753, albeit about twice the amount paid in the same period in England.[22]

If the Corn Laws did not loom large in Scottish experience of bounties, three certainly did, much preoccupying the Convention of the Royal Burghs from at least mid-century. Most was paid out to fisheries, then to whaling and linens (though linens also received significant amounts of non-bounty subsidies). Each will be briefly considered.

---

20 TNA, CUST24/19.

21 In an act passed soon after the Union: 5 Anne, c. 29, § 10. Christopher A. Whatley, 'Salt, Coal and the Union of 1707: A Revision Article', *Scottish Historical Review*, 66/1 (1987): pp. 26–45.

22 BL, Add Mss. 35,906, fols 41–2; TNA, T64/274/67. Over 98 per cent of Scottish oatmeal bounties were paid at Edinburgh.

The same act at the Union which extended the Corn Laws to include oatmeal, also brought England and Wales into line with Scottish encouragement for the herring fisheries – Scotland already had a bounty, which in the year before Union cost £28,452.[23] Bob Harris and Anna Gambles have both powerfully argued the need to view fisheries policies in relation to patriotic and national as well as economic and political themes.[24] What might be added here is a little statistical detail and context, though evidence from the first half of the eighteenth century has not been found. By one probably incomplete report, a little over £600,000 was paid out in bounties to support the herring and cod fisheries between 1751 and 1782, a clear majority upon Scotland.[25] By another comprehensive and consistently compiled report, just over £1.0m was provided in bounties to British herring fisheries between 1765 and 1797, with 62.6 per cent being paid out in Scotland.

As the final row of Table 7.7 shows, Scotland's share of British herring fisheries bounties rose significantly in the second half of the eighteenth century to very nearly 70 per cent, giving weight to Gambles's observation that 'British fisheries legislation seems to have privileged Ireland and Scotland through what amounted to regional fiscal subsidies'.[26]

A bounty on whaling was introduced in Britain in 1733. None, however, was claimed in Scotland until 1750, when the bounty was doubled, its effects there being 'quite dramatic'.[27] By 1760 about £8,000 was being claimed there annually, certainly more than being claimed for corn, but significantly less than for the fisheries. Nonetheless, in November 1766 a petition to the Convention of the Royal Burghs from Scottish Greenland whalers urged a renewal of bounties thereon for a trade asserted to be of 'the greatest advantage to Britain in general'

---

[23] 5 Anne, c. 29, § 6; Edward Hughes, *Studies in Administration and Finance, 1558–1825: With Special Reference to the History of Salt Taxation in England* (Manchester, 1934), p. 243.

[24] Bob Harris, 'Scotland's Herring Fisheries and the Prosperity of the Nation, c. 1660–1760', *Scottish Historical Review*, 79/1 (2000): pp. 39–60; Bob Harris, 'Patriotic Commerce and National Revival: The Free British Fishery Society and British Politics, c. 1749–58', *EHR*, 104 (1999): pp. 285–313; Gambles, 'Fisheries Policy'; also James R. Coull, 'Fishery Development in Scotland in the Eighteenth Century', *Scottish Economic and Social History*, 21/1 (2001): pp. 1–21.

[25] *Third Report from the Committee Appointed to Enquire into the State of the British Fisheries, and into the Most Effectual Means for their Improvement and Extension* (London, 1785), appendices 3–4 in *Sessional Papers*, vol. 53, pp. 171–3.

[26] Gambles, 'Fisheries Policy', p. 292.

[27] Gordon Jackson, 'Government Bounties and the Establishment of the Scottish Whaling Trade, 1750–1800', in John Butt and John T. Ward (eds), *Scottish Themes: Essays in Honour of Professor S.G.E. Lythe* (Edinburgh, 1976), p. 50.

Table 7.7 Bounties spent upon British herring fisheries, 1765–96 (£)

	1765–70	1770–86	1787–96	Totals
England	151,310	151,104	85,168	387,582
Per annum	16,812	9,444	8,517	12,112
Scotland	172,545	277,682	197,710	647,937
Per annum	19,172	17,355	27,768	20,248
Total	323,855	428,786	282,878	1,035,519
Per annum	35,984	26,799	28,288	32,360
% England	46.7	35.2	30.1	37.4
% Scotland	53.3	64.8	69.9	62.6

Note: periods taken from original report; there is insufficient information to change them.
Source: *Report Respecting the British Fisheries* (London, 1798), pp. 218–25, in *Sessional Papers*, vol. 118, pp. 506–13.

and 'to those petitioners in particular'.[28] In fact, Scottish whalers received £304,187 in bounties on this trade in the second half of the eighteenth century, some 15.6 per cent of total British whaling bounties of £1.96m. This was slightly disproportionate to Scotland's 13.3 per cent share of the tonnage of shipping clearing for that trade, and of course much larger than Scotland's share of British trade and customs receipts.[29] Much of the bounty went to Scottish east coast ports, stimulating their economies.[30]

Finally, note needs to be made of the impact of linen bounties upon Scotland. Linen was certainly a favoured product there. The Board of Trustees for Fisheries and Manufactures, instituted in 1727, spent £236,000 on Scotland's linen industry before 1815.[31] Additionally, bounties on linen exports were available from 1743; by 1748 some £14,540 was dispersed in Britain, 40 per cent of it in Scotland.[32] Scotland's linen industry prospered under these stimulants, its output doubling every 20 years from 1730 to 1800,

28 *Extracts from the Records of the Convention of the Royal Burghs of Scotland, 1759–79* (Edinburgh, 1918), pp. 220–21.

29 TNA, BT6/230, fol. 76; *An Account of the Number of Ships Which Have Been Employed in the Whale Fishery, to Davis's Streights, and the Greenland Seas* (London, 1785), in *Sessional Papers*, vol. 53, pp. 509–11; Jackson, *Whaling*, p. 265.

30 Jackson, 'Government Bounties', p. 61.

31 *States of the Annual Progress of the Linen Manufacture, 1727–1754*, ed. R.H. Campbell (Edinburgh, 1964), pp. v–vii, 141; Alastair J. Durie, *The Scottish Linen Industry in the Eighteenth Century* (Edinburgh, 1979), p. 29; Henry Hamilton, *The Industrial Revolution in Scotland* (Oxford, 1932), ch. 4.

32 *CJ*, vol. 25, pp. 719, 749.

and its share of British linen output fluctuating about a rising trend to 31 per cent in 1790.[33] Perhaps £240,000 was provided for the export from England and Wales of British linen between 1743 and 1771. If this was 70 per cent of the British total, then Scotland may have received £100,000, or about £3,400 per annum.[34]

The foregoing discussion has hurriedly sketched an overview of bounties, the commodities involved, the absolute and relative levels of expenditure involved as well as the inevitable regional patterns of payments. Why and how bounties were created and implemented has not been considered. Initially this is done by looking at the specific case of bounties for hemp and flax, before discussion is widened out in the conclusion.

Hemp and flax, whether as raw materials or semi-processed ('dressed'), had long been judged to be of national importance, the cordage industry in relation to Britain's naval power, including fishing nets, while a strong domestic linen industry would reduce imports and create substantial employment. A bill to encourage hemp and flax growing was considered at Westminster in 1662, but failed. Further similar efforts in the seventeenth century also came to nothing, though duties on imported linen, initially to raise revenue, then to be prohibitory, encouraged the development of the British and Irish linen industries.[35] As has been seen, in Scotland state aid helped in this, something that was also the case in Ireland where £234,000 was expended by the publicly funded Linen Board between 1711 and 1800.[36] Bounties on the export of certain types of British and Irish linens from Britain provided encouragement in another way. The growth of the shipbuilding industries in Britain was no less marked, with the state's active role being concentrated upon the expansion of the Royal Navy and the naval stores bounties. Developments in the linen and cordage industries depended upon adequate supplies of hemp and flax and while there was considerable production in Ireland, there was much less in England

---

33 Mitchell, *British Historical Statistics*, p. 352; Harte, 'English Linen Trade', p. 104; Alastair J. Durie, *The British Linen Company, 1745–1775* (Edinburgh, 1996), pp. 1–5.

34 These estimates contain some assumptions which may prove unwarranted. *Report From the Committee Appointed to Enquire into the Present State of the Linen Trade, in Great Britain and Ireland* (London, 1773), p. 46, in *Sessional Papers*, vol. 25, p. 436.

35 Joan Thirsk, 'Agricultural Policy: Public Debate and Legislation', in Joan Thirsk (ed.), *The Agrarian History of England and Wales, V, 1640–1750: II, Agrarian Change* (Cambridge, 1985), pp. 339–41.

36 Conrad Gill, *The Rise of the Irish Linen Industry* (Oxford, 1925), ch. 4; Thomas J. Kiernan, *History of the Financial Administration of Ireland to 1817* (London, 1930), pp. 165–79.

and Scotland and imports from overseas began to grow in the 1740s, leading to calls for the need for more domestic production.[37]

In Scotland the Board of Trustees had sought to address this by providing premiums upon domestically produced flax, paid according to the acreage sown. But in 1749 the scheme was abandoned because the costs became unbearable, not least because of strong suspicions of widespread fraud.[38] For a while the market was left to its own devices, but in 1764, at the behest of American trading interests, a bounty was instituted for 21 years on imported hemp and flax from Britain's American colonies.[39] Probably the initial bounty provided insufficient inducement, while it was quickly thrown into doubt by deteriorating relations between Britain and the American colonies. Only £5,560 in total was claimed on the bounty between 1766 and 1772.[40] Parliament quickly responded by passing in 1767 an act to establish a fund of £15,000 per annum to encourage British growing and processing of hemp and flax, to be paid for by increased duties on certain foreign imported cambrics and lawns.[41] This was an important development, not least because the funds were to be made available across Britain and led the state to attempt a new mode of economic support in England and Wales, though it eventually petered out in the 1790s. Why, then, was the fund instituted?

The first sight in Parliament of the idea of statutory support for domestic hemp and flax production is a petition submitted to the Commons on 31 January 1767 from the gentlemen, clergy, freeholders, growers and dealers in hemp and flax of parts of Lincolnshire. Their concern was not that American supplies might be unreliable but rather the opposite, that plentiful cheap supplies would render their own efforts uncompetitive, arguing that because Americans 'pay nothing for their lands' they needed no bounty. The petition was ordered to lie on the table, but seemingly out of the blue at the start of May it was referred to the Commons' main committee dealing with public revenue. Three days later the Commons received a second petition about supplies of hemp and flax, from Scotland's Convention of the Royal Burghs, arguing that importing raw materials from Europe cost the nation £1m annually and made it dependent

---

37 Schumpeter, *English Overseas Trade Statistics*, table xvi; Durie, *Scottish Linen Industry*, p. 35; William Ellis, *The Modern Husbandman, or the Practice of Farming* (4 vols, London, 1744), vol. 3, pp. 93–5.

38 Durie, *Scottish Linen Industry*, p. 69.

39 4 George III, c. 26; Peter D.G. Thomas, *British Politics and the Stamp Act Crisis: The First Phase of the American Revolution, 1763–1767* (Oxford, 1975), p. 67.

40 'Parliamentary Diaries of Nathaniel Ryder', ed. P.D.G. Thomas, *Camden Miscellany, 23*, *Camden*, 4th series, 7 (1969): pp. 295, 298; *St James's Chronicle*, 12 December 1775, p. 1.

41 7 George III, c. 58.

on foreign powers. Only a week later a bill was introduced by the Chairman of the Committee of Ways and Means to establish a fund to encourage domestic hemp and flax production. Ten petitions against this proposal came into the Commons over the following month, from London, Bristol, Exeter, Norwich, Northamptonshire, Kidderminster, Tiverton, Wakefield, and Halifax and Bradford, arguing that the new duties would raise their raw material costs – no comment was passed on the fund. But the bill passed in the Commons, though there was a division (28:39) on one amendment, and sailed through the Lords.[42]

As the record in the *Journals* hints, if notionally a governmental measure, the act arose from considerable non-governmental preparation.[43] Mostly this was in Scotland, particularly in the Convention of the Royal Burghs and the Board of Trustees. The Board had recently received a report from Lord Kames, one of its members, on the need to improve domestic flax production. On the orders of the trustees this report was published anonymously in 1766, its arguments then being employed by the Convention in pursuit of statutory funding of a bounty.[44]

The Convention took up the issue when presented with a petition in July 1766 from the Edinburgh Linen Society suggesting an application to Parliament for a bounty on the culture of flax and hemp in Great Britain. The Convention consulted various Scottish counties and burghs in preparing a memorial, which was printed and distributed to the royal burghs, 'requiring them in the name of the convention to instruct their respective representatives to do all in their power to support the burrows' application to parliament for obtaining a parliamentary encouragement to promote the culture of flax & hemp in Great Britain'.[45] The memorial noted the importance of linen both in its own right, and to the wool, cotton, sailcloth and cordage industries. It claimed that imported raw materials would be more expensive than those domestically produced, and that foreign sources were inherently 'uncertain and precarious'. Not only might war interrupt supplies, but perhaps Russia, Holland and other nations might in the future bar exports in line with the 'maxim of conduct firmly established amongst all commercial states to discourage the exportation of the materials

42 *CJ*, vol. 31, pp. 98, 334, 337, 345, 352, 368–9, 379, 385, 390, 398, 402, 403, 417.

43 There was nothing new in this. For some similar earlier activities see Trevor Griffiths, Philip Hunt and Patrick K. O'Brien, 'Scottish, Irish, and Imperial Connections: Parliament, the Three Kingdoms, and the Mechanization of Cotton Spinning in Eighteenth-Century Britain', *EcHR*, 61/3 (2008): pp. 625–50.

44 [Henry Home, Lord Kames], *Progress of Flax-Husbandry in Scotland* (Edinburgh, [1766]).

45 *Records of the Convention of the Royal Burghs*, pp. 186, 205–8 (quote at 208).

for carrying on any manufacture in their rude state'. The costs to Britain of these raw material imports were put at £1.3m per annum, saving which would advantage all, 'the labourer, the tenant, and the landholder'. Arguments were advanced as to why American supplies were unlikely to meet British needs adequately and of the practicability of extending hemp and flax cultivation in Britain. A bounty was 'no doubt the most effectual method that can be devised' to achieve the desired end.[46]

Meanwhile, the Edinburgh Linen Society had sent two representatives into England 'with a view to interest the manufacturers and others concern'd to join the application from this country', a move endorsed by the Convention. Probably they made a connection with the interests in Lincolnshire that presented the first petition to Parliament in 1767. Joseph Gee of Lincolnshire wrote a number of works at the time about hemp, flax and linens, noting in 1766 the moves afoot in Scotland and in April 1767 issuing a broadsheet abstract of reasons for the legislation then under consideration.[47] To mobilize support, the Convention wrote to some English towns, to MPs and to Townshend, the Chancellor of the Exchequer – the Board of Trustees separately wrote to members of the ministry and Scottish parliamentarians. The Convention's London agent was instructed to wait on Townshend, presumably to discuss the proposal, and to present their petition to Parliament. Their letter to him developed some additional lines of thought, not least the potential cost of a bounty, judging that one proposal would involve expenditure of £120,000 annually, 'a sum which it's thought the parliament would not chuse to grant towards promoting any one species of manufacture however usefull and important'.[48] But they thought that Parliament might agree to an annual charge of £45,000, two-thirds to England (Wales was ignored or subsumed within England), one third to Scotland. In Scotland the sum might be dispersed by a newly instituted board. No mention was made as to how the sum might be administered in England. Funding was proposed to come from an additional duty on German and Russian linens.[49]

---

46 'Memorial with Respect to the State of the Linen and Hempen Manufactures in Great Britain', 27 October 1766: *Records of the Convention of the Royal Burghs*, pp. 209–19.

47 Joseph Gee, *Considerations on the Expediency of a Bounty upon Hemp and Flax of Home Growth* ([London, 1766]), p. 1. This is dated 24 October 1766 from Gainsborough, Lincs. Gee had earlier complained that Ireland had passed many laws to support its linen industry, but this was inequitable because Ireland did not 'bear a proportionably equal share ... of the Publick Expence'. Joseph Gee, *Observations on the Growth of Hemp and Flax in Great Britain* (1765), p. 4. Joseph Gee, *An Abstract of Reasons for Encouraging the Linen Manufactory* ([London, 1767]).

48 *Records of the Convention of the Royal Burghs*, pp. 221–38, quote at 231.

49 *Records of the Convention of the Royal Burghs*, pp. 229–33.

In fact, the act established a much smaller fund of £15,000 per annum and made no provision for its administration. Even so, the Convention thanked those parliamentarians who had supported the bill, and Townshend at length for an act 'so necessary for securing the independency of the British navy, as well as rendering the linen manufactory permanent', though his death in September 1767 may have disrupted preparations of ways to distribute the fund.[50] Certainly nothing appears to have been decided until 1770 when it was agreed to split the fund, £7,000 to go to Scotland via the Board of Trustees, £8,000 to England via means to be decided.[51] Durie has considered what was done in Scotland, with £127,000 being spent between 1773 and 1815, an annual average of nearly £3,000.[52] His view was that 'much better use of the Flax Fund was made in Scotland by the Board ... than was the case south of the Border, where it seems largely to have been frittered away'.[53] Certainly the English fund appear to have been untouched through the 1770s, but then, in the midst of the American war, with the 1764 bounty a dead letter, statutory provision was made for using the fund in England and Wales that led to significant and productive effort.[54] The key points were:

1. £8,000 annually was to be distributed by the Board of Trade;
2. the bounty was 3d a stone for hemp, 4d a stone for flax, both dressed;
3. claims were to be made to a JP, to be forwarded to the next quarter sessions;
4. to counter fraud, two sureties were to be provided of treble the value of the claim;
5. justices were to advertise the bounties at the Michaelmas quarter sessions;
6. names of claimants were to be published by justices;
7. justices were to submit yearly statements to the Board of Trade, who were to arrange payment with the Treasury;
8. the Board of Trade was to prepare annual summaries for Parliament;
9. the scheme was to run for five years from 1 August 1782.

The reasoning behind this scheme seems clear: using an existing local administrative framework would help keep costs down, the state small, and frauds difficult to commit unnoticed. Abolition of the Board of Trade in 1782 required administrative oversight to pass to a Privy Council committee. In

50 *Records of the Convention of the Royal Burghs*, pp. 272–3.

51 10 George III, c. 40.

52 Durie, *Scottish Linen Industry*, p. 29.

53 Durie, *Scottish Linen Industry*, p. 108.

54 21 George III, c. 58.

Table 7.8 Largest county shares of bounties for hemp and flax in England and Wales, 1783–94

County	%
Lincolnshire	20.2
Somerset	16.7
Yorks West Riding	14.0
Yorks East Riding	11.5
Dorset	8.1
Norfolk	6.8
Devon	5.0
Sub-total	83.3

Source: See note 58.

1786 management of the scheme passed to the Treasury and extended down to 1794.[55]

To establish the new system, in December 1781 the Board of Trade wrote to the clerks of the peace in English and Welsh counties, including copies of the act and *Directions for the Raising of Flax*, a 24-page pamphlet authored by the Scottish Board of Trustees, first issued in 1744, with further editions in 1750, 1763 and 1772.[56] In total, 462 copies of the *Directions* were distributed, with most counties sent six, ten or 15 copies, though Lincolnshire received 20 and Yorkshire as a whole 50.[57] These efforts appear to have been successful, the first claims being made at the midsummer quarter sessions in 1783 and payments being agreed in London the following year. Annual summaries for the period 1783–94 are available, with a gap for the 1787 claims.[58] A total of £76,597 was paid out, an annual average of nearly £7,000, with a peak of over £10,000 for the 1790 claims. Claims were submitted from 26 English counties and three Welsh (totalling just £153), but most came from just six counties (see Table 7.8).

Bounties were paid for the production of 451,229 cwt of flax, 164,267 cwt of hemp, respectively perhaps 18.5 per cent and 3.3 per cent of domestic needs.[59]

---

55 26 George III, c. 43.

56 *Directions for Raising Flax ... Re-printed by Order of the Lords Commissioners for Trade and Plantations* (1781). A similar pamphlet was published when the Irish Linen Board was established in 1711: *Directions for the Sowing and Preparing of Flax* (Dublin, 1711).

57 TNA, BT6/99, fols 1–5.

58 Parliamentary Archives, HL/PO/JO/10/7/681, 703, 740, 760, 849, 867, 894, 921, 945, 974, 1006.

59 Using import of flax and hemp data in Schumpeter, *English Overseas Trade Statistics*, pp. 57–8.

Such levels of output were significantly greater than in Scotland. Moreover, if Scotland produced 17 per cent of British flax from 1787 to 1793, it consumed 24 per cent of the monies spent upon flax and hemp bounties.[60] Far from being frittered away, south of the border the money appears to have obtained the intended results for a while, rather more productively indeed than in Scotland.

Though the total numbers of claimants is unknown, in any one year there were certainly many hundreds and at the peak perhaps a few thousand. For example, in 1784 about 200 claimed in Somerset and 340 in the East Riding.[61] Consequently, most of the claims were for small sums, usually a few pounds. Little wonder that the authorities in Somerset quickly observed that the new system 'was a work of much time, and consequently much trouble'.[62] Indeed, the expenses of the clerks of the peace were sometimes questioned at the centre. As the Privy Council committee pointed out to the East Riding, their clerk's expenses could render the bounty 'inadequate to the wise purposes for which it was intended' and reduced the clerk's charge.[63] Administration costs were recorded in the annual surveys from 1786, consuming thereafter nearly 12 per cent of the cost of the scheme.

The 1786 act expired in 1794 and a bill to continue it was introduced the following year by George Rose, Pitt's right-hand man, and passed through the Commons. But it was rejected in the Lords, probably because in the same session an act to ease the importation of flax was passed.[64] Two broad factors were likely at work here. The first is suggested by the fact that in England and Wales the highpoint of claims was in 1790, hemp and flax production falling by 49 per cent between then and 1794. For example, in the Lindsey part of Lincolnshire 507 claimed the bounty for the 1790 crop, but only 205 for 1794.[65] This implies that farmers responded positively to the advent of the bounty, but soon decided that other crops were more profitable to cultivate and/or that claiming the bounty was more trouble than it was worth. Ultimately the bounty was a relatively minor factor alongside broader market forces.[66] Second, while the bounty was attractive to many farmers, they mostly produced on a small scale, either because

60 Durie, *Scottish Linen Industry*, p. 107.

61 TNA, PC1/16/11, fols 3–6, 12–17, 38.

62 TNA, PC1/16/11, fol. 1v. Somerset's claims were the highest of all counties for 1783, but none appear in the summaries for the following two years.

63 TNA, PC/1/16/25, fol. 22r. See also fols 24–5 for similar letters to Sussex and Dorset. For the reduction, BT6/99, fol. 17 – second foliation.

64 The Lords rejected the bill on 26 June 1795: *LJ*, vol. 40, p. 509; 36 George III, c. 4.

65 Lincolnshire Archives Office, LQS B/7/2-8.

66 David Grigg, *The Agricultural Revolution in South Lincolnshire* (Cambridge, 1966), p. 77.

they were unwilling to turn over more of their land to these crops or because their farms were small – the bounty may well have been particularly attractive to smallholders.[67] Because each claim was subject to some fixed administrative costs, particularly to guard against fraud, overheads took up more of the fund than was usual or, probably, as was politically acceptable. Given these factors, with the scheme reaching the end of its life at the start of a major war, legislators may well have reasoned that it was better for Britain to produce food and depend upon imported flax and hemp. The future was left to the market.

The case of hemp and flax supplies brings out clearly a number of features common to trade bounties in eighteenth-century Britain. By way of a conclusion these can be briefly considered under four headings: the reasons why bounties were used; how they were enacted; what their effects were; and what reactions they elicited.

Bounties were rarely merely economic in aim, often also serving military and political purposes. As has been seen, it was believed that improving hemp and flax supplies would simultaneously aid Britain's economic and military might, a point that was shared with a number of other bounties, such as naval stores, while fisheries and whaling helped ensure adequate supplies of sailors and shipwrights. Nor were political objectives insignificant. As has been seen, bounties were a means by which central government sought to strengthen its links to particular parts of Britain or her empire, including Ireland, as well as to specific interests. For example, the Corn Law of 1673 was in part justified in terms of making a new tax palatable to landowners upon whom it 'principally lyeth' and though it is unclear why it was revived in 1689 it seems likely that the new and vulnerable regime was looking to buy support from vital English landed and commercial interests.[68]

Economic reasons for bounties were of course especially powerful. Often they were aimed at new or vulnerable areas of the economy, effectively aiming to lower entry costs or risks.[69] Some also sought to develop a division of labour between the economies of Britain and her colonies as 'primarily militaristic conceptions of empire gradually gave way to commercial ones'.[70] Often this was associated with a desire to increase self-sufficiency by reducing dependence upon

---

67 Joan Thirsk, *English Peasant Farming: The Agrarian History of Lincolnshire from Tudor to Recent Times* (London, 1957), pp. 41, 77, 137.

68 25 Charles II, c. 7, § 31.

69 Jacob Viner considered the 'infant industry problem' as part of one of the few overviews of bounties in eighteenth-century Britain: *Studies in the Theory of International Trade* (New York and London, 1937), pp. 69–72.

70 Nancy F. Koehn, *The Power of Commerce: Economy and Governance in the First British Empire* (Ithaca, NY and London, 1994), p. 65.

European sources of supply, especially those that were vulnerable to the closure of the Baltic Sound. This might be framed in terms of import substitution and balance of trade. Some bounties were aimed more clearly at the internal economy, especially those relating to cordage, linens, silk, hemp and flax. Job creation and the hope of exports were powerful motives here.[71] Additionally, price stabilization appears to have been one factor behind the Corn Law of 1689, the preamble asserting that exporting corn when the domestic price was low 'hath been a great Advantage, not only to the Owners of Land, but to the Trade of this Kingdom in general'.[72] The variability of harvests because of the weather was a risk not only to farmers and landlords, but also to corn merchants to whom, Josiah Tucker asserted, it 'is a kind of Lottery, in wch there are a few Prizes & many Blanks'.[73]

Because bounties involved public revenues, proposals for them either emanated within the executive or required support there. Thus, for example, the bill for the naval stores act of 1705 was introduced by William Blathwayt, a member of the Board of Trade, while in 1722 the bill for the bounty on silk was introduced and carried from the Commons to the Lords by Walpole.[74] But many bounties were promoted outside of central government, as the establishment of the hemp and flax fund in 1767 showed. Colonial interests were behind both the earlier import bounty on those materials, as well as the indigo bounty enacted in 1748.[75] In 1742 the Commons asked for several accounts relating to the linen trade, but the fact that this request was soon followed by 16 petitions, most from Scotland, suggest that the initiative was largely non-governmental.[76] But such proposals depended upon obtaining adequate support in Westminster and Whitehall. One striking point is that the total number of bounties was not very large, but that there were few attempts which made it into Parliament only to fail.[77] The implication is that interests considering a bounty knew that they had to obtaining backing from ministers or departments such as the Treasury

---

71 See for example the arguments in 'Observations of London Merchants on American trade, 1783', *American Historical Review*, 18/4 (1913): p. 779.

72 1 William and Mary, c. 12, § 1.

73 HMC, *Eleventh Report, Appendix, Part IV. The Manuscripts of the Marquess of Townshend* (1887), p. 372.

74 *CJ*, vol. 15, p. 490; vol. 20, pp. 710, 741.

75 C. Robert Haywood, 'Mercantilism and South Carolina Agriculture, 1700–1763', *South Carolina Historical Magazine*, 60/1 (1959): pp. 18–20.

76 *CJ*, vol. 24, pp. 182, 189, 190, 193, 194, 212.

77 Julian Hoppit, ed. *Failed Legislation, 1660–1800: Extracted from the Commons and Lords Journals* (1997), items 85.023, 87.015, 90.005, 90.020, 97.015, 103.017, 143.011 – only the last of which relates to a new bounty.

or Board of Trade, which appears to have been made by private application rather than public petitioning and pamphleteering. If such support was not forthcoming the proposal did not proceed any further. To the executive, bounties might provide a valuable bargaining chip in negotiation with powerful interests. Often enough, 'What one Clause gives in Bounties, other Clauses take away in Duties, Excises, and expensive obligatory Conditions'.[78] This chapter has tended to consider bounties in isolation, but in practice they were part of dense networks of duties and regulations.

Judging the success or not of bounties is not straightforward. At one level the considerable sums expended indicate some success. But, the uptake on some bounties was modest, usually because they offered relatively slight aid in relation to market forces. Thus they did not enable Britain to be consistently self-sufficient in corn after population began to rise significantly from 1750, while the indigo bounty of 1748 probably offered limited help to South Carolina producers, relative price swings between it and rice being more important.[79] Further, bounties on imports of products from colonial America were rendered more or less meaningless from 1775. A further weakness was the potential for fraud that bounties offered – particularly of re-landing goods on which bounties had already been paid and adulteration of one sort or another.

Bounties were also liable to a self-generating problem, whereby their aim to stimulate certain activities might succeed sufficiently to generate unbearable calls on the public purse, a problem first manifested in the Corn Laws. In 1748, the cost of the corn bounty exceeded £200,000 for the first time and two years later £300,000. Payment systems came under enormous strain, with significant arrears accumulating. This threatened not just the well being of corn merchants, as in some ports and their hinterlands bounty payments had become important parts of circuits of credit.[80] In the 1760s the same problem happened with the herring fisheries bounties in Scotland which were 'thunder-struck' as a consequence.[81]

Such problems first generated public debate over bounties, for until then they had only been discussed occasionally. The strain on the massive corn bounty debentures in 1749 and 1750, pointing up total costs involved, was the immediate context of Townshend's attack on corn bounties in 1751, initiating a dispute that was to rage for a century. In part the debate's importance was confirmed by the timing of Adam Smith's intervention, coming just three years after the corn

78 *Third Report from the Committee Appointed to Enquire into the State of the British Fisheries* (London, 1786), p. 97 in *Sessional Papers*, vol. 53, p. 139.

79 Robert C. Nash, 'South Carolina Indigo, European Textiles, and the British Atlantic Economy in the Eighteenth Century', *EcHR*, 63/2 (2010): pp. 363, 375–6.

80 Barnes, *Corn Laws*, pp. 23–4; TNA, T1/351/47, 49, 59.

81 *Third Report of the British Fisheries*, pp. 81, 232 in *Sessional Papers*, vol. 53, p. 123.

laws had been settled on a new basis through acts passed from 1770 to 1773.[82] To Smith the new 'system ... [was] in many respects better than the ancient one, but in one or two respects perhaps not quite so good'.[83] There is no space here to detail the issues at stake: they tended to centre on the questions of who actually benefited and who actually paid, of their weight relative to market fundamentals and of unintended consequences, including market distortions and fraud. Too few, however, have noted that Smith himself distinguished between different types of bounties, some of which, especially those motivated by considerations of national defence, were broadly acceptable.

A second major stimulus to debate over bounties came in the 1760s with tensions between Britain and her American colonies. Several bounties had been specifically devised to encourage specialization or complementarities between Britain and her colonies. But if colonies could not be depended upon to play their part then the policy would have to be rethought. One consequence was to bring into focus Britain's economic relations with Ireland. Notably, British interests began to question the Irish Parliament's voting of considerable sums to help its trade and industry, including subsidies to particular individuals and places.[84] Given Ireland fell partly within Britain's trade regulations, benefited from Britain's linen bounties and had lower labour costs, British manufacturers began to argue that Ireland was being unduly favoured. This was clearly noted in 1751, but came to a head in 1785 when Pitt proposed the harmonization of British and Irish trade regulations. Robert Peel was sure that Irish manufacturers enjoyed too many advantages, but Josiah Wedgwood spoke particularly loudly. He thought it inevitable that Ireland would use its public funds to mount an attack upon one of Britain's prime export trades and that Britain was in no position to win 'a Warfare of Bounties' with Ireland.[85] Yet Pitt's measure failed,

---

82 [Charles Townshend], *National Thoughts, Recommended to the Serious Attention of the Public. With an Appendix, Shewing the Damages Arising from a Bounty on Corn* (London, 1751); Richard D. Sheldon, 'Practical Economics in Eighteenth-Century England: Charles Smith on the Grain Trade and the Corn Laws, 1756–72', *Historical Research*, 81 (2008): pp. 636–62. This provides a useful introduction to the nature of the debate between 1750 and 1776. For the new legislation, Barnes, *Corn Laws*, pp. 41–4.

83 Smith, *Wealth of Nations*, part 2, pp. 50–51.

84 Eoin Magennis, 'Coal, Corn and Canals: Parliament and the Dispersal of Public Moneys 1695–1772', *Parliamentary History*, 20/1 (2001): p. 74; Kiernan, *Financial Administration of Ireland to 1817*, pp. 165–79.

85 *Report from the Committee Appointed to Examine ... Several Petitions of the Manufacturers of, and Traders and Dealers in, the Linen Manufactury* (London, 1751), in *Sessional Papers*, vol. 19, pp. 25–44; *Minutes of the Evidence Taken before a Committee of the Whole House of Commons ... to Consider ... the Adjustment of Commercial Intercourse between Great Britain and Ireland* (London, 1785), p. 184 in *Sessional Papers*, vol. 51, p. 185.

not least because of opposition in Ireland; the warfare of bounties was to continue to 1801.[86]

Bounties grew in scope and cost in eighteenth-century Britain, constituting a small but important element of public funding. That they have been rather hidden from view hitherto is due partly to a preoccupation with military spending and the Corn Laws, to the use by historians of figures of net revenue, and to their place within a complex system of duties encouraging a case-by-case approach. Yet if bounties were more important than has usually been appreciated, they were sometimes directed at non-economic ends, particularly in relation to national defence and encouraging connections within Britain and her empire. As such, they were often assessed by political and imperial criteria as well as by general considerations of costs and benefits, helping to explain their survival well into the nineteenth century despite their often limited economic impact.

Vivien E. Dietz, 'Before the Age of Capital: Manufacturing Interests and the British State, 1780–1800' (Ph.D. thesis, Princeton University, 1991), ch. 3; Robert D.C. Black, 'Theory and Policy in Anglo-Irish Trade Relations', *Journal of the Statistical and Social Inquiry Society of Ireland*, 18/3 (1950): pp. 312–26.

[86] David R. Schweitzer, 'The Failure of William Pitt's Irish Trade Propositions 1785', *Parliamentary History*, 3/1 (1984): pp. 129–45; Paul Kelly, 'British and Irish Politics in 1785', *EHR*, 90 (1975): pp. 536–63.

Chapter 8

Investigation as a Prelude to Regulation: Information, Investigation and the Abolition of the Slave Trade

Ian Barrett

The formal political processes through which regulations were decided upon in the eighteenth century have received extensive, but selective treatment. Our knowledge of the constitutional and political contexts surrounding the petitioning process is broad, as is the work done on formal constitutional processes within Parliament.[1] This chapter explores an area of this process which has received comparatively little attention: the role of data collection and investigation.

One of the most striking features of recent historiography has been the problematization of the concept of 'knowledge' in understanding social, cultural and political phenomena. Historians have questioned both the circumstances surrounding the production, transmission and consumption of particular knowledge, and have also rethought the theoretical basis of how we relate knowledge to 'reality' and to political agency. Both these strands of research have yielded insights which have transformed our understanding of political history. However, most of the historiography of social inquiry focuses on the striking development of what Oz Frankel terms 'print statism' in the mid-nineteenth century.[2] The scale of the data collection, the breadth of the public distribution of the reports, and the connection with emerging concepts of a 'science of society' all combined to provide a qualitatively new role for information in the public sphere. Little attention, however, has been paid to

---

1 Joanna Innes, 'Legislation and Public Participation 1760–1830', in David Lemmings (ed.), *The British and Their Laws in the Eighteenth Century* (Woodbridge, 2005); Peter Jupp, *The Governing of Britain, 1688–1848: The Executive, Parliament and the People* (Abingdon, 2006); Roland G. Thorne (ed.), *The History of Parliament: The House of Commons 1790–1820* (4 vols, London, 1986).

2 Oz Frankel, *States of Inquiry: Social Investigations and Print Culture in Nineteenth-Century Britain and the United States* (Baltimore, MD, 2006).

the role of investigation, inquiry and information collection in the period before the emergence of this large-scale 'print statism'.

A key focus here are the various forms of parliamentary inquiry. Parliamentary investigations spanned the whole range of legislation that came before the House. They included social inquiries spurred on by reports of problems such as high prices and acute poverty, examinations of foreign trade and imperial questions, considerations of fiscal and economic issues and the investigation of grievances. They could constitute an attempt to collect evidence prior to legislating, or the assessment of claims and counter-claims after legislation had been introduced and contested. It has been estimated that approximately 10–20 inquiries occurred per session during the period, with the number rising in the wake of the pressing social and economic issues resulting from the end of the Napoleonic wars.[3]

This chapter examines one particular set of parliamentary investigations, those into the regulation and abolition of the slave trade.[4] The objective is to examine the role of investigation in the discursive and structural organization of the political campaigns for and against regulation and abolition. This draws on a historical literature which increasingly questions the neutrality of both the processes through which knowledge is created, and the media through which it is presented. Both create restrictions which affect how that information can be used and translated into different formats.[5]

The Organization of Investigations

William Pitt proposed the first investigation in 1788 after agreeing with Wilberforce to take on measures to abolish the trade in the Commons. Pitt intended to use the investigation to collect evidence with which to attack the trade and pursue the object of abolition.[6] Opponents of abolition would rather the issue had just gone away, but as that was not an option, seemed generally content to have some sort of investigation. The planter Lord Penrhyn

3 Innes, 'Legislation and Public Participation', p. 125.

4 This draws on work undertaken for my Ph.D. thesis, 'Cultures of Pro-slavery: The Political Defence of the Slave Trade, c. 1787 to 1807' (King's College, London, 2009), which was kindly supported by the AHRC and the Scouloudi Foundation.

5 See, for example, Christopher A. Bayly, *Empire and Information: Intelligence Gathering and Social Communication in India, c. 1780–1870* (Cambridge, 1996); Mary Poovey, *A History of the Modern Fact: Problems of Knowledge in the Sciences of Wealth and Society* (Chicago, IL, 1998).

6 John Ehrman, *The Younger Pitt: The Years of Acclaim* (London, 1969), p. 393.

is reported to have said in the Commons on 9 May 1788 that 'The charges against the slave trade were either true or false. If true, the trade ought to be abolished; if false, justice ought to be done to the characters of those who were concerned in it'.[7]

An Order in Council was issued on 11 February 1788 instructing the Board of Trade to consider 'the present State of the African Trade, particularly as far as relates to the Practice and Manner of Purchasing or obtaining Slaves on the Coast of Africa, and the Importation and Sale thereof'. It also instructed the Board to investigate the 'Effects and Consequences of this Trade' in Africa and the West Indies, and on the 'general Commerce of this Kingdom'.[8]

The resulting investigation was led by Lord Hawkesbury, one of the breed of career administrators who had risen in the ranks during the period of Lord North's administration. Hawkesbury had been chairing the Board of Trade since 1786 when it had been revived to consider the issue of economic intercourse between America and the West Indies after the American War. Historians have tended to look favourably on his conduct in leading the investigation. One recent study characterized him as 'hard-working and surprisingly fair' even though he was a 'reliable supporter' of the merchant groups most linked to the slave trade. An older account suggests that he was 'disinterested' and 'objective'.[9]

Objectivity can, of course, be a chimeral concept. Even though Hawkesbury could be said to have been 'objective' in his own terms, and seems to have approached his task disinterestedly, the investigation was structured in such a way as to offer anti-abolitionists significant advantages in terms of controlling both the flow of information and the results of the inquiry. Even if investigations are not deliberately framed so as to reach a particular conclusion, the outcome of such inquiries is inevitably closely linked to three factors – first, the framing of the initial questions for inquiry, and the unspoken assumptions behind those questions; secondly, the methodology used for collecting data; and thirdly the language and format used in presenting the results.

Hawkesbury interpreted the terms of reference broadly. He drew up extensive heads of examination, covering dozens of questions which he proposed

---

7 *Cobbett*, vol. 27, p. 501. Stephen Fuller felt it showed a lack of leadership amongst abolitionists. William Perkins Library, Duke University, Durham, NC, Stephen Fuller Letterbooks, vol. 1 (FF5642), fol. 167, Stephen Fuller to Jamaican Committee of Correspondence [hereafter 'Fuller Letterbooks (Duke)'].

8 BL, Add. Mss 38416 [hereafter 'Liverpool Papers'] fol. 11, 'Order in Council'.

9 Adam Hochschild, *Bury the Chains: Prophets and Rebels in the Fight to Free an Empire's Slaves* (Boston, MA, 2005), p. 153; Dale H. Porter, *The Abolition of the Slave Trade in England, 1784–1807* (Hamden, CT, 1970), pp. 34–44.

be investigated as part of the inquiry.[10] Just under half of the heads deal with 'Commercial Questions', by which Hawkesbury meant the size, structure and profitability of the slave trade. The economic case against abolition was inherent even in these initial draft questions. Many of them inevitably point towards the enormity of the financial interests at stake, inquiring into the overall size of not only the British trade, but that of her competitors, and in particular French attempts to increase her share of the total trade by paying bounties on imports of enslaved Africans into French colonies. Many of the questions are largely rhetorical: 'Is not the price of [slaves] already higher in the British West Indies than it is in the Foreign? ... [If Britain were to abolish the trade] would not the supply of manufactures and foreign goods now exported from hence to Africa fall to the share of some other European nation? ... Is there any reason to suppose that Africa could produce other Goods and Commodities?'

The questions dealing with non-commercial issues are generally less loaded, but Hawkesbury's attitudes do come through. For example, the first five lines read: 'The state of the countries from whence the slaves are brought', 'The nature of their government', 'The Civil rights of their subjects', 'Their religious principles' and hence 'Whether in all these respects they can be supposed to be in a better or a worse situation, than when employed as slaves in our islands'. This opens the door wide to a mitigating defence of the process of enslavement. There are also fairly loaded questions regarding the possible use of European labour as an alternative to African, especially given the weight of contemporary opinion to the effect that the West Indian climate precluded hard manual labour by Europeans. Several of the questions deal with the success (or lack of it) of missionaries in Africa and the West Indies, such as the question of whether 'their condition of slavery so debase their minds as to render them less capable of instruction'.

Whilst it would be overstating the case, therefore, to suggest that Hawkesbury had loaded the questions before the inquiry, it appears that from the outset it was significantly easier for anti-abolitionists to put forward a coherent, argued case about the deleterious effects of abolition than it was for abolitionists to put together a convincing opposition. No doubt this was partly a product of Hawkesbury's previous experience of investigations such as these. Over the previous few years, he had been addressing the issue of the prohibition placed on economic intercourse between the West Indies and the United States of America. This investigation had given him particular knowledge of the economic life of the West Indies, and the nature of the American intercourse question meant

10 Liverpool Papers, fols 13–19, 'Heads of Examination proposed by Lord Hawkesbury to the Committee for Trade and Plantations on 12 February 1788'.

that he was used to considering issues such as the threat of foreign competition, the impact of regulatory changes on homeland revenue and the consequences of such changes on producers and manufacturers providing goods for export. He had also developed a series of contacts amongst the West Indian merchant community from whom he had sourced information.[11] Coming from this background of mercantile investigation, the way in which he envisaged such an investigation proceeding was determined by the form in which he perceived the argument to be structured. Although Hawkesbury did make inquiries as to the ethical status of slavery – asking the bishop of London to comment on its conformity with scripture – the issue was investigated, overall, through the mental framework of an economic statesman.

Anti-abolitionists had significant advantages in procuring, organizing and presenting their evidence. Individuals with relevant information on particular topics were sought out by the Board. The agents of the West Indian assemblies were asked for information on the treatment of the enslaved, the economic and living conditions in the West Indies, details about commercial arrangements, prices, import and population statistics. These requests were also sent to the governors of the West Indian islands.[12]

A problem for the Board was the difficulty of procuring detailed information from sources not readily available in England. They relied on the colonial agents to answer their questions on conditions in the West Indies, but the agents had to plead ignorance on many questions. There was undoubtedly also a fear here amongst the agents of accidentally presenting evidence which might prove unfavourable to their employers in the future. Stephen Fuller, the agent for Jamaica, wrote to the Board explaining that 'having never been in Jamaica myself, I am obliged to collect evidence from different gentlemen who have resided there'.[13] He relied on a network of contacts in England to provide him with information. The principal of these was Edward Long, the author of the noted *History of Jamaica*. Fuller sourced his reprints of what he (Fuller) called the Jamaican *Code Noir*, presented as a four-column table showing the chronological development of the Jamaican legal code relating to the treatment of the enslaved. But Long seems to have had a major role in preparing and editing all the answers provided by Fuller. Fuller noted in a letter expressing his thanks to Long that his 'style & knowledge of the subject will be visible in every part

11 'A state of the allegations and evidence ... purporting to shew the distressed state of His Majesty's Sugar Colonies etc.' in *Sessional Papers*, vol. 49, pp. 73–108.

12 TNA, BT3/1, fols 184, 189, 193, 199, 201, 202, William Fawkener to agents of the West Indian Assemblies, various dates.

13 Fuller Letterbooks (Duke), vol. 1, fol. 186, Fuller to Fawkener, 1 March 1788.

of it'.[14] Fuller also drew on evidence provided by planters resident in England, notably William Chisholme, who is jointly named with Fuller and Long as the author of the answers in the report.

The evidence presented in 1788 on conditions in Jamaica is therefore a collaborative product, drawing on evidence from British resident planters and on the research undertaken by Long. This was supplemented by responses sent directly from a Committee of the Council of Jamaica. This was partly on Fuller's suggestion. He had noted that it was inappropriate to rely on him for evidence as he did not have access to the information required to answer many of the questions, and suggested that Hawkesbury write directly to the governors of the islands.

Requests for details about the process of enslavement and conditions on the coast of Africa were channelled in the first instance to the Company of Merchants trading to Africa, rather than to sources in Liverpool and Bristol. There was considerable institutional overlap between the African Company and institutions in Liverpool and Bristol, and the Company had representatives from both towns on their committee. The African Company responded rapidly, establishing a subcommittee to consider their response and William Fawkener (the secretary to the Board) attended to explain the circumstances behind the inquiry.[15] It was clear, however, that the African Company was unwilling to provide any detailed evidence regarding methods of enslavement, conditions on slaving vessels or the socio-economic conditions on the African coast. The office produced a short, platitudinous report within a week of the first inquiry, followed up with specific information requested by the investigators on white people who had travelled to the coast of Africa.[16]

The African Company also sent copies of the terms of reference to Bristol and Liverpool for the relevant bodies to formulate a response. Liverpool was already well organized in this regard through their team of delegates based in London. John Tarleton attended African Company meetings and so had prior knowledge of the nature of the evidence being sought by the investigators.[17] Bristol bodies were less well informed, but on receiving the information from the African Company, held a large meeting of interested parties and drew up a memorial to the Board emphasizing the importance of the slave trade to British commerce, which they voted to support by sending delegates to London to give

14 Fuller Letterbooks (Duke), vol. 1, fol. 201.

15 TNA, Minutes of the Company of Merchants Trading to Africa, 14 February 1788.

16 Liverpool Papers, fols 24–8, Company of Merchants Trading to Africa to Lord Hawkesbury, 19 February 1788; *Sessional Papers*, vol. 69, pp. 80–82, 86–9.

17 Frank E. Sanderson, 'The Liverpool Delegates and Sir William Dolben's Bill', *Transactions of the Historic Society of Lancashire and Cheshire*, 124 (1972): pp. 57–84.

evidence. They sent James Baillie, John Anderson and Richard Miles to London, and collected evidence locally which they forwarded to them.[18]

A number of issues under consideration lent themselves particularly to statistical consideration. One immediate issue was the size of the enslaved population in the West Indies and the rate at which enslaved Africans were transported across the Atlantic. A detailed year-by-year account of imports and exports of enslaved Africans was procured for the Board of Trade by Stephen Fuller, who had drawn up the account 13 years earlier during a dispute over duties levied on imports of enslaved Africans into Jamaica.[19]

The treatment of mortality rates during the middle passage seems at this stage to have been largely circumstantial. Captains of slaving vessels presented largely impressionistic evidence. James Penny, for example, reported that mortality rates reflected the constitution of those taken on board, which varied according to their place of embarkation. Hence, he reported, whilst 'Those Negroes from the Gold Coast and Whydah, who feed on Indian Corn, have in general little or no mortality', those from the Bight of Guinea were, on average, subject to a mortality rate of about 8.5 per cent over the course of a voyage.[20]

There was, however, more detailed consideration of the rates of mortality amongst seamen, mainly because of the efforts of Thomas Clarkson in analysing muster rolls of slaving vessels from Liverpool and Bristol. He presented a letter explaining his researches to the Board of Trade, and presented the statistical evidence in detail, along with comparative figures for East Indian, West Indian, Newfoundland, Greenland and Peterborough trades from Bristol. The rhetorical effect of the data being laid out and presented in this coherent, systematic format was powerful, and spurred the committee into detailed investigation into seamen mortality. They called in witnesses, mainly from philanthropic groups dealing with the relief of seamen, to give evidence on the documents from which Clarkson had drawn up his table, the muster rolls – the manner in which they were drawn up, their accuracy, and what conclusions it was appropriate to draw from them.[21]

The issue of plantation mortality emerged as a central consideration early in the investigations. Slave populations in the West Indies generally suffered from an excess of deaths over births, and the deficit was maintained through

18 Bristol Record Office, SMV/2/4/1/2, Papers of the Society of Merchant Venturers, fol. 74, Jeremiah Osbourne to William Gordon, 15 April 1789; *Sessional Papers*, vol. 69, p. 90.

19 Fuller Letterbooks (Duke), fols 188–9, Fuller to Jamaican Committee of Correspondence, 5 March 1788.

20 *Sessional Papers*, vol. 69, p. 116.

21 *Sessional Papers*, vol. 69, pp. 144–204.

continued imports of Africans. Abolitionists argued that the death rate could be reduced by improving conditions on the plantations, whereas anti-abolitionists argued that negative population growth was a structural feature of the plantation system and could not be altered. This made statistics on population growth and decline highly significant in the context of wider debate. Anti-abolitionists were keen to source population data which would demonstrate both that the excess of deaths over births was sizeable and that the gap was due to disease particular to the climate rather than through other reasons.

The data available on this issue was highly limited. Jamaican population statistics in the Board of Trade report were largely static, drawn from earlier estimates based on poll tax records.[22] The data about overall population over time was extensive, but of little relevance to the debate over mortality given continuing population increase through imports and re-exports. The main rhetorical effect of these statistics was to emphasize the discrepancy between white and black populations, and hence the potential fragility of the West Indian social system. Calculations were also made as to the total capital value of the enslaved population of the West Indies.[23] Samuel Estwick, agent for Barbados, did present six estate accounts showing annual numbers of births and deaths on several estates. One estate showed births equalling deaths, and hence the population remaining static; three showed a substantial decrease in populations and two an increase.[24]

It was hard, from the evidence available in the Board of Trade report, to come to meaningful conclusions about the decline or growth of population on West Indian estates. The genius of William Pitt's 1791 speech was his imaginative reworking of available statistics, a feature that he developed further in 1792. He used aggregate statistics for population growth, making adjustments for imports and re-exports.[25] The growth was negative, but the rate of decline was shown to have slowed as time went on until it was roughly stable towards the end of the century. The effect of this use of statistics was powerful. Fuller noted that in 1792 'Mr Pitt ran away with the minds of many of the young members, by his positive assertions from his own calculations'.[26] Fuller put his faith in authenticated accounts from individual plantations to rebut Pitt's 'positive assertions'. He

---

22 *Sessional Papers*, vol. 69, pp. 262–4.

23 *Sessional Papers*, vol. 70, pp. 271–88.

24 *Sessional Papers*, vol. 69, pp. 292 and 304–5.

25 *The Debate on a Motion for the Abolition of the Slave Trade in the House of Commons on Monday and Tuesday April 18th and 19th 1791, Reported in Detail*, ed. W. Woodfall (2nd edn, London, 1792), pp. 105–8.

26 Fuller Letterbooks (Duke), vol. 2, fol. 310, Fuller to Jamaican Committee of Correspondence, 6 June 1792.

hoped that close engagement with the minutiae of estate account data would prove his point that the population of 'sugar works' declined approximately 2.5 per cent per annum, with smaller reductions in towns and pens.[27] Procuring such reports was difficult, however, and Fuller continued to bemoan the lack of data with which to rebut Pitt's calculations.[28]

The Arrangement and Editing of Evidence

The collation of the large amounts of data involved in the investigation involved a considerable amount of clerical work, for which William Fawkener and Stephen Cottrell were hired as clerks. Witness evidence was collated in a manuscript minute book arranged by witness, and correspondence was similarly collated.[29]

Stephen Fuller hoped that by being collected together under the auspices of an official investigation, the authority of the evidence collected would be enhanced:

> What the Agent says or writes, or the Planter, goes for very little; they are both interested. But Lord Hawkesbury's report will be a collection of matter from all parties, concerned & unconcerned, and made by a Committee of Council under no influence whatsoever, but that of the preservation of the Trade & Commerce of this Country, and of justice due to individuals holding their possessions under the sanction of the Laws. I am perfectly clear in it that our dependence lies chiefly on that report.[30]

As it turned out, the information gathered by the Board was not collated into an officially approved narrative. The presentation of the 1788 Board of Trade report was characterized by a hidden editorial hand, the evidence being copied largely unchanged from the minuted responses of witnesses and documents received. The report is, however, reorganized under category headings and then sub-questions. On the first mention of a witness, they were introduced with a short detail of their background and their connections with the trade. After this, each question or issue was introduced by a heading, and the relevant parts of the evidence of each witness or informant was extracted and reproduced with a

---

27 Fuller Letterbooks (Duke), vol. 2, fols 72–9, Fuller to Jamaican Committee of Correspondence, 4 May 1791.

28 Fuller Letterbooks (Duke), vol. 2, fol. 312, Fuller to Bryan Edwards, 6 June 1792.

29 TNA, BT6/11.

30 Fuller Letterbooks (Duke), vol. 1, fol. 329, Fuller to John Grant, 3 December 1788.

small note of their name in the margin. The effect, therefore, was a compendium of contributions for each subject under consideration. There was no editorial comment or narrative on the part of the investigators. There was no attempt made at considering the various sources of evidence and weighing them with a view to forming a conclusion on the various points. That this had been the editorial decision was explicitly acknowledged in a note at the end of the report, when it was suggested that it was 'improper for them to offer any Observations on the Degree of Credit to be given to the various Evidence taken on a subject of this Nature'. It was suggested that it was the reader's responsibility to judge the 'weight' of each contribution. This format placed the onus on the reader of the report to consider the validity of many of the claims put forward on each issue, and the main information with which they had to do this was the small biographical sketches provided at the beginning of each person's evidence.

These sketches can be read as signifying the value of evidence in differing ways. One could take the view that a significant exposure to the slave trade implies experience and knowledge, which adds to the weight of the evidence delivered. It is clear that Lord Hawkesbury interpreted the evidence in this way when using it for his speech on Sir William Dolben's 1788 proposal to introduce limits on the number of enslaved people who could by law be packed into slave ships travelling across the Atlantic. He prepared manuscript notes for his speech in which he considered his responses to a number of questions posed by proponents of the bill, and outlined his own objections to both details of the bill and some of the accusations resting behind it. Some of his responses relied on the detailed evidence provided by slave captains about the detailed working of the ships. For example, he defended the quality of ventilation provided in under-deck 'appartments' used to confine enslaved people.[31] This information seems to have come from James Penny, an Africa merchant of 18 years' standing and 11 voyages, and one of the delegates sent from Liverpool to further the port's opposition to abolition.[32] Hawkesbury was not just taking slave traders' assertions uncritically or manipulating the evidence. In his notes he specifically attacked the calculations produced by Liverpool merchants of the estimated profit and loss on voyages before and after regulation, arguing that they deflated the figures for the amount of profit they earned on each slave transported so as to make regulation seem worse than it would actually be.[33]

Alternatively, these biographies could be read as a measure of how interested each witness was in the continuance of the trade and in avoiding regulation.

---

31 Liverpool Papers, fols 188–95, Memorandum by Lord Hawkesbury [1788].

32 *Sessional Papers*, vol. 69, pp. 11, 116.

33 Liverpool Papers, fol. 201, Memorandum by Lord Hawkesbury on the profitability of the slave trade, [1788].

This was clearly how abolitionists read them, and it was an important part of abolitionists' political strategy to suggest that readers should interpret them in the same manner.

Nine further investigations were undertaken over the course of the agitation, producing a total of 21 reports. These were all undertaken by parliamentary committees, either committees of the whole House, which cross-examined witnesses at the bar of the House, or by select committees. The structure of these investigations was rather different from those of the Board of Trade. Parliamentary committee investigations were formally structured as a forum for the presentation of evidence to support a petition or counter-petition. Witnesses were brought forward by those presenting petitions. In the case of anti-abolitionists this was by the counsel for the petitioners, after a careful selection process for witnesses. The counsel then examined each witness, before allowing them to be cross-examined by other members of the committee. These investigations therefore lacked a formal agenda for inquiry or a procedure for selecting sources of information. The shape of the inquiry depended on the strategies employed by the counsel in questioning their witnesses and the committee members in cross-examining.

There was a concerted and sustained effort on the part of lobbyists to organize witnesses so as to maximize the effectiveness of their evidence. The West Indian agents regularly came together to co-ordinate the evidence as each island was taken separately.[34] Admirals and military men who had been to the West Indies were preferred as witnesses, because they had social authority, and several could be found who would give favourable evidence.

Select committee reports shared some characteristics with that prepared by the Board of Trade Committee. Initial questions were posed to each witness requesting brief biographical details which might be regarded as pertinent to their authority as witnesses. Unlike the Board of Trade report, the evidence was not split into headings, but rather reproduced verbatim the series of questions posed to and answers given by each witness, noted down in shorthand during committee hearings.[35] It has been wrongly suggested that this format was laid down by parliamentary procedure, and that select committees were forbidden from expressing opinions on subjects referred to them, being forced merely to reprint evidence verbatim.[36] This misconception stems from a text on

34 Somerset Record Office, DD/DN/510/52, Papers of Stephen Fuller, 'Slave Trade – Plan for Session 1794', 28 January 1794.

35 For the shorthand notes see Parliamentary Archives, London, HO/PO/JO/10/7/786, fols 209–15.

36 Porter, *Abolition*, p. 75.

parliamentary procedure dating from the 1760s, and clearly was not being followed by the mid-1780s.[37]

The Publication of Investigations

The lack of a covering report to accompany printed evidence is unsurprising given the divisions within the committee over the fundamentals of the question, but highlights the fact that the production of a commonly agreed narrative was impossible to produce because of the level of conflict. This, in turn, influenced the way the reports were used in the public sphere. There are a number of aspects of the presentational format of the printed reports which meant that these reprints could serve abolitionist aims more effectively than anti-abolitionist. I will outline briefly how these reports were reprinted and reused, and then consider the problems facing anti-abolitionists.

The Board of Trade report was printed and published, but not distributed widely. John Ranby, an anti-abolitionist pamphleteer, noted in 1791 that it was 'but little known or attended to'.[38] The prohibitive expense restricted its distribution, but major libraries such as the Bodleian bought copies, and Fuller sent a copy to Jamaica.[39] It was, however, used by pamphleteers as a source of evidence. Ranby published a pamphlet in 1791 which reprinted extracts from both abolitionist and anti-abolitionist evidence, offering criticism of the former. Its low cost made access to the evidence possible on a much wider level than previously.[40]

---

[37] The rule is taken from the 'Liverpool Tractate', a procedural manual dating from c.1762. See Orlo C. Williams, *The Historical Development of Private Bill Procedure and Standing Orders in the House of Commons* (2 vols, London, 1949), vol. 1, pp. 27–8, 31. For two reports from May 1786 offering commentary on evidence collected see the 'Report from the committee to whom the petition of the principal persons concerned in the pilchard fishery ... was referred', *Sessional Papers*, vol. 49, pp. 65–72, and the 'Report from the Committee to whom the petition of the Right Honourable Anthony James Earl of Newburgh ... was referred', *Sessional Papers*, vol. 5, pp. 497–502.

[38] John Ranby, *Observations on the Evidence Given before the Committees of the Privy Council and House of Commons in Support of the Bill for Abolishing the Slave Trade* (London, 1791), p. iii.

[39] The Bodleian purchased a copy for £1, 11s, 6d in 1789: Bodleian Library, *A Catalogue of Books Purchased for the Bodleian Library in 1789. With an Account of Monies Collected for That Purpose* ([Oxford], [1789]), p. 12.

[40] It was on sale second hand for 3s in 1796. James Edwards, *A Catalogue of Books, in All Languages, and in Every Branch of Literature, Collected from Various Parts of Europe. ... Now on Sale at J. Edwards* ([London], 1796), p. 263.

These reports were used as databases of evidence from which pamphleteers, and those making speeches could select suitable or impressive evidence. One publication produced soon after the report appeared to cater specifically to this use. It broke the report down into topics, and then into statements of opinion or fact such as 'Africa – Agriculture – No property in land, but what arises from immediate occupancy'. Next to each of these was tabulated the page references of evidence that 'affirmed', 'refuted', 'agreed' and 'disagreed' with the statement.[41] Prospective authors keen to argue a point could easily locate the relevant supportive evidence.

Abolitionist pamphleteers tended not to make reference to the Board of Trade report. The numerous summaries and abstracts and abridgements they produced during the campaign tended to draw on the evidence given to parliamentary committees. There were sound reasons for this. As suggested earlier, the Board of Trade investigation had been tightly managed by anti-abolitionists, as they had both control over the flow of information to the investigators, and a favourable set of assumptions underlying the investigation. Later inquiries in Parliament enabled abolitionists to present their own evidence by calling witnesses in defence of the claims put forward in their petitions. Through the work of Thomas Clarkson and others, witnesses had been identified in the outports who were willing to come to London and give evidence which contradicted the assertions of the planters and those who had given evidence of favourable conditions on the slave ships.[42]

The exposure of acts of barbarism and poor treatment on the part of planters and slave traders (such as the famous denunciation of Captain Kimber by Wilberforce in 1792) became a powerful and heavily used motif within abolitionist discourse.[43] It was particularly potent because highly graphic reports of physical and sexual abuse were both readily transmittable through written, spoken or visual media, and could be easily understood by individuals across

---

41 *Abstract of the Evidence, Contained in the Report of the Lords of the Committee of Council, Relative to the Slave-Trade, and the Treatment of the Slaves in the Sugar Islands: Also an Abridgement of Such of the Colonial Laws, as Relate to the Treatment of the Slaves* ([London], 1790). It is not clear who authored the abstract. It was not produced corporately by either the West India Committee or the Abolitionist Committee. It may have been produced by the Committee itself, although I have not been able to locate proof of this.

42 On Clarkson's witnesses see Thomas Clarkson, *History of the Rise, Progress and Accomplishment of the Abolition of the African Slave Trade by the British Parliament* (rev. edn, London, 1839), pp. 180–242.

43 See, for example, Brycchan Carey, *British Abolitionism and the Rhetoric of Sensibility: Writing, Sentiment and Slavery, 1760–1807* (Basingstoke, 2005); Henrice Altink, 'An Outrage on All Decency: Abolitionist Reactions to Flogging Jamaican Slave Women, 1780–1834', *Slavery and Abolition*, 23/2 (2002): pp. 107–24.

the social spectrum. Such reports could be fitted into wider condemnations of the slave system in various ways. For example, they could be used in the context of providentialist theology to demonstrate that the nation was at risk of divine intervention through sanctioning such behaviour. This usage helped contribute to a sense of moral panic amongst some about the potential for such chronic abuse to bring retribution upon the nation.[44] Equally, reports of abuses could reflect experiences of populations undergoing socio-economic changes within Britain, particularly industrialization.[45]

This was to prove a severe problem for anti-abolitionists in terms of using the results of parliamentary investigations in the public sphere. It was very difficult to assert convincingly that accusations made by abolitionist witnesses were false; the result of personal grudges or merely isolated incidents. The anti-abolitionist strategy of relying on social standing to enhance the credibility of the witness evidence given at their behest was limited by the nature of that evidence. Bland assertions that the enslaved were well treated held little rhetorical power even when delivered by socially respectable witnesses such as the senior naval figures persuaded by Stephen Fuller to give evidence. Most of this evidence was general and non-specific: it consisted of assertions of general good treatment, or idealized descriptions of conditions on ship or in the West Indies. A well-known example is James Penny's evidence on slave-ship conditions. He reported an extremely favourable picture of life on board, complete with 'country food', the provision of pipes and tobacco, musical instruments and games of chance. 'If the weather is sultry and there appears the least perspiration on their skins, when they come upon deck, there are two men attending with cloths to rub them perfectly dry, and another to give them a little cordial'.[46] Such generalized evidence, even when not so clearly ludicrous, had little rhetorical power in the wider public sphere.

Conclusion

This has been a detailed analysis of the data collection and printing processes undertaken by a particularly important set of parliamentary investigations. I would like to conclude by drawing some more general points about the nature of the relationship between information and political lobbying in the campaign over slave trade abolition.

---

44 Christopher L. Brown, *Moral Capital: Foundations of British Abolitionism* (Chapel Hill, NC, 2006), pp. 333–90.

45 Seymour Drescher, 'Cart Whip and Billy Roller: Or Antislavery and Reform Symbolism in Industrializing Britain', *Journal of Social History*, 15 (1981): pp. 3–24.

46 *Sessional Papers*, vol. 69, p. 117. Reprinted in Hochschild, *Bury the Chains*, p. 154.

Information ran through political networks in chains of communication – a letter might be recopied several times before being sent to an MP, read out in Parliament, reprinted in a report of the debate and then reused in a pamphlet again. This transfer of information between media could have effects on both its inherent meaning, and on its reception. Take, for example, the use of information drawn from letters. The reading practices associated with merchant letters in this period emphasized the role of trust and creditworthiness in evaluating letters' contents. Such bonds of trust could only exist in the context of relationships developed over a period of time. When letters were quoted, even given a named author, the social web of relationships surrounding the letter-writer was broken and the information had to be evaluated using quite different criteria. In the case of parliamentary investigations, attempts were made to replace this personal knowledge with brief biographical sketches with which the reader could evaluate the authors' veracity and qualifications. Much ink was spilled and time spent debating the qualifications of these observers. Abolitionists were highly successful in many cases in discrediting the testimony of their opponents. It became clear that neither social authority nor first-hand personal knowledge would do as qualifications for witnesses.

This presented anti-abolitionists with a significant problem in terms of evidence and how to validate their truth claims. It was a problem they never really solved. 'Impartial' witnesses were drawn in, specifically from the Navy, and initially this seemed to bolster their credibility. However, whilst both sides tried to boost their reputation for impartiality, abolitionists were particularly successful in discrediting anti-abolitionist witnesses and sources of information – an air of suspicion hung over anti-abolitionist evidence of all kinds.

In the context of this highly politically charged situation, the validity and usefulness of data became contested in itself, and there was a parallel political contest over how data should be read, and how truth claims should be assessed. We need to be sensitive to the ways in which contemporaries decided who was telling the truth, and certainly need to question deeply the notion of rational critical debate. Most reading in political situations must inevitably have been deeply inflected by the readers' political position and sense of self-identity.

Political information, therefore, is made effective or ineffective partly by the political identities of those reading it. Anti-abolitionism as a political identity suffered from several weaknesses in comparison with abolitionism. On a local level, as David Turley has shown, abolitionism was incubated amongst other developing cultures of middle-class civic authority and in the context of nonconformist religion.[47] It developed an independent life of its own – a shared culture based on clear moral principles and a strong visual language.

Local anti-abolitionism never developed the same independent political coherence – it was always more closely linked to the institutions from which it emerged. This was partly linked to the nature of anti-abolitionist lobbying institutions. Because lobbying was undertaken primarily through institutions with limited social constituencies, and because of the nature of anti-abolitionist petitioning, a national anti-abolitionist campaign with a coherent language and message was not feasible. Institutions mediated the relationship between Parliament and 'public', and lobbied through channels and in formats which were established by constitutional precedent. Because anti-abolition was, by its essence reactive – a counter-petitioning movement – its campaign was conceptualized around groups who were economically threatened by abolition. This immediately limited the social breadth of the anti-abolitionist movement.

To appreciate fully the connections between data, knowledge and political debate, therefore, we need to understand the ways in which political identity and the underlying assumptions behind different types of media shaped the ways in which political actors determined truth and interpreted evidence.

47 David Turley, *The Culture of English Antislavery, 1780–1860* (London, 1991).

Chapter 9

Facing Uncertainty: Markets, Norms and Conventions in the Eighteenth Century

Philippe Minard

The question of honesty in exchange constituted a major concern for manufacturers and businessmen in the eighteenth century who are all confronted with the problem of 'opportunism', as today's economists would put it: does the product match the buyer's expectations or the seller's promises? How can they assure themselves that there are absolutely no hidden defects, invisible or undetectable at the moment of purchase and only later to be revealed, much to the despair of the buyer? How can all dishonest or fraudulent behaviour be avoided?

According to the *laissez-faire* advocates, those questions should not even be asked: the liberal political economy solves the problem by the argument of the automatic neutralization of dishonest behaviour, thanks to the competition of the market. But if we turned towards the grass-roots practitioners, the answer is rather different. Among those engaged in manufacturing and commerce, opinions on norms and regulations were in fact greatly divided. Contrary to the commonplace *cliché*, manufacturing regulations were far from being opposed by all traders, simply because they were afraid of counterfeiting and dishonest suppliers. The source of many disputes and misunderstandings can be explained through study of these rival perspectives.

In France, the textile industry, which was one of the most important producers at the time, was heavily regulated. Colbert's initial laws, renewed and enlarged all over the eighteenth century, combined all the local and regional regulations about the various fabrics into one consolidated code. It set the standards of fabrication for textiles in the whole kingdom: the size of the pieces, quality of the raw materials, number and section of yarns, dyeing and finishing. All the locally produced goods had to be inspected by experts in the trade. If the pieces were of good quality, and made according to regulations, they received an inspection mark: this seal of lead guaranteed both their conformity to the official standards and its origin, since it bore the name of the place of fabrication and inspection.[1] In England, such a system existed, to a lesser extent, for some textile products, notably in Yorkshire, and also for leather in some places like London. In both countries, it was increasingly brought into question by *laissez-faire* advocates, putting forward several kinds of arguments: expenses, delays, lack of flexibility of the standards and so on. Above all, liberals rejected the idea that inspections and quality stamps could help to suppress deception. But the question remained highly disputed all over the century. And in England, in mid-century, we can see norms and inspections re-introduced in the West Riding of Yorkshire woollen industry, because the practitioners themselves called for them. In London also, at the end of the eighteenth century, new controls were introduced in the leather trade.[2]

So, the issue is not as simple as we have been told for years: the practitioners of trade, and some economists as well, did not take lightly the question of the social organization of confidence. Analysis of the actual functioning of the markets can enlighten us about the long-standing persistence of the quality regulations, standards and specification of products so violently denounced by free-trade reformers. Rather than considering these regulations as incongruities or archaisms, this chapter will instead be trying to understand the needs to which they answer.[3]

Automatic Neutralization of Dishonest Behaviour?

The problem of fraud and honesty in commerce was in no way beyond the purview of eighteenth-century authors and practitioners. In order to

[1] Philippe Minard, *La fortune du colbertisme. Etat et industrie dans la France des Lumières* (Paris, 1998); Minard, 'Colbertism Continued? The Inspectorate of Manufactures and Strategies of Exchange in Eighteenth-Century France', *French Historical Studies*, 23/3 (2000): pp. 445–64; and Minard, 'Réputation, normes et qualité dans l'industrie textile française au XVIIIe siècle', in Alessandro Stanziani (ed.), *La qualité des produits en France, XVIIIe–XXe siècles* (Paris, 2003), pp. 69–92. Professor Minard thanks William Biashop for his assistance in translating this piece.

[2] Philippe Minard, 'L'inspection des draps du West Riding of Yorkshire, ou le jeu des normes au XVIIIe siècle', in Gérard Béaur, Hubert Bonin and Claire Lemercier (eds), *Pour une histoire de la fraude et de la contrefaçon* (Genève, 2007), pp. 621–38; and Minard, 'Disputes about Quality and Quality-Control among the London Leather Trades at the End of the Eigtheenth-Century', unpublished paper. See also re-evaluations by William J. Ashworth, 'Quality and the Roots of "Expertise" in Eighteenth Century Britain', *Osiris*, 25 (2010): pp. 231–54.

[3] See Dominique Margairaz and Philippe Minard (eds), *Revue de synthèse*, special issue: 'Le marché dans son histoire ', 127/2 (2006); and Philippe Minard, 'Norme, istituzioni e regolazione dell'economia. Nuovi approcci del mercato in Francia, secoli XVIII–XIX', *Studi storici*, special issue: 'La storia economica delle società dell'Europa preindustriale', 50/3 (2009): pp. 695–716.

understand how contemporaries might have perceived it, one has to remember the importance of the mental mindset they had inherited: the secular regulation of trades is steeped in scholastic thought and the Thomist representation of commerce and merchants. Its constant concern with protecting the consumer is based on the idea that 'selling something more expensively or buying something cheaper than what it is worth, is in and of itself unjust and illegal'. Yet the intrinsic value of a commodity is a variable that can be difficult to perceive – whence the uncertainty in fixing the 'just price'.[4] In Thomas Aquinas's *Summa Theologicae* (1273), fraud was addressed in three ways: first of all in terms of the falsity of volume or weight measurements, which plays on the quantity of the merchandise. Secondly, in terms of the alteration of the product, the modification of its substance through tampering or any other procedure that dilutes its purity and hence its quality. Finally, in terms of a false qualification by which the seller claims that his merchandise is attributed with qualities superior to the ones it actually has.[5] These last two 'defects' are related to situations of information asymmetry. It is because of these types of fraud that corporative, municipal or royal regulations attempted to raise protective barriers by imposing certain specifications or thresholds of guaranteed minimal quality: producers and merchants must only supply 'good and honest products' (*une 'marchandise loyale et marchande'*), as all regulations and instructions for merchants repeat over and over again.[6]

Against the grain of this long-lasting neo-Aristotelian heritage, eighteenth-century economic thought proceeded with a rehabilitation of commerce and merchants grounded in a general theory of individual interest. What about the question of dishonest practices and falsification in this framework? Classical

---

4 Raymond de Roover, *La pensée économique des scolastiques* (Paris, 1971); Diana Wood, *Medieval Economic Thought* (Cambridge, 2002); André Lapidus, 'Norm, Virtue and Information: The Just Price and Individual Behaviour in Thomas Aquinas's Summa Theologiae', *European Journal of the History of Economic Thought*, 1/3 (1994): pp. 435–73.

5 These are precisely the questions discussed in the twentieth century by economists such as Carl Alsberg, 'Economic Aspects of Adulteration and Imitation', *Quarterly Journal of Economics*, 46/1 (1931): pp. 1–33; Edward Chamberlin, 'The Product as Economic Variable', *Quarterly Journal of Economics*, 67/1, (1953): pp. 1–29. See Stanziani, *Qualité des produits*, and Alessandro Stanziani, *Histoire de la qualité alimentaire, XIXe–XXe siècle* (Paris, 2005).

6 'When there has been no sample, the merchandise must ordinarily be honest and saleable', according to the *Instruction sur les affaires contentieuses des négociants, la manière de les prévenir ou de les suivre dans les tribunaux* (2nd edn, Paris, 1789). 'Good faith must reign in all operations relating to sales', according to the jurist Jean-Baptiste Denisart – *Collection de décisions nouvelles et de notions relatives à la jurisprudence actuelle* (Paris, 1763–64), vol. 4, p. 796, quoted by Jean-Yves Grenier, 'Une économie de l'identification. Juste prix et ordre des marchandises dans l'Ancien Régime', in Stanziani, *Qualité des produits*, p. 60.

liberal political economy solved the problem of deceit quite easily. First, by making it a question of the agent's responsibility, as did the French economist and reformer Vincent de Gournay: 'It is a major error to think that, as many would have us believe, it is as easy to deceive people who have an interest in not being deceived. The buyer is never forced to buy. It therefore befalls him to be careful about what he buys. It's his business'.[7] Secondly, by asserting that in the end, competition pulls the rug out from under the feet of ill-intentioned agents who might be tempted to take advantage of an ill-informed buyer by deceiving him on the price or quality of merchandise. This is the lesson of the fable of the duped consumer and the merchant crook, a famous text in which the liberal minister Turgot explained how the market automatically neutralizes dishonest behaviour: it is not in the seller's best interest to deceive his client, because his client would then move on to another supplier; the crook would therefore be punished for his trick.[8] Adam Smith later takes up this reasoning, and we know how successful he was to be.[9] At the end of the century, this idea has become commonplace.[10]

The whole logic stems from the idea that the seller needs to preserve his reputation to continue to do business. Yet this all heavily relies on one dubious hypothesis: the market is understood as transparent, and agents as perfectly informed. In other words, the idea that competition is capable of dissuading sellers from deceiving and of keeping buyers vigilant is only true if agents have access to sufficient information about local market conditions. Liberal reasoning therefore presupposes a buyer who is well-informed about both price and quality, and/or in a position to verify what it is that she's buying.

But what about non-visible defects? And what happens when distance or lack of time keep the buyer from making these verifications? In this case, the second aspect of liberal reasoning is not respected. In short, as soon as the hypothesis of the market's transparency is abandoned, competition no longer systematically puts a stop to opportunism, and the automatic neutralization of dishonest

---

7 Jacques Vincent de Gournay, *Traités sur le commerce de Josiah Child avec les Remarques inédites de Vincent de Gournay, texte intégral d'après les manuscrits conservés à la Bibliothèque municipale de Saint-Brieuc*, ed. T. Tsuda (Tokyo, 1983), p. 257.

8 Turgot, 'Éloge de Vincent de Gournay' (1759), in *Écrits économiques*, ed. B. Cazes (Paris, 1970), p. 87.

9 'The real and effectual discipline which is exercised over a workman, is not that of his corporation, but that of his customers. It is the fear of losing their employment which restrains his frauds and correct his negligence', Adam Smith, *An Inquiry into the Nature and Causes of the Wealth of Nations*, ed. E. Cannan (New Rochelle, NY, 1966), p. 145.

10 Abraham Lloyd Eldridge, sheet-maker in Gloucestershire, 'Minutes of evidence taken before the committee, to whom the bill, respecting the laws relating to the woollen trade, is committed', *PP*, 1802–03 (VII), pp. 381–2 (pp. 875–6).

practices is less certain. The economist Georges Akerlof, studying the impact of information asymmetry among agents, has demonstrated how a doubt about the objectivity of the goods being exchanged, and quite precisely an uncertainty about their quality, can profoundly alter the framework of the exchange, to the point of making all balance impossible.[11]

In the actual concrete conditions of eighteenth-century markets, it is very doubtful that the crook would be punished for his deception as quickly as Turgot claimed: because of the length of the economic channels; because of the delays in the orders, especially because of the huge number of middlemen between manufacturers, merchants, retailers and end-of-the-line consumers. The commercial chain was very long, from the weaver in the countryside of Brittany to the trader in Saint-Malo port, then to the one in Cadiz, and then at last to the retailer in Mexico City or Lima. And anyway, was it always immediately possible for the customer to go somewhere else to do business?

Turgot's argument assumed that the deceived customer had enough economic information to be able to find his way quickly in the market, in his best interest. But of course not all the economic agents were this familiar with the conditions of the market. It seems very bold to believe Turgot's implicit hypothesis that the information could be gathered quickly and easily, and even that there was some economic stability to make this gathering possible. In France in the eighteenth century, the reality actually presented fragmented markets, substantial differences in price between regions and difficult travel conditions. Moreover, the competing goods were insufficiently homogeneous to allow easy substitution. In fact, it is difficult to find a more imperfect competition.[12]

So, in such a context, the problem of good faith in the labels and marks was far from trivial. Whence the '*choc des opinions*' among practitioners, for and against regulations and inspections. Whence the fairly nuanced position of Dean Josiah Tucker. In his 1757 *Instructions for Travellers*, he began by developing the argument of well-understood interest as an indication of an economy's proper functioning:

---

[11] George A. Akerlof, 'The Market for "Lemons": Quality Uncertainty and the Market Mechanism', *Quarterly Journal of Economics*, 84/3 (1970): pp. 488–500. See also Joseph Stiglitz, 'The Causes and Consequences of the Dependance of Quality on Price', *Journal of Economic Literature*, 25 (1987): pp. 1–48.

[12] For an analysis of a situation of 'imperfect competition' in the contemporary economy, see Jean Gabszewicz and Isabel Grilo, 'Price Competition when Consumers are Uncertain about which Firm Sells which Quality', *Journal of Economics and Management Strategy*, 1/4 (1992): pp. 629–50. It shows that in such a case the liberal ideal of perfect competition is a product of utopian economics.

> The self-love and self-interest of each individual will prompt him to seek such ways of gain, trades and occupations of life, as by serving himself, will promote the public welfare at the same time. The only thing necessary to be done by positive institutions is to enforce the observance of voluntary contracts

But he quickly adds that precisely because of this, the law must punish fraud, which constitutes a breach of contract: 'If the goods should prove to be worse than they appeared, having flaws or blemishes concealed within, or if they should be short of measure, weight, etc., the seller ought to make ample reparation to the buyer, and be subject likewise to some fine, or mark of infamy'. This is why, in his comparative essay on commerce in France and Great Britain, he pronounces himself in favour of 'public inspectors' that would ensure that exporters would not dupe their foreign clients: 'That so the buyer, in seeing the mark and seal of the Office, may confide in that, and be assured that he is not deceived by what is out of sight'.[13]

This demonstrates how much this question was not easily solved, and should in no way be over-simplified. Let's try to understand what the norms and regulations were useful for.

Regulative Construction of Trust

First of all, the regulations are the basis for a system of information: the artisan and manufacturing world developed a veritable culture of discernment among products. This 'economy of identification' is of course linked to the social structure of an Ancien Régime world marked by the importance of social taxonomies and the notion of honour.[14] The phenomenon can be observed in two ways: on the one hand, the hierarchization of consummations must reflect the interests of consumers (hence the obsession with classifying products); on the other, the

---

13 Josiah Tucker, *Instructions for Travellers* (1st edn, 1757), reprinted in *The Collected Works of Josiah Tucker*, (London, 1993), vol. 3: 'Economics and Social Policy', pp. 48–9; *A Brief Essay on the Advantages and Disadvantages which respectively attend France and Great-Britain, with regard to Trade* (edn of 1753), ibid., vol. 1, 'Certain proposals', § 14, pp. 121–2. On Tucker, see Philippe Minard, 'France "colbertiste" versus Angleterre "libérale"? Un mythe du XVIIIe siècle', in Jean-Philippe Genet and François-Joseph Ruggiu (eds), *Les idées passent-elles la Manche? Savoirs, représentations, pratiques, France-Angleterre, Xe–XXe siècles* (Paris, 2007), pp. 197–210.

14 Jean-Yves Grenier, 'Une économie de l'identification', pp. 25–53; John Styles, 'Manufacturing, Consumption and Design in Eighteenth-Century England', in John Brewer and Roy Porter (eds), *Consumption and the World of Goods* (London, 1993), pp. 527–54.

signature of a product and the producer's mark put his personal dignity at stake. Thus, we can appreciate the importance of appellations that indicate not only a product's provenance, but also the specific qualities associated with the mark.[15]

In textile production, for example, the infinite declension of denominations that takes up hundreds of pages of the *General Collection of Regulations* (*Recueil général des règlements* [Paris, 1730]) corresponds to the concern for identifying each type of fabric, knowing that each element of this nomenclature refers to particular specifications and to qualities that are proper to it. As Nicolas Desmarest, the Champagne inspector of manufactures explains in 1779:

> Without this infinite nomenclature of fabrics whose regulations properly enclose their definitions, it would not be possible to get along. It is thanks to this simple code that such and such a fabric is known, that it is ordered, manufactured, prepared, expedited, and sold, that complaints are authorized, that defaults are appreciated: those who ask for the suppression of regulations want business to have neither language nor dictionary[16]

By imposing precise specifications and by ensuring that these are respected through inspections by inspectors or *garde-jurés*, a regulated economy gives its support to trade by contributing to the construction of trust. As Forbonnais says:

> the good faith of a nation has an obvious interest in keeping the buyer protected from what the eye cannot see; this certainty facilitates consummations. This is why it is not possible to be too careful and rigorous in our attention to the fact the seals and marks only designate what really exists.[17]

At the very least, one can affirm that 'this correspondence of the work of industry maintained by the execution of regulations simplifies all operations

15 The term 'mark' (*marque*) refers to several types of stamping: 'In terms of negotiation and manufacture, is said of certain characters that are applied and printed on several types of merchandise, either to know the place where they were manufactured, or to make the workers who manufactured or prepared them guarantees of their solidity, or to make known that they were seen and visited by officials from the police of manufactures, or else to serve as proof that the rights imposed by this police have been well and duly followed', according to the definition of Jacques Savary des Bruslons, *Dictionnaire universel de commerce* (Amsterdam, 1726), column 672.

16 Archives départementales Marne, C 468, no. 3: report from inspector Desmarest, 15 mai 1779: 'Réflexions sur les mémoires qui ont été remis à Monsieur l'Intendant par les marchands et fabricants de Reims et de Troyes au sujet du plan d'administration intermédiaire entre le système réglementaire et la liberté indéfinie'.

17 François Véron de Forbonnais, *Éléments du commerce* (Leyde, 1754), vol. 1, p. 278.

and makes them much less expensive': in other words, the existence of norms lowered the transaction costs.[18] The regulation therefore sustains a specific social organization of confidence.

Let us take a French example with the '*bretagne*' fabrics and their lasting success in the Spanish and American markets. At the end of the seventeenth century, fabrics made in the bishopric of Saint-Brieuc in Brittany, had spread into Spain and Spanish America under the generic name of '*bretagnes*'. The wholesalers in Saint-Malo, who controlled their exportation, made the fabric a true label of reference, a leading product sought out even by foreign competitors, and inspiring many an imitation and counterfeit. The study of the factors that allowed '*bretagnes*' fabrics to gain prominence in a relatively open colonial market reveals that decisive advantages were to be found on the supply side of things. The merchants were able to maintain a grasp on a strong commercial niche – that of high quality fine fabrics, just below the narrower market for 'super-fine' fabrics of extremely high quality. But in their range of quality, the '*bretagnes*' were not the least expensive. It is therefore their irreproachable quality that allowed these fabrics to gain the dominant position. The Saint-Malo traders had quite a few indisputable trump cards: the quality of the local linens, the secular practical knowledge of Breton weavers, and the quality of the region's laundering. To these qualities, they added the very profitable strategy of a rigorous normalization of qualities: for each variety of the fabrics – the 'narrow' or 'ordinary' fabrics, and the finer 'wide' fabrics – they defined standards of quality and dimensions that guaranteed the identity and quality of the product for their clientele with no uncertainty. The fortune of the *bretagnes*, when compared to the competing Silesia fabrics, therefore depended on the trust and respect for norms indicating very precise qualities and inscribed into the regulations of fabrication.[19]

This then is the argument for official certification and preventive inspections in stamping offices: the system of regulations plays the role of a police of economic behaviour, guarantees the honesty of the labels, the respect of specifications and standards of quality; in short, it acts as a reducer of uncertainty. A merchant could not check the quality and size of every piece of cloth he bought. The

---

18 Archives départementales Marne, C 468, 'Réflexions', fol. 7.

19 Jean Tanguy, 'La production et le commerce des toiles "bretagnes" du XVIe au XVIIIe siècle. Premiers résultats', *Actes du 91e Congrès National des Sociétés Savantes* (Paris, 1969), pp. 105–41; André Lespagnol, *'Messieurs de Saint-Malo': une élite négociante au temps de Louis XIV* (rev. edn, Rennes, 1997), vol. 1, pp. 427–44, and Lespagnol, 'Des toiles bretonnes aux toiles "bretagnes". Conditions et facteurs d'émergence d'un "produit-phare" sur les marchés ibériques', in Jacques Bottin and Nicole Pellegrin (eds), *Échanges et cultures textiles dans l'Europe pré-industrielle*, Revue du Nord Hors series (Villeneuve d'Ascq, 1996), pp. 179–92.

pieces of woollens or linens were folded and packed away: so he had to rely on samples and labels. Moreover, it was impossible to check the cargo of any sale when one bought from a distance, whether directly or through brokers, based on samples inspected beforehand. But the multiplication of middlemen as the volume of trade increased only compounded the risks of deception and diffused responsibility.[20] So trading always included a problem of confidence: traders were afraid of dishonest suppliers, and no amount of liberal prophesizing about perfect markets would allay those fears.[21]

The smooth functioning of commercial operations was dependent on a social organization of confidence, which the market itself could not provide. In order to be able to trade in acceptable conditions, it was necessary to have common references, collectively accepted standards that could guarantee a minimal level of trust between partners. Trade, especially international, long-distance trade, needed the security that came with official standards and official certification. Unwanted surprises when unpacking bundles of cloth could thereby be avoided. Controls and certification of standards in the marking offices were therefore useful for guaranteeing trust: the *gardes-jurés* and the inspectors did for the merchants what the merchants could not do themselves.[22]

But norms and specifications are not just made through imperial fiat. The rules guaranteeing these standards of quality, as we have seen, predated their codification by the state. The state, in other words, was registering customs that were already established. The system of marks and control of manufacturing ratified accepted qualities and common standards about which trading parties had already reached *de facto* agreement through a process of coordination. In the

---

20 Thus, a merchant at Amiens denounced the dishonest behaviour of some of his colleagues who deceived foreign customers by sending excellent samples to obtain orders, and then provided goods of increasingly poorer quality – Archives nationales, Paris, F[12] 676/A, Pailleux, Amiens, correspondence with the Bureau of Commerce, 1778–79.

21 The struggle against counterfeiting was a continual worry for the manufacturers. In 1824, for instance, a bill was introduced 'to repress alterations or substitutions of names on manufactured goods' – Archives Nationales, AD XI 62, report by Lemoine des Mares, 25 June 1824, printed pamphlet.

22 'They would lose too much time if they were obliged to measure off every piece that they buy' – Archives départementales Nord C 7982, report of the *subdélégué* Crendal, Valenciennes, 29 June 1778. 'The cloth is brought for the merchants to buy several hundred pieces at a time, and quantities of it are bought every day. How would it be possible to measure them all? It would cause the merchant, not only great annoyance, but also an enormous expense, by forcing him to employ more people for the purpose, whereas with a stamping office the cloth is gauged exactly, the merchant has no worries, and for the cost of two sols a piece [the stamp tax], he avoids an expense which would become burdensome and useless' – Archives Nationales F[12] 1429, Crommelin, inspector at Valenciennes, 18 February 1792.

case of the *bretagnes* fabrics, one can note the slow process of defining a generic product, which led to the negotiation of a norm by Saint-Malo exporters that was ratified in 1676 by a regulation and reinstated in 1736.[23]

Here the conceptualization provided by the School of the Economics of Conventions proves very enlightening.[24] This school proposes to analyse the foundations and origins of the agreement which, in any given society, institutes and legitimizes the market, as well as the description of the objects to which this founding convention applies. However, it also seeks to study the description of the rules through which this convention is objectified by implicated agents, constituting the normative and cognitive framework available to them for obtaining the knowledge base on which they will make their decisions and act.

The eighteenth-century system of control and the mark of conformity I am dealing with can therefore be read in an entirely different way than it was by its liberal detractors: codified rules officialized and generalized the application of what we might call 'quality covenants', which the various economic agents had already tacitly recognized. In fact, it seems that no exchange, no agreement between the participants would have been possible without a prior common framework, a founding covenant that would do away with all suspicions and all factors of uncertainty: in this case, the covenant concerned the quality of the goods now regulated, ratified and officialized by the royal administration, which was developing a concept of market policing.[25]

This is exactly what the inspector Desmarest explained in his already cited 1779 report. The merchants and manufacturers in Reims and Troyes, he writes,

> all think that uniformity in the fabrication of each fabric known and adopted by the trade must also be maintained for the advantage of the negotiator and the consumer. It's thanks to this uniformity that different parties have attached a fixed idea to such and such a denomination of fabrics, and it is based on this convention that the merchant and the manufacturer receive commissions from

---

23 Lespagnol, *Messieurs*, p. 439.

24 *L'économie des conventions*, special issue of *Revue économique*, 40/2 (1989); André Orléan, *Analyse économique des conventions* (Paris, 1994), pp. 9–40; Robert Salais, 'À la recherche du fondement conventionnel des institutions', in Robert Salais, Élisabeth Chatel and Dorothée Rivaud-Danset (eds), *Institutions et conventions* (Paris, 1998, 'Raisons pratiques', no. 9), pp. 255–92; Olivier Favereau and Emmanuel Lazega (eds), *Conventions and Structures in Economic Organization: Markets, Networks and Hierarchies* (Cheltenham, 2002), esp. pp. 213–52.

25 François Eymard-Duvernay, 'Conventions de qualité et formes de coordination', *Revue économique*, 40/2 (1989): pp. 329–59, and Eymard-Duvernay, 'La qualification des produits', in Robert Salais and Laurent Thévenot (eds), *Le Travail. Marchés, règles, conventions* (Paris, 1986), pp. 239–48.

> their correspondents and that they satisfy them. It's thanks to this convention that the functioning and operations of trade are simplified.[26]

A similar process is witnessed in the West Riding of Yorkshire, where the Stamping Acts of 1709 and 1725 regulated the size of the woollen pieces, in order to forbid over-stretching which causes fallows to form in the pieces and makes the cloth uneven and less resistant. To avoid any hidden defect, the laws set a minimum breadth and a maximum length for the cloth to have when it is wet, that is to say when it is reduced to its smallest size. When the pieces left the mill, they had to be measured and marked. The manufacturer had to weave or sew his name along one of the edges of the piece, and the fuller not only had to stamp the trademark along the other side, but he also had to keep a registry for the seal. If a buyer suspected that he had been deceived, he had two weeks to commission a second opinion. The 1725 law created positions for salaried searchers charged with supervising the seal's operations and with visiting all manufacturing sites to catch any excessive stretching: in mid-century there were about 50 of these searchers overseeing a zone whose radius was around 15 miles to the south and west of Leeds, and they were charged with supervising about 80 mills.[27]

In the 1760s, a series of petitions called for a better enforcement of the laws: petitioners underlined the importance of the local production's reputation, for it was their reputation that provided a way of guaranteeing confidence and maintaining long-standing buyers. 'Shoddy work', 'false measurements' and fraudulent stretching of the cloth harmed the credit of clothiers all over West Riding. Norms are in effect a point of reference in international exchange. Whoever does not respect the usual specifications places themselves at risk of losing their business. 'The merchants abroad know that cloth is made in Yorkshire to a particular breadth, and expect to have it so', explained a Leeds clothier: the deceitfulness of a few would necessarily threaten the reputation of the whole group: whence the need for norms and controls.[28]

The modalities through which trust is generated vary with the nature of the product and the configuration of the various markets, but the general framework and principles remain the same. Here we see something very similar to what the

---

26 Archives départementales Marne, C 468, no. 3, 'réflexions' cited above. The words 'it's based on this convention' were added in between two lines by the inspector.

27 7 Anne cap. 13: *An Act for the better ascertaining the lengths and breadths of woollen cloths made in the County of York* (1709); 11 Geo. I, cap. 24, *An Act for the better regulating the manufacture of cloth in the West Riding of Yorkshire* (1725); *CJ*, vol. 21, p. 246, 28 February 1728/29. See Minard, 'L'inspection des draps du West Riding of Yorkshire'.

28 *CJ*, vol. 30, p. 91, 7 February 1765; *CJ*, vol. 30, 19 March 1765, p. 262–267 (report of select committee).

sociologist Laurent Thévenot called 'investments of form': some codifications that contribute to the stabilization of exchange and of the relations between agents. One could say that something like automatic relations are made possible through these investments, which allows them to avoid continually having to enact evaluations or renegotiations concerning the qualities or the truth of the announced labels and specifications.[29]

In the end, the official stamp provides the solution for a situation fairly close to what I would call 'an economy of quality': when supply and demand are principally defined by quality, and when an asymmetrical relation of information keeps the client, unlike the seller, from being able equally to evaluate available qualities and from easily separating the good from the bad, the exchange depends on a social organization based on confidence rather than on the forces of the classical market.[30]

Yet the regime of regulation does not work without certain disadvantages, and this is what explains the diversity of opinion among tradesmen.

Uses and Limits of Norms

The scope and efficiency of the mechanisms just explained are effectively limited: it is a question of markets and of types of products; the degree of uncertainty that can be tolerated, and, inversely, the need for confidence – all of which vary according to the type of merchandise under consideration.[31] Yet the regulatory

---

29 Laurent Thévenot, 'Les investissements de forme', *Cahiers du Centre d'Études de l'Emploi*, 1985, no. 29: 'Conventions économiques', pp. 21–72. See also Thévenot, 'Économie et formes conventionnelles', in Salais and Thévenot, *Le travail*, pp. 195–218, and Thévenot, 'Conventions of Co-ordination and the Framing of Uncertainty', in Edward Fullbrook (ed.), *Intersubjectivity in Economics* (London, 2002), pp. 181–97. The question of the role of trade marks in the social construction of contemporary markets would benefit from a development of the ideas proposed by David M. Higgins and Geoffrey Tweedale, 'The Trade Marks Question and the Lancashire Cotton Textile Industry, 1870–1914', *Textile History*, 27/2 (1996): pp. 207–28, and Mary Wilkins, 'The Neglected Intangible Asset: The Influence of the Trade Mark on the Rise of the Modern Corporation', *Business History*, 34 (1992): pp. 66–95.

30 Lucien Karpik's analysis, even though it applies to a certain type of offer (in this case, a service: lawyers) offers interesting points of comparison: 'L'économie de la qualité', *Revue française de sociologie*, 30/2 (1989): pp. 187–210.

31 One can distinguish between three categories of goods in terms of the information asymmetry: 'search goods' for which information is obtained during an examination of the product before purchase; 'experience goods' whose quality is experienced by consummation or use; 'faith goods', which attributes authority to a knowledgeable third party since their

regime that functioned in France took only one commercial situation into account: a situation in which competition mainly concerned not price, but quality. Colbert only envisioned a competition over guaranteed minimum quality for top-of-the-line products. As we have seen, this was a question of defeating foreign competition by offering the best fabrics possible, on the basis of constraining specifications and a fixed minimum quality.[32] It was also a question of guaranteeing an invariably fixed quality: to maintain confidence in long-distance markets, product specifications had to stay stable in a sustained way. By forbidding the producer from varying these characteristics and from going below certain norms, the regulation of course limited the price-elasticity of the market, and concentrated competition on the superior quality of the product. In the end, it is as if the products were destined to a unique consumer whose demand was fixed once and for all. In short, if on the one hand it is clear that stabilizing conventions into regulations offers the advantage of the predictability of actions (everyone knows what to expect), on the other hand it presents the disadvantage of stabilizing products in their momentary state.[33]

All markets cannot function in this manner. Over the course of the eighteenth century, in France, the development and especially the diversification of textile consumption led this 'economy of quality' to be placed in doubt by getting rid of the former market dichotomy on which the whole system relied. The Colbertian regulations essentially encompassed top-of-the-line production, and/or products for exportation; daily fabrics of poor quality were for the most part left to peasant auto-consumption. Yet in the eighteenth century, the evolution of the domestic demand, linked among other things to the original characteristics of French demographic growth, made this bi-partition more and more inappropriate: goods of intermediate quality have no place in it. It is, however, on mid-line products that fashion and the economy of 'novelties' play. Here we can observe a double movement. On the one hand, merchants certainly felt the necessity of expanding into semi-luxury goods, a privileged terrain where the rising urban classes could imitate elite consumption (with 'Indian' cotton fabrics most notably). On the other hand, we can see products that used to be auto-consumed or fabricated on command, enter into the market; this is the fruit of the heightened integration of peasants into the channels of a moneyed

---

quality cannot be estimated by a mere consumer either before or after the purchase because the prohibitive cost of the acquisition of this knowledge. The plating industry and silversmith trade belong to this third category: see Philippe Minard, 'Le bureau d'essai de Birmingham, ou la fabrique de la réputation au XVIIIe siècle', *Annales HSS*, 65/5 (2010), pp. 1117–46.

32 Coarse cloth did not go through these commercial channels, and its consumption was limited to peasant households.

33 Robert Salais, 'postface', in Stanziani, *Qualité des produits*, p. 284.

economy. This diversification of the textile economy signals the end of the unique consumer and the product that was dedicated to her.[34] The same consumers can buy merchandise that belongs to varying levels of quality.

For some goods and for some markets, then, the economy of quality underpinning the regulatory system became meaningless, because in that type of market everything depended on price elasticity, not on a marginally superior quality. So there were actually several different kinds of markets, which followed very different laws: there were many different 'worlds of production', and each one was organized around particular goods, commercial conditions and specific covenants.[35] There was the price elasticity on one hand, competition for quality on the other. These were two different commercial universes, and of course, they did not follow the same rules.

The divisions in opinion on regulations become clearer, then. At the vanguard of the fight for regulation we find those whose business worked well only if the quality of the goods was maintained, if the standards remained fixed. These people benefited from an official authority enforcing the respect of the quality covenant. On the contrary, all those who were bothered by regulations belonged often to another 'world of production', the world of light clothes, of novelties, of fashion, of middle or ordinary quality. For them, standards changed rapidly and so were less important than the selling price.

This offers a primary explanation for the diversity of opinions that we find. But there is another important cause, because not everything can be explained solely by the nature of the product. The position of a given economic agent in the exchange network changed everything as well: everything depended on whether you were dominant or dependent.

The play on regulations and standards of production was an integral part of the permanent balance of power underpinning exchanges. Each participant's dream was to be able to impose upstream rules on his employee or supplier, while he himself, downstream, would escape all regulations. For example, the same

34 Daniel Roche, *The Culture of Clothing: Dress and Fashion in the Ancien Regime* (Cambridge, 1994).

35 Robert Salais and Michael Storper, *Worlds of Production: The Action Frameworks of the Economy* (Cambridge, MA, 1997). These two economists intend to 'confront the actual characteristics of inequality, diversity and heterogeneity in economic situations, and inquire into the existence of several possible worlds of production and on the ways ... they interact in many real worlds of production' (p. 10). Each of the four 'possible worlds of production' is defined by the combination between a form of economic coordination, a type of product and a register of action. I have not taken this analogy further here, since the purpose is not to write an industrial and commercial history of France, but to relate the discourse and debates of political economy to their roots in the real problems of economic activity.

manufacturers opposed, on the one hand, the creation of any rule on the number of threads in the warp and in the weft of a piece of woollens, and demanded, on the other hand, the benefit of a regulation codifying and guaranteeing the high quality of their wool supply. Any regulation was good as long as it did not create constraints on oneself but affected everybody else, especially suppliers. Freedom for myself, constraint for everybody else: that was the doctrine.[36]

There was, therefore, a specific role for the repeated invocation of regulations by the very people who sought to evade them selectively. Regulation actually existed within a curious dialectic relationship between the collective and the particular. The necessity for quality could be universally recognized as a guarantee for preserving the market outlets and reputation of a manufacturer or trader, but everyone was secretly hoping at the same time to escape this restriction while competitors would respect it, or be forced to respect it. The collective advantage of maintaining standards could be strangely conflated with the individual hope of receiving the dividends of fraud. After all, the comparative advantage derived from fraud existed only if competitors were forced to follow the rules that the crook did not respect.[37]

But in the proto-industrial universe, it is the commercial game between producers and merchants that wins out, and this game is fundamentally unequal. The merchants hold the key to it, because they control the circuits. And it so happens that the norms imposed by regulation prove to be a weapon in the service of the strongest. Whether the merchant buys a semi-finished product from the fabricant (*Kaufsystem*), or whether the fabricant-merchant furnishes the primary material to be worked by the weaver (*Verlagssystem*, or putting-out system), in either case, the business person buys fabric or pays a salary based on the guaranteed minimum quality. The inspection done at the stamping office allows the buyer or the taskmaster to 'unmask the false fabricant', the worker who is not working hard enough or who is trying to limit her sweat.[38] And it

---

36 The inspector at Elbeuf, in 1763, was not fooled by this double game: 'The manufacturers want to be as independent as possible, but they want the opposite for their employees and the outworking spinners, whom they would on the contrary wish to subject without hindrance to the whims of their master carder-spinners in the countryside': Archives Nationales, F^{12} 737, Vallon de Boisroger to Trudaine, Elbeuf, 5 January 1763.

37 Erhard Friedberg, *Le pouvoir et la règle. Dynamiques de l'action organisée* (Paris, 1993), p. 170.

38 The expression comes from a former *garde-juré* at the stamping office for sail canvases in Rennes in 1767 – Archives Nationales, F^{12} 738, Pierre Jean Colliot de la Bussonnière, Rennes, 1 July 1767. In 1781, the Rennes merchants underline the benefits of regulations on a population of extremely dispersed spinners and weavers: 'The producers, numbering more than 2000 and spread throughout the countryside at 6 or 7 *lieues* from the centre of Rennes, have been on the one hand encouraged to do better, and on the other held back in

is clear that the massive ruralization of spinning and weaving only heightened producers' dependence on merchants who controlled the textile market. So, both as a means of putting pressure on prices, or as a supplementary guarantee as to the quality of a product, the official norm can constrain the worker and the producer to the advantage of the employer or the merchant.

In some cases, this dialectic game of rules can prove quite perverse. In the West Riding of Yorkshire, it sometimes happened that the merchant deliberately bought, with full consciousness, cloths that had been marked as bigger than they actually were, simply because he paid less for them. According to certain accounts, he then stretched them himself before selling them off: 'It is the merchant's interest, if he has bad designs, to have the cloth narrower than it is stamped, because he can stretch it more'.[39] In fact, the small-scale merchant-clothier did not have a choice: he was stuck between the risk of being fined and the loss of his business. If he wanted to sell his product, he had to submit to the demands of the merchant who was looking for under-dimensioned, less expensive pieces; but he also had no way of responding if the merchant demanded a further cut in price, because he himself was doing something illegal: 'The merchant does not always pay for the quantity of cloth delivered, which the clothier would rather submit to than to go to law, because he is subject to a penalty'.[40]

This is the source of a curious paradox: knowing that these norms aimed to protect the buyer against the deceit of the seller, one might have thought that, as a result, clothiers would be the first to be against regulations that prevent them from deceiving. It so happens that this is not at all the case. Far from being hostile to regulated specifications, clothiers, quite to the contrary, demanded their rigorous enforcement as a way of avoiding the situation of finding themselves hostage to the fraud the merchants imposed on them. This was for a very simple reason: strict verification during stamping would free them from any potential blackmail from merchants. In sum, in the present case, the norm is liberating as long as it is actually applied. One must therefore carefully discern the one who has an interest in the existence of the standard (the merchant who uses it to exert pressure on the clothier) from the one who has a vested interest in the strict application of the standard through actual verification (the clothier, as a way of evading of the merchant's blackmail).[41]

---

fear of fines' – Archives Nationales, F[12] 654, mémoire de juin 1781, signed by 12 merchants from Rennes.

39 See testimonies given by different clothiers to the select committee: *CJ*, vol. 30, pp. 262–7, 19 March 1765 (quote: David Farrer's testimony, p. 265).

40 Ibid., John Senior, manufacturer, p. 263.

41 Minard, 'L'inspection des draps du West Riding of Yorkshire'.

Finally, the obligation of passing all production through the stamping offices offers another advantage. We know that the concentration of merchandise, their physical grouping at sites of collective sales such as urban markets or supply centres, provide the advantages of comparison and choice to the buyers, who are informed as to available qualities and quantities. In areas without such a site, the stamping office, which makes production visible, fulfils its function: when the office is open, one or several times a week, the office works as a marketplace does. Thanks to this obligated concentration of rolls of fabric, it plays the role of a market for quotations and commercial information. Buyers who are present evaluate the quantity and quality of the arrivals, before they are eventually put on sale as they leave the office; the confrontation between product supply and demand gives birth to the market price. Conversely, in the *kaufsystem* that existed in West Riding, the public exhibition of cloths in a marketplace or a drapers hall could also, in some cases, liberate the clothier from an isolated interaction with one sole buyer by establishing a minimum of competition.

All this helps to explain these bizarre differences of opinion on regulation. Clearly, the world of manufacture and commerce was anything but a unified whole. On the contrary, everybody's interests changed with the nature of the product, with their position, whether strong or weak, in the commercial process. But many needed the visible hand of norms and regulations to run their business.

Conclusion

What lessons can be drawn from all of this? First, we can see to what extent exchange cannot be reduced to the contract of sale. To the contrary, all previous social conditions, norms and tacitly accepted rules must be taken into account since they constitute the common framework that allows for the exchange: the agreement is made possible by a preliminary agreement (whether unacknowledged or objectified) about the forms of agreement. French historian Jean-Pierre Hirsch has formulated this in other terms: the market, he says, 'needs other laws than the ones usually designated by the name of the "laws of the market"'.[42] This is not just a nice play on words, just for fun. This is the crucial acknowledgement that the market is not an absence of rules, quite simply because everything is not purely contractual in a contract.

---

42 Jean-Pierre Hirsch, *Les deux rêves du commerce. Entreprise et institution dans la région lilloise, 1760–1840* (Paris, 1991).

So, in addition, if we put ourselves on the more general level of a reflection on capitalism, we are brought to deny the claims of neo-liberal ideology: the hypothesis of absolutely free competition posited by the model of general equilibrium under the name of 'pure and perfect competition' not only presupposes an impersonal market, but also the homogeneity of goods being exchanged, which thereby become easily interchangeable. In short, when the exchange takes place, everyone knows what is being bought and what is being sold, and the problem of quality is always associated with price. In real life, things do not work frequently or automatically this way.

The eighteenth-century debates should not, therefore, be read through distorting lenses: the discussions did not bear so much on the principle of the rules as on the realm where they were applied, their pertinence and their zone of effectiveness. This was not a debate on principle, but on opportunity. And consequently, the true stakes for the actors were not about the existence of the rules, but about knowing who had the power to set them.

Chapter 10

Regulating Wages in Eighteenth and Early Nineteenth-Century England: Arguments in Context

Joanna Innes

This chapter explores a deregulatory shift which took place between the late eighteenth and mid-nineteenth centuries. In the late eighteenth century, there were on the statute book several acts authorizing justices of the peace to regulate wages – in general, under the sixteenth-century Statute of Artificers, or in particular trades, under new acts passed between 1721 and 1773. By contrast, during the next half century, attempts to obtain new authority for wage regulation were rejected, and most older statutes were repealed. By 1830, it was an article of faith in government circles that public authorities must not interfere in setting wages. Magistrates who sanctioned local wage agreements so as to contain disorder during the Swing riots which swept southern England in that year received 'testy memoranda' from the Home Secretary telling them to stop breaking the law.[1]

Policy developments in this period in relation to wage regulation specifically have never been the subject of focused study. Such accounts as have been supplied have mainly been framed within larger narratives of transition: from an older order, sometimes described as 'paternalistic', or alternatively as attuned to the values of small producers, towards a new, capitalistic social order, under which the state sought only to defend capitalists' freedom to deploy capital as they chose. These narratives of transition have their origins in stories told in the nineteenth and early twentieth centuries by people who often had one foot in the policy-making process. They derive from heroic narratives of the removal of obstacles to progress, from the laments of those who deplored change, and, finally, from histories of lost practices compiled in the late nineteenth or early

---

[1] Peter Jones, 'Swing, Speenhamland and Rural Social Relations: The "Moral Economy" of the English Crowd in the Nineteenth Century', *Social History*, 32 (2007): p. 281.

twentieth centuries at a time when state regulation was once again contemplated, so there was reason to revisit the past.[2]

Clearly change is central to this chapter: change is its subject, and undoubtedly the period saw larger intellectual, cultural and economic changes which helped to shape policy. Changes in official discourse furthermore reshaped the terrain on which arguments had to be made. Still, some problems arise from framing an account of policy shifts primarily within a narrative of transition. First, there is a danger that we might romanticize and traditionalize 'pre-transition' circumstances; secondly, we might oversimplify divisions of opinion, pigeonholing people as just for or against an older order; thirdly, we might over-estimate the impact of changes in law and government.

By way of corrective I stress first that England throughout this period was a highly commercial society, widely perceived as the site of clashing interests, played out within an international market economy. Those who sought wage regulation drew upon a heritage of ideas and practices, but their object was to manage change. The ways in which they sought to do this were diverse: some hoped to raise wage levels; some to stabilize them; some to keep them down.

Secondly, I stress heterogeneity. Within the English economy there co-existed various systems of production and exchange, some globally, some locally oriented. Some changed radically during the period, others less. The project of regulating wages did not have the same meaning in all settings; the potential for instituting it varied, as did the kinds of people who supported it. Opinion was heterogeneous in other respects too: some people were more ideological, others more practical. When wage regulation became the subject of dispute, not all who shared sides shared world-views. Not everyone found it easy to take sides:

---

2 We lack a modern historiography bridging the gap between the period covered by on the one hand, Walter E Minchinton (ed.), *Wage Regulation in Pre-Industrial England* (Newton Abbott, 1972) – reprinting works by Tawney (1914) and Kelsall (1938, 1942) – and Michael Roberts, 'Wages and Wage-Earners in England, 1563–1725: The Evidence of Wage Assessments', (D.Phil. thesis, University of Oxford, 1981); and, on the other hand, that recently surveyed by Sheila Blackburn, *A Fair Day's Wage for a Fair Day's Work?: Sweated Labour and the Origins of Minimum Wage Legislation in Britain* (Aldershot, 2007). Intervening conflicts have mainly been explored by labour historians, including Sidney and Beatrice Webb, *The History of Trade Unionism, 1666–1920* (Edinburgh, 1920); John L. and Barbara Hammond, *The Skilled Labourer* (new edn, London, 1979); Rodney Dobson, *Masters and Journeymen: A Prehistory of Industrial Relations 1717–1800* (London, 1980); John Rule, *The Experience of Labour in Eighteenth-Century Industry* (London, 1981) and Adrian Randall, *Riotous Assemblies: Popular Protest in Hanoverian England* (Oxford, 2006). For older studies, note the cluster of articles on this theme in *EHR* and *Economic Journal* 1898–1900.

what they wished for and what they thought practicable did not always mesh. In accounting for change, we need to acknowledge both diversity and uncertainty.

Thirdly, I stress certain continuities running through the period. At no point did authorities play much of a role in determining wages. They acted occasionally, in specific settings, and what they did was usually either to affirm what they took to be going wage-rates, or to try to mediate. Their actions were epiphenomenal to other kinds of 'wage-regulating' process: the formation of consensus among employers, or the making of agreements between employers and workers. When authorities lost the formal right to participate in these processes, they did not always stop acting (as we know because in 1830 the Home Secretary had to tell some of them to desist), and when they did stop acting, other, extra-official collective processes often continued. Continuities in this regard help to explain why there was always dissent from what became orthodoxy – always people who thought that officials could potentially help by nurturing wage agreements. Doctrinaire political economists may have needed a lot of convincing, but it did not require an enormous shift in the ideas of other key actors for alternative ideas to make headway on the parliamentary agenda in the late nineteenth and early twentieth centuries.

The Context: Wage Relationships

Through the eighteenth and nineteenth centuries, most English people were largely or wholly dependent for their support on wages – or 'prices' for piece-work, sometimes also termed wages – earned by themselves or other household members. Wage-workers worked across all sectors of employment: in the public services (especially the army and navy), in agriculture, manufactures, mining, construction, commerce, transport and services (especially domestic service). Some worked for wages set by the day or the week; some on piece rates. Some, especially those called 'servants' (both servants in husbandry and domestic servants), worked for annual wages, and had most of their remuneration in board and lodging. Wages were often only part of a package that included other perks; in a cash-poor economy, people were often 'paid' in credit or goods rather than cash. From wages might be subtracted rental charges, for space or tools, or fines and deductions. A worker might need to pay assistants from his or her wages. Disputes between employers and workers often focused on other elements of remuneration or conditions of work.[3]

---

[3] For wage-workers, John Rule, *The Labouring Classes in Early Industrial England, 1750–1850* (London, 1986). For wages, Donald Woodward, *Men at Work: Labourers and Building Craftsmen in the Towns of Northern England, 1450–1750* (Cambridge,

Through the eighteenth and early nineteenth centuries, wages were supposed to be agreed at the point of hiring. As such, they might reflect an employer's judgement of the capacities of a particular worker and the needs of the moment, or some kind of established rate – though even those could be treated as norms, and varied. Some employers determined what wages to pay with only the lightest reference to the wider economy. The government, above all, rarely varied what it paid soldiers and sailors, relying instead on targeting promising recruitment pools. But most employers operated in the context of tight budgets, and many had to compete to sell goods or services, so had reason to be sensitive to the implications of what they paid for their positioning within two different markets.

The setting for competition, however, varied from place to place. Some employers operated within what were in effect bounded labour pools, alongside a known and limited set of fellow employers. Insofar as farmers relied on daily or weekly waged workers, they could recruit only within walking distance, and sometimes drew only on their own parish. Usually they knew their competitors: opportunities to start new enterprises in rural England were limited. Farmers in the same parish often met formally in the parish vestry; this could operate informally as an employers' organization or labour exchange. Information and opinions about wages must often have been shared there or in other places where such men met (for example, in local towns on market days). Sometimes agreements may have been made.[4]

A complication, both an advantage and a disadvantage for the employer, was that the parish was also a relief unit: parishes were responsible for relieving people with 'settlements', and initially that remained the case even after the New Poor Law of 1834 shifted decision-making in welfare-cases towards larger unions. Settlement laws helped to tie down labour, which potentially helped to keep wages down, but might produce a local labour-surplus. Farmers and other local employers had to decide how to balance wage decisions against what these might entail in relief costs. These arrangements helped to focus collective attention on employment practices.[5]

1995); Leonard D. Schwarz, *London in the Age of Industrialisation: Entrepreneurs, Labour Force and Living Conditions, 1700–1850* (Cambridge, 1992), esp. pp. 157–229; Peter Scholliers and Leonard D. Schwarz (eds), *Experiencing Wages: Social and Cultural Aspects of Wage Forms in Europe since 1500* (Oxford, 2003).

[4] For relevant insights, Bernard Eccleston, 'Malthus, Wages and the Labour Market in England 1790–1830', in Michael Turner (ed.), *Malthus and His Time* (Basingstoke, 1986), pp. 149–53 and Robert C. Allen, *Enclosure and the Yeoman* (Oxford, 1992), pp. 49–54, 292–300.

[5] *The Diary of Thomas Turner 1754–1765*, ed. D. Vaizey (Oxford, 1984), pp. 238–9, for a suggestive parish dispute, turning on the relationship between employment and relief.

By the early nineteenth century, it is clear that these issues also pressed in some industrial parishes harbouring large groups working in low-wage industries. Ratepayers who found themselves subsidizing low-wage industry had an interest in encouraging employers to pay a living wage (or, as it was expressed in Coventry 'a living price').[6] In the later nineteenth century, employers who expected their workers to draw on relief or charity to survive were criticized as 'parasitic'. One argument then made for legal minimum wages in these settings was that this might force employers out of parasitism. The remedy ultimately endorsed under the New Poor Law was the denial of relief to people in work. Later, it could be argued that this had failed, so other approaches should be tried.[7]

Skilled workers might hope to enjoy less trammelled mobility than the relief-dependent. There were some other bars to movement, but the practice of restricting urban employment to freemen declined in this period. Resident workers, organized in trade clubs, sometimes tried to maintain closed shops, but it was hard for them to achieve complete control. Even small-town labour markets were therefore usually quite open.[8] Yet at any given moment, employers in a town or region might regard the workforce as given, and feel too that they knew the scale of competition. Especially if they were producing goods or services primarily for local markets, they might then think it possible and advantageous to agree with fellow employers what wages they would standardly pay, or at what prices they would sell: in effect, they made anti-competition agreements.[9] Employers sometimes equally found themselves pushed individually or collectively by organized workers to agree to 'fair' rates. Many employers did make such agreements, and in conditions of price stability, these might prove enduring.[10]

In some circumstances, even employers in expanding industries, operating with flexible labour pools and low levels of fixed as opposed to circulating capital,

---

Most studies have a later focus: e.g. Anne Digby, 'The Labour Market and the Continuity of Social Policy after 1834: The Case of the Eastern Counties', *EcHR*, ns. 26 (1975): pp. 69–83.

6 E.g. Alfred Temple Patterson, *Radical Leicester: A History of Leicester 1780–1850* (Leicester, 1975), pp. 104–5, 115–17, 220–27, 130–31, 138, 178–9, 291–3.

7 For parasitism, Blackburn, *Fair Day's Wage*, pp. 78, 113.

8 Michael J. Walker, 'The Extent of the Guild Control of Trades in England c.1660–1820: A Study Based on a Sample of Provincial Towns and London Companies', (Ph.D. thesis, University of Cambridge, 1986).

9 Guilds sometimes served as employers' organs in these regards. See e.g. pamphlet headed 'October 30, 1782. At a general meeting of the Society of Master Carpenters (London) ... specially summoned to receive the report of the committee appointed for revising the prices of day work, the following list was unanimously approved, and ordered to take place from Christmas last' – copy in the Eighteenth-Century Collections on-line database.

10 E.g. Webbs, *History of Trade Unions*, pp. 74–5.

and producing goods for sale in competitive national or international markets – conditions that obtained in most textile industries throughout the period, and from the later eighteenth century pre-eminently in cotton textiles – at least contemplated entering into wage agreements with other employers in the region, or with workers. They too might see benefit in stabilizing competition between producers, in maintaining good relations with their workforce and standards of living within communities. But the more these circumstances applied, the harder wage agreements were to forge, and the more precarious when forged.[11]

Statute Law to 1777

At the start of the eighteenth century, only the Elizabethan Statute of Artificers and a Jacobean amending statute authorized justices of the peace to regulate wages. The original statute was loosely drafted: it applied to agricultural workers, yet not to them only. There was ambiguity as to whether rates 'assessed' and published by quarter sessions represented maxima or minima. Many county benches occasionally published 'assessments' for agricultural and other workers through the seventeenth and into the early eighteenth century. Probably the rates specified (to the extent they were observed) served as norms. In years of price inflation, as the late sixteenth and early seventeenth centuries were, publication of rates may have been welcomed by employers as an aid to containing pay. Through the middle years of the eighteenth century, prices were more stable; this may help to explain why assessments became less common – though there is a cultural dimension to be considered too; arguably English culture changed in ways that made public enunciation of norms seem less evidently proper.[12] In East Sussex, wage assessments were issued annually until 1787, but by then the practice attracted little notice, and had an anachronistic air. In the 1790s, tables setting out county wage assessments were antiquarian curiosities – seen as models for possible new initiatives by some, but to others, of interest only as sources of historic price data.[13]

Did eighteenth-century 'price stability' really suffice for wages to stabilize? Did they not come under pressure, for example at times of bad harvest, when

11 For example, *PP*, 1818 (IX), pp. 12–15; Norman Murray, *The Scottish Hand Loom Weavers 1790–1850: A Social History* (Edinburgh, 1978), pp. 192–4.

12 Roberts, 'Wages and Wage Earners', is the most recent study. Minchinton, *Wage Regulation*, pp. 228–34 reprints a list of eighteenth-century wage assessments compiled by Kelsall, probably incomplete.

13 *Annals of Agriculture*, xxv, 305; Frederick M. Eden, *The State of the Poor* (3 vols, London, 1797) vol. 3, pp. xc–cx.

food prices shot up? Wage levels were not invariant, even when they were most stable, but employers often judged it wise to maintain norms so long as the underlying trend was level – fearing that wages once raised would be hard to lower. They could hope to help workers cope with hard times in other ways: by varying other elements of remuneration, by supporting extensions of credit, or by organizing charitable relief.[14]

During the early eighteenth century, English borough justices also issued occasional assessments.[15] For much longer, into the early nineteenth century, they sometimes adjudicated wage disputes. Whether they did this under statute, or simply to keep 'the peace' is probably not something they always felt the need to clarify, especially since they commonly proceeded by reconciling disputants. In 1777, as such disputes multiplied – probably reflecting food-price hikes in the 1760s and 1770s – Middlesex magistrates considered at length whether they had legal power to act, ultimately deciding by 13 votes to five that they had 'absolute jurisdiction'.[16]

Although magistrates sometimes acted without specific authority, through the middle eighteenth century, there nonetheless issued several new statutes, authorizing magistrates to regulate wages in particular trades. These dealt with London tailors (1721, revised 1768), woollen broadcloth weavers, concentrated in the west of England (1756), and silkweavers in Spitalfields, in the East End of London (1773, revised 1792 and 1811). Parliament contemplated similar provision in relation to hatters (1777) – but no such clause figured in the final act.[17]

The aims of those who sought legislation varied. In the case of the tailors, the proposal came from master tailors, seeking to restrain the wages of a privileged elite within the workforce.[18] In the case of the hatters also, it came from London masters, who claimed that workers had breached previous informal wage agreements. Journeyman in the north however made counter-representations,

---

14 Dr Johnson expressed conventional wisdom: Samuel Johnson and James Boswell, *A Journey to the Western Isles of Scotland and The Journal of a Tour to the Hebrides*, ed. R.W. Chapman (Oxford, 1970), pp. 337–8.

15 For Canterbury, Maidstone and Lincoln examples: Minchinton, *Wage Regulation*, pp. 233–4.

16 Dobson, *Masters and Journeymen*, ch. 6.

17 Tailors: 7 Geo I St 1 c. 13 (1721), 8 Geo III c. 18 (1768); Weavers: 29 Geo II c. 33 (1756); Spitalfields: 13 Geo III c. 68 (1773), 32 Geo III c. 44 (1792), 51 Geo III c. 11 (1811). Proceedings on the hatters' bill can be traced in *CJ*, vol. 36. The list is not exhaustive. I have, for example, omitted haulers and carriers, including coalheavers and porters.

18 *CJ*, vol. 19, p. 416 (7 February 1720/21) for the master tailors' petition. For 'tailors' as an elite among garment makers, Schwarz, *London*, pp. 186–94; for their activities, Dobson, *Masters and Journeymen*, ch. 5.

and headed off this attempt.[19] In the case of west-of-England woollen weavers, by contrast, the demand came from rank-and-file weavers, who sought to maintain wages. The next year, employing 'clothiers' struck back, claiming that so many different kinds of woollen cloth were fabricated that justices' broad prescriptions were meaningless; they got the offending clause repealed.[20] The Spitalfields Act emerged by a different route. It embodied an attempt to keep the peace between weavers and masters, by both maintaining and constraining wages. Masters who supported it argued that regulation was feasible in a manufacture primarily oriented towards a protected domestic market, while conceding that things were different for more export-oriented industries.[21]

All these initiatives grew out of intractable industrial disputes. That they took legislative form reflects the declining importance of the Privy Council, which might once have managed them alone, and the growing importance of Parliament. In the case of provincial workers, applications to Parliament possibly also tracked growing sophistication and determination. In 1726, West-Country weavers were advised by gentry whom they consulted that there was no point in applying to Parliament, which would never meddle with wages. They therefore petitioned the Crown. Their case was referred to the Board of Trade – a sub-committee of the Privy Council. The Board directed the parties to bring their dispute before local justices. County benches across west-of-England woollen counties did set weaving rates in this context.[22] Thirty years later, weavers who tried to get justices to act on the basis of such older assessments sought legal advice; they were told that the Elizabethan act had not specified adequate remedial procedures. They therefore turned to Parliament, seeking new law.[23] Identification of deficiencies in the drafting of older legislation provides one explanation for eighteenth-century resort to Parliament.

The tailors', woollen weavers' and hatters' acts all originated under private-bill procedure: applicants first petitioned, then adduced witnesses and written

---

19 *CJ*, vol. 36, pp. 118–19 (5 February 1777). For the hatters act as passed: 17 Geo III c. 55 (1777).

20 Repeal: 30 Geo II c. 12 (1757). Proceedings can be traced in *CJ*, vol. 27.

21 *PP*, 1818 (IX), p. 44.

22 Proceedings in *CJ*, vol. 27, and Julia de Lacy Mann, 'Clothiers and Weavers in Wiltshire in the Eighteenth Century', in Leslie S. Pressnell (ed.), *Studies in the Industrial Revolution* (London, 1960), pp. 67–71; Mann, *The Cloth Industry in the West of England from 1640–1880* (Oxford, 1971), pp. 108–18. Parliament did engage with concerns over wages after unrest among Devon and Somerset weavers in 1726, but acts resulting did not regulate wage levels (12 Geo I c. 24; 13 Geo I c. 23): the view that Parliament would not meddle with wages may reflect discussion then. Proceedings in *CJ*, vols 20, 21. Parliament wanted to know what the Council had done: *CJ*, vol. 20, pp. 746–7 (20 February 1726/27).

23 Mann, *Cloth Industry*, pp. 111–12, for weavers' proceedings in this instance.

evidence in support. If the case were 'proved', and no persuasive counter-case made, Parliament usually approved such bills, probably using drafts supplied by the petitioners. In the face of counter-representations, Parliament had either to choose sides or attempt a compromise.[24]

The Spitalfields Act of 1773 was unusual in embodying a compromise agreed outside Parliament.[25] It passed against the background of several years of violent conflict in the London district of Spitalfields. In order to restore peace, magistrates finally prevailed upon the parties to accept a concordat. The act empowered magistrates to fix wages in the trade; it also limited the number of apprentices that any one master might employ to the traditional two. Wage regulation under the Spitalfields Act was a laborious exercise, conducted over days of meetings between representatives of masters and workers. Hundreds, even thousands of prices for different products had to be agreed.[26]

In immediate context, Parliament's sanction for official involvement in wage fixing usually aimed at dispute resolution. Information about how regulatory processes operated over the longer haul is patchy. In the case of the London tailoring trade, masters clearly struggled to maintain set rates; some saw advantage in breaching limits so as to have first call on labour. Tailoring rates were specified in a simple way within the act; magistrates were empowered to vary them. They did so several times in the century, at the request of masters who thought that the old rates were untenable; they wanted legal sanction to pay higher rates, but also hoped by securing a new ruling to hold a new line.[27] The work involved in setting wages under the Spitalfields Act discouraged frequent revision. Magistrates oversaw this process only at intervals of years. It seems unlikely that wages were always paid exactly as specified, with no individual variation, and more probable that regulated prices served as norms.[28]

---

[24] Orlo C. Williams, *The Historical Development of Private Bill Procedure and Standing Orders in the House of Commons* (2 vols, London, 1948); David L. Rydz, *The Parliamentary Agents: A History* (London, 1979), esp. 42–6; 86–8.

[25] Uniquely, it (and later amending acts) were introduced not by petition, but by order; the first was steered through Parliament by an alderman; the second by the chairman of the Middlesex Bench; the third by the Vice President of the Board of Trade, George Rose, on whom see further below. *CJ*, vol. 24, p. 320 (18 May 1773); vol. 47, p. 733 (25 April 1792); vol. 66, p. 107 (21 February 1811).

[26] For context, Steinberg, *Fighting Words*, ch. 3; for the disturbances, Walter J. Shelton, *English Hunger and Industrial Disorders* (London, 1973), pp. 192–9; Dobson, *Masters and Journeymen*, pp. 86–8 details the manoeuvres of the authorities.

[27] Dobson, *Masters and Journeymen*, pp. 65, 66, 72. See also note 41.

[28] Prosecutions brought against masters and workmen who breached rates (Steinberg, *Fighting Words*, p. 64) show that they were not universally observed. Gravenor Henson, *Henson's History of the Framework Knitters*, ed. S.D Chapman (Newton Abbot, 1970),

That they achieved something is suggested by the fact that years of turbulence in Spitalfields were followed by decades of harmony, despite further ups and downs in the trade (though government also sought to protect employment in other ways, for example by maintaining barriers against imports of French silk in the Anglo-French trade treaty of 1786).[29]

The Revival of Interest in Rural Wage Assessments 1792–1800

In the autumn of 1795, the young Bedfordshire magistrate and radical Whig Samuel Whitbread junior moved for leave to bring in a bill to restate and refine magistrates' power to set wages in agriculture. Whitbread intended his rates to be minima; he meant his bill to be the first instalment of a package of measures to help the poor. The prime minister, William Pitt, may have wished chiefly to pre-empt this larger scheme. Be that as it may, Pitt did take seriously the bid to shape policy implicit in the wage-regulation proposal, sought advice on its merits, and came down against it. In parallel he assembled a think-tank of experts to devise alternatives. When Whitbread followed through on his proposal, Pitt was primed to counter him in a long and ambitious speech.[30]

Whitbread's proposal did not come from left field. Rather, it gave expression to ideas that had been disputed across southern England for several years. It sought to deal with a chronic problem, but also to manage a crisis. It piqued Pitt because it contributed to a radical Whig attempt to represent the government as floundering amidst crisis. The issues it raised were ones that Pitt found it hard to resolve. Just what it was possible and wise for government to attempt by way of regulating economic relations was still very much in debate. In fact when Pitt brought in his own package of proposals, a year later, there lurked within them the notion that parishes might determine an appropriate minimum wage, and subsidize those paid less – an idea that attracted its own share of abuse.

In the background to Whitbread's proposal lay the rising trend in prices that had characterized recent years. From the 1770s this had stimulated concern about the falling value of agricultural wages, and more generally about rural

p. 382, says there was much speculation in the measurement of work – one way in which employers could have adjusted costs.

29 John Ehrman, *The British Government and Commercial Negotiations with Europe* (Cambridge, 1962), pp. 46–7, 57–61.

30 John R. Poynter, *Society and Pauperism: English Ideas on Poor Relief, 1795–1834* (London, 1969), pp. 62–76; Thomas Ruggles, *The History of the Poor* (2nd edn, London, 1797), pp. 394–410; TNA, PRO 30/8/307–8.

workers' living standards and 'happiness'.[31] The situation reached near crisis when a bad harvest raised prices in 1789–90; crisis broke in 1795–96, when even agricultural regions experienced 'absolute shortage': sometimes grain simply could not be had; not merely how much but what to eat was in question. The 'principal inhabitants' of parishes struggled simultaneously to manage food supply, radically increased demands for relief and workers' demands for higher wages.[32] Given that it was widely agreed that the value of the agricultural wage had fallen, there was a case for increasing wages, though not to the level needed to purchase at famine prices; food shortage had to be managed in other ways. Communities debated by how much wages should be increased. And how could local agreements be made to stick, under continuing pressure from workers? Could magistrates play a part in brokering and stabilizing agreements? If that would help, did they have power to act? Was the Statute of Artificers (as amended) still fit for purpose, and even if so, was it still law, after being ignored for decades? These issues were debated within communities, in farmers' clubs on market days, and among magistrates across the south of England. Some county benches decided to issue wage assessments under the Statute of Artificers; some doubted their legal powers, but issued informal advice; some concluded that interfering would be controversial and do more harm than good.[33]

---

31 E.g. David Davies, *The Case of Labourers in Husbandry Stated and Considered* (Bath, 1795). Davies favoured the setting of a minimum wage. For other signs of concern, Joanna Innes, 'Power and Happiness: Empirical Social Enquiry in England', in Joanna Innes, *Inferior Politics: Social Problems and Social Policies in Eighteenth-Century Britain* (Oxford, 2009), pp. 159–60, 169–70; Anne Mellor, *Mothers of the Nation: Women's Political Writing in England 1780–1830* (Bloomington, IN, 2000), pp. 74, 110.

32 Roger Wells, *Wretched Faces: Famine in Wartime England, 1793–1801* (Gloucester, 1988). Wells collects instances of farm-worker militancy over wages in 'The Moral Economy of the English Countryside', in Adrian Randall and Andrew Charlesworth (eds), *Moral Economy and Popular Protest* (Basingstoke, 2000), pp. 229–31.

33 Gregory C. Smith, '"The Knowing Multitude": Popular Culture and Evangelical Revival in Wiltshire 1739–1850', (Ph.D. thesis, University of Toronto, 1992), p. 128 [Wiltshire, 1792]; [William Windham],*The Windham Papers* (2 vols, London, 1913), vol. 1, p. 108 [Norfolk, 1792]; David Eastwood, *Governing Rural England: Tradition and Transformation in Local Government 1780–1840* (Oxford, 1994), pp. 110–11 [Oxford, 1794–95]; M. Neuman, *The Speenhamland County: Poverty and the Poor Laws in Berkshire 1782–1834* (London, 1982), pp. 80–85 [Berkshire, 1795]; S. and B. Webb, *English Poor Law History: Part I, The Old Poor Law* (London, 1927), p. 174 [Suffolk, 1795]; C.N. Howard, 'The Justices of the Peace and County Government: Northamptonshire, Cambridgeshire and the West Riding 1730–95', (Ph.D. thesis, Johns Hopkins University, 1976), p. 248 [Cambridge, 1795]; Wells, *Wretched Faces*, p. 207 [Hampshire, 1795?]; John Acland, *Answer to a Pamphlet by Edward King* (Exeter, [1796]), pp. 25–6 [Devon, 179?]. The Whitbread papers in the Bedfordshire Record Office contain a Hertfordshire resolution on wages from

Whitbread stressed that he meant to respect market forces; Pitt argued that his proposal still went too far in tampering with them – though Pitt's own scheme when presented was also rejected with contumely. The Whigs revived the issue during the next harvest crisis, in 1800, but made little headway.[34] The argument that government should not interfere in domestic markets was gaining ground, and debates over this principle – which raged even more fiercely within the political classes in the crisis around 1800 than they had five years earlier – helped to entrench that notion in some minds. But the principle was disputed, and its proponents were sometimes hard pushed to defend it.[35]

Wage Regulation in Crafts and Manufactures 1775–1814

During the late eighteenth and early nineteenth centuries, employers continued sometimes to show interest in what statutory wage regulation might do for them. However, new applications for wage regulation statutes in a craft and manufacturing context were mostly made in the name, and sometimes at the instigation of workers. The Spitalfields Act provided vital inspiration. Those who found the model attractive included local elites who hoped such arrangements might bring peace to their communities, ratepayers seeking defences against industrial 'parasitism' and workers seeking leverage against employers. All applications in the name of workers ultimately failed, and tentative approaches in the name of employers were also rebuffed. Initial rebuffs took place against a background of division and uncertainty in government and Parliament. Subsequently, general prejudice against 'interference' gained ground, though it always comprehended diverse viewpoints.

An early instance of an application prompted by the Spitalfields Act came from framework knitters in 1778, repeated with modifications in 1779. There were links between London framework knitters (many of whom worked in silk) and silk weavers, which may have helped diffuse the idea. A committee of knitter delegates from the south and Midlands collected funds to support application costs. The campaign centred on Nottingham, where it gained support not only from workers but also from some employing hosiers, shopkeepers and local MPs. Other hosiers counter-petitioned, and rallied some workers, who said they

---

1795: Whitbread 1/11. The Suffolk proposal prompted Arthur Young to invite discussion in his periodical *Annals of Agriculture*.

34 *CJ*, vol. 55, pp. 171, 180, 186–7, 216 (12–14 February 1800); *Parliamentary Register* (12 vols, London, 1797–1802), vol. 12, 463–9 (11 February 1800).

35 For divisions and tensions within Parliament and government, Wells, *Wretched Faces*, esp. ch. 14.

had been misled by designing men but now appreciated that wage regulation would not help. Doubting whether magistrates could be trusted to withstand employer pressure, the committee initially proposed that wage rates should be specified in the text of the act. Both proponents and opponents of regulation found determined support in the Commons: over a two-year period there were three divisions on the bill, though in the end it failed.[36]

Further applications came only at the end of the century. By then, circumstances had changed in several respects. First, prices had continued to rise, stimulating strikes whenever boom conditions permitted, especially in 1792 and in the late 1790s. Secondly, two episodes of harvest crisis (1795–96 and 1800–1) had encouraged hard thinking about the rights and wrongs of interference in domestic markets. Thirdly, the outbreak of the French Revolution had made government and Parliament nervous about both popular assertiveness and utopian schemes.[37] These pressures did not all press in the same direction.

Against a background of political unrest and worker militancy, Pitt in 1799 asked his two secretaries to the Treasury to bring into Parliament a general act against workers' 'combinations'.[38] This was modelled on an act arising from a papermakers' dispute in 1796. That had banned combinations, but, in contrast to some other dispute-resolving acts, had not provided for wage regulation. The historian John Orth suggests that its attraction as a model was that it 'made not thinking about [wages] that much easier'. In fact, the two elements had not always been conjoined, and it would have been surprising if government had joined them, given Pitt's recent resistance to Whitbread's proposals. If he had not wished to affirm justices' power to regulate agricultural wages, how much less likely was he to do so in relation to all trades. In principle in any case these powers were still extant, if only in the vague, procedurally problematic form in which they had been cast by the Statute of Artificers.[39]

Historians have argued that, however adventitious in origin, the Combination Act marked a watershed in official attitudes. John Orth concludes, after reviewing the literature, that, both as first passed, and as amended but largely affirmed in 1800, the Act, though only marginally more oppressive than existing common law and statute, did mark a decisive turn against dealing with labour collectively,

---

36 Proceedings can be followed in *CJ*, vol. 36, and more fully in Henson, *Henson's History*, pp. 383–416.

37 For strikes, Dobson, *Masters and journeymen*, pp. 154–70. For debates, see Wells, *Wretched Faces*.

38 John V. Orth, *Combination and Conspiracy: A Legal History of Trade Unionism, 1721–1906* (Oxford, 1991), ch. 4.

39 For Middlesex justices' continuing activity, see *The Times*, 9 November 1804.

and a conscious turn against wage regulation.[40] However, it is not clear that the act's proposers (who had assembled it in a hurry) had committed themselves to any further reaching programme. At the time, its implications for the future of labour regulation in general and wage regulation in particular were unclear.

A first point to stress in this connection is that wage regulation can serve, and had most commonly served, to hold wages down. The Combination Act was pro-employer in orientation – but some employers continued to see wage-regulation as an attractive technology of control.[41] Pitt himself, in opposing Whitbread's bill, stressed that what he opposed was the use of regulation to maintain or increase wages: he exempted from his strictures acts meant to contain pressure from workers.[42] It was also possible, from a more neutral, managerial standpoint to suppose that the Combination Act positively necessitated further regulatory measures. For if workers were to be dissuaded from organizing to help themselves, was it not crucial to have ways of addressing their grievances? In any case, if anyone ever supposed that, unlike all previous, trade-specific combination acts this one would exterminate combinations, they were soon disappointed. Trade organizations, pressure on employers to raise wages or improve working conditions and various coercive tactics all continued to operate, so that the challenge of managing such conflicts remained acute.

Even as the Combination Act passed through Parliament, two trade groups sought statutory wage regulation to solve their problems. These were the main groups from which such proposals would emanate in later decades: silk and cotton weavers. Though workers in other manufacturing contexts showed equal concern to defend their interests through years of war-induced economic stress and industrial restructuring, they proceeded in different ways; framework knitters, notably, did not renew their former application.[43]

Quite why silk and cotton weavers persistently favoured wage regulation is unclear – not least because they were differently placed; circumstances within each industry also changed over time. Persistence probably had a cultural

---

40 Orth, *Combination*, pp. 57–67, esp. pp. 59–60.

41 For attempts by master tailors to adjust wages upwards but then hold the line, by application under the Tailors Act, *Morning Chronicle*, 28 January 1801; see also *The Times*, 14, 28 January 1801.

42 [William Woodfall] *An impartial report of the debates ... 1796* (4 vols, London, 1796), vol. 3, pp. 29–30. This approach was contested by John Howlett in *Examination of Mr Pitt's Speech* (London, 1796), pp. 22–4.

43 Randall, *Riotous Assemblies*, chs 9–11 for a recent overview. For the knitters' next application, see *PP*, 1812 (II), p. 203ff: the resulting bill (printed at several stages) would have required masters to publicize prices, but not to obtain any sanction for them; cf. for 1843, Patterson, *Radical Leicester*, pp. 384–5.

dimension: the strategy became a habit. At the start, it perhaps mattered that these groups could not – as woollen workers for example could – call upon a historic arsenal of regulatory statutes. Through to the 1810s (until blocked by the repeal of relevant acts) woollen workers harassed manufacturers who tried to change production regimes by prosecuting them under laws passed over the centuries to shape England's premier manufacture.[44] No such option was open to silk and cotton weavers. In cotton weaving, in addition, conventional apprenticeship constraints had been broken in the 1780s and early 1790s, as the industry boomed on the back of the mechanization of cotton spinning, and new workers flooded in. Cotton weavers were therefore ill placed to defend what workers in other trades often saw as a crucial bastion of workers' power. Yet, silk and cotton industries differed in important respects. The silk industry enjoyed protection from foreign competition, and catered primarily for a domestic market. The cotton industry, by contrast, was in important part export-oriented; cotton textile manufacturers saw great potential to expand sales in competitive global markets.[45]

In fact the two campaigns flourished in rather different social milieu. Coventry tended to take the lead in provincial silk campaigns: the 1799 application came from Coventry alone.[46] It may be significant that, like Nottingham, Coventry was a parliamentary borough and that this encouraged the political uptake of local trade concerns. Both in 1799 and in 1818 (when a second application was made in the name of Coventry ribbon weavers), the project was backed by at least one local MP, and enjoyed broad support within the city. In 1799, when mass signing of petitions was becoming *de rigueur*, the Coventry application was reportedly signed by 12,000, an impressive total given a city population of 21,000. The 1818 application was supported by local ratepayers, who feared that the ribbon industry was becoming parasitic, by the mayor and corporation and by local manufacturers. When it failed, its prime mover, Peter Gregory (a weaver who was also an 'undertaker', organizing production for manufacturers) led a successful strike to force employers to accept price 'lists'; this again enjoyed broad local support.[47]

---

44 Randall, *Riotous Assemblies*, pp. 253, 264–7; similarly for framework knitters p. 276.

45 Sir Frank Warner, *The Silk Industry of the United Kingdom: Its Origin and Development* (London, 1921); Stanley D. Chapman, *The Cotton Industry in the Industrial Revolution* (London, 1972).

46 John Prest, *The Industrial Revolution in Coventry* (Oxford, 1960); Peter Searby, 'Paternalism, Disturbance and Parliamentary Reform: Society and Politics in Coventry, 1819–32', *International Review of Social History* (1977): pp. 198–22.

47 *Whitehall Evening Post*, 6 July 1799; *PP*, 1818 (IX), pp. 16, 38–9; *Hansard*, vol. 40, p. 337 (13 May 1819); Searby, 'Paternalism', pp. 203–5, 208–9.

Cotton weavers also sometimes mustered broader support within their communities, but less broad support and less often.[48] Initial leadership was supplied by Bolton fancy-weavers, some working as putting-out agents. They constructed an impressive network among rank-and-file weavers across several counties, later also in Scotland. Even so, it took some time for the penny-a-week paid by their members to fuel a fighting fund sufficient to pay the costs of an attorney and parliamentary counsel, and witnesses' expenses. In 1799, prime evidence for the Coventry weavers came from 'Walter Brind esq.'. By contrast the cotton weavers' witnesses were mainly working men.[49]

There was no consensus within Parliament or government as to how to deal with these end-of-the-century applications. The Coventry bill passed the Commons – as private bills, supported by local members, usually did – but was blocked in the Lords by the Lord Chancellor, who argued that the Combination bill, then in process, should be considered first; he also said that he himself favoured only individualistic forms of bargaining. Once withdrawn, this bill was not re-introduced.[50]

Pitt probably had prior knowledge of the cotton weavers' organization, whose democratic structure and geographical reach had caused the government some anxiety.[51] What the weavers brought to Parliament in 1800 was a request for the establishment of two kinds of regulatory machinery: a regime of wage regulation (whose precise mechanisms remain unclear), and a system of arbitration, empowering representatives of employers and workers quickly and cheaply to settle one-to-one disputes about contractual terms and the quality of work performed. Pitt met with weaver delegates and offered to support their

---

48 There are many accounts, including Hammonds, *Skilled Labourer*, ch. 4; Duncan Bythell, *The Handloom Weavers: A Study in the English Cotton Industry during the Industrial Revolution* (London, 1969); Geoffrey Timmins, *The Last Shift: The Decline of Handloom Weaving in Nineteenth-Century Lancashire* (Manchester, 1993); John Bohstedt, *Riots and Community Politics in England and Wales 1790–1810* (London, 1983), ch. 6; Katrina Navickas, *Loyalism and Radicalism in Lancashire, 1798–1815* (Oxford, 2009); J.C.F. Barnes, 'The Trade Union and Radical Activities of the Carlisle Handloom Weavers', *Transactions of the Cumberland and Westmorland Antiquarian and Archaeological Society*, 78 (1978): pp. 149–61; Richards, 'State and Early Industrial Capitalism'. For the Scots, Murray, *Scottish Hand Loom Weavers*. For a participant's account, Alexander Richmond, *Narrative of the Condition of the Manufacturing Population and the Proceedings of Government Which Led to the State Trials in Scotland* (London, 1824).

49 *CJ*, vol. 54, p. 548 (22 May 1799); vol. 55, pp. 485–94 (8 May 1800).

50 Proceedings can be traced in *CJ*, vol. 54; see report in *The Star*, 9 July 1799.

51 In Privy Council papers, correspondence about the weavers is mixed with information about radical conspiracies, TNA, PC 1/44/155, 161, 1/45/164. For law officers' advice that weavers' proceedings were lawful: HO 43/11 ff 216, 222.

arbitration scheme, if they would drop the wage-regulation proposal. With his backing, the Arbitration Act passed into law.[52] Though ready to go some way to meet the weavers' wishes, Pitt thus continued to question the merits, and obstruct the passage of wage-regulation proposals.

Yet, in the same period at least potentially conflicting signals were being emitted by another senior legal figure, Kenyon, Lord Chief Justice of the Court of King's Bench. Kenyon was at this time irritating Pitt by advocating – contrary to ministerial policy – that justices of the peace respond to dearth by overseeing the sale of grain. He believed that empowering magistrates visibly to uphold social justice would promote order. He took a similar line in relation to wage disputes, advocating that they be either brought to the courts, or submitted to Parliament. Lancashire cotton weavers, who had read one of his judgements in the press, cited him as inspiration for their strategy.[53]

Pitt's long-serving senior Secretary to the Treasury, George Rose, who had helped bring in both Combination Acts, also was not securely on board the non-interference bandwagon. Rose probably first met weavers in 1800, concluding that they were men with whom one could do business; he maintained cordial links with them until his death, almost 20 years later.[54] During 1807–9, as Vice President of the Board of Trade under the Portland ministry, Rose coordinated the response to the weavers' renewed campaign for wage regulation – only to conclude, after laborious examination, that 'it was impossible to devise any method by which effectual relief could be afforded to those persons who had suffered so much and so patiently'.[55] At the Board of Trade shortly after, Rose dealt similarly sympathetically with master ropemakers who sought a wage-regulation statute, though he advised them that the cotton weavers' experience

52 *CJ*, vol. 55, pp. 262, 485–94 (5 March, 8 May 1800). For a later account, based on hearsay but consonant with known facts: *PP*, 1824 (V), pp. 51, 544. The act was 39 and 40 Geo III c. 90.

53 For grain, Douglas Hay, 'The State and the Market in 1800: Lord Kenyon and Mr Waddington', *Past and Present*, 162 (1999): pp. 101–62. For labour, see e.g. ropemakers' case reported in *The Times*, 23 February 1799. For the weavers, PC 1/44/155, bundle dated 29 April 1799, Papers relative to an association of weavers at Bolton, *An Address to the inhabitants of Bolton and places adjacent* (1799), p. 6. They cite remarks by Kenyon reported in the press (e.g. *The Star*, 20 February 1799).

54 *Hansard*, vol. 20, p. 433 (5 June 1811): Rose says he had held a correspondence with them for four or five years, probably circa 1804–10; for his attitude in 1804, *Hansard*, vol. 1, p. 473 (13 February 1804); see also BL, Add. Mss 42774, fol. 365.

55 Bythell, *Handloom Weavers*, pp. 153–5, considers Rose to have been insincere. For an interesting though not necessarily reliable account, *PP*, 1834 (X), pp. 423, 425, 442. I quote *Hansard*, vol. 20, pp. 433–4 (5 June 1811).

showed that such applications were unlikely to succeed.[56] Rose does not seem to have been clearly either pro-employer or pro-worker. Rather, an admirer of what had been achieved in Spitalfields, he continued to believe that official adjudication had the potential to promote both social justice and good order.[57]

By 1810, the climate had become more hostile to such notions. Big employers, and MPs responsive to them, were increasingly set on clearing away obstacles to their own advance. Some MPs (including Whitbread) had lost faith in legislative interference.[58] Some (like Rose) had struggled, through years of industrial turbulence, to develop new forms of regulation sensitive to a changing environment, but had achieved little (bar the first factory act, the Health and Morals of Apprentices Act of 1802, which was, exceptionally, championed by a leading industrialist, giving it a credibility that most such proposals lacked).[59] The cause of non-interference was making headway for a mixture reasons, but in part by default, not least because MPs quailed before the prospect of arbitrating mounting numbers of manufacturing disputes.

At about this point, a new strain of anti-regulatory sentiment began to form. A nodal figure was Francis Place, a retired businessman and political fixer, with a background both as an organizer of militant London trades and within anti-statist, Painite radicalism. Place questioned whether any official action was likely to advance the interests of working people. He thought they must fight their own battles. As he put it in 1835, the business of the working man 'should be to care for himself, his relatives, for his class, and to give himself no trouble what the rich may think of him ... [It was hopeless to look to] a power from above to "shake the temple of tyranny to its foundations"'. He argued also that workers must intelligently assess market conditions: some trades simply would not support high wages. There were groups of workers to whom his approach offered little. But his views were echoed by some other radicals, also products of the metropolitan trade world; some though not all of these had shared his business success. They were echoed too by a group of radical intellectuals with whom he now mixed: Jeremy Bentham, James Mill and a man soon to emerge as a tireless radical MP, scourge of big-spending government and closed corporations, Joseph Hume.[60]

---

56 TNA, BT 5/19, pp. 337–8.

57 *PP*, 1834 (X), p. 442, for a (perhaps rose-tinted) reminiscence. See also n. 25 above.

58 Dean Rapp, *Samuel Whitbread (1764–1815): A Social and Political Study* (New York, 1987), pp. 228–9.

59 Joanna Innes, 'Origins of the Factory Acts: the Health and Morals of Apprentices Act 1802', in Norma Landau (ed.), *Law, Crime and English Society, 1660–1830* (Cambridge, 2002), pp. 230–55.

60 Graham Wallas, *The Life of Francis Place 1771–1854* (4th edn, London, 1923) remains useful for long passages in Place's own words. Iorwerth J. Prothero, *Artisans and*

A complex set of alignments was thus taking shape, for and against official participation in the management of labour. On one side, most big and some small businessmen; political economy ideologues; some men with roots in militant unionism; and some radical literati. On the other; some more cautious small businessmen and tradesmen; workers in some overstocked, volatile and low-wage industries, and their more or less bullish sympathizers in the world of government, Parliament and philanthropy. A heterogeneous set of alliances – but with some similarities to those which formed for and against state intervention in the later nineteenth century.

A trade-boom in 1810 brought the usual increase in strikes; war-linked disruption of trade followed closely. Together these developments intensified agitation among craft and manufacturing workers. The result demonstrated Parliament's growing determination to restrict the tools they made available to contending parties. In 1811, master tailors applied to Parliament for the renewal and strengthening of their powers; their application ran into the sand. Place, who had run a tailor's shop, gave evidence against them.[61] In 1812, English and Scottish cotton weavers, despairing of obtaining new laws, in parallel brought court cases under old wage-regulation statutes (the Statute of Artificers in England, a similar statute in Scotland), aiming to force magistrates to regulate wages. Unexpectedly, the Scottish court ruled in favour of the weavers. The government responded in 1813 with a bill repealing the relevant clauses of both acts.[62] In parallel, Rose and Place found themselves on opposite sides on the issue of apprenticeship. Rose (who retired from the Board of Trade in 1812) was persuaded, despite his initial reluctance, to present a petition and chair the resulting committee on behalf of a body of tradesman who argued for the reform and strengthening of apprenticeship laws, whose deficiencies they had discovered in bringing prosecutions. Place organized publicity for a group who

---

Politics in Early Nineteenth-Century London: John Gast and His Times (Folkestone, 1979), pp. 172–5, details the development of his strategy. Place sometimes struck a different note (e.g. Wallas, *Life of Place*, pp. 217–18) but the passage quoted seems to me characteristic; it comes from 'Handloom Weavers and Factory Workers: A Letter to James Turner, Cotton Spinner', pp. 7–8 in John A. Roebuck (ed.), *Pamphlets for the People* (London, 1835); see also J.R. McCulloch, whom Place saw as a key ally, *An Essay on the Circumstances which Determine the Rate of Wages and the Condition of the Labouring Classes* (Edinburgh, 1826), esp. section VI. For other associates, William Thomas, *The Philosophic Radicals: Nine Studies in Theory and Practice, 1817–1841* (Oxford, 1979); Ronald K. Huch, *Joseph Hume, the People's M.P.* (Philadelphia, 1985).

61 *Hansard*, vol. 20, p. 589 (12 June 1811). Subsequent proceedings can be traced in *CJ*, vol. 66; Wallas, *Life of Place*, pp. 201–2.

62 1 Maule and Selwyn 190, *The English Reports* (Edinburgh, 1900–32), vol. 105, p. 71; Murray, *Scottish Handloom Weavers*, p. 187.

responded by pressing for the repeal of the apprenticeship clauses of the Statute of Artificers. Among others, he brought into play some Whigs who had recently launched an assault on the government's use of trade restriction as a weapon of war. Repeal won out, and so legal options were further restricted – to both practical and symbolic effect.[63]

Repeal Grand Finale: 1824

The climax to this sequence of repeals came in 1824. By that time there had developed a broad liberal consensus on economic issues among people who otherwise disagreed: Tory ministers and officials, an ambitious, rising section of the Whig opposition, and radical intellectuals who admired Bentham and Ricardo.[64] They agreed on the need to strip down and rationalize the mass of tariffs and taxes that had accreted around the economy during a quarter of a century of war (in this regard scorning the memory of the now deceased Rose, whom they portrayed as the mad architect of a grotesquely over-elaborated fiscal-military state).[65] They also agreed on the need to remove the meddling hand of officialdom from the domestic economy – though they differed over what they hoped would emerge when the state was stripped back.

In this context, they combined to support two epochal repeals. First, the repeal of the Spitalfields Acts, that is, the dismantling of the iconic wage-regulation regime. It was argued that the acts had failed to maintain living standards: Spitalfields workers were as distressed and demoralized as any. Moreover, if the acts had helped to maintain wages, then they had helped disperse the industry into cheaper regions. If English silk producers were to penetrate global markets, like their counterparts in the cotton industry, then, it was argued, they needed freedom to respond to market forces. Lowering of import barriers shortly afterwards was intended to affect the necessary jolt – but the challenge proved too strong; instead of forging ahead, the industry lost ground.[66] Secondly, these men supported the repeal of the Combination Act. Some among them may have thought this would discourage conspiracy and violence, and usher in an era

63 *Hansard*, vol. 27 (27 April 1814), p. 570. Thomas K. Derry, 'The Repeal of the Apprenticeship Clause of the Statute of Artificers', *EcHR*, 3 (1931): pp. 67–87; Prothero, *Artisans and Politics*, ch. 3.

64 Barry Gordon, *Political Economy in Parliament, 1819–1823* (London, 1976) and *Economic Doctrine and Tory Liberalism, 1824–1830* (London, 1979).

65 See e.g. *Hansard*, vol. 35, pp. 1018–20 (13 March1817); ns. vol. 12, pp. 53–4 (3 February 1825).

66 5 Geo. IV c. 66 (1824). Steinberg, *Fighting Words*, chs. 5–6.

of individualism and harmonious industrial relations. Place and his friends by contrast aimed to set workers free to assert themselves, to claim their fair share of such wealth as the market economy might generate. Henceforth the state was not to arbitrate: employers and workers were to work out their own future.[67]

Aftermath

The importance of maintaining a free market in labour and allowing wages to find their own level was variously theorized across the nineteenth century, but it long retained both a political and an intellectual hold. There were attempts to formulate counter-theories, but they failed to achieve intellectual prestige.[68]

Yet, officially endorsed or not, agreements about wage rates continued repeatedly – in some contexts routinely – to be made by economic actors in various settings. Farmers in village-England continued to come to understandings with one another about rates they would pay; small-town businessmen made non-competition agreements. Some manufacturers voluntarily endorsed wage-maintenance schemes; while organized labour battled to bring others to terms, under the eye of governments who increasingly accepted that these struggles were compatible with, indeed provided a testing ground for market forces.[69] All this being so, the idea that officially sponsored initiatives might in certain circumstances make a benign contribution – reducing friction in bargaining, assisting in the containment of labour militancy, helping workers poorly placed to pressure employers to make their case, or combating 'parasitism' – was, beneath the carapace of orthodox economic argument, always latent: ready, given the right circumstances and the right constellation of forces, to re-emerge.[70]

---

[67] 5 Geo. IV c. 96 (1824). Orth, *Combination and Conspiracy*, pp. 68–9; Prothero, *Artisans and Politics*, ch. 9.

[68] Noel W. Thompson, *The Real Rights of Man: Political Economies for the Working Class, 1775–1850* (London, 1998), pp. 42, 96–9. For orthodoxy as block to policy innovation, José Harris, *Unemployment and Politics: A Study in English Social Policy, 1886–1914* (Oxford, 1972); Blackburn, *Fair Day's Wage*.

[69] Swing riots produced wage renegotiation in some parishes, as noted at the start of this chapter. For industry, Prest, *Industrial Revolution*, pp. 53–63, though cf. pp. 88–93; Mark Curthoys, *Governments, Labour, and the Law in Mid-Victorian Britain: The Trade Union Legislation of the 1870s* (Oxford, 2004).

[70] For later initiatives: Lawrence Goldman, *Science, Reform and Politics in Mid Victorian Britain: The Social Science Association 1857–1886* (Cambridge, 2002), pp. 213–21; Blackburn, *Fair Day's Wage*.

Chapter 11

The Transition to Factory Production in the English Wool Textile Industries: Individual and Family Desires for Labour Regulation, 1720–1850

Paul Minoletti

The wool textile industry had been carried out for almost as long as there had been human settlements, and had been subject to regulation at least as early as the twelfth century.[1] Herbert Heaton concludes that almost from the beginnings of the industry until the nineteenth century, when the state abandoned all attempts at controlling the quality of goods, focusing instead on supervising the conditions of labour, regulation of the wool textile industry on a national level was motivated by two primary considerations. First, the real and genuine desire to keep English cloths at a high and uniform quality and to maintain the good name of English fabrics at both home and abroad, and secondly, the desire to get revenue for the state from the industry.[2] However, there had also long been legislation concerned with the national labour market, such as the 1563 Statute of Artificers. Further, Parliament was willing to intervene in local labour markets, for example the legislation passed in 1756 to set piece-rates for Gloucestershire weavers.

The existence of legislation did not necessarily translate into regulation being enacted, with local interpretations of legislation and customary expectations often differing significantly. The extent and type of regulation which was actually enforced can largely, but not exclusively, be explained through the self-interest of workers, employers and other interested parties of all classes, and the social, political and economic power they enjoyed in their locality. Until the 1833 Factory Act, under which inspectors were appointed by a national body, any labour regulation passed in Parliament was dependent on the local magistracy for

---

1 Herbert Heaton, *The Yorkshire Woollen and Worsted Industries: From the Earliest Times up to the Industrial Revolution* (Oxford, 1920), p. 3.

2 Heaton, *Yorkshire Woollen and Worsted Industries*, pp. 124–5.

its implementation, who were responsive to the desires of local actors. However, despite wool textile production long having been organized for national and international trade, regional variation in the application of regulation was becoming increasingly difficult to maintain. Rapid technological change threatened the interests of certain workers, who were hostile to a potential loss of earnings or employment, but resistance to more efficient technology (e.g. the spinning-jenny, the fly-shuttle, the gig-mill) resulted in a loss of trade and decreased earnings and employment when other regions adopted the superior technology. The occupational structure of West Riding woollens, where division of labour was the least advanced, ensured there was the least opposition to new technology and the least clamour for the fixing of piece-rates, showing the importance of an understanding of the political and social situation when trying to determine the economic efficiency of competing systems of industrial organization.

The desire of domestic production workers for regulation of technology or wages reflected the monetary effect this would have on family income, but workers' responses to the advent of factory production was not so simple. Domestic workers cherished their freedom and strongly resented the controls over their behaviour and use of time that factory work entailed. It also created a significant shift in attitudes towards women's work as in some sectors women began to threaten male occupations, and long regular hours worked away from home conflicted with their ability to perform the mothering and domestic tasks expected of them. Parliament was never completely opposed to the regulation of labour; even in the supposed heyday of *laissez-faire* in the early nineteenth century. There was initial doubt over whether to repeal the apprenticeship laws, and acts regulating factory labour were passed in 1802 and 1819.[3] This chapter begins by charting the course of labour regulation as the eighteenth century progressed, and how this was shaped by the economic self-interest of the actors involved. The later part of this chapter considers how regulation according to age and gender was increasingly desired as factory production became predominant. Whilst there has been superb scholarship looking at each of the two main wool textile producing areas which has included discussion of workers' desires for regulation and how this was influenced by industrial structure,[4] there has been

---

[3] Although the 1802 Health and Morals of Apprentices Act primarily applied to parish apprentices, some of its provisions affected employment conditions for all workers, and many members of Parliament wished to see its provisions extended to all children working in factories. See, Joanna Innes, 'Origins of the Factory Acts; The Health and Morals of Apprentices Act, 1802', in Norma Landau (ed.), *Law, Crime and English Society, 1660–1830* (Cambridge, 2002), especially p. 251.

[4] See Pat Hudson, *The Genesis of Industrial Capital: A Study of the West Riding Wool Textile Industry c.1750–1850* (Cambridge, 1986); Theodore Koditschek, *Class Formation*

little written that explicitly contrasts the two regions in this context. Historical investigations of the evolution of regulation on a national scale have tended to focus on regulation of trade, rather than that which directly affects labour.[5] Most research by historians on the transition to the factory and the effect this had on gender ideology and family decision-making has focused on the more heavily-researched cotton industry.[6] This chapter represents a modest attempt to fill some of these gaps.

The growth of the woollen industry in the eighteenth century was particularly concentrated in the West Riding of Yorkshire.[7] At the start of the century the west of England (principally Gloucestershire, Wiltshire, Somerset and Devon) dominated woollen cloth production, but by the end of the century was already in rapid decline relative to the West Riding, and not long after the Napoleonic Wars it entered absolute decline.[8] The worsted industry, previously centred in Norfolk and the surrounding area, showed even more spectacular growth in the West Riding. Having been relatively unimportant there until the late seventeenth century, it then expanded rapidly, particularly with the expansion of 'stuff' manufacture from the middle of the eighteenth century onwards.[9] Unlike the worsted trade around Norwich, the West Riding trade was highly centralized with the trade dominated by a small number of wealthy entrepreneurs typically employing proletarianized domestic workers in specific processes, and this was increasingly so as the eighteenth century progressed.[10] The west-of-England woollen trade was organized along similar lines to the worsted trade in the West Riding, whereas the West Riding woollen trade was still dominated by small clothiers, who owned the materials they worked on and

and Urban-Industrial Society: Bradford, 1750–1850 (Cambridge, 1990); Julia de Lacy Mann, *The Cloth Industry in the West of England, from 1640 to 1880* (Oxford, 1971).

5 For example, see Raymond L. Sickinger, 'Regulation or Ruination: Parliament's Consistent Pattern of Mercantilist Regulation of the English Textile Trade, 1660–1800', *Parliamentary History*, 19 (2000): pp. 211–32.

6 For example, see Joyce Burnette, *Gender, Work and Wages in Industrial Revolution Britain* (Cambridge, 2008); Anna Clark, *The Struggle for the Breaches: Gender and the Making of the British Working Class* (London, 1995); Sylvia Walby, *Patriarchy at Work: Patriarchal and Capitalist Relations in Employment* (Cambridge, 1986).

7 Throughout this chapter the 'West Riding' is taken to include some of the border areas of Lancashire where wool textile production was also carried out.

8 Adrian Randall, 'Work, Culture and Resistance to Machinery in the West of England Woollen Industry', in Pat Hudson (ed.), *Regions and Industries: A Perspective on the Industrial Revolution in Britain* (Cambridge, 1989), p. 175.

9 Hudson, *Genesis*, p. 27.

10 Hudson, *Genesis*, pp. 19, 27; David T. Jenkins and Kenneth G. Ponting, *The British Wool Textile Industry, 1770–1914* (London, 1982), pp. 8–9.

performed most processes from buying the raw cloth to selling it with only the assistance of their family and perhaps a few journeymen.[11] Even by the start of the nineteenth century, it remained common for West Riding clothiers to own small plots of land which they would farm, in contrast to the wage-dependent workers that characterized West Riding worsted and, particularly, west-of-England woollens.[12] Surviving evidence from the West Riding in the eighteenth century regarding the cost of domestic machinery suggests that it was within the reach of a worker wishing to start-up, or move up in the trade, and there was considerable social mobility in the woollen branch of the trade.[13]

These differences in industrial structure were highly significant in determining the desire for regulation amongst both workers and employers. Aside from some preparatory and finishing work, all the production processes in West Riding woollens could be performed at home within an extended family production unit, thus there was relatively little incentive for these workers to oppose new technology, since they stood to benefit from any increase in productivity at a given stage in the production process; whereas workers focused on one specific process stood to lose from labour-saving developments, encouraging them to demand regulation to prevent technological change. Similarly for these workers any decrease in wages in one process gave no benefit to family income, encouraging demands for wage regulation. The opportunity for social mobility in West Riding woollens also reduced a binary self-identification between employees and masters, encouraging cooperation. The conflict of interest between masters and workers in West Riding worsted and west-of-England woollens made employers more keen to enact regulation to try to get workers to behave as they wished.

Due to the industrial structure, embezzlement of materials by domestic workers was a recurrent problem for employers in West Riding worsted and west-of-England woollens. Acts against embezzlement were introduced in 1610 and 1702, and were sometimes enforced. For example in August 1764, according to the *Leedes Intelligencer*, 'Lydia Longbottom, of Bingley, was publickly whipt thro' the market at Wakefield, for reeling false and short yarn ... the town bailiff carrying a reel before her'.[14] And it was the opinion of Josiah Tucker, a rector from Bristol writing in 1757, that in general sufficient checks existed to provide, '... a tolerable Security against Impositions', by textile workers.[15]

11 *Report and Minutes of Evidence, on the State of the Woollen Manufacture of England PP*, 1806, (III), p. 1040; Jenkins and Ponting, *British Wool Textile Industry*, p. 8.

12 *PP*, 1806 (III), pp. 602, 934; Hudson, *Genesis*, p. 19.

13 *PP*, 1806 (III), pp. 1040–41; Hudson, *Genesis*, p. 30.

14 Cited in Heaton, *Yorkshire Woollen and Worsted Industry*, p. 419.

15 Josiah Tucker, *Instructions for Travellers* (Dublin, 1757), p. 30.

However, prosecutions were rare, with masters not finding it worthwhile to take on fraudulent workers by themselves through the regular legal channels, which were cumbersome and frequently too overstretched to care about an issue which could seem trivial and for which it was difficult to prove guilt. In the West Riding an informal group of worsted employers banded together around 1775 to employ inspectors to safeguard the interests of the worsted masters. The success of this initial step led to the authority of their group being sanctioned by the Worsted Act of 1777, which fixed new penalties for workers found to be embezzling and receivers of stolen goods, and agents and putting-out merchants were made responsible for false-reeled and short-weight yarn. It also stated that material given out to spinners had to be worked up within eight days, or else the spinners could be committed to the House of Correction for one month as punishment.[16]

There was an apparent deterioration in relations between clothiers and workers in the west of England in the eighteenth century, leading Gloucestershire clothiers in 1774 to successfully petition Parliament for renewed legislation with higher penalties. It did not provide any new provision for inspection and had little effect, whereas the 1777 Worsted Act seems to have ultimately succeeded.[17] Further, Herbert Heaton notes that even the generally successful Worsted Committee had to deal with the ignorance, apathy or actual hostility of the magistrates. The worsted industry covered a wide area, in much of which the spinning of yarn was merely a by-occupation for agricultural workers, and in these parts justices could be unaware of all the details of complicated textile legislation. Even though the Worsted Committee regularly printed digests of the law and sent deputations to the justices, local authorities did not always side with them. Indeed, in some cases even if the magistrate accepted the defendants were guilty, they refused to prosecute since they claimed that the laws were arbitrary or irrelevant.[18]

From the start of the eighteenth century there were strikes and rioting over wage-rates from West Riding worsted workers, especially wool-combers (wool-combing was a preliminary stage required for worsted production) and the clothworkers (i.e. those employed in the finishing processes) in Leeds woollens.[19] There was a similar desire to enforce both formal (i.e. codified by law) and informal (brought about by protest and 'collective bargaining by riot') regulation of wage levels and payment type amongst the woollen workers in

---

16 Heaton, *Yorkshire Woollen and Worsted Industry*, pp. 418, 420–21; Ivy Pinchbeck, *Women Workers and the Industrial Revolution* (2nd edn, London, 1969), pp. 146–7.

17 Mann, *Cloth Industry*, p. 114; Pinchbeck, *Women Workers*, p. 146.

18 Heaton, *Yorkshire Woollen and Worsted Industry*, pp. 428–9.

19 Heaton, *Yorkshire Woollen and Worsted Industry*, pp. 316–17.

the west of England. West-of-England clothiers complained to Parliament in 1718 and 1724 that weavers, 'threatened to pull down their houses and burn their work unless they would agree with their terms', showing a strong desire to standardize piece-rates.[20] The riots in Wiltshire and east Somerset in 1726–27, in Wiltshire in 1738 and in Gloucestershire in 1727 and 1756 were all by weavers objecting to the level of wages, or unfair practices by employers (such as truck payments or using false measures) which reduced earnings.[21] Despite the riots of 1726–27 attracting much sympathy from country gentlemen, and even some clothiers, the only regulation of the acts passed in an attempt to address the weavers' grievances which was consistently observed was the obligation to pay weavers by the yard, and even this merely applied to the superfine branch of the Wiltshire trade.[22] The acts had also prohibited truck payments and arranged for the fixing of wages by the magistrates but these provisions were widely ignored, despite in 1728 an order for the rate of wages being made at the Michaelmas quarter sessions.[23] No regulation was introduced in response to the Wiltshire riots of 1738. Although an act directing the justices to set piece-rates was introduced in 1756 following the Gloucestershire riots, this was ignored by many of the clothiers and repealed in 1757 following their complaints.[24]

These events show an ideological willingness to accept the validity of regulation of wages amongst sections of the ruling classes, and huge desire for them to do so on the part of workers, but limited concern at a national level as to whether regulation was actually applied. The dispersed nature of the weavers and illegality of combinations of workers attempting to increase wages also made it difficult for them to combine apart from at sporadic junctures, and so, unlike the trade unions of the mid-nineteenth century, they were unable to maintain consistent pressure on employers. The wool-combers in the West Riding had a union in existence well before 1741 and they were able to fix piece-rates, as well as use a national ticket system that enabled them to work in union-controlled shops elsewhere in the country.[25] However, it is unclear

---

20 Cited in E.J. Hobsbawm, *Labouring Men: Studies in the History of Labour* (2nd edn, Trowbridge, 1968), p. 7.

21 Mann, *Cloth Industry*, pp. 108–9.

22 Mann, *Cloth Industry*, p. 109. The obligation to pay weavers by the yard was a response to employers frequently lengthening the warp (i.e. the length of the piece of cloth) by several yards whilst continuing to pay the same price for the piece.

23 John L. and Barbara Hammond, *The Skilled Labourer, 1760–1832* (London, 1919), p. 157.

24 Hammond and Hammond, *Skilled Labourer*, pp. 157–9; Mann, *Cloth Industry*, p. 110.

25 Heaton, *Yorkshire Woollen and Worsted Industry*, p. 318.

how long this particular union lasted and to what extent they could flout the law preventing them from wage bargaining. And we know that in 1791, that is before the introduction of the Combination Acts which provided an increased legal barrier to unionization, certain Halifax wool-combers were prosecuted for having conspired to raise their wages.[26] While some leniency regarding combinations was expressed throughout the eighteenth century, unions had to act in a climate whereby they could face prosecution if local interests against them were strong enough (since Halifax was a key centre of the worsted industry, and by this time the Worsted Committee had considerable power, the interests of employers here can be expected to have exercised considerable power over the local magistracy).

Eighteenth-century unions expended much of their effort on trying to limit the labour supply. Women's employment as weavers had been attacked in the fifteenth and sixteenth centuries, and at Cullompton in Devon the male serge weavers enforced a ban on women weavers for just under a century until 1825.[27] There were sporadic outbursts of violence at households of weaving couples in Essex around the 1730s, with women weavers being accused of causing wages to fall and decreasing the quality of cloth.[28] However, there seems to have been relatively little desire to completely exclude women from weaving. Since weaving could be performed at home women could combine it with mothering duties and household chores, diminishing male resistance to it. The fact that weaving had traditionally been men's work does not appear to have led to significant gender conflict over women entering the trade. Attempts by weavers to control entry to their trade primarily focused on trying to enforce apprenticeship regulations. The sixteenth-century 'Act Touching Weavers', which specifically stated that nobody could become a weaver without being apprenticed, and the 1563 Statute of Artificers which controlled entry to the trade, were theoretically still in force throughout the eighteenth century (not being repealed until 1809, and 1813 respectively), but these rules were already being widely disregarded by the beginning of the century, especially in the west of England, and fell into further disuse as the century progressed.[29] Despite

---

26 Heaton, *Yorkshire Woollen and Worsted Industry*, p. 432.

27 Hammond and Hammond, *Skilled Labourer*, p. 162; Ephraim Lipson, *The History of the Woollen and Worsted Industries* (London, 1921), p. 57.

28 Pamela Sharpe, *Adapting to Capitalism: Working Women in the English Economy, 1700–1850* (Basingstoke, 1996), p. 33.

29 *Minutes of Evidence Taken before the Committee, to Whom the Bill, Respecting the Laws Relating to the Woollen Trade, Is Committed, PP*, 1802–03 (VII), p. 787; Heaton, *Yorkshire Woollen and Worsted Industry*, p. 301; Mann, *Cloth Industry*, p. 105; Pinchbeck, *Women Workers*, pp. 159–61.

this, wherever workers were able to organize they frequently tried to attempt to enforce some kind of apprenticeship regulation.[30]

Unsurprisingly, given women's lower tendency to unionize and their dispersed location, spinners (who were almost exclusively women and children) had few means of exerting pressure to try to regulate their widely fluctuating wages.[31] By contrast clothworkers seem to have had the most success in limiting entry to their trade of any branch in the eighteenth century, benefiting from, and perpetuating an all male workforce who worked together in shops, making communication between these workers easier than for dispersed domestic workers such as weavers and spinners. This increased the levels of trust needed for effective unionization, and they also benefited from performing a vital stage in the production process. Thus, in Wiltshire and Somerset by the end of the eighteenth century they were able to impose high entry fees on journeymen from elsewhere, with the resultant limitation on worker numbers meaning that their earnings, in Wiltshire at least, had almost doubled.[32]

As well as attempting to set piece-rates and limit entry to the trade, workers frequently tried to prevent the introduction of new technology. Industrial structure was again important here for determining workers' attitudes: labour saving technology faced relatively little opposition from West Riding woollen weavers, who would typically benefit from increased productivity in spinning, weaving and so on, since they would sell the cloth themselves; whereas the West Riding worsted and west-of-England woollen workers, employed in one specific branch of the trade, would naturally oppose any developments which threatened to reduce demand for their labour. The higher level of opposition, particularly violent opposition, from west-of-England workers compared to West Riding worsted workers probably reflected the stronger growth of the West Riding worsted trade, which helped to compensate for technological unemployment.

The flying-shuttle, an invention which increased the productivity of weavers, first appeared in the West Riding woollen industry around 1763–64. Although there was some initial resistance to it, including a riot against it in Leeds in 1770, it had been completely accepted by the end of the 1770s.[33] The much later introduction and spread of the flying-shuttle in the west supports Adrian Randall's view that, 'The rebellious culture of the west-of-England woollen workers undoubtedly had an impact on innovators. Their tradition of violence

---

30 Alfred P. Wadsworth and Julia de Lacy Mann, *The Cotton Trade and Industrial Lancashire, 1600–1780* (Manchester, 1931), pp. 116, 343–4, 362, 366, 368–9; Malcolm I. Thomis and Jennifer Grimmett, *Women in Protest, 1800–1850* (London, 1982), p. 72.

31 Mann, *Cloth Industry*, p. 109.

32 Mann, *Cloth Industry*, p. 109.

33 Hudson, *Genesis*, p. 42; Mann, *Cloth Industry*, p. 140.

deterred all but the most determined from confrontations over machinery'.[34] The first evidence we have of it being introduced in the west of England is at Trowbridge in 1792, resulting in a riot. A clothier from Stonehouse tried to introduce it in 1793–95, but was persuaded by other Gloucestershire clothiers to withdraw it, due to their fear of worker opposition.[35] Around 1798, when trade was good and enlistment in the army had led to a real shortage of weavers, it was adopted by the majority of Gloucestershire weavers, but was still far from universal there by 1803. Elsewhere in the west of England 'it was hardly known' by this time and faced continued worker opposition.[36]

It seems that the nature of worsted fibre made it unsuitable for use with spinning-jennies (invented c.1764–65, and first used in the cotton industry), whereas woollen fibre was extremely well suited to it, and the jenny was increasingly used in West Riding woollens in the 1770s, where the domestic jenny dominated as the method of spinning woollen yarn until well into the nineteenth century. Since the jenny could be used at home, and the weaving family production unit benefited from cheaper and more plentiful yarn there was little opposition.[37] In contrast, in the west of England worker opposition ensured that it did not become common until the early 1790s, despite the first attempt at introducing it to the region being in 1776.[38] In that year 12 Shepton Mallet clothiers, having successfully quelled opposition by local weavers, introduced jenny machinery. However, the fear of this machinery was so great that the machinery was destroyed by a mob, mainly from Frome and Warminster.[39] By the spring of 1781 at least one jenny and carding engine had been set up in Frome, but these were destroyed by a Whit Monday mob. At Keynsham in 1790 the colliers and their wives attempted to destroy the jennies being introduced, and dragoons had to be sent in to deal with the rioters.[40]

The geographical mobility displayed by the mob at Shepton Mallet in 1776, many of them travelling 15–20 miles, displayed a powerful willingness among members of the labouring classes to protect their self-interest, even if this was ultimately doomed to failure. Unlike in the West Riding, where labour saving technology in weaving and spinning benefited woollen workers, in the west of England it provoked fierce resistance from communities who stood to suffer. The strong opposition of men to spinning machinery, which would affect female

34 Randall, 'Work, Culture and Resistance', p. 192.

35 Mann, *Cloth Industry*, p. 140.

36 *PP*, 1802–03 (VII), p. 575; Mann, *Cloth Industry*, pp. 140–41.

37 Hudson, *Genesis*, p. 42.

38 Randall, 'Work, Culture and Resistance', p. 176.

39 Mann, *Cloth Industry*, p. 123; Randall, 'Work, Culture and Resistance', pp. 192–3.

40 Mann, *Cloth Industry*, pp. 125, 128.

employment, stands in contrast to the opposition many men had to women's work after the transition to factory production. Domestic spinning was no threat to male jobs, and neither did it interfere with traditional expectations regarding their childbearing and child-rearing role. The importance of male self-interest in influencing their attitude towards regulating the determinants of female employment can be seen even more clearly in cotton-spinning. In 1779, jennies in and around Blackburn with more than 24 spindles were destroyed by men and women, as were some carding machines and water-frames. All of the machinery attacked was selected because it could not be used within the home.[41]

The transition from domestic to factory production marks a change in how workers were motivated to try to enforce regulation regarding new technology. Under the domestic system, workers' attitudes towards regulation was fairly clearly motivated by narrow economic self-interest, albeit that there may have been a level of initial resistance excessive to the actual threat to their earning capability due to imperfect knowledge or hostility to change generally. However, the shift to factory production meant that changes in family earning capability no longer provided such a clear guide to workers' attitudes. There was great hostility from the labouring classes, as evidenced by the well-known difficulty the early factory masters had in attracting labour.[42] The separation of work and home was particularly important for attitudes regarding women's work, and many men (and women) no longer fought to defend women's earning capability.

The government investigations of 1802–03 and 1806, which interviewed workers and employers in the west of England and the West Riding, in response to the petition of the west-of-England clothiers to repeal all restrictive legislation on the wool textile trades, are extremely revealing for why workers in both regions were so resistant to being forced to abandon the domestic system of production.[43] The distance required for travelling to work in factories each day could be up to six miles, representing a major loss of time in the day when compared to a putting-out merchant coming to visit individuals or hamlets.[44] Many weavers expressed their concern as to how their children and wives could earn an income, since factories were not thought to offer the chance for the family production unit to survive, or to provide much alternative work for wives and children.[45] Even if male wages were higher in the factories, which was not

---

41 Wadsworth and Mann, *Cotton Trade*, pp. 374–5.

42 Stanley D. Chapman, *The Early Factory Masters: The Transition to the Factory System in the Midlands Textile Industry* (Newton Abbot, 1967), p. 156.

43 *PP*, 1802–03 (VII), pp. 495–877; *PP*, 1806 (III), pp. 567–1041.

44 *PP*, 1802–03 (VII), pp. 557, 566, 589.

45 *PP*, 1802–03 (VI), pp. 563, 592; *PP*, 1806 (III), pp. 643, 673, 938.

necessarily the case, it was believed that family income would decline.[46] This problem was seen as particularly acute for the youngest children, with workers expressing dismay at factories rarely being willing to employ children under the age of eight or nine.[47]

The abandonment of the family production unit was not just feared for potential effects on income, but also on the possible negative moral effects of children no longer being supervised by their fathers, as well as factories themselves sometimes being perceived as immoral places, since they featured, 'A great many people, men and women, getting together, and great irregularities I understand take place'.[48] At a meeting of the woollen workers around Huddersfield in 1806 it was 'resolved unanimously':

> That the domestic system is highly favourable to the cultivation of paternal, filial, and fraternal affections, the springs of family happiness, and to the cultivation of good, moral, and civil habits, the sources of public tranquillity; that the factory system tends to the prevention of these affections and habits, and leads youth sooner into the strongest temptations, by which they are in danger of being corrupted, even to their ruin.[49]

Given the later campaigns to reduce factory hours, it is striking that some workers objected to the fact that factory work did not enable them to work long enough hours, whereas at home, 'We work all our leisure Time how we like there'.[50] Even if the number of hours worked at the factory was no different there was also strong opposition by workers to being told at what time they could start and finish.[51] In the West Riding, where, unlike in the west of England, the small clothiers typically enjoyed a close relationship with any journeymen working for them and annual contracts were common, it was felt that factory owners would be far more willing to discard workers when trade was bad, amplifying cyclical unemployment.[52] The closeness of the relationship between domestic

---

46 *PP*, 1802–03 (VII), p. 863; *PP*, 1806 (III), p. 616.

47 *PP*, 1802–03 (VII), p. 567.

48 Testimony of William Child, a journeyman weaver from the West Riding, *PP*, 1806 (III), p. 705.

49 *PP*, 1806 (III), p. 1042. See also, *PP*, 1802–03 (VII), pp. 566, 592; *PP*, 1806 (III), pp. 643, 714.

50 Testimony of Cornelius Bancroft, a weaver from Bradford (Wiltshire), *PP*, 1802–03 (VII), p. 572.

51 *PP*, 1806 (III), pp. 697, 705, 719.

52 *PP*, 1806 (III), pp. 670, 698. In the west of England the large clothiers had no such relationship with their journeyman, and it was felt that the shift to the factory might actually

master weavers and journeymen in the West Riding was described thus by Joseph Coope, a weaver from Pudsey (a village around six miles from Leeds), 'Our men and masters are in general so joined together in sentiment, and, if I may be admitted to use the term, love to each other, that they do not wish to be separated if they can help it'.[53] The testimony of John Wallington, a clothier of over 30 years at Dursley (Gloucestershire), to the 1802–03 Report suggested that hostility to factory production was the primary reason for opposition to the flying-shuttle. He stated that in his area they were first introduced in workshops, creating much alarm amongst the workers, but once a delegation was sent to speak to the 3–4,000 assembled on Hartley Common who explained they could use them at home, the opposition died down and the workers soon began to use them voluntarily.[54] The strength of workers' opposition to the factory is further indicated by John Phillis, a weaver from Shepton Mallet, stating that he would rather have half the level of work (and therefore income) at home than to work in a factory.[55] Defence of the merits of the domestic system was not limited to the weavers: they enjoyed considerable support from various classes, and despite the two full-scale parliamentary investigations of 1802–03 and 1806, and contrary to the expectations of the west of England masters, it was not until 1809 that the repeal of all the restrictive legislation finally took place, despite the obvious impracticalities of continuing with the old system of apprenticeship. Indeed, although the committee who undertook the 1806 investigation did not recommend any legislation to prevent factory production, they gave this assessment of the benefits of domestic production:

> ... it affords to men of steadiness and industry to establish themselves as little Master Manufacturers, and maintain their families in comfort by their own industry and frugality; and to the encouragement which it thus holds out to domestic habits and virtues ... [we also note] its favourable tendencies on the health and morals of a large and important class of the community.[56]

The often violent protests of 1802 against the gig-mill in Wiltshire and Somerset revealed similarly mixed responses to regulation. The workers believed it to be prohibited by an Act of Edward VI, and an inconclusive legal action had been

---

reduce cyclical unemployment since employers would now have a higher level of fixed capital invested, *PP*, 1802–03 (VII), p. 563.

53 *PP*, 1806 (III), p. 637.

54 *PP*, 1802–03 (VII), pp. 793–4, 811.

55 *PP*, 1802–03 (VII), p. 563.

56 *PP*, 1806 (III), p. 578.

brought against a Wiltshire clothier who had tried to introduce it in 1794.[57] The confusion was due to whether the machinery now being used in the gig-mill was the same as that prohibited by the act. In Gloucestershire it had long been used for coarse cloth, and at the end of the eighteenth century its use had been extended to fine cloth without much opposition.[58] In contrast, in Wiltshire and Somerset it was fiercely resisted and remained rare until after the end of the Napoleonic Wars.[59] However, it should be noted how temporary labour market conditions considerably affected workers' desire to protest: a few Wiltshire masters had experimented with gig-mills right at the end of the eighteenth century without too much unrest, but demobilization led to an over-stocked labour market, leading to the riots of 1802.[60] It is also significant that Wiltshire and Somerset clothiers were able to send their cloths to Gloucestershire gig-mills, limiting the extent to which Wiltshire and Somerset workers could prevent their use.[61]

The other main development to affect the finishing processes of the woollen industry was the introduction of the shearing-frame. It was first patented in 1787, and another patent was granted in 1794, but as was the case with the gig-mill it did not become widespread in Wiltshire and Somerset until after 1815.[62] Although it was in use in the West Riding by the end of the eighteenth century, the Institution (the organization of the croppers, the workers threatened by the shearing-frame) fought powerfully against it, and were particularly successful in preventing its introduction to the Leeds area. Around 1799 a mill employing the shearing-frame at Holbeck had been burned to the ground by the local populace, and violent protest continued against it, culminating in the Luddite attacks of 1812.[63] The Institution also used strike action and violent protest, with some success, in an attempt to spread the use of the gig-mill in the West Riding.[64] Unlike the small master weavers that typified West Riding woollens, the finishing workers did not stand to benefit from labour-saving technology, and so responded in the same way as workers employed on the same processes in the west of England.

Of all the Luddite protests of 1811–12 (in Yorkshire, Lancashire and the East Midlands), Thomis and Grimmett find only one clear example of Luddite

---

57 *PP*, 1806 (III), p. 571; Mann, *Cloth Industry*, p. 141.

58 Mann, *Cloth Industry*, pp. 141–2; *PP*, 1802–03 (VII), p. 747.

59 Mann, *Cloth Industry*, pp. 150–51.

60 *PP*, 1802–03 (VII), pp. 646, 672–3, 674, 678.

61 *PP*, 1802–03 (VII), pp. 831, 863; *PP*, 1806 (III), p. 959.

62 Mann, *Cloth Industry*, pp. 150–51; Malcolm I. Thomis, *The Luddites: Machine Breaking in Regency England* (Newton Abbot, 1970), p. 54.

63 Thomis, *Luddites*, p. 54.

64 *PP*, 1802–03 (VII), p. 743; *PP*, 1806 (III), pp. 830–37, 901, 963.

hostility to women's work, at Pentridge in Derbyshire.[65] The acceptance of women's work by the Lancashire Luddites, who were primarily handloom weavers resisting attempts to shift their work to the factory, reflected the fact that women could perform this work at home, as well as the dispersed nature of the weavers and the ease with which their trade could be learnt, making exclusion of certain groups from the labour force extremely difficult to achieve. This contrasts with cotton mule-spinners, who had a powerful union from early in the nineteenth century, and almost all of their strikes 1800–40 featured opposition to women working, leading to their near total exclusion.[66] Whilst this was partially a way of protecting male privilege, they also excluded the Irish and males unrelated to members of the union, suggesting that gender was primarily seen as another way of limiting the labour supply, therefore increasing the wages of the existing members.

Carol Morgan has highlighted how the question of their domestic role was not the most important issue for women in the 1830s and 1840s. Rather, these women saw their interest as being aligned with their husbands at this time, and their priorities were adequate wages for their families and education for their children.[67] This can be seen in the movement that brought about the Factory Acts of the 1830s and 1840s. The 1833 act banned children aged less than nine from working in factories, and limited the number of hours children aged nine to 12 could work. The act of 1844 placed further restrictions on child labour, excluded women from night work and stated that their hours should be limited to 12 per day. The short hours movement enjoyed further success with the 1847 act, which limited women's and children's factory work to ten hours per day. Sylvia Walby argues that all the protective legislation which treated women workers separately from men should be seen as patriarchal rather than reformist.[68] However, this fails to see how the acts of 1844 and 1847 built on the act of 1833. Since female and child labour was so integral to factory textile production, restrictions on this type of labour helped reduce hours for all workers, and it was much easier to get support from the ruling classes for such reforms when compared to campaigns for restrictions on male labour.[69]

---

65 Thomis and Grimmett, *Women in Protest*, p. 69.

66 William Lazonick, 'Industrial Relations and Technical Change: The Case of the Self-Acting Mule', *Cambridge Journal of Economics*, 3 (1979): p. 236.

67 Carol Morgan, *Women Workers and Gender Identities, 1835–1913* (London, 2001), p. 41.

68 Walby, *Patriarchy*, p. 101.

69 Beatrice L. Hutchins and Amy Harrison, *A History of Factory Legislation* (2nd edn, London, 1911), pp. 50–51, 65.

There is no doubt that many working men supported the exclusion of women, for example in 1841 a deputation from the West Riding Short-Time Committee to Peel and Gladstone called for 'the gradual withdrawal of all females from the factories'.[70] It was often claimed that it was unnatural for women to work, and that preference should be given to males.[71] Unfortunately, there is very little surviving evidence on working-class women's attitudes to work during this period. However, what little we have suggests that many women were willing to accept a diminution in their work opportunities relative to those of men, if this was seen as benefiting the family. Michael Anderson concludes from his study of Preston cotton workers in 1851 that, 'Only before they had their first child did women work because they wanted to'.[72] Similarly, amongst the cotton workers of Stockport and the framework-knitters of Leicester women's level of employment decreased once their children were old enough to go out to work.[73] Since it would have been easier to combine mothering and domestic responsibilities with factory work once children had left the home, this shows a strong resistance to factory work by mothers, and it seems that they were driven to do this work by family income requirements.

In 1849 a survey of cotton textile operatives by the factory inspectors found that just under 55 per cent of women supported the reduction of women's factory labour to ten hours per day. Only 70 per cent of men questioned supported the reduction; hence there was no dramatic difference in preference by gender. Moreover, it can be expected that wives of male factory operatives who did not work in factories themselves would have been even more supportive of the reduction than the factory women surveyed. Angus Reach, who undertook extensive tours of the Lancashire and Yorkshire textile districts in 1849, found that:

> ... a very powerful stimulus has been given to increased neatness at home by the additional evening leisure time which the Ten Hours Bill has ensured to the women. 'I have now time to clean my house, and I do it, too, every evening', is the

---

70 Pinchbeck, *Women Workers*, p. 200.

71 Wanda Neff, *Victorian Working Women: An Historical and Literary Study of Women in British Industries and Professions, 1832–50* (London, 1929), p. 37.

72 Michael Anderson, *Family Structure in Nineteenth-Century Lancashire* (Cambridge, 1972), p. 72.

73 R. Burr-Litchfield, 'The Family and the Mill: Cotton Mill Work, Family Work Patterns and Fertility in Mid-Victorian Stockport', in Anthony S. Wohl (ed.), *The Victorian Family: Structure and Stresses* (London, 1978), p. 191; Nancy Grey Osterud, 'Gender Divisions and the Organisation of Work in the Leicester Hosiery Industry', in Angela V. John (ed.), *Unequal Opportunities: Women's Employment in England 1800–1918* (Oxford, 1986), pp. 58–9.

> phrase I have heard repeated a hundred times by the tenters and female weavers. 'Before I was so tired that I could do nothing but just eat my supper and go to bed', they generally added.[74]

Since it was widely believed by the working-class during the campaign in the 1840s for the ten-hour day that a reduction in working hours would not permanently reduce wages, it is unsurprising that there was strong support for it from both genders.[75] Of course, women without a man to support them stood to lose from legislation which made males more attractive to employers, and this point was made by both working women and their defenders in the press.[76] However, this was not the situation for most working-class women and family and community identities seem to have been more important than any notions of gender solidarity at this time.

The 1833 Factory Act was the first piece of factory labour legislation to have a real impact on how employers treated their workers and whom they chose to employ.[77] The Factory Acts of the 1830s and 1840s were the result of the support of the majority of the working-class in textile areas for restrictions on their hours, combined with a widespread sentiment amongst the ruling classes that no longer saw work as beneficial for women and children, as it had done previously.[78] Whilst a few employers, such as Henry Ashworth (a paternalist cotton manufacturer near Bolton), maintained a strong ideological attachment to having complete freedom as to how to treat their workforce, many employers also followed their economic self-interest with regard to factory legislation: large urban manufacturers using steam engines, who employed relatively low numbers of young children and were less susceptible to production interruptions than water-powered mills, gave support to the 1833 Factory Act since it gave them a competitive advantage.[79]

---

74 Angus B. Reach, *Manchester and the Textile Districts in 1849*, ed. C. Aspin (Rossendale, 1972), pp. 10–11.

75 Jane Humphries, 'Class Struggle and the Persistence of the Working-Class Family', *Cambridge Journal of Economics* (1977): p. 252.

76 Pinchbeck, *Women Workers*, pp. 199–201.

77 Clark Nardinelli, *Child Labour and the Industrial Revolution* (Bloomington, IN, 1990), p. 107; Pinchbeck, *Women Workers*, p. 184.

78 *PP*, 1806 (III), p. 1035. Hutchins and Harrison, *History of Factory Legislation*, pp. 65–6.

79 Rhodes Boyson, *The Ashworth Cotton Enterprise: The Rise and Fall of a Family Firm* (Oxford, 1970), p. 157; Howard P. Marvel, 'Factory Regulation: A Reinterpretation of Early English Experience', *Journal of Law and Economics*, 20 (1977): pp. 380, 388, 392.

Industrial structure determined the self-interest of workers, and thus was vital for determining their attitudes towards regulation. Whilst attempts to set wages or prevent the introduction of labour-saving technology were more common in the west of England, we also see this attitude amongst West Riding workers employed in worsted and the finishing processes of the woollen industry, where they faced the same labour market conditions as the west-of-England workers. The recourse to violent protest reflects the strength of feeling amongst the workers, but also the difficulty they had in combining due to their dispersed nature and the illegality of unionization until the repeal of the Combination Acts in 1824. Although enthusiasm amongst the ruling classes for regulation of labour reached a low point around 1800, it was never fully extinguished, and revived dramatically from around the 1830s as interest increased in the nature of factory work. This period also saw the introduction of nationally appointed inspectors, meaning that the strength of local interests no longer had so much influence on how regulation was enforced. The shift to factory production was also instrumental for attitudes towards regulation amongst the labouring classes, who expressed strong hostility to the lack of control this meant they would have over their work patterns and the breakup of the family work-unit. This meant the workers' attitudes towards regulation could no longer be so comprehensively explained by the effects any change would have on family income. The movement of industry away from the domestic sphere was particularly important for attitudes regarding women's work: men and women had fought to defend women's ability to earn income within the home, but the attitudes of working-class families were significantly different towards work which was much more difficult to combine with domestic and mothering responsibilities.

Chapter 12

Rent Seeking or Skill Creating? Apprenticeship in Early Industrial Britain

Jane Humphries

Apprenticeship has long been contentious. Did it bar entry to trades and so secure monopoly rents as Adam Smith famously contended, or did it contribute positively to the performance of the early modern economy as some modern economic historians have dared to suggest? The restoration of apprenticeship's reputation requires a defence against charges that it was exclusive and anti-meritocratic: time spent in indentures serving only to limit the supply of skills. Rehabilitation also involves specifying the ways in which it contributed to growth and efficiency. Possible channels include training, mobility and lifelines to the socially excluded. This chapter investigates the case for and against apprenticeship in the context of eighteenth- and nineteenth-century Britain, a context which provides something of a natural experiment since the repeal of the Statute of Artificers and the decay of the guilds enables the comparison of regulatory regimes. In the early eighteenth century both the law and the power of the guilds supported apprenticeship. By the nineteenth century both had disappeared. Apprenticeship no longer conferred an exclusive (albeit irregularly and incompletely policed) right to practice a trade.

The chapter focuses on two issues. First, it explores changes in the popularity of apprenticeship over time. Evidence for a structural break with the repeal of the Statute of Artificers might suggest that it was not training that attracted lads but access to trades whose supply was artificially limited and whose returns were thereby inflated: indentures constituted a barrier to entry that raised rents once apprenticeship was completed. In this case, the incentive to complete an apprenticeship would disappear alongside the legal basis for such rents, and its popularity would decline sharply. In contrast, the persistence of apprenticeship across the legal regimes suggests that potential apprentices valued the training irrespective of the institutional context and thought that the years of service paid off in terms of skill-related higher earnings post-indentures even as the latter no longer limited supply.

Second, the chapter presses the case for rehabilitation by examining the extent to which apprenticeship was anti-meritocratic and hence inefficient. Were prosperous or well-connected families able to transmit economic advantages regardless of their descendants' aptitude? Alternatively, were the skilled trades accessible to boys from humble backgrounds if they exhibited enterprise and willingness? If so, scarce training would have been more widely distributed and better matched to ability. This is no trivial issue. Economists have argued that matching talent to opportunity enhances economic performance. In the continental European literature, the extent to which apprenticeship was an instrument for the dynastic transmission of human capital has been an issue in the debate about the openness of guilds. Its measurement has usually involved the calculation of the proportion of masters with fathers who were masters in an earlier cohort. However, the pursuit of an apprenticeship did not necessarily signal the aspiration to become a master, especially in the English context. A better test of the extent to which apprenticeship distorted the distribution of training must focus not on access to mastership but apprenticeship. This involves an examination of the ways in which apprenticeship indentures barred entry, including whether all boys had to pay premiums and whether or not they had some pre-existing relationship with their master, most obviously kinship.

The investigation makes use of findings about the extent of and motivation for apprenticeship extracted from working-class memoirs presented in detail in *Childhood and Child Labour in the British Industrial Revolution*.[1] It uses both quantitative and qualitative evidence to begin to answer these questions and complements other recent research based on apprenticeship indentures.[2]

Did 1814 Provide a Structural Break in Apprenticeship?

Historians have agreed that apprenticeship declined during industrialization, but the timing and causes remain unclear.[3] Studies based on company records

1 Jane Humphries, *Childhood and Child Labour in the British Industrial Revolution* (Cambridge, 2010), p. 256ff.

2 See Chris Minns, Tim Leunig and Patrick Wallis, 'Networks in the Premodern Economy: The Market for London Apprenticeships, 1600–1749', *Journal of Economic History* (forthcoming); Tom Marshall, 'Were There Any Limitations on Who Could Undertake an Apprenticeship?', unpublished paper presented in the Graduate Student Seminar, Nuffield College, Oxford, 2010.

3 See George Unwin, *The Gilds and Companies of London* (London, 1908); John L. Hammond and Barbara Hammond, *The Town Labourer, 1760–1832* (London, 1917); Olive Dunlop and Richard D. Denham, *English Apprenticeship and Child Labour: A*

have identified the seventeenth and early eighteenth centuries as marking decline with considerable leeway for variation by trade.[4] Decline has been associated with the diminishing control of the guilds a century or so before the industrial revolution but also (as noted above) with the repeal of the Statute of Artificers in 1814, which removed the legal requirement to serve an apprenticeship before practising a trade. Dunlop suggested that 1800 marked the end of apprenticeship's influence over the generality of trades,[5] while more recently Lane has argued for a more gradual retreat, unaffected by the repeal of the Statute of Artificers.[6] Snell identified decline with a reduction in the years of actual service, and the growth of illegal apprenticeships as revealed in settlement examinations.[7] His evidence suggested a different chronology for guilded towns and rural areas. For London, Schwarz contended that apprenticeship survived the decline of the guilds and the repeal of the Statute of Artificers, but withered alongside the reorganization and de-skilling of the semi-skilled trades in the nineteenth century: a position close to that adopted both here and in *Childhood and Child Labour in the British Industrial Revolution*.[8]

History (London, 1912); Keith D.M. Snell, *Annals of the Labouring Poor: Social Change and Agrarian England, 1660–1900* (Cambridge, 1985); Keith D.M. Snell, 'The Apprenticeship System in British History: The Fragmentation of a Cultural Institution', *History of Education*, 25 (1996): pp. 303–22; Annemarie Steidl, 'Silk Weaver and Purse Maker Apprentices in Eighteenth- and Nineteenth-Century Vienna', in Bert De Munck, Steven L. Kaplan and Hugo Soly (eds), *Learning on the Shop Floor: Historical Perspectives on Apprenticeship* (Oxford, 2007), pp. 133–57.

4 See Michael J. Walker, 'The Extent of Guild Control of Trades in England, c. 1660–1820: A Study Based on a Sample of Provincial Towns and London Companies', (Ph.D. thesis, University of Cambridge, 1986); John R. Kellett, 'The Breakdown of Guild and Corporation Control over the Handicraft and Retail Trade in London', *EcHR*, 10 (1957–58): pp. 381–94; William F. Kahl, 'Apprenticeship and the Freedom of the London Livery Companies 1690–1750', *Guildhall Miscellany*, 7 (1956): pp. 17–20. For a recent study based on the Cordwainers' Company in eighteenth-century London, which acknowledges the difficulties of working out from company records to evaluate trends in either the arrangement of apprenticeship indentures or their completion, see Giorgio Riello, 'The Shaping of a Family Trade: The Cordwainers' Company in Eighteenth-Century London', in Ian A. Gadd and Patrick Wallis (eds), *Guilds, Society and Economy in London 1450–1800* (London, 2002), pp. 141–59.

5 Dunlop, *English Apprenticeship*, pp. 224, 236; see also Thomas K. Derry, 'The Repeal of the Apprenticeship Clause of the Statute of Artificers', *EcHR*, 3 (1931–32): pp. 67–87.

6 Joan Lane, *Apprenticeships in England, 1600–1914* (London, 1996).

7 Snell, *Annals of the Labouring Poor*.

8 Leonard D. Schwarz, *London in the Age of Industrialization: Entrepreneurs, Labour Force and Living Conditions, 1700–1850* (Cambridge, 1992), pp. 216–21.

Several authors suggested that although traditional apprenticeship declined, adaptations survived. Snell, for example, proposed that apprenticeship became more casual with apprentices serving less time, being less likely to take out formal indentures, and becoming more likely to quit prematurely. He found that the duration of apprenticeships declined from the mid-eighteenth century, especially after 1780, with 1811–20 seeing most change.[9] Charles More identified several different types of apprenticeship, each with its own history.[10] Where small-scale production units flourished, artisan apprenticeship, in which masters personally taught apprentices, as in Dunlop's archetype, survived. Where masters had withdrawn from production and workers were organized in trade unions, apprentices were increasingly taught by journeymen in a capitalist form of training, which usually involved strict limitations on apprenticeship numbers.[11] In both surviving types of apprenticeship, the apprentice usually lived out and received some wages. Apprenticeship could also take an exploitative form involving years of poorly paid work without either training or entry restrictions. What light do the autobiographies cast on the extent, chronology and possible degeneration of apprenticeship?

For the early industrial working class, apprenticeship was a common experience.[12] Overall, 277 boys (45 per cent of the sample) served apprenticeships. This figure may underestimate the proportion apprenticed as it counts all autobiographers who did not explicitly record such service as not apprenticed. Some autobiographers possibly neglected to mention their apprenticeship though given its importance frequent omission seems unlikely. On the other hand, it may include a few informal apprenticeships. Table 12.1 summarizes the frequency of apprenticeship by cohort, defined with reference to the standard chronology of industrialization.[13]

---

9 Snell, *Annals of the Labouring Poor*; see also Peter Rushton, '"The Matter in Variance": Adolescents and Domestic Conflict in the Pre-industrial Economy of Northeast England', *Journal of Social History*, 25 (1991): pp. 89–107; Hugh Hanley, *Apprenticing in a Market Town: The Story of William Harding's Charity, Aylesbury, 1719–2000* (Chichester, 2005).

10 Charles More, *Silks and the English Working Class, 1870–1914* (London, 1980).

11 More, along with other authors, follows the Webbs in seeing the enforcement of apprenticeship as dependent on the authority and power of journeymen and so likely to be undermined by easy entry of new employers, reorganization of trades and the introduction of machinery and alternative sources of labour, see Sidney and Beatrice Webb, *Industrial Democracy* (London, 1902), p. 479.

12 The data extracted from the working-class autobiographies was checked for demographic and occupational representativeness. I discuss the problems and advantages of drawing on this source material in Humphries, *Childhood and Child Labour*, pp. 14–24.

13 Four boys have no cohort, including two who were apprenticed.

Table 12.1 Frequency of apprenticeship by cohort (per cent)

Cohort	1627–1790	1791–1820	1821–1850	1851–1878	All cohorts
% apprenticed	68.3	56.0	36.3	26.6	44.9
All cases	123	150	171	169	613

The autobiographies record high levels of apprenticeship in the first cohort with more than two thirds of boys indentured, a figure consistent with Peter Rushton's estimate for the north-east in the seventeenth and eighteenth centuries and Steven Rappaport's for London in the mid-sixteenth century.[14] Thereafter levels fell, with the decline particularly precipitate between the second and third cohort, consistent with Snell's view that the period after 1815 saw most rapid change.[15] However, even as late as the fourth cohort, more than a quarter of all boys pursued the traditional path to skilled status.

Was apprenticeship a substantive experience that moulded boys' lives or a mere formality with little consequence? Although some boys were not formally indentured and others did not complete their time, the vast majority of those apprenticed served out their contract and worked as journeymen and/or masters in their chosen trade. Of the 277 boys who held apprenticeships, only 57 (20.6 per cent) were known to have not served their time. Of the remainder 188 (67.9 per cent) reported fulfilling their contracts, or (rarely) ending their indentures by agreement, while the fate of the rest is uncertain though many surely also served as contracted. Do completion rates mirror the decline in apprenticeships, suggesting, as did Snell's settlement data, that as well as fading in importance apprenticeship was becoming more casual?

Table 12.2 summarizes the evidence on completion rates by cohort. Occasionally, it may not be clear whether apprenticeships were completed. Upper-bound estimates assume that indefinite cases did complete; lower bounds assume non-completion as the default and are about 10 per cent lower across all cohorts. Non-completion was hard to conceal, so the upper bounds are likely more reliable, but to err on the conservative side, I report the lower bounds.

There are few benchmarks with which to compare these figures. Premature quits are difficult to quantify from corporate records because not all apprentices are listed, even if they completed and took the freedom of the city in the Livery

[14] Rushton, '"The Matter in Variance"'; Steven Rappaport, *Worlds within Worlds: Structures of Life in Sixteenth-Century London* (Cambridge, 1989).

[15] The decline is not affected by the assignment of zeros in cases where apprenticeship was neither claimed not ruled out. Dropping all such cases the sample still shows a downward trend in the proportion of boys apprenticed.

Table 12.2 Frequency of completed apprenticeships by cohort (per cent)

Cohort	1627–1790	1791–1820	1821–1850	1851–1878	All cohorts
% completed	67.9	67.9	70.9	64.4	68.0
Number apprenticed	84	84	62	45	275

Company associated with their trade. Many died; others returned home or migrated to other expanding centres.[16] However, completion rates computed on the basis of corporate records for the late Middle Ages or early modern London are much lower than those calculated for the autobiographers.[17] Further, completion rates inferred from checks on residence, also for early modern London, are also lower.[18] On the other hand, apprentices in the 1920s exhibited higher completion rates than the autobiographers.[19] Therefore, although completion rates appear to have varied historically by time and place, in the eighteenth and early nineteenth centuries, premature quits, the sign of unravelling contracts, do not seem to have been widespread or to have increased dramatically over time, findings that receive further attention in *Childhood and Child Labour*.[20]

[16] See note 3 above.

[17] Hovland's 2001 survey of the records of the Goldsmith's Company of London 1444–1500 provides one standard. She found retention rather lower than achieved by modern universities, with 56 per cent of the apprentices dropping out. As about 10 per cent of apprentices died before they could complete their term, this suggests a comparable completion rate of about 48 per cent, see Stephanie R. Hovland, 'Apprenticeship in the Records of the Goldsmith's Company of London, 1444–1500', *Medieval Prosopography*, 22 (2001): pp. 89–114. Rappaport, *Worlds within Worlds* found that 40 per cent of mid-sixteenth-century London brewers' apprentices finished their term, but, again adjusting for the proportion that died, suggests a 47 per cent completion rate. For the same time, he calculated a 55 per cent completion rate for London carpenters. Schwarz reported similar drop-out rates, while Ben Amos found an even lower rate for early modern Bristol apprentices, but she was looking explicitly at the attainment of citizenship rather than the completion of apprenticeship, see Leonard D. Schwarz, 'London Apprentices in the Seventeenth Century: Some Problems', *Local Population Studies*, 38 (1987): pp. 18–22; Ilana K. Ben Amos, *Adolescence and Youth in Early Modern England* (New Haven, CT, 1994). For evidence on completion rates for silk weavers and purse makers in eighteenth- and nineteenth-century Vienna, see Steidl, 'Silk Weaver and Purse Maker Apprentices'.

[18] Patrick Wallis found that by the seventh year of their term only 38 per cent of apprentices remained resident with their masters and inferred similarly low completion rates, see Patrick Wallis, 'Apprenticeship and Training in Premodern England', *Journal of Economic History*, 68 (2008): p. 841.

[19] Bernard Elbaum, 'Why Apprenticeship Persisted in Britain but not in the United States', *Journal of Economic History*, 44 (1989): pp. 337–49.

[20] Humphries, *Childhood and Child Labour*, p. 261ff.

Moreover, although duration appears to have been shorter than in the late Middle Ages and to have declined over the industrial revolution, the trend was neither dramatic nor statistically significant.[21] However, the variance of apprenticeship terms did increase over time, suggesting that while many contracts retained traditional periods of service (five or seven years) an increasing proportion deviated from standard practice. On the other hand, there was no clear trend in mean age of apprenticeship or the variance around this mean.[22] So although the autobiographical evidence corroborates Snell's conclusion from settlement data that apprenticeship declined in importance, with changes particularly marked in the decades after Waterloo, it does not support his suggestion that shorter-term apprenticeships and younger apprentices gained in popularity. The main finding from the autobiographical evidence is that long after ceasing to be a legal prerequisite to practice a trade apprenticeship remained common, experienced by more than one quarter of all working-class boys.

Many autobiographers regarded apprenticeship as important but prosaic; it was what happened in certain working-class *milieu*. Apprenticeship was the birthright of boys from artisan backgrounds whose families, while not rich, were relatively comfortable. Their fathers and grandfathers had been apprenticed, often in the same or a related trade, and their indentures represented their 'appointed station in life' as Thomas Okey put it.[23] However, cultural inertia played only a small part in apprenticeship's continued popularity. More important was a widespread belief in its value. A successfully negotiated apprenticeship distinguished the stable grounded working class from the *lumpen* proletariat and its absence was assumed to blight boys' prospects. Thus Robert Collyer's father, who had trained as a blacksmith after several years as a pauper apprentice in a textile factory, felt that unless apprenticed his sons would have taken 'a step down'.[24] Were these beliefs justified? Did apprenticeship provide training and enhance skills? The obvious test involves a comparison of the relative economic situation as adults of ex-apprentices with peers who had not been indentured.

[21] See Humphries, *Childhood and Child Labour*, p. 262. Snell found years served went from about 6.5 in 1750 to just under 4 in 1786, a decline possibly related to the Act of 1768 which specified the age at completion to be 21 rather than 24 as previously, see Snell, *Annals of the Labouring Poor*, p. 234ff, see also Lane, *Apprenticeship*, p. 5. Hugh Hanley found evidence in the records of Harding's Charity to suggest that few apprentices served seven-year terms even if these were agreed, Hanley, *Apprenticeship in a Market Town*, p. 94.

[22] Humphries, *Childhood and Child Labour*, p. 263.

[23] Thomas Okey, *A Basketful of Memories: An Autobiographical Sketch* (London, 1930), p. 25.

[24] Robert Collyer, *Some Memories* (Boston, MA, 1908) p. 21.

Unfortunately, autobiographical evidence on adult wages does not occur sufficiently regularly to be able to identify the earnings benefit associated with having served an apprenticeship except in an illustrative way via individual cases. However, it is possible to link autobiographers' adult occupations to the CAMSIS occupational scale, which measures both economic and social standing and can be used to identify and calibrate the effects of factors that enhanced or retarded such standing, including apprenticeship.[25]

Ex-apprentices enjoyed a higher mean CAMSIS grade as adults (50.5) than did boys who did not mention serving in this role (47.0), a 3.5 unit difference that is statistically significant.[26] Moreover, not only was the mean higher but the variance of the CAMSIS score was much lower for ex-apprentices compared with other boys, suggesting that formal training not only raised average returns from

25 Historians use a number of classification schemes to analyse occupational data, most of which are based on categorical skill hierarchies (skilled, semi-skilled, etc.). While the CAMSIS (Cambridge Social Interaction and Stratification) scales also use occupational groups as the basic units, their theoretical basis is the idea that differential association is an essential feature of social stratification arrangements. Put simply, persons sharing a similar social position, in terms of social class or status group membership, are more likely to interact socially on the basis of equality with members of the same group than with members of other groups. So, acquaintances, friends and marriage partners will all tend to be chosen much more frequently from within the same group than from without. The usual approach is to define a structure composed of a set of classes or status groups and then to investigate social interaction between them. The CAMSIS approach reverses this, using patterns of interaction to determine the nature of the structure. The crucial point is that differential association can be seen as a way of defining proximity within a social space and that this social space can be reconstructed from the distances between groups.

Although, strictly speaking, a CAMSIS scale is ordinal (or ordered interval), the large number of categories means that it can be treated as effectively continuous and reflecting a fine-grained social reality.

The original Cambridge scale was based on friendship as the central form of social interaction but more recent scales, including the historical ones, use marriage as the indicator of social distance. Prandy and Bottero report two historical versions of the scale for Britain, one for the period 1777–1865, and this has been used to develop an ordinal ranking of those occupations that occur within the autobiographical data set – Kenneth Prandy and Wendy Bottero, 'Social Reproduction and Mobility in Britain and Ireland in the Nineteenth and Early Twentieth Centuries', *Sociology*, 34 (2000): pp. 265–81. For further detail, including the replication of the scale used here, see Humphries, *Childhood and Child Labour*, p. 89 and table A4.1, pp. 121–3.

26 The CAMSIS outcomes for autobiographers who reported being apprenticed are compared with those who did not, that is non-apprenticeship is taken as the default case as in the estimates of the frequency of apprenticeship (t-stat. = 1.984 and sig. = .048). Non-parametric tests also suggest a significant difference (Man Whitney Z statistic = -2.244 and sig. = .025 and Kolmogorov-Smirnov Z = 2.035 and sig. = .001).

the early industrial labour market, it also reduced its risks.[27] As James Mullin's mother observed '... a trade ... would prevent me from falling in the world, but never prevent me from rising ....'[28] Skills insured against unemployment. As a colliery waggon-wright, Anthony Errington undertook demanding and dangerous underground work and his average earnings were not much higher than those of colliers. However, even in the slack market that accompanied the cession of hostilities in 1815 he had no difficulty in finding jobs and his social status was that of a skilled craftsman.[29] Here apprenticeships stood in sharp contrast to child labour, particularly in factories, which was widely felt to be a dead end, especially for boys. Thus Robert Collyer's parents sought 'some craft better than those we were taught in the factory', while orphan Frank Forrest, though earning good wages, reported a strong desire to get away from factory life and learn a trade.[30]

Dropping doubtful cases from the analysis increases the size of the CAMSIS gap and its statistical significance, but the most important refinement comes from excluding those boys who defaulted on apprenticeship contracts. Comparing CAMSIS outcomes for men known to have *completed* an apprenticeship (52.85), with those who both did not report apprenticeships and whose timeline left no room for such training (46.14), produces a statistically significant gap of 6.71 points.[31] Again, men who had completed an apprenticeship suffered significantly less variance around their higher occupational scores than did those without training.[32]

Cutting the data at the repeal of the Statute of Artificers does not reveal changes in the positive effect of a completed apprenticeship. Boys who served out apprenticeships both before and after *circa* 1814 enjoyed significantly higher

---

27 The standard deviation of CAMSIS scores for ex-apprentices was 19.461 and for other autobiographers it was 24.292, a difference that was statistically significant (F-stat. = 9.842 and sig. = .002).

28 James Mullin, *The Story of a Toiler's Life*, ed. P. Maume (Dublin, 2000), pp. 42–3.

29 As his editor P.E.H. Hair remarked, 'It was the regularity of employment and the fact that in his work he was largely his own master, rather than the economic advantages which gave the waggonway-wright a higher social status than the collier – Brunel University Library, Anthony Errington, 'Coals and Rails: The Autobiography of Anthony Errington a Tyneside colliery waggonway-wright, 1776–c. 1825', transcribed and ed. by P.E.H. Hair, TS (n.d.), p. 8.

30 Collyer, *Some Memories*, p. 21; Frank Forrest, *Chapters in the Life of Dundee Factory Boy: An Autobiography*, ed. J. Myles (Edinburgh, 1850), pp. 65–6.

31 T-stat. = 3.319; sig. = .001. Including cases where completion was not explicitly confirmed but it is highly likely that this does not change these findings.

32 F-stat. = 6.46; sig. = .011.

CAMSIS scores compared with those never apprenticed.[33] They also experienced lower variance around these higher scores in both eras, but the difference in dispersion was only significant post 1814.

In understanding why repeal of the Statute of Artificers might have had only muted effects on completion, it is important to remember that serving out an apprenticeship remained a legal obligation. Several autobiographers fell foul of this ruling. Dyke Wilkinson, for example, was apprenticed aged 12 in the 1830s to a rule maker in Birmingham and in rebellion for many of the ensuing years. He tried to steal his indentures, absconded several times, and when summoned failed to respond. On his second appearance before the magistrates, aged about 15, he was sentenced to two months solitary confinement.[34] Default had other ominous ramifications. An apprentice who quit prematurely not only lost out on training and broke the law but stood revealed as lacking pertinacity, a great virtue within the working class. Defaulting apprentices were downwardly mobile. A failed apprenticeship, even if not a boy's fault, blighted his subsequent career. In contrast, fulfilling an apprenticeship contract marked a lad out as honourable and dutiful, characteristics guaranteed to appeal to prospective employers.

A regression of CAMSIS scores on the outcome of the apprenticeship contract, and other explanatory variables, captures the penalty for default. This exercise distinguishes the effect of not completing an apprenticeship from never being indentured. The reference group comprises the never apprenticed. The results are reported in Table 12.3. The log of the autobiographer's own CAMSIS score is the dependent variable. Model 1, shown in the first column, focuses exclusively on the effects of apprenticeship, but models which include other determinants of human capital formation, including father's CAMSIS score (in log form), are shown in columns 2 through 3 and discussed in *Childhood and Child Labour*.[35]

In the simple model, a completed apprenticeship was positively and significantly associated with occupational outcomes. More surprisingly, failing to complete an apprenticeship had a negative effect on achieved status. Since this is in comparison with the group, which remained without apprenticeship, it cannot be ascribed to absence of training. Although in the simplest model, the non-completion of an apprenticeship was not statistically significant,

---

[33] The analysis compared boys born before and after or during 1804 to capture those training in the two different legal regimes.

[34] Dyke Wilkinson, *Rough Roads: Reminiscences of a Wasted Life* (London, 1913), pp. 17–40.

[35] Humphries, *Childhood and Child Labour*, pp. 281ff.

Table 12.3 Effect of apprenticeship and other variables on CAMSIS outcomes

	Dependent variable: log own CAMSIS score Coefficient (t-statistic)		
	Model 1	**Model 2**	**Model 3**
Constant	1.570** (86.755)	1.044** (15.842)	.917** (13.393)
Years of schooling	–	–	.026** (4.341)
Log of father's CAMSIS score	–	.362** (8.375)	.336** (7.417)
Sunday school	–	–	.073** (2.513)
Adult education	–	–	.133** (4.705)
Apprenticeship completed	.127** (4.367)	.087** (3.001)	.091** (3.060)
Apprenticeship not completed	-.053 (-1.106)	-.103** (-2.168)	-.114** (-2.391)
R^2 (adjusted)	.035	.151	.234
Sample size	606	528	482
Standard error	.330	.306	.295
F statistic	11.961	32.356	25.536

Note: Significant at the 10 per cent level *; significant at the 5 per cent level **.

the inclusion of other relevant determinants of occupational outcomes, most importantly fathers' attainments, increases both the size and t-statistic on non-completion.[36]

Individual stories bring these statistics to life. Broken indentures threatened social exclusion as well as downward occupational mobility. Even upright John Buckley, who had genuine grievances against his master, damaged his standing in the community and forewent an advantageous marriage when he absconded. On his capture and return to work out his term, his sweetheart's family forbade

[36] Where apprenticeship was not mentioned, cases were coded as 'not apprenticed' and completion was assumed unless there was evidence to the contrary. Dropping cases where apprenticeship was unlikely but possible and/or where completion was likely but not certain reduces the sample size but does not change the signs of the coefficients. See Humphries, *Childhood and Child Labour*, p. 281.

him to see her and shunned him.[37] Even worse befell other defaulting apprentices. David Haggart's apprenticeship to a millwright temporarily rescued him from a 'sinful career' and he 'formed a resolution of following my new business with honesty and zeal'.[38] However, the master's bankruptcy threw David out of work. Thereafter he followed a life of crime culminating in his murder of a turnkey in Dumfries Jail and own death on the gallows of that town in July 1821.[39] The association between broken apprenticeships and beggary found elsewhere is also apparent.[40] George Brine was apprenticed to a local butcher, the Bluecoat Charity providing a £10 premium and two suits of clothes. George exhibited no gratitude. He proceeded to run wild and after frequent visits to Dorchester jail, absconded to pursue an alternative career in petty crime. He died, like his father before him, in Sherborne Workhouse.[41]

Broken indentures represented opportunities foregone. If the contract was chosen in the first place, it was clearly desirable for breakdown to be avoided. English apprenticeship, like most efficient institutions, possessed a number of self-reinforcing mechanisms, which meant most grievances could be resolved in ways that held the agreement together with minimal recourse to expensive legal or semi-legal adjudication.[42] Threats to go public with grievances may have been sufficient to soften masters' behaviour as defamation could reduce access to apprentices (and their premiums) in the future. Symmetrically, apprentices' resisted being thought truculent or undisciplined. Moreover, their complaints frequently related to features of the contract (wardrobe, quality of food and kindliness of treatment) left implicit and so difficult to contest formally. Often the best strategy was stoicism. Henry Manton resented his bigoted master/uncle who disapproved of scientific learning and banned his apprentice/nephew from attending the Mechanics' Institute. Henry avoided confrontation and

[37] John Buckley [pseud. of John Charles Buckmaster], *A Village Politician: The Life Story of John Buckley*, ed. J.C. Buckmaster (London, 1897), p. 112.

[38] David Haggart, *The Life of David Haggart* (Edinburgh, 1821), p. 7.

[39] See also Robert Henderson, *Incidents in the Life of Robt. Henderson; or, Extracts from the Autobiography of 'Newcassel Bob', A Tyne-side Rake. To which is appended a discourse on the Prodigal Son*, ed. Rev. J. Martin (Carlisle, 1869).

[40] See Helmut Bräuer, *'... und had seithero gebetlet' Bettler und Bettelwesen in Wien und Niederösterreich sur Zeit Kaiser Leopolds I* (1996), as cited in Steidl, 'Silk Weaver and Purse Maker Apprentices', p. 150, n. 98.

[41] George A. Brine, *King of Beggars: The Life and Adventures of George Atkins Brine. A True Story of Vagrant Life* (London, 1933?).

[42] Jane Humphries, 'English Apprenticeship: A Neglected Factor in the First Industrial Revolution', in Paul A. David and Mark Thomas (eds), *The Economic Future in Historical Perspective* (Oxford, 2003).

turned to Sunday school teaching and the dissenting chapel as more acceptable activities.[43]

Where masters and apprentices were unable to reconcile, adjudication was possible from within that same network of friends and neighbours, co-religionists and extended kin that had mediated the arrangement in the first place. David Binns, placed with an uncle in the drapery business, reported 'one serious dispute' during his apprenticeship. '[My uncle] ... was imposing labour upon me that was not fit for me to undertake and that my strength was not equal to perform'. David appealed to his parents for support and they, in turn, drew on another trusted family member. 'Some correspondence took place betwixt my Uncle and my parents, which with the kind advice given us by my Uncle Joseph Binns caused the breach to be made up'. David also recalled another bone of contention, common in apprenticeship contract disputes: the quality of the food. 'Another cause of dispute was during a bad harvest about 1817, when nearly all the corn in the country was spoiled and [bread] being so bad [that] it all run together like paste ....'[44] Such disputes and their means of reconciliation provide an unvarnished perspective on apprenticeship and the forces holding contracts together.

However, these reinforcement mechanisms increasingly operated in an environment where apprenticeship contracts were becoming less effective in preventing premature quits. Repeal of the Statute of Artificers was one blow, fading guild controls another. Moreover, industrial structure was changing to provide more berths for journeymen, creating greater opportunities for senior apprentices to hold up their masters and, organizational changes in production made it harder for journeymen themselves to exclude potential work mates who had not completed their apprenticeships.[45] The increasingly common practice of paying wages to apprentices calibrated to their seniority and skills testifies to the threat of premature quits. Is there evidence from the autobiographies of a faltering institution?

As already noted, completion rates showed only a small decline in the fourth cohort and so do not suggest an institution in decay. A regression of CAMSIS outcomes on measures of human capital provides more insight. The hypothesis of structural change is tested by establishing the loss of fit involved in restricting the parameters, as in a pooled sample combining all cohorts compared with an unrestricted model that estimates the parameters separately for cohorts 1–3 and cohort 4, as in Table 12.4.

---

43 Henry Manton, 'Alderman Manton's Reminiscences', *Birmingham Weekly Mercury*, 15 November 1902–14 March 1903.

44 Bradford Central Library, Archives Department, David Binns, untitled, MS and TS (n.d.), p. 5.

45 Snell, *Annals of the Labouring Poor*; Elbaum, 'Why Apprenticeship'.

Table 12.4 Occupational determination regressions

	All Cohorts	Cohorts 1, 2 and 3	Cohort 4
Constant	.917**	.792**	1.259**
Years of Schooling	.026**	.020**	.032**
Sunday Schooling	.074**	.071*	.071*
Adult education	.133**	.159**	.073*
Completed apprenticeship	.090**	.114**	.068
Not completed apprenticeship	-.114**	-.125**	-.004
Log father's CAMSIS score	.336**	.411**	.123*
N	482	341	141
Residual sum of squares	41.386	33.223	6.998
Standard error	.2952	.3154	.2282
F statistic	25.478	20.675	5.389

Note: Significant at the 10 per cent level *; significant at the 5 per cent level **

The results of sub-dividing the sample in 1850 and estimating separate regressions are intuitively plausible. The impact of apprenticeship in terms of both the positive effect of completion and the negative effect of premature quits faded after mid-century in contrast to the positive effect of schooling, which increased in importance. The effect of Sunday school attendance was similar in both sub-periods while adult education and father's CAMSIS score declined. However, an F test for structural change did not reject the null hypothesis that the coefficient vectors are the same in the two sub-periods.[46] Thus although apprenticeship was a fading force, it appears to have survived the dismantling of its legal and guild underpinnings and continued to contribute to boys' occupational advance. Those boys and their families who persisted in believing that the training provided by an apprenticeship was of value were probably correct in their judgement.

Were There Barriers to Obtaining an Apprenticeship?

Early modern Britain was not an egalitarian society and its institutions often functioned to reproduce existing hierarchies. Apprenticeship was no exception. The ability to obtain an apprenticeship especially in a desirable trade depended

[46] $F(7, 468) = 1.971$ compared with the critical value 2.01 for 5 per cent significance. Subdivision of the data according to other potential structural breaks between cohorts or different legal regimes produced similar results. For an overview of the relevant test, see William H. Greene, *Econometric Analysis* (London, 1997), pp. 343–53.

Table 12.5 Apprenticeship by fathers' occupational group

Fathers' occupational group	Proportion of sons' apprenticed: % (total number of all sons)
Agriculture	41 (137)
Mining	19 (53)
Factory	25 (36)
Domestic manufacturing	51 (75)
Trades	60 (97)
Casual	30 (40)
Clerical	50 (16)
Soldiering	33 (12)
Sea	67 (30)
Services	55 (64)
All known	45 (560)

on family wealth and connections; after all premiums needed to be paid and appropriate masters located. Fathers who had benefitted from apprenticeships would be able to earn more and so support sons' apprenticeships, whereas fathers with no training or rent element in their wages would not be so equipped. Disadvantage was transmitted inter-generationally as in the standard model of a dynastic poverty trap.[47] Indeed, the Statute of Artificers, by way of a property qualification and rules about the social standing of apprentices, had sought to restrict access to apprenticeships in certain occupations to the sons of freemen, and particularly to exclude the sons of labourers or men engaged in husbandry. If selection depended on wealth and connections rather than merit, the result would not maximize the return to training. Did apprenticeship function in such a socially unfair and economically inefficient way? The answer involves an investigation of the background of boys who secured apprenticeships and the way in which barriers to entry functioned.

The autobiographical evidence confirms that boys, whose fathers had enjoyed apprenticeships, as indicated by their practice of a skilled occupation, were themselves more likely to be apprenticed. Table 12.5 reports that boys whose fathers were themselves domestic manufacturers, tradesmen, mariners and service providers, all of whom were likely to have served an apprenticeship themselves and to have earned above average wages, had greater than a 50/50 chance of being indentured.[48] However, although the sons of skilled fathers were

47 Kaushik Basu, 'Child Labor: Cause, Consequence, and Cure, with Remarks on Labor Standards', *Journal of Economic Literature*, 37 (1999): pp. 1106–8.

48 Formal testing suggests that the null hypothesis of no relationship between chances of apprenticeship and fathers' occupational group can be rejected ($\chi^2 = 43.545$; sig. = .000).

more likely to be able to access apprenticeship, they did not possess a monopoly. Boys with fathers in all occupational groups became apprenticed.

The Statute of Artificers has been described as the most comprehensive expression of the pro-agrarian character of English economic policy but the Elizabethan property qualifications were soon overtaken by inflation and other restrictions appear to have been readily breached.[49] As a result, apprenticeship had long provided a route out of agriculture not only for the sons of yeomen and farmers (perhaps younger sons) but also for the sons of men lower down the rural hierarchy. Many autobiographers travelled this route. More surprising still, even boys whose fathers had no skills and laboured in the harsh casual sub-sector of the labour market could strive to obtain some training. Twelve such boys out of the 40 in the database obtained apprenticeships.

Thus although apprenticeship undoubtedly contributed to occupational inertia, the autobiographical evidence suggests that it could also provide opportunities to disadvantaged boys. How these opportunities were provided and second chances institutionalized deserves attention.

Apprenticeship as an institution involved the exchange of training for labour services. The apprentice remunerated the master himself by work performed in the course of training. A lad who could credibly commit to compensate a master for his training could secure a berth on his own account and without the need for the support of others. By definition then apprenticeship liberated children from reliance on either parental altruism or intra-familial implicit contracts. In this sense, apprenticeship itself was a force against the dynastic persistence of occupational privilege. Thus James Choyce, who on being left fatherless at an early age, could see 'no better prospect than to follow the plough all the days of my life', and was sufficiently emboldened '... to leave my friends and native place and try my fortune in foreign climes'.[50] Choyce left his home at the age of 16 and bound himself apprentice in the Southern Whale Fishery, eventually becoming master of a whaler.

Choyce achieved the first step on his career ladder without the help of friends and family. One manifestation of the difficulty such a move involved would be a high frequency of apprenticeship to fathers or other family members. The autobiographical sources do not always reveal a boy's relationship with his master, although it is evident that the vast majority of apprentices, 76 per cent of those for whom there is information (182 cases), were apprenticed to non-kin. Nine per cent of boys were apprenticed to their fathers, a cheap alternative,

---

[49] Margaret G. Davies, *The Enforcement of English Apprenticeship: A Study in Applied Mercantilism, 1563–1642* (Cambridge, MA, 1956), p. 5.

[50] James Choyce, *The Log of a Jack Tar; or The Life of James Choyce, Master Marriner* (London, 1891), p. 3.

which sometimes locked them into stagnant trades and contributed to dynastic deprivation. William Farish's parents, for example, desired to apprentice him to his grandfather's trade of carpentry, but his weaver father could not raise the funds and, too short for the army, William fell back on the loom.[51] Apprenticeship to a family member was not however a complete dud, for although such boys scored lower on the CAMSIS scale than did their peers apprenticed to non-kin, the difference was not statistically significant. Boys were also apprenticed to brothers, uncles, grandfathers, stepfathers and other kinsmen. Although numbers are too small to draw strong conclusions, it is interesting that while boys apprenticed to step-fathers and grandfathers did worse than boys apprenticed to non-kin, those apprenticed to uncles and brothers did better. Those placed with distant kin or family acquaintances did best of all, suggesting the wisdom of searching the periphery of kinship networks for promising openings.

The surprisingly low frequency with which boys were apprenticed to their own fathers and the apparent interest in obtaining a placement that enabled boys to learn the latest techniques and be able to produce new products testifies to English apprenticeship's resilience to entropy. It was an outward-looking institution within which boys were placed to advance themselves and not just fill their fathers' boots.

An obvious obstacle to poor boys access to apprenticeship was the need to provide masters with a premium payable up-front before training commenced. Premiums were not always a prerequisite to obtaining an apprenticeship but by the eighteenth century had become common. Still boys could get round excessive premiums, and this was essential if the poor were to have access to skills in the absence of capital markets. Premiums were variable though a hierarchy, related to the status of the trade and the value of its raw materials, which was widely recognized in the advice books of the day.[52] Thus, impecunious boys could target trades with low premiums, though these were not the cherries of the apprenticeship market. Premiums could also be paid in instalments or by boys' families providing services in kind. W.E. Adams's grandmother bound herself to pay his £15 premium in instalments from her washtub earnings.[53] Wider kin and friends sometimes provided financial assistance. William Lawrence's father borrowed his £20 premium from a friend, a bad investment

[51] William Farish, *The Autobiography of William Farish: The Struggles of a Handloom Weaver. With Some of his Writings* (London, 1996), p. 18.

[52] See Joseph Collyer, *The Parent's and Guardian's Dictionary, and the Youth's Guide, in the Choice of a Profession or Trade* (London, 1761); Robert Campbell, *The London Tradesman* (London, 1747).

[53] William E. Adams, *Memoires of a Social Atom* (London, 1903), p. 82.

as Lawrence absconded to join the army![54] Orphan Frank Forrest's landlord proved a real friend, helping the lad to find a master and then '... generously offering to be one of my securities at the same time paying for one half of the expenses of the legal document'.[55] Exceptionally likely lads could signal their potential, as did the entrepreneurial James Lackington, who, while working alongside his journeyman father, so impressed the master that he agreed to take James apprentice 'without any premium and to find me in everything'.[56] Masters were persuaded to take boys 'In consideration of love and affection' as the apprenticeship contract frequently phrased it. Such generosity was rare.[57] More often, the only way to overcome capital constraints was to agree to serve additional years, thereby repaying masters who took an apprentice without the conventional sweeteners. Such agreements stretched the trust essential to the contract, requiring masters to rely on older apprentices working out an elongated contract that lay outside the reinforcing bounds of custom and whose origin was shrouded in the past. Nonetheless such customized arrangements were not entirely absent in the autobiographical database, enabling even the most unprepossessing candidates as well as the Lackingtons of this world to get a foot on the ladder. Thus James Dawson Burn, self-described in his autobiography as a 'beggar-boy' who spent his peripatetic youth around feckless and vagrant adults, late in life, finagled himself an apprenticeship. This he regarded as his 'one act of wise determination ... the grand turning point in my existence ... the halfway house between the desert of my youth and the sunny lands of my manhood'.[58]

Another way in which poor but ambitious boys could access apprenticeships was by obtaining charitable sponsorship. Private charities were very active

54 Sergeant William Lawrence, *The Autobiography of Sergeant William Lawrence. A hero of the Peninsular and Waterloo Campaigns*, ed. G.N. Bankes (London, 1886), p. 2.

55 Forrest, *Dundee Factory Boy*, p. 66.

56 James Lackington, *Memoires of the Forty-Five First Years of the Life of James Lackington. Written by Himself in Forty-seven Letters to a Friend* (London, 1794), p. 44.

57 In a sample of 861 apprenticeship contracts for Kent between 1730 and 1779, Tom Marshall found only 23 sealed by 'Love and Affection' though a further 266 involved 'No consideration', that is did not appear to involve the payment of a premium, see Marshall, 'Were There Any Limitations?'.

58 Burn did pay a premium (which he obtained from a woman of his acquaintance in a not altogether honourable way!) but also hammered out a customized apprenticeship contract, see [James D. Burn], *The Autobiography of a Beggar Boy: in which will be found related the numerous trials, hard struggles, and vicissitudes of a strangely chequered life; with glimpses of social and political history over a period of fifty years*, ed. D. Vincent (London, 1978), p. 200.

in promoting apprenticeship.[59] Twenty-six boys (4.2 per cent of the sample) reported either their schooling or apprenticeship or both subsidized by private benevolence and the actual proportion was probably much higher. Stephen Forsdick's local school was endowed with sufficient funds to educate 40 boys and 20 girls and 'to furnish them with a suit of clothing each year'. Moreover, when they reached the age of 14, '[T]here had been provision made to apprentice them to some trade if their parents or guardians desired, ...' and since '... it cost ten pounds in those days to teach a boy a trade, ... it was considered quite a thing to get a boy into this school'.[60] Christopher Thomson was apprenticed under Cogan's Charity, which placed out poor boys as apprentices to mariners, handicraftsmen and artisans; preference to be given to the sons of freemen of Hull.[61] In addition to the expense of binding, the Charity paid 20s per year towards the apprentice's clothing. Thomson's masters did not take the money as allowed but transferred the present to the apprentice. The apprenticeship was an outdoor one with wages paid in rising increments. The wages were low but, as Thomson notes, no premium was required. Moreover boys benefited from additional perquisites: Christmas boxes and extra pay when repairing old vessels were awarded to apprentices who gained a favourable report from their masters. Consistent with the need to reward completion, at the expiration of the term £2 was awarded to the master and £4 to the apprentice 'towards his outfit in life'.[62] On obtaining indentures, Cogan's apprentices also received a bible and sometimes another book and were expected to be able to read as 'Sunday school was always open to us ... and if we could not read tolerably well the money was detained'.[63] Under this regime, Thomson completed his apprenticeship although neither suited to nor enamoured with the trade of shipwright.

Tommy Mitchell's support was less formal. After early hard unskilled labour for low wages, Tommy was '... getting older and wanted more ...'.[64] Tommy's mother was desperate to get him apprenticed.

> There was a gentleman she worked for, a Mr. Harris in Queen Square and he was Chairman of the Anchor Society. This Society apprenticed poor boys but he had been so deceived by boys who had turned out bad he said he would never

---

59 See Malcolm Graham, *Oxford City Apprentices 1697–1800* (Oxford, 1987); Hanley, *Apprenticing in a Market Town*.

60 Brunel University Library, Stephen Forsdick, untitled TS (n.d.), p. 3; see also Brine, *King of the Beggars*, p. 11; Brunel University Library, James Ashley, untitled TS (n.d.), p. 2.

61 Christopher Thomson, *The Autobiography of an Artisan* (Nottingham, 1847), p. 60.

62 Thomson, *Autobiography*, p. 60.

63 Thomson, *Autobiography*, p. 61.

64 Reference library, Bristol, Thomas B. Mitchell, 'Tommy's Book' (n.d.), p. 2.

> recommend another, but Tommy's mother used her influence with him and other gentlemen connected with the Society so one day good news was brought home – he said he would try me for my mother's sake. So now they had to find a master for me and Tommy's father found a man in business as a Whitesmith, Bellhanger and Gasfitter in Bath Street … Now Tommy bade goodbye to the Forge Hammer and piling *to learn a trade*.[65]

The gratification in this last phrase is palpable.

More important still as a facilitator of apprenticeships in the lower reaches of the market was the Poor Law. The origins of apprenticeship, as widely noted, were intertwined with the Elizabethan Poor Law: '… although apprenticeship was adopted primarily in the interests of trade and manufactures, it was regarded by the Government with additional favour as a partial solution of the problem of pauperism'.[66] Historians have sometimes been scathing in their evaluation of poor law apprenticeship placements, dismissing them as little more than a device (because apprenticeship constituted a head of settlement) to rid a parish of destitute, or potentially destitute children. At best pauper apprenticeship secured some basic (albeit probably loveless) fostering; at worst it exposed children to exploitation and abuse. Examples of both outcomes can be found in the autobiographical evidence.[67] However, even boarding out by the parish authorities was not always a desolate experience, and some lucky boys found love and support as the result of a parish placement.

Nor were pauper apprenticeships as worthless in terms of training as has sometimes been suggested. The classic account of apprenticeship, while careful to distinguish training from boarding out, made clear the potential importance of this lifeline to the destitute. Poor law documents from a large number of parishes with a range of economic bases confirm that pauper apprenticeship was very frequent. Apprenticeship registers suggest that between 10 and 20 per cent of all apprentices had premiums paid by the overseers. 'The total number [of children] who acquired their training and start in life by this means must have been very large'.[68]

Snell's investigation of the biographical information contained in settlement examinations shows that those apprenticed by the parish or charity, although undoubtedly restricted in choice of occupation, generally were taught the trade and later practised it.[69] Important recent work by Honeyman has extended the

65 Mitchell, 'Tommy's book', p. 4, my emphasis.

66 Dunlop, *English Apprenticeship*, p. 68.

67 See Humphries, *Childhood and Child Labour*.

68 Dunlop, *English Apprenticeship*, p. 250.

69 Snell, *Annals of the Labouring Poor*.

rehabilitation of parish apprenticeship. He demonstrates that poor law officials were not universally brutal and uncaring, obsessed with securing placements for pauper children beyond their own ratepayers' remit, but sometimes dutiful and responsible, checking on the welfare of children whom they had placed at distance and cognisant of the dangers of abuse.[70]

The autobiographers' parish apprenticeships were not mere time fillers. Stradley, for example, worked as an armourer in the navy and at the Royal Arsenal Woolwich for most of his life, while the fathers of Flockhart, Collyer and the Unfortunate Genius all brought up families by the trades they had learned.[71] Turning to the charity boys, Ashley supported his large family by lifelong application to his trade, and although Thomson worked only temporarily as a shipwright, the skills he learned spilled over into his other pursuits (ship's carpenter, veneer sawyer, strolling player, stenciller, painter and stationer).[72] Tommy Mitchell, though his apprenticeship was hard and even dangerous, obtained skills that enabled him to become a successful small-scale businessman.

The decline of the family-based trades and the retreat of the Old Poor Law adversely affected parish apprenticeship in the late eighteenth century.[73] Poor law officials had to deal with apparently increasing numbers of impoverished children while keeping rates down. At the same time, a new demand for child workers arose from the location of water-powered factories far from existing centres of population. Supply and demand created a systematic traffic in pauper apprentices between many urban centres and the early cotton factories. It is possible, as Honeyman argues, that even children batch apprenticed to the early textile factories, learned tolerance of routine and some skills, which helped them earn a living in later life.[74] Nonetheless, long before 1834, the Old Poor Law

---

[70] Katrina Honeyman, *Child Workers in England, 1780–1820: Parish Apprenticeships and the Making of the Early Industrial Labour Force* (Aldershot, 2007).

[71] Local History Library, Blackheath, John Stradley, 'Memoires of John Stradley, 1757–1825', TS, as précised in John Burnett, David Vincent and David Mayall (eds), *The Autobiography of the Working Class: An Annotated Critical Biography* (Brighton, 1984–89); Robert Flockhart, *The Street Preacher, being the Autobiography of Robert Flockhart, late corporal 81st Regiment*, ed. T. Guthrie (Edinburgh, 1858), p. 2; Collyer, *Some Memories*, p. 3; [Factory Girl], *The Unfortunate Genius* (London, 1853), p. 9.

[72] Ashley, untitled, TS; Thomson, *Autobiography*.

[73] Byung K. Song, 'Agrarian Policies on Pauper Settlement and Migration, Oxfordshire, 1750–1850', *Continuity and Change*, 13 (1998): pp. 363–89; Joan Lane, 'Apprenticeship in Warwickshire Cotton Mills, 1790–1830', *Textile History*, 10 (1979): pp. 161–74; Mary B. Rose, 'Social Policy and Business: Parish Apprentices and the Early Factory System, 1750–1834', *Business History*, 21 (1989): pp. 5–32.

[74] Honeyman, *Child Workers*.

had ceased to act in a symbiotic way with the apprenticeship system to provide a supply of skilled labour, and to breach if not overcome the barriers to social mobility embedded in deprived origins.

Several well-known autobiographies relate the fate of children 'apprenticed' from workhouses in London and Liverpool to textile manufacturing establishments at the end of the eighteenth century.[75] Lesser-known accounts suggest that the traffic was more widespread.[76] Children were sent to work in factories not only from the large metropolitan workhouses. Robert Collyer's parents, both the children of sailors lost at sea, met after being sent to the same West Riding textile factory. Collyer senior was sent from London: 'He told me they gave him the free choice to go or stay and wanted him to stay; but he said "I will go". And so it was he went out, not knowing whither he went, was bound apprentice, and served his time'.[77] However, Collyer's mother hailed from Norwich suggesting this strategy was a widespread response to maritime orphanage. Moreover fragmentary evidence suggests that alongside the appearance of batch apprenticeship to factory industry, more traditional placements also became less attractive. Thomas Sanderson, with the collaboration of his father, was to be apprenticed by the poor law authorities of Sheffield but he 'cut off running', preferring to make his own arrangements with a shipwright in his native Bishopwearmouth.[78]

The burgeoning market for child labour crowded out traditional pauper apprenticeships as illustrated by the history of the Marcroft children, orphaned around 1820 in Middleton Lancashire. 'At this period, the system of the Poor Law and the customs of the overseers were very irregular, and much favouritism could be carried on by the officials'.[79] Children in this flourishing area of family farms and hand-loom weaving were hired out to farmers and weavers. The Marcroft children were placed in four different families: Betty to weaving; Frank to be a boatman; Sally to be a farmer's girl; and Joseph to be a collier. None were formally apprenticed. 'The career of each child was much varied.

[75] [Robert Blincoe], J. Brown, *A Memoir of Robert Blincoe, an orphan boy sent from the workhouse at St. Pancras London* (Manchester, 1832); Anon., 'Some passages in the Life of a London Parish 'Prentice at Litton and Cressbrook Mills. Written by Himself', ed. J.R. Stephens, *Ashton Chronicle*, 19 May, 2 June 1849.

[76] As Honeyman, *Child Workers*, also argues.

[77] Collyer, *Some Memories*, p. 13.

[78] Thomas Sanderson, 'The Life and Adventures of Thomas Sanderson, As written by himself, in 1861, in the 53rd year of his age', in Thomas Sanderson, *Chips and shaving of an Old Shipwright; or, the Life, Poems, & Adventures of Thomas Sanderson; Author of 'Freaks of Fancy', &c.* (Darlington, 1873), p. 16.

[79] William Marcroft, *The Marcroft Family* (Manchester, 1889), p. 17.

Like pieces of timber from a wreck on a troubled sea, no person can tell when and where they would come to rest'.[80] Sally, despite being a clever textile worker, without parental protection foundered in a sexually-predatory environment. She became pregnant by a local weaver. Marriage was mooted but thwarted by his father's opposition to a poor and friendless daughter-in-law. Sally was removed to her parish of settlement to have her illegitimate child and after a sojourn in a terrifying lunatic asylum *cum* workhouse, eventually, with the help of her brother, sought independence as a hand-loom weaver.[81]

Although pauper apprenticeships were discouraged for the first decades of the New Poor Law, children continued to be placed with families seeking cheap labour. The demand for boy labour from the rapidly expanding coal industry provided one important outlet. Thus, Thomas Ince was taken out of Wigan Workhouse into service with a collier, and George Lloyd after only a few weeks' care was handed over by the Cardiff authorities to a collier looking for a boy to assist him in underground work.[82] George, it transpired, was too young to work underground. He was passed on carelessly to become 'apprentice' to a shoemaker even though this contravened his original master's agreement to return the boy if the placement was unsuccessful. Eventually George ran away and after several adventures found a better situation, still as a collier's boy but with a decent family, a placement that resembled the boarding out of earlier times.

Conclusion

The emphasis of modern economics on the importance of human capital in growth and development has provided economic historians with a conundrum. Without evidence to show growth in formal education, and its markers in terms of literacy or numeracy, the first industrial revolution appears mysterious. Apprenticeship's contribution to human capital in industrializing Britain may provide the answer. No dinosaur of a corporate cretaceous, apprenticeship remained the main vehicle through which training was accessed and delivered long after the Repeal of the Statute of Artificers deregulated the child labour market. In earlier work I explained its resilience by its chance development of

---

80 Marcroft, *Marcroft Family*, p. 17.

81 Marcroft, *Marcroft Family*; see also Lucy Luck, 'Straw-Plait Worker', in John Burnett (ed.), *Useful Toil: Autobiographies of Working People from the 1820s to the 1920s* (London, 1974).

82 Thomas Ince, *Beggar Manuscripts: an Original Miscellany in Verse and Prose* (Blackburn, 1888); Brunel University Library, George Lloyd, 'The Autobiography of "George Brawd"' (n.d.), p. 12.

characteristics which overcame many of the basic difficulties associated with contracts for a commodity as tendentious as training to be delivered over a long period of time and largely paid for by labour services.[83] It was a 'smart institution' that adapted to changing circumstances and new needs. Here I have used another (albeit controversial) source, working-class autobiographies, to support and develop these arguments. Apprenticeship was not *either* rent seeking *or* skill creating; it was both. However with the disappearance of the customary and legal barriers to entry associated with apprenticeship, its material foundation rested increasingly on the worth of the training it provided. The Repeal of the Statute of Artificers is seen here as less a blow against corporate power than a deregulation of the child labour market, an interpretation in keeping with Honeyman's recent emphasis on the responsibility towards pauper apprentices that an earlier regime had required. The transition to the new Poor Law also adversely affected the child labour market and apprenticeship's role therein. While the New Poor Law put pressure on children, even young children, to contribute to family subsistence, by discouraging pauper apprenticeship it ceased to offer those children the protection of indentures. The burgeoning market in child labour was the other side of the coin from the decline in apprenticeship. In this changing environment, apprenticeship became increasingly associated with the payment of graduated wages, more routinized training provided by journeymen not masters and eventually links to formal education, as some of the later autobiographers describe.[84] However, this is a story for another day.

83 Humphries, 'English Apprenticeship'.

84 John Finney, *Sixty Years' Recollections of an Etruscan* (Stoke-on-Trent, 1902); Peter Taylor, *Autobiography of Peter Taylor* (Paisley, 1903).

Further Reading

Julian Hoppit

A large secondary literature exists on the themes addressed by this volume, from the venerable to the new. What follows provides a selection of works judged to be more significant to the field, including those that have proved controversial, or which provide effective introductions to or surveys of their fields. The focus is mainly upon works in which questions regarding regulation – introduction, operation and consequences – are central. This means that many important works of economic history whose focus lies elsewhere are not considered.

The Nature and Performance of the British Economy, 1660–1850

The transformation of Britain's economy into the world-leading industrial power by the Great Exhibition of 1851 was extraordinary, whether or not one chooses to employ the concept of an 'industrial revolution'. Two fine general introductions are: Roderick Floud and Paul Johnson (eds), *The Cambridge Economic History of Modern Britain, Vol. 1: Industrialisation, 1700–1860* (Cambridge, 2004); Martin J. Daunton, *Progress and Poverty: An Economic and Social History of Modern Britain, 1700–1850* (Oxford, 1995). Some sense of the quantitative dimensions of economic change is essential in this area. For many years the national accounts framework provided the main means of estimating economic performance quantitatively. Nicholas F.R. Crafts, *British Economic Growth During the Industrial Revolution* (Oxford, 1985) was an important revision, arguing for slow growth but significant structural change. The conceptual and evidential limits to such an approach have encouraged the development of very different perspectives, notably demographic by Edward A. Wrigley in *Continuity, Change and Change: The Character of the Industrial Revolution in England* (Cambridge, 1988) and a collection of his essays in *People, Cities and Wealth: The Transformation of Traditional Society* (Oxford, 1987). A compendium of relevant statistics is provided in Brian R. Mitchell, *British Historical Statistics* (Cambridge, 1988).

State Formation in Britain, 1660–1850

Clearly the nature of government and the authority it could command profoundly influenced its capacity to regulate parts of the economy. There are now several important general works on 'state formation'. A fine prelude to the period covered by this volume is Michael J. Braddick, *State Formation in Early Modern England, c. 1550–1700* (Cambridge, 2000). Earlier developments are placed in a European context in Thomas Ertman, *Birth of the Leviathan: Building States and Regimes in Medieval and Early Modern Europe* (Cambridge, 1997). For the long-view, see Philip Corrigan and Derek Sayer, *The Great Arch: English State Formation as Cultural Revolution* (Oxford, 1985) and Philip Harling, *The Modern British State: An Historical Introduction* (Cambridge, 2001). On the growth of legislation see Julian Hoppit, 'Patterns of Parliamentary Legislation, 1660–1800', *HJ*, 39/1 (1996): pp. 109–31. For an emphasis upon the practices of governance, Peter Jupp, *The Governing of Britain, 1688–1848* (London, 2006).

As rich a work as any, if hard to digest as a whole, is Paul Langford, *Public Life and the Propertied Englishman, 1689–1798* (Oxford, 1991). An important question that Langford considers is the extent to which regulation was produced by policies generated within the executive, or in response to demand from interests beyond government. It is too easily assumed that regulation was produced only by the former. The significance of the latter is argued for in [Tim Keirn and Lee Davison], 'The Reactive State: English Governance and Society, 1689–1750', in Davison, Tim Hitchcock, Keirn and Robert B. Shoemaker (eds), *Stilling the Grumbling Hive: The Response to Social and Economic Problems in England, 1689–1750* (Stroud and New York, 1992), pp. xi–liv. Some qualifications, and much else, are offered in Joanna Innes, *Inferior Politics: Social Problems and Social Policies in Eighteenth-Century Britain* (Oxford, 2009). The debate over the 'Victorian revolution in government' was worn out long ago, but it did raise important points about conceptualizing policy formation. See: Oliver Macdonagh, 'The Nineteenth-Century Revolution in Government: A Reappraisal', *HJ*, 1/1 (1958): pp. 52–67; Henry Parris, 'The Nineteenth-Century Revolution in Government: A Reappraisal Reappraised', *HJ*, 3/1 (1960): pp. 17–37. A recent extended survey of this important period of evolution of government is the introduction to Arthur Burns and Joanna Innes (eds), *Rethinking the Age of Reform: Britain 1780–1850* (Cambridge, 2003).

Particularly important work has been done on the growth of the central 'fiscal-military' state. Peter G.M. Dickson, *The Financial Revolution in England: A Study in the Development of Public Credit, 1688–1756* (London, 1967) remains foundational. Patrick K. O'Brien has produced many important essays on related themes, such as 'The Political Economy of British Taxation, 1660–1815', *EcHR*, 41/1 (1988): pp. 1–32, while John Brewer, *The Sinews of Power: War, Money and the English State, 1688–1783* (London, 1989) fizzes with information and ideas. A body of work has considered Britain as a composite state, such as Glenn Burgess (ed.), *The New British History: Founding a Modern State, 1603–1715* (London, 1999) and Sean J. Connolly (ed.), *Kingdoms United? Great Britain and Ireland since 1500: Integration and Diversity* (Dublin, 1998), including works on the effects of the Unions of 1707 and 1801 such as Iain McLean and Alistair McMillan, *State of the Union: Unionism and the Alternatives in the United Kingdom since 1707* (Oxford, 2005). For the imperial aspects of this see Jack P. Greene, *Peripheries and Centre: Constitutional Development in the Extended Polities of the British Empire and the United States, 1607–1788* (New York, 1986).

The changing nature of local government across the period has been less well served. Important differences between England and Wales on the one hand and Scotland on the other complicate matters. For an introduction see David Eastwood, *Government and Community in the English Provinces, 1700–1870* (Houndsmills, 1997). Urban government has been well explored in Joanna Innes and Nicholas Rogers, 'Urban Government, 1700–1840', in Peter Clark (ed.), *The Cambridge Urban History of Britain, 1550–1840* (Cambridge, 2000), pp. 529–74. Various points can be gleaned from Sidney and Beatrice Webb, *English Local Government from the Revolution to the Municipal Corporations Act* (9 vols, London, 1906–29), though they are inclined to decry earlier practices. For Scotland, see Ann Whetstone, *Scottish County Government in the Eighteenth and Nineteenth Centuries* (Edinburgh, 1981).

General Views of State and the Economy in Britain, 1660–1850

Fine introductions are provided by Barry Supple, 'The State and the Industrial Revolution, 1700–1914', in Carlo Cipolla (ed.), *The Fontana Economic History of Europe*, vol. 3 (London, 1971), pp. 301–57 and Ron Harris, 'Government and the Economy, 1688–1850', in Floud and Johnson (eds), *Cambridge Economic History*, vol. 1, pp. 204–37. Patrick O'Brien has written a number of general essays on this theme, including 'Political Structures and Grand Strategies for the Growth of the British Economy, 1688–1815', in Alice Teichova and Herbert Matis (eds), *Nation, State and the Economy in History* (Cambridge, 2003), pp. 11–31.

Mercantilism has provided an important framework for analysis, especially for the first half of our period, most notably in Eli F. Heckscher, *Mercantilism*, trans. M. Shapiro (2 vols, London, 1935) and the final volume of Ephraim Lipson, *The Economic History of England* (5th edn, 3 vols, London, 1929–31). The importance of the growth of international trade, and the regulatory framework and military power that helped to structure it, has been emphasized in several 'grand narratives', notably by Braudel and Wallerstein, and most recently Ronald Findlay and Kevin H. O'Rourke, *Power and Plenty: Trade, War, and the World Economy in the Second Millenium* (Princeton, NJ, 2007). Necessarily these operate at a high level of generalization, with important causal connections sometimes loosely specified. Mercantilism's utility as a concept has been vigorously doubted by Donald C. Coleman within his (ed.), *Revisions in Mercantilism* (London, 1969) and 'Mercantilism Revisited', *HJ*, 23/4 (1980): pp. 773–91. The mirror to mercantilism is the literature on *laissez-faire*. For a brief introduction see Arthur J. Taylor, *Laissez-Faire and State Intervention in Nineteenth-Century Britain* (London, 1972). A more modern framework has been provided by 'new institutional economists', notably Douglass C. North, *Structure and Change in Economic History* (New York, 1981), esp. chs. 11 and 12. The approach informs Lars Magnusson, *Nation, State and the Industrial Revolution: The Visible Hand* (Abingdon, 2009), though he is mainly concerned with nineteenth-century Europe. Important criticisms of the economic history of new institutional economists are made in Stephan R. Epstein, *Freedom and Growth: The Rise of States and Markets in Europe, 1300–1750* (London, 2000).

Economic Ideas and Economic Regulation

A stimulating discussion of ways of thinking about connections between economic ideas and political action is provided in the introduction to Mary O. Furner and Barry Supple (eds), *The State and Economic Knowledge* (Cambridge, 1990). In *The Wealth of Nations* (1776), Adam Smith extolled the benefits of freer trade and less regulation by condemning the distortions produced by what he conceived as the 'mercantile system'. The intellectual clarity and power of his views have significantly influenced all subsequent research into the relationship between ideas and action in this area. For the first half of our period see especially Terence W. Hutchison, *Before Adam Smith: The Emergence of Political Economy, 1662–1776* (Oxford, 1988); Lars Magnusson, *Mercantilism: The Shaping of an Economic Language* (London, 1994); Joyce O. Appleby, *Economic Thought and Ideology in Seventeenth-Century England* (Princeton, NJ, 1980). For Smith and his ideas in context see Istvan Hont and Michael Ignatieff (eds), *Wealth and Virtue: The Shaping of Political Economy in the Scottish Enlightenment* (Cambridge, 1983). Donald Winch takes this context as his starting point in his very important book *Riches and Poverty: An Intellectual History of Political Economy in Britain, 1750–1834* (Cambridge, 1996), moving into the later period in *Wealth and Life: Essays on the Intellectual History of Political Economy in Britain, 1848–1914* (Cambridge, 2009). Within an older tradition, still valuable are Lionel C. Robbins, *The Theory of Economic Policy in English Political Economy* (London, 1952) and Alfred W. Coats (ed.), *The Classical Economists and Economic Policy* (London, 1971), particularly the editor's introduction.

'Political economy' was not an established area of intellectual endeavour until the early nineteenth century. Relevant to economic regulation was the development of a related strand of quantitative enquiry, first as 'political arithmetic', later as statistics. William Petty was a key figure at the outset of this development, for whom see now Ted McCormick, *William Petty and the Ambitions of Political Arithmetic* (Oxford, 2009); wider context is provided by Paul Slack, 'Government and Information in the Seventeenth Century', *Past and Present*, 184 (2004): pp. 33–68. The topic is opened up in stimulating ways by Mary Poovey, *A History of the Modern Fact: Problems of Knowledge in the Sciences of Wealth and Society* (Chicago, 1998) and a very useful but rather neglected survey of sources is Stanley H. Palmer, *Economic Arithmetic: A Guide to the Statistical Sources of English Commerce, Industry and Finance, 1700–1850* (New York, 1977). The later period is dealt with in Michael J. Cullen, *The Statistical Movement in Early Victorian Britain* (Hassocks, 1975).

Regulation and Markets

Governments set many of the broad terms within which exchange takes place. Property rights are one aspect of this, much emphasized by new institutional economists. A foundational text for them was Douglass C. North and Barry R. Weingast, 'Constitutions and Commitment: The Evolution of Institutions Governing Public Choice in Seventeenth-Century England', *Journal of Economic History*, 49/4 (1989): pp. 803–32. Their approach has inspired much further work, for example David Stasavage, *Public Debt and the Birth of the Democratic State: France and Great Britain, 1688–1789* (Cambridge, 2003) and Hilton L. Root, *The Fountain of Privilege: Political Foundations of Markets in Old Regime France and England* (Berkeley and Los Angeles, CA, 1994). A fine critical review of property rights theories is provided by Joshua Getzler, 'Theories of Property and Economic Development', *Journal of Interdisciplinary History*, 26/4 (1996): pp. 639–69. North and Weingast's argument that property rights became more secure after 1688 rests on thin foundations, something made clear by work by legal historians on property rights in practice, including Joshua Getzler,

A History of Water Rights at Common Law (Oxford, 2004) and Rande W. Kostal, *Law and English Railway Capitalism, 1825–1875* (Oxford, 1994). Intellectual property rights were also vitally important, especially via patents, for which the standard account is Christine MacLeod, *Inventing the Industrial Revolution: The English Patent System, 1660–1800* (Cambridge, 1988).

Governments also provide the standards for exchange, including the money supply, for which see Christopher E. Challis (ed.), *A New History of the Royal Mint* (Cambridge, 1992), though serious shortages occurred in places into the nineteenth century. Weights and measures were also more irregular than is usually appreciated until the 'imperial system' gradually became established after 1824. See Julian Hoppit, 'Reforming Britain's Weights and Measures, 1660–1824', *EHR*, 108 (1993): pp. 82–104. Standards for some commodities were also set by the customs and excise services, for which see William J. Ashworth, *Customs and Excise: Trade, Production, and Consumption in England, 1640–1845* (Oxford, 2003). Other attempts to regulate standards, notably the assize of bread, were weakening, for which see Christian Petersen, *Bread and the British Economy, 1770–1870* (Aldershot, 1995).

Revenue raising by government influenced various markets to a greater or lesser extent. In addition to the works by O'Brien and Brewer cited earlier, there is a classic work on customs duties by Ralph Davis, 'The Rise of Protection in England, 1689–1786', *EcHR*, 19/2 (1966): pp. 306–17. Also helpful is John V. Beckett and Michael Turner, 'Taxation and Economic Growth in Eighteenth-Century England', *EcHR*, 43/2 (1990): pp. 377–403. There is no effective general account of the influence of smuggling and evasion on revenue legislation. Calls for the streamlining, rationalization and cheapening of government were important influences on policy at various points, especially from the late-eighteenth century. Generally see Philip Harling, *The Waning of 'Old Corruption': The Politics of Economical Reform in Britain, 1779–1846* (Oxford, 1996).

Local authorities were much involved with overseeing the workings of retail exchange, especially markets rather than shops or fairs. See, for example, John A. Chartres, 'The Marketing of Agricultural Produce', in Joan Thirsk (ed.), *The Agrarian History of England and Wales, Vol. 5: 1640–1750, part 2* (Cambridge, 1985), pp. 406–502. The growth of towns set particular challenges here. A fine study of the capital's markets is Colin S. Smith, 'The Wholesale and Retail Markets of London, 1660–1840', *EcHR*, 55/1 (2002): pp. 31–50. The coincidence of growth of exchange outside of markets and local food shortages sometimes led to attempts to enforce older regulations. There is a large literature here, including the classic article by Edward P. Thompson, 'The Moral Economy of the English Crowd in the Eighteenth Century', *Past and Present*, 50 (1971): pp. 76–136, that prompted much further work, including Adrian Randall and

Andrew Charlesworth (eds), *Moral Economy and Popular Protest: Crowds, Conflict and Authority* (Basingstoke, 2000).

Profound changes took place in Britain's infrastructure in this period. The government was rarely directly involved in this. The Post Office was an important exception. We lack a modern history of it in the eighteenth century, but see Kenneth Ellis, *The Post Office in the Eighteenth Century* (London, 1958). For the nineteenth century, Martin J. Daunton, *Royal Mail* (London, 1985). Most changes to the infrastructure were enabled by local acts of Parliament, initiated by a variety of bodies. For roads, see William A. Albert, *The Turnpike Road System in England, 1663–1840* (Cambridge, 1972). Thomas S. Willan, *River Navigation in England, 1600–1750* (Oxford, 1936) has still not been surpassed. The provision of legislation for canals has been less well considered, but see John R. Ward, *The Finance of Canal Building in Eighteenth Century England* (Oxford, 1974). For railways, see Kostal's book cited earlier.

Regulation, the Land and the Sea

The authoritative survey regarding agriculture for the first half of the period is Joan Thirsk, 'Agricultural Policy: Public Debate and Legislation', in Thirsk (ed.), *Agrarian History*, vol. 5, part 2, pp. 298–388. The succeeding volume in this series is very deficient by comparison. Enclosure legislation was a major way in which Parliament affected land use in England and Wales. For an introduction to the extensive literature see Michael Turner, *Enclosure in Britain, 1750–1830* (Basingstoke, 1984). Parliament also passed many private estate acts, for which see Dan Bogart and Gary Richardson, 'Making Property Productive: Reorganizing Rights to Real and Equitable Estates in Britain, 1660–1830', *European Review of Economic History*, 13/1 (2009): pp. 3–30.

Governmental measures sometimes directly affected agriculture, notably through the Corn Laws, for which see Donald G. Barnes, *A History of the English Corn Laws from 1660–1846* (London, 1930). The repeal of the Corn Laws was one of the most significant battles between different ideas of regulation and different economic interests: Boyd Hilton, *Corn, Cash and Commerce: The Economic Policies of the Tory Governments, 1815–1830* (Oxford, 1977); Norman McCord, *The Anti-Corn Law League, 1838–46* (London, 1958). Government also stepped in to manage cattle disease, providing considerable amounts of compensation: John Broad, 'Cattle Plague in Eighteenth-Century England', *Agricultural History Review*, 31/2 (1983): pp. 104–15. And it provided some support for the relatively short lived Board of Agriculture: Rosalind Mitchison, 'The Old Board of Agriculture (1793–1822)', *EHR*, 74 (1959): pp. 41–69.

Fisheries and whaling were a persistent concern of governments before and through this period. See the references to works by Harris, Gambles and Jackson in Hoppit's essay in this volume.

Regulation and Labour

At the broadest level, there was considerable concern through this period with the size of the labour force. Initially, political arithmetic provided a particular spur, for which see above. Theories of population for the first half of the period warrant more study, but see James Bonar, *Theories of Population: From Raleigh to Arthur Young* (London, 1931). The question grew in significance from the middle of the eighteenth century, for which see David V. Glass, *Numbering the People: The Eighteenth-Century Population Controversy and the Development of Census and Vital Statistics in Britain* (Farnborough, 1973) and Andrea Rusnock, *Vital Accounts: Quantifying Health and Population in Eighteenth-Century England and France* (Cambridge, 2002). Malthus's *An Essay on the Principle of Population*, first published in 1798, along with the establishment of the census in 1801, profoundly influenced the terms of debate for the next half century. For an introduction to Malthus see William Petersen, *Malthus* (London, 1979). The question of population size initially raised questions about immigration, later of emigration. See Daniel Statt, *Foreigners and Englishmen: The Controversy over Immigration and Population, 1660–1760* (Newark, DE, 1995) and Alexander Murdoch, *British Emigration, 1603–1914* (Basingstoke, 2004). In the context of debates over the old Poor Law from c.1780, especially its cost, there was also considerable anxiety about whether labour was sufficiently mobile within Britain. See John R. Poynter, *Society and Pauperism: English Ideas on Poor Relief, 1795–1834* (London, 1969).

How labour might be rewarded and treated was a constant source of unease. One aspect was the debate over high or low wages, for which see John Hatcher, 'Labour, Leisure and Economic Thought before the Nineteenth Century', *Past and Present*, 160 (1998): pp. 64–115, and of wage regulation, for which see the chapter by Innes in this volume. A related theme was patterns of consumption, as in the contemporary debate over 'luxury'. Despite these concerns, the relative absence of sumptuary regulation was an important feature. The Poor Laws were internationally distinctive, and the subject of much legislation. For an introduction to a very large literature see, Paul Slack, *The English Poor Law, 1531–1782* (Basingstoke, 1990); Rosaline Mitchson, *The Old Poor Law in Scotland: The Experience of Poverty, 1574–1845* (Edinburgh, 2000); Peter Dunkley, *The Crisis of the Old Poor Law in England, 1795–1834: An Interpretive*

Essay (New York, 1982). Conditions of employment began to generate considerable concern from the late-eighteenth century. This has particularly been addressed in relation to the 'factory acts', for which see Robert Q. Gray, *The Factory Question and Industrial England, 1830–1860* (Cambridge, 1996), and mechanization, for which see Maxine Berg, *The Machinery Question and the Making of Political Economy, 1815–1848* (Cambridge, 1980). The quality of labour related to a variety of questions, notably apprenticeship, for which see the chapter by Humphries in this volume.

Regulation and Capital

Private capital markets were directly influenced by the money supply, for which see the volume edited by Challis cited above. The recoinage of 1696 and the suspension of cash payments in 1797 were the two most significant events relating to the money supply in our period. The former has not yet been adequately studied, but see Ming H. Li, *The Great Recoinage of 1696–9* (London, 1963). On 1797, see John H. Clapham, *The Bank of England* (2 vols, Cambridge, 1944). Private capital was increasingly liable to be influenced by the state of public finances, for which see the references above to books by Dickson and Brewer, and for the later period Patrick K. O'Brien, 'The Impact of the Revolutionary and Napoleonic Wars, 1793–1815 on the Long-Run Growth of the British Economy', *Review*, 12/3 (1989): pp. 335–95. The Bank of England came to play an important role as a lender of last resort. For an introduction see Huw V. Bowen, 'The Bank of England during the Long Eighteenth Century', in Richard Roberts and David Kynaston (eds), *The Bank of England: Money, Power and Influence, 1694–1994* (Oxford, 1995): pp. 1–18. On monetary thought and policy see Frank W. Fetter, *The Development of British Monetary Orthodoxy, 1797–1875* (Cambridge, MA, 1965).

Company formation was heavily regulated for much of the period, especially in relation to questions of exclusive privileges (monopolies), joint-stock enterprise and limited liability. A major contribution was made by Ron Harris, *Industrializing the English Law: Entrepreneurship and Business Organization, 1720–1844* (Cambridge, 2000). The earlier period is considered in Kenneth G. Davies, 'Joint-Stock Investment in the Later Seventeenth Century', *EcHR*, 4/3 (1952): pp. 283–301. Legal requirements also framed the winding up of companies and of retail credit: Ian P.H. Duffy, *Bankruptcy and Insolvency in London in the Late Eighteenth and Early Nineteenth Centuries* (New York, 1985); Paul H. Haagen, 'Eighteenth-Century English Society and the Debt Law', in Stanley Cohen and Andrew Scull (eds), *Social Control and the State*

(Oxford, 1983), pp. 222–47; V. Markham Lester, *Victorian Insolvency: Bankruptcy Imprisonment for Debt, and Company Winding-up in Nineteenth-Century England* (Oxford, 1995).

Three Kingdoms and Empire

Initially, Britain and Ireland were governed by one monarch, but three parliaments. The abolition of the parliaments at Edinburgh and Dublin changed the nature of governance significantly and regulation varied between the three kingdoms across the period. There was, for example, considerable use of public funds to stimulate activity in Scotland and Ireland, especially the linen industry: Eoin Magennis, 'Coal, Corn and Canals: Parliament and the Dispersal of Public Moneys 1695–1772', *Parliamentary History*, 20/1 (2001): pp. 71–86; Conrad Gill, *The Rise of the Irish Linen Industry* (Oxford, 1925); Toby Barnard, *Improving Ireland? Projects, Prophets and Profiteers, 1641–1786* (Dublin, 2008); Alastair J. Durie, *The Scottish Linen Industry in the Eighteenth Century* (Edinburgh, 1979). Scotland and Ireland's place within Britain's navigation laws also changed across the period and were important considerations at the unions. For two different interpretations of 1707 see Christopher A. Whatley and Derek J. Patrick, *The Scots and the Union* (Edinburgh, 2006) and Allan I. Macinnes, *Union and Empire: The Making of the United Kingdom in 1707* (Cambridge, 2007). On Scotland's place within the empire see Tom Devine, *Scotland's Empire, 1600–1815* (London, 2003). For Ireland's relationship to England and then Britain see Kevin Kenny (ed.), *Ireland and the British Empire* (Oxford, 2004).

Perceptions and conceptions of economic prospects were a key driver in the development of the British empire across this period, for which see: David Armitage, *The Ideological Origins of the British Empire* (Cambridge, 2000), ch. 6; Donald Winch, *Classical Political Economy and Colonies* (Cambridge, Mass, 1965); Bernard Semmel, *The Rise of Free Trade Imperialism: Classical Political Economy, the Empire of Free Trade and Imperialism 1750–1850* (Cambridge, 1970). There are many relevant essays in four of the five volumes of the Oxford History of the British Empire: Nicholas Canny (ed.), *Vol. 1: The Origins of Empire: British Overseas Enterprise to the Close of the Seventeenth Century* (Oxford, 1998); Peter J. Marshall (ed.), *Vol. 2: The Eighteenth Century* (Oxford, 1998); Andrew Porter (ed.), *Vol. 3: The Nineteenth Century* (Oxford, 1999); Robin W. Winks (ed.), *Vol. 5: Historiography* (Oxford, 1999). All of these point to the very rich literature which exists in the field. Particularly important works that consider the changing nature of empire in the eighteenth century are Vincent T. Harlow, *The Founding of the Second British Empire, 1763–1793*

(2 vols, London, 1952–64) and Peter J. Marshall, *The Making and Unmaking of Empires: Britain, India, and America c. 1750–1783* (Oxford, 2005).

The nature of economic relations between Britain and empire has often been considered within the framework of mercantilism in general, or the navigation laws more specifically. See, for example, Lawrence Harper, *The English Navigation Laws: A Seventeenth-Century Experiment in Social Engineering* (New York, 1939); Sarah Palmer, *Politics, Shipping and the Repeal of the Navigation Laws* (Manchester, 1990). Often the efforts of particular interests have been studied. For a wider account see Michael G. Kammen, *Empire and Interest: The American Colonies and the Politics of Mercantilism* (Philadelphia, PA and New York, 1970). For most of our period, the empire in Asia related to the activities of the East India Company, for which see Lucy Sutherland, *The East India Company in Eighteenth-Century English Politics* (Oxford, 1962). Peter J. Marshall has also produced many invaluable works, but for an introduction see his *Problems of Empire: Britain and India, 1757–1813* (London, 1968). Imperial relations were challenged by the rise of free-trade ideology. There is a large literature on the adoption of free trade, crisply introduced in Anthony Howe, 'Restoring Free Trade: The British Experience, 1776–1873', in Donald Winch and Patrick K. O'Brien (eds), *The Political Economy of British Historical Experience, 1688–1914* (Oxford, 2002), pp. 193–213 – a volume containing other essays relevant to the themes of this collection.

Imperial matters were often critical to the many wars fought in this period, challenging the government's ability to protect property on the seas and in the colonies. For the former see Patrick Crowhurst, *The Defence of British Trade, 1689–1815* (Folkestone, 1977) and Nicholas A.M. Rodger, *The Command of the Ocean: A Naval History of Britain, 1649–1815* (London, 2004). For government's reaction to a failure to protect property, Mary B. Norton, *The British-Americans: The Loyalist Exiles in England, 1774–1789* (London, 1974). Dramatically, near the end of our period Parliament legislated to dissolve property in persons, slaves, within Britain's empire. There is a vast literature on this. The classic work is Eric Williams, *Capitalism and Slavery* (Chapel Hill, NC, 1944), which provoked a torrent of further studies, much of which is engaged with in two recent important studies: David B. Ryden, *West Indian Slavery and British Abolition, 1783–1807* (Cambridge, 2008); Nicholas Draper, *The Price of Emancipation: Slave-Ownership, Compensation and British Society at the End of Slavery* (Cambridge, 2010). On the politics of the earlier growth of the slave trade see William A. Pettigrew, 'Free to Enslave: Politics and the Escalation of Britain's Transatlantic Slave Trade, 1688–1714', *William and Mary Quarterly*, 64/1 (2007): pp. 3–38.

Primary Sources

The increasing availability online of printed primary sources and finding aids has dramatically transformed the ability to do research on the topics covered in this volume. Though most resources require a subscription, they are often available through university libraries. Web addresses have not been provided because of their length and the rapidity of changes in online provision, but all should be found easily via search engines.

The key finding aid to works published before 1800 is 'The English Short Title Catalogue' (ESTC). This is freely available, via the British Library's online catalogues, whose main catalogue provides a good means of finding most nineteenth-century titles. The ESTC contains 460,000 titles, which can be searched in various ways. Many bills and acts are included.

Much parliamentary material, including the *Journals* of both houses, debates, 'blue books' (i.e. official papers and reports from 1801) and earlier reports, is available in the 'House of Commons Parliamentary Papers', published by ProQuest, though in fact it does contain material from the House of Lords. Other debates are freely available in *The Parliamentary History of England ... to 1803*, ed. William Cobbett via the Oxford Digital Library, part of Oxford University Library Services. *Hansard's Parliamentary Debates* for the post-1803 period are also freely available at 'Historic Hansard' via Parliament's website.

The contents of two great libraries, focusing upon literature relating to Britain's economy, are available as 'The Making of the Modern World: The Goldsmiths'-Kress Library of Economic Literature, 1450–1850', published by Gale Cengage Learning. This is different to but complements the same publisher's 'Eighteenth-Century Collections Online' (ECCO), though this collection contains all types of literature, not just relating to economic matters. The earlier period is covered in similarly general ways by 'Early English Books Online, 1475–1700' (EEBO), published by Chadwyck-Healey and ProQuest. The ESTC usually notes when works are available in these three collections.

A number of newspapers and serials from the period can now be accessed through '17th and 18th Century Burney Collection Newspapers', published by Gale Cengage Learning. 'British Periodicals', published by ProQuest provides access to many serial publications from the period covered by this volume, as does 'Eighteenth-Century Journals', published by Adam Matthew Digital.

A variety of useful sources, including the *Statutes of the Realm* before 1714, are freely available at 'British History Online', published by the Institute of Historical Research.

Finding aids for archives are now very good, with the major repositories providing online catalogues: The National Archives, the National Archives of

Scotland, the Public Record Office of Northern Ireland, British Library and Parliamentary Archives. Holdings of many English and Welsh archives can be searched through the powerful 'Access to Archives' (A2A).

Index